Pittsburgh

O H I O

Cincinnati

W. VIR- GINIA

A N A

Louisville

K E N -

K Y

Brent—*Here we built the shantyboat in the fall of 1944 and lived for two years. Then we began the drifting voyage*

Payne Hollow—*the first long stop, an entire summer*

Owensboro—*Near this place our boat was caught in the ice*

Bizzle's Bluff *on the Cumberland River where we spent another summer*

The third winter of drifting, on the swift Mississippi, took us to

Natchez, *where we lay over for ten months*

New Orleans *was reached in March 1950*

Distance from Brent 1385 miles

Shantyboat Journal

My river is the Ohio, whose channel from the first has borne the dreams of men. . . .

. . . To live with the river, to watch it through the changing seasons, to go with it on its long journey to the sea.

—*Shantyboat*

Shantyboat Journal
Harlan Hubbard

with illustrations by the author

Don Wallis, Editor

THE UNIVERSITY PRESS OF KENTUCKY

Scholarly publisher for the Commonwealth,
serving Bellarmine College, Berea College, Centre
College of Kentucky, Eastern Kentucky University,
The Filson Club, Georgetown College, Kentucky
Historical Society, Kentucky State University,
Morehead State University, Murray State University,
Northern Kentucky University, Transylvania University,
University of Kentucky, University of Louisville,
and Western Kentucky University.

Editorial and Sales Offices: Lexington, Kentucky 40508-4008

Library of Congress Cataloging-in-Publication Data

Hubbard, Harlan.
    Shantyboat journal / Harlan Hubbard ; Don Wallis, editor ; with
illustrations by the author.
      p.   cm.
  ISBN 0-8131-1868-9 (acid-free paper) :
  1. Mississippi River—Description and travel. 2. Ohio River—
Description and travel. 3. Bayous—Louisiana. 4. Shantyboats and
shantyboaters—Mississippi River. 5. Shantyboats and shantyboaters
—Ohio River. 6. Hubbard, Harlan—Diaries. I. Wallis. Don, 1943-
.   II. Title.
F 354.H73 1994
917.704'33—dc20   93-42398

Contents

Editor's Preface

Harlan Hubbard was a thorough keeper of his journal. He wrote an entry, usually a long entry full of details, for almost every day during the *Shantyboat Journal* years. He kept his journal in a series of hard-backed notebooks. The hard backs of these books were useful, for Harlan rarely had a table or desk to write on; he often wrote while sitting on the deck of the houseboat as it drifted, or in the johnboat as he fished. Every once in a while his pencil point makes a sudden wavy squiggle on the page, thanks to the rocking of the boat or a fish biting on the line.

Harlan had started keeping his journal in 1929, inspired perhaps by the journals of Thoreau, a great influence on his life. He kept his journal regularly until 1968. Keeping his journal was of essential importance to Harlan, as a way of examining his life; he had no thought of putting it to any other purpose. But he discovered another use for his journal when, having suffered an attack of appendicitis during the Mississippi River stretch of his shantyboat journey, he found himself in a hospital for a five-day stay. "The five days passed quickly enough," Harlan recalled in *Shantyboat*. "Desirous of turning them to account by producing something positive, some fruit which would not have ripened in ordinary times, I began the writing of this narrative of our river life." He used his journal as the basis for *Shantyboat* and its sequel, *Shantyboat on the Bayous,* and, later, for *Payne Hollow.*

The journal books were stowed away in the attic of the Hubbard home at Payne Hollow. One day a visitor, Vince Kohler, discovered them and, after Harlan read a few passages to him, recognized their value. He had them typed, and Harlan and Anna reviewed the nearly million-word typescript, correcting it and making a few—a very few—changes in wording and phrasing. Vince Kohler and David Ward then edited the first sixteen years of the journals, and Harlan Hubbard's *Journals 1929-1944* was published in 1987 by the University Press of Kentucky.

In editing the *Shantyboat Journal* I have tried to preserve a sense of the unfolding of a story, as well as Harlan's day-by-day recording of his vision of the world. For the story's sake I have organized the material into sections and chapters and have given them titles, and I have inserted here and there in the text passages from *Shantyboat* and *Shantyboat on the Bayous* to provide some continuity and to reinforce or extend the meanings of events and observations. I told Harlan I would do this, and he approved; my goal was to edit the text in a way he would like, and I believe he would have liked it.

Harlan would have had one complaint, though. He had forgotten (he told me this) how glorious the journals were; when they were freed from his attic and he read them anew, he felt *every word* in them should be published. But that would have required a book of too many pages, so I have had to edit out several thousand words. It was a vexing job, for I found meaning in nearly all of those words. For those who would like to read Harlan's journals complete and unedited, they are preserved, in both handwritten and typewritten form, in the University Archives at the University of Louisville, where there is an extensive collection of Hubbard materials. In making the deletions, I did not always use the customary ellipses—three or four dots—for to do that would have inflicted upon the pages black dots swarming around like flies, unacceptable in a book by Harlan Hubbard, a wild and natural soul but a very neat and orderly man, who valued simplicity above all.

Introduction

"Sometimes I long to write a river book," Harlan Hubbard wrote in his journal on September 4, 1939, "a book of the Ohio, which shall itself flow through the pages, and the very smells and sounds shall be there, too. For so it flows through my heart. . . ."

When Harlan wrote this he was thirty-nine years old, a solitary soul, restless and lonely, an artist frustrated at the failure of his work to gain recognition. He lived with his widowed mother in Fort Thomas, Kentucky, a suburb of Cincinnati, making his living by working part-time as a carpenter. He longed for a new life. Whenever he could he went to the river, making long canoeing trips on the Ohio, taking long walks in the hills and woods of the valley, painting river scenes and valley landscapes. This is how he wanted to live. "Perhaps when I give myself completely to the river, I will be able then to write a true river book," he wrote in completing the journal entry above. But later on the same day he wrote: "I know that the aspiration for a higher life will never be satisfied."

Five years later Harlan gave himself completely to the river, and his new life began. He was no longer alone; he had married a remarkable woman named Anna Wonder Eikenhout, a librarian and an accomplished musician. Harlan was forty-three years old, Anna was forty-one. Together, they made their home on the river's shore for two years, at Brent, Kentucky, a shantyboat community; then for four and a half years they drifted down the Ohio and the Mississippi in the tiny houseboat—their "shantyboat"—that Harlan had built, living a free-flowing, natural, river way of life.

This is the story told in Harlan's *Shantyboat Journal*. It begins as Harlan and Anna take their lives to the river. Now in Harlan's journal, the "I" and "my" have become "we" and "our," and despair has turned to joy and hope: "The whole day was morning. Now, when the stars are shining, the stars of winter, and we await the moon's rising over the hills directly across the river, there is the same exhilaration and our aspirations seem almost realized." They would be fully realized by the end of Harlan and Anna's drifting river journey. And Harlan would write his true river book.

Shantyboat: A River Way of Life (1953) is that book. It is perhaps the best book ever written about life on a river, for it has the river's real life in it, the feel of the river, the river's true presence. It is written as Harlan's river art is painted, from the river's point of view. "The river is a world in itself. . . . The river air is softer, a little misty always. . . . On sunny days the pale yellow shores seem afloat on the heavy blue water. In the mild air, the migrating birds lingered, softly whistling fragments of their summer songs."

The *Shantyboat Journal* is the rich and abundant raw material out of which the book was made—the day-to-day rendering of Harlan and Anna's great adventure, rendered completely, directly, immediately, and intimately, in the moments they were living it. And so perhaps it is the *Shantyboat Journal* that is Harlan's truest river book, fulfilling his longing, for the river flows through its pages as it flowed through his heart: "I recline in the stern of the johnboat these summer evenings in the twilight, looking at the sky, water and hills, absorbing the forms and colors, the character and details, making it all a part of my very bones." "I feel the river strongly. Its course through the green valley and all the life it flows by. . . . The green hills of June and the summer evening sky, these and the river are part of the earth on which I live." "I look at the river and the single aspect of earth and sky, and seem close to the heart of the earth."

The *Shantyboat Journal* is, on one level, an adventure story, an entertaining and amazing traveler's tale. On another level it is the story of the transformation of a life. The seeds of change are sown on the river's shore at Brent, before the voyage begins. It is here that Harlan, until now a solitary and restless soul, settles his life and shares it with another: "We had supper as usual by the open fire—always so pleasant, with warmth and rest and good things to eat." "Above all, comradeship, quiet talk, perhaps none at all, sometimes serious discussion, often laughter—it would sound strange to a solitary wanderer on the beach at night." Harlan had once been that solitary wanderer. Now: "Indoors by the fire, lantern and candle burning, the dog asleep under the stove. Here is contentment, peace and cheer."

Drifting down the river, Harlan and Anna deepen their life together, sharing the pleasure and joy they take in their journey, and sharing the challenge of its rugged demands: their river way of life was free-flowing but it was a life of hard work and peril, too. They drifted in winter, when the current was strong enough to carry them swiftly down the river; often the river was wild and dangerous. They were adrift, at the mercy of the river. They endured floods and storms, and once the river froze over, entrapping their boat in ice. "Sometimes," Harlan wrote in his journal, "it takes an amount of faith to shove off." Yet always their work, and even their peril, was rewarding to them; they took pleasure in all of it. With their boat dangerously trapped in the ice, Harlan celebrates his evening activity: "In the last light of a fine sunset I cut firewood for the night and morning"; Harlan loved cutting wood in that fine sunset light. And on the wild and treacherous Mississippi, in a winter flood and fog so thick they are helpless to move their boat from its hazardous mooring, Harlan and Anna calmly play music together: "How satisfactory it is to send forth the music of Brahms into the woods." "These days of fog and flood, especially here in our exposed position, so open to storms, might be called trying. We seldom feel that they are, just a trace now and then. With the Brahms on our side and so much else, we could easily put through a winter of fog."

In summer, when the river's current slackens and they can no longer drift, the Hubbards make long stays on land. On their journey they take their time, and they fully discover their place in the world—the river's place, graced with rich bottomland soil in which they grow elaborate gardens, and generous people with whom they become good neighbors and friends. They join themselves to the river community. It is an expansive, outward-reaching movement in their life, and it surprises and gratifies them: "It is but 3 weeks today that I first came into this valley, yet we are well acquainted with the inhabitants." "Our relations with these country people are an important part of our living here."

But the essential movement of this journey is inward. Harlan and Anna make a marriage and a household on their drifting boat. The little boat is the domestic center of it all. "Light snow during the night, freezing rain this morning. We can stay in and be snug as a rabbit in his nest. . . . Our woodbox is filled with walnut now, and its fragrance when burning hangs about the outside of the boat. Good firewood, too, and a joy to split." Harlan, out on the river in his johnboat to gather fire-wood on an island, is moved by the sight of the houseboat, tied to the shore: "When I looked across at our boat, against a long, unbroken line of willows, a desolate shore, it was hard to believe that inside it could be so warm and cheery. So dry and clean. What marvels these modest fires and lamps can produce. And Anna working away inside or writing a letter, not bothered at all by the wind and mud outside. In really congenial circumstances."

The journey down the river is the middle of the story the *Shantyboat Journal* tells. The beginning is on the river's shore at Brent, where "the whole day was morning," and "our aspirations seem almost realized." The ending of the story—in the bayous of Louisiana, after their river journey is completed—affirms the promise of the beginning. Harlan celebrates his birthday: *"January 4, 1951—* The warmest, sunniest birthday I can remember. . . . Anna's love and attention set this day apart. Yet even that is my daily lot. . . . I am 51 years old today. As I was painting I was sure that what I could do, what I could see and how I could express it were worth even longer years of living. My writing is an unknown factor but it may amount to something. It is another expression of what I have felt and lived for. The creation of an environment in which it is possible to do this work, which allows the necessary time and freedom, peace of mind, happiness and security—this in itself is a success which is not always achieved."

The Hubbards learned on their shantyboat journey how to live together a full and self-sustained life. In a sense, their journey never ended: they extended it for the rest of their lives, living a river way of life on the land. They returned to the Ohio River and settled at Payne Hollow, Kentucky, a remote country place on the river's shore. In his book *Payne Hollow* (1974), Harlan wrote: "We were both led on by a common desire to get down to earth and to express ourselves by creating a setting for our life together which would be in harmony with the landscape." In this way the Hubbards lived at Payne Hollow for nearly forty years, until their deaths, Anna's in 1986, Harlan's in 1988. They had, as Wendell Berry has written, "fashioned together a life that is one of the finest accomplishments of our time." It began on the river, in their shantyboat days.

—Don Wallis

I

A River Way of Life

September 13, 1944 – December 31, 1946

1

To Build My Own Boat on the River Shore

To build my own boat on the river shore, and drift down the Ohio to the unknown Mississippi, and on southward to the river's end—I cherished this prospect for so many years, even after reaching an age when the dreams of youth have been usually abandoned, that it became more like a dreamed-of or imagined adventure than a definite plan of action; so I did not recognize the opportunity when at last chance found the right combination of circumstances; not until Anna said, "Now we can build the boat we have so often talked of, and drift down the river."

September 13, 1944 I do not know just why I call this place home. I feel no strong attachment to it, or desire to return when away. Yet it is the center of the universe, the standard of comparison for the rest of the earth, the one place in which the stars are just right and the sun rises correctly. When I leave it, part of me remains behind, and all is joined in one when I return. I was welcomed by the song of four birds. I had not thought of them when away, but when they sang here I realized how fine they were: the Carolina wren, tufted titmouse, summer tanager and white-eyed vireo.

September 27 This evening a lightning bug flashed in the darkness. Previously I had almost seen one, out of the corner of my eye, but could not be sure. This one swung his lantern the second time, quite close to me, so there was no doubt. . . .

3

I have taken the first steps in a project long dreamed of—the building of a houseboat on the river. I am not sure whether houseboat or shantyboat is the better term, but when built I suppose there will be no doubt as to which is more suitable. So far I have located some fine timbers for the gunwales and possibly for the planking, but I will not describe it until it is at hand to work with. Lumber is difficult to find now, good or bad, and expensive. Other conditions would seem to make this time not propitious for the enterprise, but we know that it is right for us. I have gathered a quantity of information, instruction and advice, all of which I must sort over, like a pile of old lumber, using what seems best and most suitable to me. . . .

October 5 We are in the midst of preparations and preliminary work for the houseboat we intend to build on the riverbank below Brent. Today the material for the hull was hauled from Covington after considerable delay and unloaded in the small flat strips of ground between the railroad and highway, just south of the Four-Mile Light. Yesterday afternoon I worked at these timbers at the old building being torn down in Covington. The rear wall is against the Suspension Bridge and the building extends west to the first street. The lots toward the river have been cleared and as I worked on the third floor, the floor above and roof already torn down, I watched the river through the holes which were windows. . . .

October 6 We were up very early for I mistook the moonlight for dawn. Again. However, it was well, as we were busy from then. . . . The job was to get the planks cleaned up and down the hill. With the added help of Harry Haas we got the long timbers down the hill, all but one, which was the bridge across the railroad ditch. Four of them we carried the short distance down on the rocky shore, where we planned to build. The *General Ashburn* came up with a double lockage tow when we were finishing our lunch and two naval craft passed down. In the afternoon Mitchell and I slid the short planks down the hill, the last long one after the section of flooring, loose pieces, tools, etc. had been carried down. It was still early in the afternoon when we stopped work, with all our material and gear down the hill, though quite scattered about. . . .

There is a dipper dredge working at the Cincinnati Water Works landing and the little motor towboat *Bejac* is towing the barge of spoil up to our landing. The river is at pool, not so clear. . . .

I see and hear all the familiar sounds and landmarks, trains running, whistles, lights on boats and shore, but it is different now, for I feel that I am living on the river shore at last. Soon we hope to live on the river itself.

This morning in the half light, a remembrance of spring in the warm moist air, I heard a robin in full song, far off, a brief song which stopped short as if he remembered that this was autumn after all. A cardinal sang a few notes from another quarter and the Carolina wren loud and clear.

This is the day we begin a new venture, facing now the true direction.

October 7 All seems a new world.

While dinner was cooking, I explored the hillside above camp. After dinner of green beans, mashed potatoes and fried ham, we worked all afternoon on our camp, which is almost a house, back against the trees on the rocks, 14 feet long, a shed roof sloping toward the bank, high enough to sit in comfortably at least, roll roofing on top and back, canvas that can be rolled up on front and sides.

October 8 It was a bright night after the moon rose and quite cool. We slept in our shack. In the morning we worked about camp, though not strenuously. Donnie came down after dinner, or rather before, staying until it was eaten; in fact, he had dessert of stewed pears and toast with us. He is a tall thin boy, 15 years old, thoughtful and quiet, and observant of more than one realizes. We do not know just who he is, but it will be revealed, no doubt. . . . We had a quiet afternoon on this quiet day, fixing and arranging about camp, reading, a walk down the shore and supper, baked sweet potatoes in our new fireplace.

October 9 Before daylight rain pattered on our new roof. . . . I was busy here building up cribbing of stone and railroad ties, for the construction of the hull, which we have finally decided to build right side up. It is in line with our own judgment and inclination, too. The ties came from the railroad embankment and nearby driftpiles. Not much of value from drift yet. Donnie helped for two hours in the afternoon and we carried over the rest of the planks. I ripped one of the 20-foot ones for streamers. When Anna returned the tools were put away, I had washed hands and face and built a fire. It is good to see the planks laid out straight and level on the uneven, sloping rocky shore. Even a boat is begun by digging in the earth.

October 10   Now that the material is at hand I feel no doubt or indecision about how to proceed. At first there were many questions—whether to build the boat upside down and turn it over after the bottom was on or whether to start right side up. The authorities disagreed, but now I feel that we are following the best course, all things considered. It is exciting, the river just below. I can already see the hull floating. The river will rise up and take it, muddy and swift then, with drift running, and all these heavy timbers, one of which is a load for three men, will be light on the rough water.

October 11   Last evening, by special invitation delivered by Donnie, along with a bag of pears and tomatoes, we called on the Detisches, our neighbors. It was 8:30 before we arrived and we found Andy and Donnie in the kitchen, Andy by the range and Donnie working at a jig-saw puzzle under the lamp on the table. Sadie was asleep but not gone to bed, just resting after a day of carrying her weight around. These puzzles are their winter pastime and they showed many of them to us, all worked out and pasted on paper. We enjoyed the conversation and their commonplace, ordinary events of houseboat life sound like adventures to us on the threshold. They told tales of ice and flood, and boats and runaway barges in collision with their boat. We acquired useful information, both about building and maintaining a boat, and life on board. A steamboat whistled for the lock. Through the windows it looked like one of the DPC boats. It was cozy and warm there, and they were friendly and hospitable, but about 9:30 we lit our lantern and walked down the rocky shore to our little house.

October 12   Sadie called on us this morning as she walked down the beach picking up driftwood, piling it into the boat which Donald rowed. He was down off and on with his puppy, Ring, on one trip bringing us a pumpkin. This was from a vine which came up of itself on the bank near their boat. We hope to have a riverbank garden sometime.

We continued work on the bottom planks. Donald strolled down in the morning late and I had him help me plugging nail holes with wood pegs. With Anna painting, we stopped work about 5 o'clock with all the planks ready, two coats of paint on all bottoms and edges. Donald stayed for lunch, in all working about 3 hours. The first part of the morning I made two trips to Brent, borrowing two jacks and buying some red oxide roof paint, with which we will paint the hull. I am pleased with the color, almost an Indian red or Mars violet.

October 13   We awoke to another cloudy morning. It had rained some before daybreak and there was a trace through the morning, but at last the day established its gray quietness, as settled as sunny weather. As it darkened, the sky cleared until it was all stars. We worked hard. . . . Today we decided on the angle of the rake and the method of construction there. This meant some thinking and discussion, and revision of our first ideas. Now we are satisfied with our design, the rakes cut.

Sadie was down a while. She enjoys the construction of a boat, this kind of boat, and is a good practical hand.

Mid-October, yet we bathe in the river, and live out of doors with just a cooking fire. Our fireplace has been very successful. The tin stove I rigged up hasn't been needed.

October 14   This was the morning of fog coming down over the river at daybreak. When we looked out, the *E. D. Kenna,* which had passed in the darkness, was in at the bank, the head of the tow on the rocky point at Three-Mile. A hundred yards below us was the sternwheel diesel, *R. W. Turner,* with a loaded barge of oil. After the fog cleared, the day was of the kind we expected in this month— warm, sharp sunshine, light breeze and cloudless sky. We conditioned the last of the bottom planks, except the four we used to cradle the boat. We cut the rake end of the streamers and set up the shoe gunwales, nailed on the first plank. So now it looks like a boat, and we can proceed with the bottom.

October 17 We came down to the river again late yesterday afternoon, a fine autumn day after the first heavy frost. Each time I come to the river shore, there is a relaxing and expanding within, and I am again in tune.

Today we continued work on the boat, nailing on the bottom planks, with Donald's help, using two jacks to raise and hold them against the gunwale, inserting a strand of cotton soaked in white lead between. Holes for the 5 spikes on each end must be drilled, the 3 into each streamer driven. It was a three-man job, and by evening 12 planks were on, but the nailing not all completed.

A warm welcome from Sadie yesterday. Her voice rings along the shore like the Carolina wren's. A redbird sang like in the spring this morning, early in the fog, and the song sparrow.

October 18 Foggy mornings are regular now, and welcome, too, for they mean a fine day. Even though we expect it, when the sun breaks through it is so cheerful and encouraging, for in the thickness of the fog we could not entirely believe it would come about.

We put on the remaining bottom planks except the end one which must be beveled, and also the first plank on the rake. So now it looks quite like a boat.

October 19 Later, these foggy mornings, the sun appears, a white disc. All had seemed to be in a deep sleep, but now, when you can see shreds of fog above and light breaking through, almost blue sky, though the water and shores are all but concealed, it is like the edge of sleep, when one must hold his eyes shut or be wide awake. Then the shore across appears, where you had forgotten one was, only its bare outlines and mass revealed. Then in the afternoon, when the sun is behind you, to look across through the clear air, it is like a shore in a dream, no wind stirring. The higher hills are bright with autumn trees.

Today we put on the last plank at the end and the first one of the other rake. So now, the caulking, plugging and painting, though all has had at least one coat, are to be done. Then the hull will float, if it must, and we will be easy of mind.

October 22 The river rose swiftly for some 2 hours and I decided to work all day at making the bottom watertight. . . . Donald helped a while and we finished caulking the bottom except for the seam at the angle of the rake at one end. There are still some nails to drive and holes to plug, but now, in the evening, the river seems to be at a standstill.

October 23 The river was stationary last night, but began to rise slowly this morning and continued so all day. It was a whip for me and I worked steadily all day. . . . By evening the bottom was tight and the hull ready to float.

There was the usual fog this morning, but it dispersed early, with a fine effect up the shore to the south, shore and hills emerging from the fog, the river still shrouded.

We were visited by Bill Edwards, "drifting" in his johnboat. He was impressed with the stoutness of our hull, offered some suggestions, both in completing and in criticism of work done so far. He is Jim's brother and John's. They are true river people and love the river in their own way more deeply perhaps than I do, and more simply and directly. The river takes them to her closely and reveals her secrets.

I bathed in the river at evening, very handy now and close to the fire. We cooked and ate out of doors by lantern light. In the foggy morning, however, it was pleasant to sit inside with a fire in the fireplace. Soon the sun was shining in, too. Our location is most favorable. The sun shines on us as soon as it rises and we have shade in the afternoon.

October 24 Last night was warm and cloudy, and rain seemed imminent. The river rose steadily and in the searchlights of passing boats, as they swept the water, we could see much drift running, right past our beds, it seemed. If we live on a boat there will be many nights like this.

A little rain fell before daybreak, and I was up before it was light, thinking it might be a rainy day. However, the clouds disappeared, and it turned out to be a mild, springlike day, with warm sun all through. The river rose all day, in the afternoon when mea-sured, about one inch an hour.

I went up to look at Bill Edwards' homemade lines, as we must procure some. In the afternoon we painted the sides and bottom and now it is ready for water, though we would like to put caulk-ing compound in the seams over the oakum. How different from Bill Edwards' way of working. When I visited him this morning he was straightening out nails, putting on a variety of bottom planks, driftwood, etc. outgauged with a hatchet, the rakes cut that way, the rotten edges of the gunwales chopped away. Yet I viewed it all with respect and felt like an amateur.

The Detisches visited us this afternoon, first Sadie, who was much interested in our work, followed by the pup, Ring. Then Andy wandered down, not very well these days. Donald was putting in coal, up on the hill, but later when tending to their boats, he drifted down, standing up in the bow with an oar for a paddle, landing at our doorsteps.

October 25 We enjoy Sadie's company and conversation, and she understands our working and living on the riverbank, perhaps herself a little longing for a new boat, afloat, with adventures ahead. She is kind and thoughtful and of sound judgment. . . . The river neither rose nor fell all day, like a cup brim full. Late in the after-noon Sadie yelled down, "The river is fallin'." I looked at my mark and sure enough it had; but not more than 1/4 inch. By evening it had fallen about an inch. No drift was running, and the river itself seemed more at ease.

We worked today at the upper gunwale plank. It was very pleas-ant working in the warm sunshine and south wind, spring weather, on the platform of the hull, directly over the water. The work itself was a joy, figuring the most advantageous way to use the remain-ing material, making long cuts for the rakes and splicing. There was just enough to complete the hull. That is, sides and planking. For keelsons, I have already used some oak driftwood.

Anna went up the hill in midafternoon to peel pears for can-ning, and now I am here alone in the twilight, listening to the lapping of the current against the rocks, and voices across the river, a few crickets, maybe just one.

October 30 On our walk up the hill last Friday night in the bright light of the three-quarter moon, first up our path to the railroad, experiencing again that feeling of elevation which is in such contrast to the descent to the railroad from above, for there you feel that the lowest level has been reached; then walking down the deserted highway and up the Altamont road, all good for night walking, we talked of our boat, planning the cabin, our living arrangements, and did well, too, abandoning old ideas for new ones which were radical changes.

We came down again this morning, hauled by J. M. in his car, for he picked us up soon after we had left the house with our packs, for it was not early. Jim came down to the shore with us and looked at the boat, an incongruous figure with his overcoat and shiny shoes. Our relations with our friends are strained by our unconventional behavior, but somehow none of them, or no one else for that matter, ever offers criticism or advice, though some of them probably desire to. . . .

A full moon rose, not yet quite dark, clear over the hill, a dull, golden ball. The night was bright, the moon shining in our shelter so no lantern was needed. We were talking about our house, what a fine balance between shelter and out-of-doors, just as much of the first as we needed in'this season and weather, and nothing shut out or seen through windows.

October 31 I was up early this morning. Daybreak was beginning to show above the hills across the river, above the rising fog, which had not yet concealed the far shore. The unfamiliar stars of early morning were beginning to dim. In the half light I stumbled along the rocky shore, ax on shoulder like Robinson Crusoe, getting into burrs and mud left by the falling river. My object was useful driftwood. I walked down to the waterworks pier, and looked along the line left at the river's highest point, as I came back, for now it was lighter. I found nothing valuable but all of it is curious and suggests a tangible relic, so much of the human life along the river and what grows there, like branches of birch from headwaters in mountain country.

Our work on the boat today continued the streamers up the rakes, bolting the two pieces at the angle, and spiking the rake planks to these extensions, which were of oak pieces which I had salvaged. First we had two planks to place on one rake. Anna painted these and the other parts of the hull so far unpainted. So far the decks and cabin are things talked of and planned, but we cannot believe they will ever come to pass. The hull as it now is seems complete.

The day was warm and still. We bathed in the river at midday. The water was cold, so our bath was short, but the warm sun was good. Just then two boats passed, *Wacouta* down and *Tennessee.* . . .

We walked up to Brent in the evening light and returning saw the full moon rise over the Ohio hills. As we ate our supper it shone directly into our shack, making other light unnecessary, though we lit the lantern to read a few pages of *Livre de mon ami,* and to see to write these words.

I ceased my hammering to watch Anna as she moved about the stony beach, tending the fire and cooking, setting the rude table with camp tinware as carefully as if it were fine china and silver upon a linen cloth. She was tall and slender, fair-haired. I marveled that she could keep her clothes so neat and clean; even her camp slacks were smart and trim. Then I thought, momentarily, that the approaching months of shantyboating and riverbank might be a trying ordeal to one so constituted, but I was confident that she would evolve a pattern of living which, while still giving scope to my wild longings, would satisfy her innate delicacy, her femininity and self-respect.

November 1 This morning was a rare one, with no fog, and the red ball of the sun rising behind broken clouds. The day was warm with a south wind, but no further signs of rain. We had little to show for our day. On the boat, only a little caulking, and another coat of paint over the part that was painted yesterday. I spent some time poking around in driftpiles for suitable material but found little of value. The best find was a sack of tomatoes, some that had ripened in Dellie's garden down the track after frost had killed the vines. We were pleased to glean these small red fruits, down in the tangle of vines and weeds in a squatter's garden. . . .

Even though I did little work on the boat, I thought about it, and now have the construction of decks and floor in mind. A plan that you are satisfied with is the first requirement. It is so in painting. I realized this evening, as I was bathing on the shore below, that I can do nothing after all but represent what I see, allowing for the shortcomings of my means and materials. Form and color need not be exaggerated, except as simplicity is necessary.

November 2 I was out early this morning, carrying usable driftwood up the stony beach. I also got a long 2x6 and some sheathing from the mill and began building the long deck. Everything takes more time about a boat. All is curves and angles, and in my case it all must be figured out as it progresses, and I cannot go ahead as from a plan. Yet the work is a joy and I would like to take even more time than I do, and do more careful work.

November 8 We went ahead with our construction, set up posts, notched in the plates and set the carlings, which I had shaped yesterday. It went quickly, and was a joy to see it growing, almost like the unfolding of a flower, into the shape we had planned. Yet the proportions were a surprise to us, for we had made no careful drawings or measurements beforehand. The diesel towboat *Jim Martin* passed down when this structure was being raised. The pilots must watch our progress.

November 9 We awoke in the night to hear light rain pattering on the roof close overhead. We were warm and dry, and as all was shipshape outside, we welcomed the rain. There seemed to be a steady passage of boats through the night, and their searchlights flashed into our cabin like lightning. Sometimes the pilot held the light steady, as if examining our layout. It is difficult to identify boats at night, but I could tell the *Sam P. Suit* by its whistle and exhaust, the *John W. Hubbard* by its whistle and appearance in the lights along the guard.

November 13   I came down today by way of Dodsworth Lane, where I picked up pears and walnuts, arriving with a pack on my back about 11 a.m. Fine day, after a heavy fog which reached the hilltops. It is good to get into the country and on the hilltops, a necessary change from the river and an experience valuable on its own account.

November 14   A warm morning, no fog, sun rising behind broken clouds, all signs of the rain which began to fall before nine o'clock. It was quite steady, hard at times, until mid afternoon, when the sun came out. Between showers in the morning we managed to get the head log on the small deck, using the 4x4 that was the highway sign post, but as it was not long enough, piecing it out with a 4x6 of oak which I had found in a driftpile. Anna swept out the boat inside, repiling all the boards neatly, the first of many sweepings, probably.

A leisurely dinner, during which it rained the hardest, and it was a good dinner, of macaroni and cheese baked with whole peppers, second growth cabbage, which is delicious food, and a sweet potato or two baked in the ashes of the breakfast fire, as was the macaroni and cheese. After this, I went up to Brent getting nails, hinges, and screws for the shutters and some strips for battens. Also fresh milk and potatoes from the store. A lot to carry, but I am quite used to packing things on my back. I had to go up the hill again, to get a bucket of drinking water, and eggs from Sadie.

Taking advantage of the clearing weather, we completed the small deck, covering it with roofing. We worked till darkness fell, then a fire inside, shaving for me and a bath for Anna, all by fire and lantern light.

Today we saw drifting down in the rain, a shantyboat, the first one we have seen traveling, with no motor, but a man in a johnboat towing it in the rain, from the dam over to the Ohio side below the dike. Then he went indoors, by the fire, whose smoke we saw coming out of the chimney, where probably his wife, for we saw someone inside through the windows, was getting dinner. They floated off into the rain and mist. . . .

November 15 It rained hard in the night, with thunder. Our roof had openings in it and rain sprinkled down on our blankets and clothes, but we slept comfortably through most of it. Daybreak was clear. . . .

It was a fine day, the rain was over and it gradually became cooler with a breeze up river. Bill Edwards came down as we were eating dinner by the fire outside. He had turned his hull over and added the upper gunwale, he said. Turning it over was an easy job, with the help of some railroad workers. He was puzzled by our boat, admiring some details, but critical of several features, such as the lack of overhang, the slightly curved roof, large windows, lack of sheer, and again the sharp angle of the rake. . . .

Several boats passed today. The *Omar* down with five lengths of loaded coal barges, the *Catherine Davis* up. The latter waited off-shore for the *Omar* to come down through the lock and the narrow channel below. She headed the tow into the bank just below us, holding it in with wheel slowly turning, steam escaping directly. I walked down and talked with one of the deck crew on the end of the tow, possibly the mate, for he asked if there was anyone who would ship with them as deckhand. I am always tempted by such offers. . . .

This evening we went over to the Detisches' boat, walking along the rough path we have already worn to and fro, carrying the lighted lantern, single file. Ring was asleep outside the door, but did not bark when we approached. Donald was alone in the kitchen, working on a jig-saw puzzle in the lamplight. Sadie and Andy were in the next room, napping, I suppose, for Andy isn't well these days. They came out into the kitchen, made us welcome and put a chunk of wood into the range.

November 23 We made the first move into the boat. I came down in the morning and set up the little cookstove. An event, for I have pictured this stove on a shantyboat for years. It promises to fulfill its destiny. However, today it was too zealous and scorched the roast and mince pie. For today was Thanksgiving Day. It was a pork roast, with sweet potatoes, peeled and baked with the meat. And cauliflower, too. The pie we baked for supper, and ate it all. . . .

In the evening we built a fire in the shack. No place will ever be quite so cozy as that, with an open fire in such a small enclosure. . . .

All work about a boat goes slowly, or seems so to me. I never accomplish as much in a day as I think I might, even if I work from dark to dark. Yet I enjoy this kind of building and it is a satisfaction to make this shell around us for protection from the kind of weather which is already here, working at shutters and doors while Anna gets dinner in the other corner, burning shavings and blocks in the cookstove.

This was a clear bright day, such as was expected. Last night we heard raindrops on our roof and waves on the shore, both seeming very close. Before daybreak, the sky was overcast, but then the clouds rolled away like a curtain from west to east, revealing all the stars and the dim light of the coming day.

November 25 A red sunrise, lighting the underside of the cloud layer, wind somewhere southerly, so we expected rain. It was quite cool, though, and it was not until after dark that we heard light rain dropping on our roof. This was in the shack, where we had supper as usual by the open fire—always so pleasant, with warmth and rest and good things to eat, sometimes even more enjoyed than the dinner at midday. Above all, comradeship, quiet talk, perhaps none at all, sometimes serious discussion, often laughter—it would sound strange to a solitary wanderer on the beach at night. . . .

November 27 The sound of light rain on the roof most of the night. Snug and comfortable inside. The morning dark and chill, wind shifting but it did not clear all day. We closed in the cabin today, though the sashes are not quite finished, and we must work awhile by lantern light for the first time. But we need the protection from the keen wind. By lantern light too, we bathed, luxury, the heat and hot water. Then supper, fun cooking and baking in the little stove.

The wind has whipped up waves, noisy on the stony shore.

I pick up coal along the shore, pumped up there with the sand when the channel was dredged. Round as gravel or boulders, formed by the same forces. I wonder what tow it was lost from, a sunken barge perhaps. It is fuel as innocent as driftwood, as much part of the river.

November 28   The transition from building a boat to living on it is gradual and never complete, I suppose, but we feel now that ours is a place to live, more than a construction project. We intend to enjoy living here as we go on with the work. This we have done right along, but never so much in the boat as during the last two or three days. Suddenly all seems new and strange. . . .

In the evening we visited the Detisches, five of us in the little kitchen, which one would expect to be crowded by the big cookstove, table and other furniture, and Sadie so big, yet there always seems to be plenty of room.

November 29   I bought a new saw yesterday, an 8-point hand saw of a make considered the best. It is a joy to have and use, cutting so fast with smoothness and ease. . . . I have used my old saw more than 20 years, 22 1/2 as I count it. Now it is narrow, so much so that the point cannot be kept straight. But it cuts well. I remember when I bought it, one Saturday evening in Newport at a time when I was working for a contractor. It seemed an extravagance, but when the salesman called it a ship saw, I could not resist.

November 30   We came up the hill this evening, and I write this in the studio with the usual difficulty. The river and shantyboat seem far away and impossible. Now living here seems right.

We were quite astonished to see, on raising the flap this morning, that the ground was covered with snow. Again the miracle of winter, a blossoming of the bare earth beyond all of summer's.

December 1   Today was not so cold as yesterday or last night, and the snow and ice were melting. I came down at 4 with a bilge pump just completed this morning, and a spike pole under my arm, like a knight on horseback with a lance. The dam had been thrown this afternoon and six feet more will float our boat, or be very close

17

to it. There are still no signs of a rise, so I will go home again. In the night I will think of the boat resting so close to the water, and early in the morning will dash down again.

December 4 I was down here part of the day alone working on the fireplace mostly. It is about complete now, and we will have the only shantyboat with an open fire.

It has been quite cold, but this afternoon is much warmer. The clear, cold air of winter, what a joy it is. I look back on those few days, from this mild weather, as I would look back on mountain country I had traversed and left behind. Yesterday morning every twig was white with frost. This morning I was pleased to find it so down here along the river. The trees across were clothed in foliage, a new flowering of the earth.

December 6 I put a long day alone on the boat, working steadily. A light rain early, but all day after that, changeless atmosphere, not cold.

A little black and white dog crawled out from under the shack when I arrived and was under foot all day. Very friendly. . . .

December 8 Again here alone part of the day, finishing the floor, the rough draft anyway. Nothing is quite complete here, but left as soon as usable, to bring some other work farther along, or begin a new project.

Clearing and colder after a day and night of steady light rain. The little dog welcomed me at our door.

The *Catherine Davis* was up, marking time at the end of the dike while the *Wm. Larimer Jones* was locked through. This boat had 7 lengths of short barges, possibly triple lockage for it took a long time. By this time the *Tennessee* was behind the *Davis,* then the *R.W. Turner* and *Omar* with a five-length tow. Then the *Donald B.* came up and overhauled the *R. W. Turner.* They were locked through together and seemed to be both hooked on to the *Turner's* loaded barge as it left the lock. Possibly not.

The wonderful sunshine after the dark rainy weather. It never seems possible at first.

December 12 River rising slowly, almost at edge of cribbing supporting boat. A fine afternoon, snow falling, the dark river so close, almost as if floating on it. . . .

Anna came down after dark direct from the city, and we had a fine evening and the first night on board. Very comfortable now, with two fires. The little dog was waiting for me under the boat and made herself right at home inside, directly under the stove most of the time. In the night she made a bed at our feet.

I think of last evening, my walk through the falling snow, up the path from the boat where the little trees grow close together, now each twig holding snow, along the railroad track past snow houses with warm-lighted windows, all level surfaces deep with snow, the shed roofs, window ledges, fence posts, tree branches. No one was out this wintry night, the much-used paths unbroken snow.

December 14 The wintry weather continues, more snow falling through the day. The snowy aspect of the hills and shore is familiar now. The sky cleared as the day went on and the sunset was cloudless. A clear winter sunset over snow. . . .

We really live here now.

Yesterday afternoon we walked up to the studio, a fine winter walk. There we printed some woodblock Christmas cards and had supper, coming back here afoot at bedtime. We could not drive back the little dog, whom we now call Skipper, so she trailed along up and back. The dog and the fires are company for us. I can't imagine the place without them.

December 15 This morning was cold. We were warm in bed, but water froze in the water bucket, even though the wood in the fireplace must have burned half the night. It was clear at sunrise with a south wind and did become warmer by afternoon. The dam was being raised as darkness came on, so the threat of high water has passed for this time. Now it has been three times that the river rose almost to our boat and then fell back. . . .

Each day that we live here, each little improvement we make increases the charm of this place. Today Anna reorganized the pantry and I finished the chimneys with a little cap and guy wires. A few more chores, the cooking of meals, chopping of wood, Anna's walk to the store, mine down the river, down the track and up along the water's edge, some reading, and by then daylight was fading. We sit by the fire in the half light which belongs to neither day nor night, then light the lantern and prepare supper.

December 16　I had a pleasant walk in the woods which grow on the hillside above here and stretch to the north unbroken for several miles. The ground was covered with snow, the trees rose dark and severe in form. I carried an ax, and the two dogs ran ahead, enjoying it greatly, for it was a treat as Ring seldom is allowed to go anywhere, and Skipper is unaccustomed to taking walks. It was a novelty to me, too, having a pair of dogs along. Many times I have walked in these woods, but now it seems new, and I found unexpected pleasure in familiar ground. . . .

I painted some in oil today, for the first time in many months. It will be a joy to come back to it now. Yet the painting will be different now, I feel, though carrying on and developing the old, for I could never do anything radically different. I also worked at a little model of our boat that I am making, and a few licks at the task of completing the cabin. There is much to be done, but it does not bother us if it is not done. The place is very convenient and comfortable.

December 18　I have enjoyed so much this continued snow and winter weather. Toward evening today I walked up to Fort Thomas after a fresh snowfall, just enough to cover all the ground again and whiten the trees. I walked down along the shore and up the hollow all the way to my destination without traversing a street. I came down the same path as darkness fell, running recklessly down hill through the woods, retracing my footprints in the snow. It is marvelous to come down the dark, rough hillside, and see the boat on the shore, no light or life showing, then at a whistle to see the door open, light shine forth, the sound of a sweet voice and fierce barking of the little dog.

*[The Hubbards make a Christmas trip by train
to visit Anna's family in Michigan.]*

December 28 Yesterday morning at 10 o'clock I came down the hill at top speed, immediately on our return from Grand Rapids. The boat was not floating then, but the bottom planks were covered. The lines Donald had put out were slack. I did not know just what to do first. I raised the center section of the floor to see how much it was leaking, but as little water came in, I built a fire and prepared to stay aboard as usual. . . . A fast-moving towboat came down, and in the waves the boat rocked, the railroad ties underneath worked out, and she was afloat. . . .

This is our second day afloat, and the change does not seem to make a great difference to us. The boat rocks some, and driftwood goes scraping by. Last night we were more exposed and heavy pieces struck us with a jolt. The headline was taut. As the river rose we gained protection from the shore and trees ahead of us, and are in little current, though some drift still strikes us. It is very heavy, seeming to cover the whole river now. For a while it seemed thicker on the other side. One whole tree went by close to us, complete with roots and branches, even mistletoe. The river is expected to reach 36 or 38 feet, which will put us over the bank. The Detisches' boat floats at 37 feet, the *Bozo* at 35. It is an old story to them, but each time awaited with apprehension, I suppose. Our boat leaks very little and we have been floating for 36 hours. . . .

Now the drift is in a stream, close to this shore. We are in to the bank, behind enough protection that little strikes us. Some of it looks dangerous as it races by, long, heavy logs. It is fun to watch, and change the spars and lines. . . .

About 9:30 p.m. We have returned from a visit to the Detisches. The moon, almost full, glows faintly through the clouds. . . . The Detisches' boat is home-like, they are friendly and hospitable.

Sadie's laugh is like the wind.

December 29 The newspaper said the river had risen 10 1/2 feet in the preceding 24 hours. It rose again last night, but not so much. However, the end of our gangplank was at the edge of the water, for the new shore is sloping gradually and a slight rise makes more difference, now that we are over the steep bank.

The morning was light, though not entirely clear. Later the clouds closed in and fine rain fell. The distant shore looked as wet as the river. Our shore was still icy, the falling rain freezing anew. Inside we are so dry and warm. . . .

After our late breakfast was over, Donald came on board to ask my help with the *Bozo*. It was leaking at the stern rake, and several inches of ice frozen in the bottom. We caulked the seams with cotton, chopped the ice away and pumped out the water. When I looked this evening, the leaks seemed stopped. Their houseboat is almost afloat, will be by morning, probably.

This afternoon I walked up the hill, crawled almost, for all the earth was coated with ice, every twig and blade of grass.

December 30 This evening is foggy. As darkness came on, the shores across disappeared, and above and below faded into the mist. We seemed alone in the world. . . .

After supper, an especially good one of baked beans, cabbage salad and good corn bread, with fruit and milk, indoors by the fire, lantern and candle burning, the dog asleep under the stove. Here is contentment, peace and cheer.

2

A River Way of Life

Time became as smooth and even as the current outside our windows, and we began to realize our true aims in coming to the river. . . .

I had no theories to prove. I merely wanted to try living by my own hands, independent as far as possible from a system of division of labor in which the participant loses most of the pleasure of making and growing things for himself. I wanted to bring in my own fuel and smell its sweet smell as it burned on the hearth I had made. I wanted to grow my own food, catch it in the river, or forage after it. In short, I wanted to do as much as I could for myself, because I had already realized from partial experience the inexpressible joy of so doing.

January 1, 1945 When we awoke and looked out the door, there was snow on every twig. The deck and gangplank were white, even the line had a ridge of snow on it. The wind blew today from the west probably, though we did not feel it under the bank. The waves rocked our boat all day. We felt more afloat than ever.

January 2 This morning one of the rarest joys in this climate, a clear sunrise over snow. . . . I feel something new in myself, as if in a faraway place.

The temperature was +4 degrees, we learned, but during the night we were warm. I did keep the fire going, the second chunk of railroad tie lasting till daybreak.

The river rose some last night and we were told to expect 50 feet. This morning it was something over 40 feet and this evening is rising quickly.

January 3 The most exciting event of today, I suppose, was the passing of the *Julius Fleischmann*. I have watched for this boat from our first coming to the riverbank, but not seeing it, decided it was out of service, and would probably never run again, since it is quite old. To my surprise and delight, this cloudy morning, its familiar whistle sounded as it passed the dam, a strange harmony of a shrill and very low note.

The river continues to rise slowly. There is little drift and a swift current. We are back in the little clearing, at an angle to the bank, so that we have trees outside the window. Birds pass by quite close. There are Carolina wrens, chickadees, song sparrows and downy woodpeckers. These are common along the shore.

It is remarkable how accustomed we have become to living on the water. The gangplank is our front walk. We notice the rise of the river, wind, current and drift, but not with anything like the concern one would expect from such new shantyboaters. Yet we mustn't take too much for granted, or feel smug in our tight boat, with the neighbors pumping away.

The boat grows slowly, but each day sees a little progress and every few days some part is completed, and our life is on a new basis.

January 7 I hear the *Catherine Davis* whistling as she comes up through the fog this morning, a wailing note that seems a voice of the river itself.

The river continues to fall and we are at the edge of the trees, sparring off at intervals day and night. The shore from the highwater line is mud, very wet. The falling river lacks the excitement and adventure of a rise.

The light today is so even, the change from night to morning almost imperceptible, and night replacing day almost unnoticed. We felt so remote, hardly making out the opposite shore all day, and no view up or down the river. Being sparred off shore so far that our gangplank would not reach to land, made it like a castle with drawbridge raised.

January 9 When I first came down here, I wrote about the daily progress of our boat, the boats that passed on the river, our other activities, that is, a sort of diary or log of a trip. It has changed now, for we live here, and our life is not as new and strange as at first. Not that we have lost any of our interest but we must now go a little deeper, be somewhat abstract and be concerned with what is here, of which we are a part. What we do on any one day is not important. The river goes on, as does time, the river is always before us, the present moment is always here. . . .

The wind blew hard all day, and we were tossed on the swell made by the north wind which has a long sweep here. Toward evening the wind died down and there was a clear sunset over the smooth river and snowy hills.

In the afternoon I helped the Detisches set two more posts under the boat and now Sadie can move around freely. It took the whole family to do the job, Sadie shouting orders from the deck, Andy coming out for a few minutes at a time for advice or inspection, and Donald and I working with blocks and jacks under the boat.

It is always exciting to climb the bank and walk along the railroad. So many possibilities are suggested by the higher elevation and signs of the great world of which we see so little under the riverbank. . . . I reach the store. How can storekeepers lead normal lives? So much goes on before their eyes. Who might open the wooden door?

January 11 Last night was very cold. We barely kept warm with no fire and when I went out I felt it was colder than other mornings. . . . Every twig and weed and grass blade was covered with frost, and when the sun shone it was a dazzling sight. The wooded hills were white, and white willows against the dark river.

Now I can see our boat from the shore, above and below, for it is outside the trees. If the fall continues I can soon walk up and down on the open shore. I wonder what the river has left in the driftpiles. . . .

January 12 The boat is now floating over the spot where it was built. The stones of our old fireplace are coming out of the water. . . .

We had a visit from Bill Edwards today. I saw him up on the

track looking down at us, and after a while he came on board, having come a little closer to the boat at each of my repeated invitations. He told us, though, that he had come down this way to see us. He approved of our boat, except for some details, and admired our way of living. He sat on the woodbox which is our step, quite at home, with his new, heavy shoes on a newspaper to keep the mud off the floor. He discoursed on the river and life on a boat with many personal experiences.

January 15 This would be a rough day anywhere, and here, exposed to the north wind, which has a long sweep up the river before it reaches us, whipping up whitecaps and tossing us about, driving the snow so that it would seem to skim along the water without touching it.

The river rose a little last night and today, so we stayed in the same position but so far from shore that our gangplank does not reach dry land. On one trip over a narrow board and a sloping gangplank all coated with ice, and holding Skipper in my arms, I lost my balance and landed in the water. There my rubber boots slipped on the stones and I sat down in 2 or 3 feet of water. When we get our johnboat, which I hope will be soon, all our work will be easier.

I cannot remember a season of so much dark, wet weather as this is. Yet it doesn't bother us as much as the city dwellers, we, or at least I, who am out so much. Almost all the wood we burn must be dug out of the snow, and has been in the water recently. Yet I enjoy getting in the firewood.

The *Jason* was down this morning and the *Gona,* a DPC boat, up. Their waves rock us, but we are used to that. However, yesterday an LST came down and in this lower stage of water it created a suction as it passed. I was trying to spar out the boat before the waves came. Spar and boat were swung out of position by the suction, and the waves coming right after, washed the boat on shore, where it pounded on the rocks until the waves passed. I could shove it off and no harm was done, but this and my tumbling into the water today made us realize that there are hazards.

January 16 The north wind continued all last night and to-day, though moderating toward evening. The air was clear and fresh, not very cold but freezing, yet no glimpse of the sun. We bobbed around in the waves, and both of us were a little sick at times, I frankly so. During the night I was up a good deal, tending the spars on the rising river, and the frozen lines. Skipper wanted to go ashore in the middle of the night, but there was a gap of several feet be-tween the end of the gangplank and shore. Skipper started down the icy incline, at that, and I was afraid she would slip into the water and I would have to move the boat inshore at once to bring her inside. However, she backed up to the deck again. Anna told this morning of the picture I made dressed in the green robe, stand-ing in the doorway, imploring Skipper not to go down the plank....

Today we made a change in our cabin, opening the pair of shutters on the land side and installing the glazed sash. It makes a striking difference and will affect our life on board immensely.

January 17 Today is calm, not a ripple on the water. . . .

I went up the hill this morning on the bicycle, bringing down a sack full of groceries, like any shantyboater. However, I have never seen one ride a bicycle.

January 18 It is fascinating to observe the drift going by our window. When we get a johnboat I will be putting out after likely pieces. As it is, quite a lot of firewood, and a good board or two, has caught on our gangplank and I have tossed it ashore, so that our landing looks real shantyboat.

January 19 A rough one all around. It rained and snowed, sleeted and hailed, coating everything with ice. The boats seemed to be trying to wash us out on the bank. A DPC down, then not one LST, but two, a mile or so apart. When an Ashland boat came down we thought the list complete but after dark I heard a whistle and the fastest moving river boat I ever saw swung around the bend. It was a DPC boat with one barge. After it passed, swiftly, close in, I heard the wash breaking as it rolled in, like combers from the sea. They dashed over the deck, the first time that happened, but lines and spars held. Opening the door of the cabin, for I was on deck, I was shocked at the spectacle. Everything was on the floor and water dashed about. First I thought it had come in a broken window, but Anna explained that it was the full pan of water on the stove. Broken glass was in most everything and a pan of soup was well mixed. However, nothing serious happened, and we were pleased that the spars held and we were not washed onto the rocky shore.

January 21 I saw a small towboat coming up the river. . . . I saw through the glasses that it was the *W. C. Mitchell,* an old boat that I had not seen for a long time and supposed was no longer running. Perhaps this was the steamboat that passed one night with a weird sound of exhaust and I had fancied it one of the old towboats, perhaps even the ghost of one no longer in existence. But now I see it could have been the *W. C. Mitchell,* which has such a sound. There was another boat coming up which turned out to be the *Julius Fleischmann.* On her heels was the *Sam P. Suit.* The river seemed itself. The new boats have indeed taken away some of its character, as did the departure of the packets. No doubt of this.

Today we made an important move, to an anchorage about 50 feet upriver from our first one. It seems that we are miles away. Here we are on a mud bank, safer in the waves, and not so far out in the river. Also, trees closer to tie to. It was fun moving the boat, which was a job for both of us, and we did it fairly well. It will be easier with a johnboat and better fittings and another line. It is strange what a difference in the view this slight move makes, even when looking across the river. . . .

The river continues to fall slowly. I was up before daylight to spar off.

We have had wonderful and sumptuous meals.

January 23 Few nights have been as clear as this, the moon three quarters. . . . The river still falls slowly. . . . I paint some this morning, with still the feeling of not quite finding the way, though I seem to be on the right track part of the time. Then there is a keen enjoyment and sense of power.

January 24 At night, when we put out our lamp, I hang a lantern outside on the corner of the boat. Somehow I feel quite proud of our light. It can be seen from far off on the river, for there are few lights on the water. As for a shantyboat, I can think of none afloat near by, in fact the first one above that I would be at all sure of is in Eagle Creek, above Ripley. The pilots see our light and turn their searchlight on our boat. Very likely they have watched our progress from the beginning and regard us as permanent. As long as the cabin has a light inside, none is needed without, for the big windows and glass door facing downriver make good beacons. Mornings I take in the lantern, burning pale in the daylight like the fading stars. It retires for the day like a faithful night watchman.

January 28 This morning the snow falls, light and fine, the earth sprinkled with this white powder. It began in the night and we walked through it from the concert. No trace of whiteness in the city, but the countryside was transformed. . . .

The music last night was a joy. It was living and clear, coming to us from the composer. The trappings of the concert hall were no hindrance this time. . . .

The river came up a little. It fell again last night. . . . It is exciting to think that it will rise again. When, we do not know, and we do not care, quite at home and prepared for either low water or high.

I worked too hard and furiously about the boat last week, trying to get the interior more or less complete, so as to get at the construction of a johnboat. But I suddenly came to myself, realizing that none of it mattered a great deal, and I was losing much by my absorption in it. We are really comfortable here, with the chores inside and out easy enough to do. All that we plan to do will make for added comfort, convenience and neatness, but will come in time, and leisure must be had for other activities and for just living, or we will miss our way.

January 29 A cold clear morning, quiet and still, but not dull silence, rather bright, breathless expectancy. And the whole day was morning. Now, when the stars are shining, the stars of winter, and we await the moon's rising over the hills directly across the river, there is the same exhilaration and our aspirations seem almost realized.

January 30 An LST down this afternoon with a great swell and suction. Earlier, the *W. C. Mitchell,* a comforting sight to match the other sinister one. . . .

We are amused by our radio, an old crystal set that Sadie gave us to use, yet today we clearly heard the weather forecast, and it may be valuable for river news when the stages are higher, rising or falling. It is impressive to hear, even faintly, a voice which you know is far off and has no visible connection with us. It seems more of a marvel in these circumstances than the complicated radio with electrical connection. But what trifling, even harmful use is made of this wonderful contrivance.

I painted some today, and the time, even with its yesterday and tomorrow, is redeemed. No other accomplishment could be as satisfactory.

What else did I do today? Woodchopping, for one thing. First shortly after I arose at 7 a.m., now in the half light of dawn. Then some after dinner and again in the twilight. The sound of an ax then.

Also, today I had a walk down the shore, to Brent for water and coal oil and a sack of groceries, visiting with Andy and Sadie on the way. We read some after each meal, I tinkered with the box in which I keep my painting stuff. No other work today, though much is to be done. But it will come in time.

I played the violin today. What a fine setting for Bach.

February 1 In the night we heard from our warm bed, for it was very cold, zero here, 4 below on the hill, the crashing and soft grating of ice floes as they broke against the boat. Daylight showed the river half covered by ice floes, not thick ice but said to be formed during the night and broken up by passing the dam. It formed a sheet of solid ice ahead of the boat, for the boat and gangplank formed a boom. I broke up the ice between boat and shore and floated it off. The running ice increased but in the afternoon was lighter. The sun was warmer but the day was cold all through, and as the sun went down, Andy sent Donald down with a boathook and advised us to shove off the sheet of ice ahead of the boat so we would not be frozen in. It was, say, 50' x 30', but it was remarkably easy to shove it loose. It floated upstream in the eddy behind Three-Mile Bar. Then it circled round and round on its center close to shore, finally joining with the ice sheet behind the bar.

We must now pull in the boat, for the river had been rising. The "monkey boat" at the dam worked out into the river and to our surprise raised the wickets which were down. The river fell about 2 feet in a short time, so I must spar off. First however I shifted the lines so we could get farther from the trees as the water fell. The headline I extended to the large poplar at the top of the bank, using two wire lines, one borrowed from Andy, in addition to our inch line. The straight-in lines (what would one call them, spring lines?) and the stern line are tied to anchors on shore which I made of the short section of railroad culverts which were rolled down the hill. So we are ready for low water. How long will it continue?

Andy talked about his experience with ice in the river, beginning with the severe winter of 1908, when he was tied up across from Pomeroy. The river was frozen over, and when it broke up with a great noise, tearing up the ice down the middle of the river, he abandoned the houseboat at night, transferring the children to a mattress laid in the deep snow. The boat was tied up to an open, gently sloping sandbar and the ice pushed the boat out on this. He had laid some plank on the shore, extending into the water under the boat for skids and the ice had shoved the boat out on these. He said it was dangerous to tie up against a steep bank.

February 2 Ice conditions were worse this morning, and made us a little uneasy. It was a cold night, down to zero at least. I was up several times, sparring off in the falling river, breaking up the ice which formed inside, new ice there, and ahead, where it floated in. When up about this I put wood on the fire, which burned all night. It was clear and still, with all the stars and a late moon. At daybreak the river was almost full of floating ice. More open water showed as the day went on, and by night, which was not so cold as the last two, the ice was scattered.

February 4 The night was warmer than the three zero ones preceding and the morning was dark and misty. A freezing rain fell, but the air became warmer and all ice melted. The river was almost full of broken ice. Yesterday it failed to thin out as the day went on, and at night, when the *Monongahela* went up, it showed almost unbroken in her searchlight. It was an impressive sight. . . . All night there is the sound of ice breaking along the side of the boat. . . . The Detisches are quite concerned about us, or perhaps just interested in a boat on the river in these conditions, which are not nearly as bad as some they have been through. I seldom appear on deck day or night without a hail from them and they are most willing to help.

February 6 Our situation is peculiar, on the outside of a bend where the ice naturally runs, yet ahead some 150 yards is a rocky point where Three-Mile Creek enters the river. There is an eddy behind this point which sometimes reaches about down to us, so that close to the shore the ice moves up or down, depending I suppose on the current. Ice gathers close packed just behind the point, and circles around below it. We are in the circle at times, and once yesterday a large sheet of ice, swinging inshore in the eddy, crashed into the side of the boat with a heavy jolt, careening the boat sharply. Everything held, however, and the hull seems to have no damage. No scratches or leaks, anyway. We are ever thankful for the stanch material and construction. . . .

Now that the ice is less, we realize the strain of the past days. Yet it is never out of our mind, for there is much ice above, and a cold spell may make conditions worse than they have been. I don't suppose that life on a boat, on this river anyway, will ever be carefree. Too much can happen, even at times which seem most secure. . . . We lead a wary, watchful existence, in which natural forces can be a danger. This takes us back toward primitive existence where such concerns are always present. It is almost absent in such a direct form in modern living, but our dangers are but shadows compared with those confronting the dwellers of cities.

February 7 The ice increased overnight and by morning the river was almost full of broken ice, soft in the mild weather. It became even warmer as the day went on, and while we were constantly surrounded by ice, we felt no concern. . . .

32

This evening we baked heart-shaped cakes.

February 9 The ice is in the past now and off our minds, although day before yesterday the river was covered with a floating mass of it, not heavy, but broken and soft, yet some chunks of it were quite thick and solid. . . . Many boats passed and we were wakened each time by the ice driven against our boat and washing past on each side. By morning, however, there was less ice than the evening before and during the day it disappeared almost entirely.

February 10 This was a morning of a new season. . . . The morning air was mild, with the song sparrow and Carolina wren tinkling away and the redbird whistling. The sun rose red behind the bare trees across the river. I was out cutting wood early, before the banks were too muddy. I breathed the morning air, listened to the birds and the *Catherine Davis* steaming past, blowing for the lock. I smelt the wood smoke from the fire I had kindled, and suddenly I felt that this was the realization of much that my life had been pointing to.

> *People ask us, "What do you do in high water?" A flood is the landsman's problem, not ours. We pull into the backwater where we are safe from wind, current and floating drift. There gently swaying between the trees, we enjoy the new outlook and the excitement of the fast-flowing river outside our harbor.*

February 13 The rain poured last night, sounding on the roof as we were off the wet, muddy bank. I was up at daybreak, for we were away from the bank too far, shifted the lines up the bank and pulled us in. I had made anchors of short sections of corrugated iron culverts from the railroad, filling them with stones, and leaning stones against them. As the river rose to a higher level, I tied the lines to trees which were now near enough. I went back to bed, for all this was done under the stars by lantern light, but there wasn't much time this night for sleep. . . .

Sadie watches us and our boat constantly and often when I appear she comes out on her porch and yells down to me. She told me today that they had next to nothing stolen since they came in 1922, yet they go away often, all of them, with the door unlocked and a good deal of truck lying about loose.

We had no alarms during this night, though the rain pelted down and I watched the rising river. Going out at daybreak I saw a great stream of drift and ice running by close in, trees and small stuff and trash, not collected into islands but strung out close to shore. We guessed that Four Mile Creek was running out, and this was proven by a signboard floating down—"Darlington Lake." The ice was thick and sometimes in cakes ten feet across. Some hit the bow with a thud. I was kept busy with the boathook for awhile, warding off ice and fishing out firewood, of which I collected enough for several days.

There was much to do in the mud today, and it is very muddy, with the ground still frozen underneath and the heavy rainfall. Also I made two trips to Grimm's, in the interest of the johnboat. I ask advice from men who have built them but always take my own ideas into account. I have built two johnboats in the past, one in 1922 and another several years later. Neither of these was designed well, and this time I want to make a good one.

February 14 We began actual work on the johnboat today, cutting the rake in the sides and setting in the ends. It looks a lot like a boat already. This is a critical time. It is almost impossible to make drawings beforehand, the thing must be almost molded by the hand, and lines and proportions decided on as one goes along. The ease of rowing, stability, buoyancy and above all grace, depend on the shaping and proportion. A johnboat can be a beautiful boat. Some are, but many are just boxes. Donald was over in the morning interested and helping. All the Detisches are concerned. A new johnboat along the river is like a new house on the street, almost like a new baby.

The Detisch family includes several chickens, one rooster and some hens, three or four of which are young. They are very tame, and all seem to have a name. Donald picks them up anywhere. They lay no eggs at present but there are hopes. Sometimes the flock wanders near our boat, scratching in the chips by the chopping block. They are so dignified.

February 15 This was a day of days. All was different somehow, the sky, air and water. The bluebirds whistled as they went by unseen, and the sun had an unusual warmth. I worked without sleeves. A strong wind blew downstream, a warm wind, ruffling the tawny water. Soon after sunrise a shower of rain came up, with broken clouds piled high and a sky such as has not been seen since summer. I worked on the johnboat both in the morning and afternoon, and most pleasant it was in the warm sun and wind, looking down over the rising river. Several boats passed, as it happened all gleaming white. The *Jason* just had a new coat. However, before dark, which came so late, the *W. C. Mitchell* came down, ancient and gray, in harmony with the sunset, which was reflected in the eastern sky and water. A bright young moon shone above the ridge to the west.

February 16 We had supper at the studio by the fireplace, which seems so open after the boxlike affair in the boat. Snow was falling fast now, and by the time we had packed the supplies we had bought ready to go, it was 9 p.m. with a couple of inches of snow on the ground. A street car passed as we approached the corner, so, rather than wait, we walked on with the wind. I carried a pack on my back and a box in my arms. Anna had a bundle under each arm. We turned off at the Altamont Road and walked down to the river in the strange white light of the snow, and along the river road, looking down at the swift water wondering how we could have our home there. At last, down over the bank, a word with Donald and a greeting from Skipper. The river had risen but we could step to the end of the gangplank and now had lights and fires and a warm, cheerful cabin.

February 17 As I was playing the violin by the window this afternoon I saw a muskrat swim by, upstream between the boat and shore, but close to the boat. I saw his course for only a few feet, then he dived under some drift under the gangplank. I had called Anna and she saw only his disappearance. But later he swam by downstream, fast, and we both had a good view. As before, he dived under drift. He was quite large, larger than our expectation anyway. Brown with coarse fur, seeming so when wet. He was fat, had whiskers, and his tail, not as broad as I thought it would be, trailed along behind. His appearance excited us as if we had seen a sea serpent. It is inspiring to know that there is wild life rarely seen along the familiar shore. I suppose they build their houses under driftpiles. How do they calculate the rise of the river?

The rising river made it necessary to move upstream a couple of rods, where the bank was more open, so that now we are close neighbors to the *Bozo*. As we have no windows facing that way our situation seems as remote as ever, for the trees extend their branches over the water towards us and the little woods on shore is unbroken. The snow now is a canopy and we can hardly see the trains. It is ever strange to me that our situation seems so unfamiliar as the river stage changes and we shift a little ways upstream or down. Even a distant view is never the same.

There was a flush of violet color at sunset and now the stars and moon shine in the still night. This has been a quiet day on board with just a short walk or two and a little woodchopping before our bath at dusk. This is almost daily and most delightful. Then supper in the darkness by the fire, a little reading, and bed.

February 19 An eventful day. Anna did a full-time washing of clothes and to see them out on a line on the riverbank made us truly live here. It went very well, too, and with a little more equipment and experience it can be very efficiently done. Where now are your electric washing machines?

The river rose during the night, and in midmorning Sadie broadcast from her porch the news that it would reach a stage of 41 feet on Wednesday, according to present indications. So we made ready to leave our landing where the trees kept us too far offshore. Donald came down to help us, but I refused the offer of their johnboat, though as it turned out I had better accepted. First there was cut wood to load on board, the spar and gangplank to take on the decks. Then we freed the wire cable that was on the stern and the shore line. We must pull the boat ahead to disconnect the wire cable that was serving as a headline. I thought we would be able to drift down the one hundred feet to our clearing, and keep control of the boat by holding to trees, but it got away from us in the strong current and we almost went on a long voyage. Fortunately I was able to catch hold of some branches with a boathook, and though not checking the boat completely, at least caused her to swing to the shore so that Donald on the other end could get a secure hold. Then of course the boat swung around. We must pull her up to the landing we had passed and turn her around. Now we are secure at our old anchorage, headed into the bank at an angle, the clearing above us and the railroad in plain view, as we are to it also. As before, we seem to have moved so much farther, and even this place is different. . . .

I delivered a letter to Andrew Detisch from Witte's store, where the postman leaves their mail. The address was: Rural Route 2, Houseboat on River, Cold Springs, Ky., all typewritten so by an insurance company.

February 20   The *Fleischmann* shoving up along the willows, the distance across seeming so much greater than at low water, though it is not much. The *Davis* was just down, and when they blew their familiar whistles, I felt close to my former self, on the hill listening to the boat whistles, picturing the whole scene and longing to be there. I had wondered if living on the river all the time would dull the enjoyment of it, but I find that I do not live here fully conscious of the river all the time. I turn within and only see it part of the time. Of course it is made conscious most of the day and night, but there are enough blank periods to keep it a fresh experience. Not the same thrill, though, of coming down a hill to the river when one has been absent for a long time.

A dull gray day, wet, whether raining or not, with the melting snow and mud. I would work on the johnboat, but it stays wet. The river rises slowly. Yet inside it is warm and cheery. We have music and reading. Baths, or rather one common bath, good things to eat, always cooked and served with grace, and eaten leisurely, hungry as we are.

I fish driftwood out of the river as it comes to us, picking out the most likely pieces. It is like catching fish for food. The wood goes from the water into the fire and in the right combinations it is a good fire.

February 21 Long since has it rained as it has the past night and day. No sky, water dripping and pouring from the overhanging mist, the air warm and wet. Unfamiliar streams of water cascading down the bank. Fog on the river, yet at times the air clear, sky broken and hills distinct. The river will rise, surely, yet for the past 24 hours has changed little. But for the rain this would have been the crest. Now who knows? We care little. This is a snug harbor.

I went up the hill on errands today, from noon until 2:30, walking up through the hollow and riding down on the bicycle. Going to town now is exciting. I walk through the streets with bad-weather clothes, carrying a pack or sack, and ride laden, same pack and sack, stared at by the conventional inhabitants. It is good that someone is different occasionally. I meet some of them casually, the plumber friend who drives alongside, window of truck open for conversation. He has felt the river's attraction, too. It is strange so many have. Tabb Craver, of all people. Then the bicycle. As I go by a soldier calls, "Raleigh." I say, "Yes." He says, "A good one." "Yes," again. Did he ride in England?

We are headed into the bank at a sharp angle and it is difficult to adjust to the direction of familiar surroundings. The railroad seems to have swung around and the river has some new bends in it. Lights which should be on boats are from cars on the highway.

Anna just remarked that a year ago tonight we were making ready to leave for New York in the morning on the F.F.V., C & O, which will go past here tomorrow at 11 a.m. That morning was as rainy as today's. As we rode by here we could not see our boat or even dream of it. . . . Anna wore the poncho which, green, looked quite well over her green coat.

February 23 A careful record if only of the weather, by one who was out in it and whom it affected in some way, would be worth writing and reading at any season.

We are in our little steep clearing, tied to small, swaying elms. It is like living in a treetop. In yesterday's wind we swung so much that I must rig a spar on the end near shore. Not a line to change

38

all day, but this morning we must be slacked off a little. It is strange how far from the river we seem, though just inside the trees. It is like being in a creek back aways from the river which is seen at a distance. The upstream boats follow the other shore, which seems so distant now, and those going down are farther from us too.

Anna baked bread yesterday, the best yet. In fact, I don't think it can be improved on.

I worked on the johnboat yesterday, beginning by lantern light, for I feared the river might reach it. Anna and I can watch each other work, for the johnboat is just outside the window. We are close to the railroad, too. The trains roar down above us and we wave at the engineer from inside our cabin. They must watch us and our progress. . . .

The end of the day is satisfactory. A pause late in the afternoon and perhaps a few lines read—some paragraphs of Thoreau's journal, a poem, or lately, Anatole France. Then I go out to chop wood for the night and morning; there is never much ahead. As I work, the light from the moon shines on the water, though the sunset light does not seem to fade. Sadie and Donald go by on the track above, walking homeward with coal they have picked up. We shout a few words back and forth. I cut stove wood, short pieces for the little firebox, hard wood, and dry if possible. . . . Then I must gather some dry twigs from the drift for kindling. All this I carry down to the boat, filling the two woodboxes and leaving the rest on deck to be covered if rain threatens. I go into the cabin, lovely with the moonlight streaming in. Firelight too, and everything in order, floor swept and mopped. We bathe with no other light, and now we are ready for supper. The candle is lit and Anna prepares the meal and sets the table about my writing. Skipper has had her supper, and lies uncomfortably in my lap, growling at something she might have heard or just fancies. The johnboat outside the window, stark white in the moonlight, has good lines so far.

February 26 Toward evening yesterday there was a suggestion of a rise, and this morning when I looked out, after daylight, too, even though a dark morning, I saw the gangplank leading into the water and the jump to shore was too much for Skipper.

February 27   In the night I looked out at a hazy moon and the rising river. By morning it was up to the bottom of the johnboat and soon it must be launched.

February 28   Yesterday the report was that the river would rise slowly until Friday, reaching 56-58 feet. It had already risen higher than in our experience here, and all was strange to us. I cut more of the slim locust trees for a harbor for us. These are the last fringe between the railroad and river. I tie lines farther uphill, and carry up the boards and a few other loose properties. We try not to accumulate belongings, though, so as to be easily moveable.

The morning showed but a slight rise. I heard rain in the night, and find the gangplank ice-coated, a treacherous walk in rubber boots. However, ashes from the stove soon fix that. I bail out the johnboat. Quite heavy drift is running.

March 1   This has been a day to mark, for I rowed the new johnboat for the first time, even though not quite complete. It promises to row and handle well, seems steady and capable of carrying a load or riding rough water.

I had my first view of our outfit from the water. Though we departed from traditional shantyboat design, we have acquired true shantyboat character. Our boat looks well and is in harmony with the shore.

I drift down a quarter of a mile and row back against the stiff current, especially strong around the drift. The shore was unfamiliar, seen from the water, and at this high stage. The piles of drift, once far back from the water, and so ancient, draped over the uneven bank, now float in a flat mass, tossing in the waves, taking the full force of the river's power.

Later we both rowed up to the Detisches', making a call in our new boat.

We rowed the johnboat for the first time. It promised to fulfill all our hopes, and soon became our mainstay on the river. In it I was a new animal, as a man on horseback is conceived to be. The johnboat was so useful that we wondered how we had ever managed without it. . . . It made us feel like real shantyboaters to call upon our neighbors by water, tying up at their deck and climbing aboard. We were becoming part of the river fraternity now, and as we sat in Sadie's cheery kitchen with perhaps half a dozen others, we ventured a few words about our own doings and opinions.

March 2   The river reached flood this morning. . . . At 52 feet, or flood stage, Three-Mile Bridge is under water.

March 3   The rain began again, from the south, Thursday night, and continued all of Friday and most of last night, clearing at this midday. The river reached flood stage, 52 feet, yesterday morning and is now about 60 feet, with higher stages to be reached.

So this is a flood. To us, this isn't significant. We are afloat, the river is always rising or falling, higher or lower as it may be. Conditions are different than they have been, but they are never the same to us, hardly, from one day to the next. When we leave here, though, and see the extent of the water, we realize that it is really high.

Last night as I walked up the track in the rain I saw many lights in California across the river, heard voices and the sound of trucks grinding, all indicating the moving out from the riverside cottages. The heavy rains had already raised the water higher than first predicted, with rain still falling, the river rising quite fast, .3 foot per hour. . . .

The weather is cool, yet spring creeps upon us. The maple buds are quite open and distant groves near the water have a new color.

The only boat I saw yesterday or today was the *American,* down this afternoon with a few empties, a small, old sternwheeler I have missed for several years. Few boats of this type are left.

Tonight we went to the symphony concert, walking through muddy yards and up the hill and from the street car terminal to Music Hall, in all about 4 miles of walking. This night the music was worth that at least. As we came down the dark road, the moon was rising in a haze and stars shone overhead.

March 4   A frosty morning, clear, warming with the sun into a fine springlike day. The groves of maple across the river color through the day, and I see tiny white flowers on the moss-like plant

41

that covers the ground in the woods. This is the first bloom, which is likely to come forth any month after a few warm days.

This fine Sunday brings many strangers down to see the flood. A few cars on the road, though it is blocked by water, boys on bicycles, horseback riders and walkers, some with guns, even bow and arrow shooters. . . .

March 5 It was a large washing today including four sheets, and seemed to turn out well. It is a satisfaction, and makes us feel independent and thoroughly at home here.

March 6 Through the night we heard the tropical rain pouring down, but I did not even look out, sleeping so soundly. In the morning, looking out into the rain and fog, I saw the river had risen, about 2 feet I guessed. Our walk to shore was afloat, the johnboat deep with rainwater. The lines, except for the long headline which reached up to a tough sycamore at the top of the bank, were close to the water, so there was work for all hands. Skipper attempted to get ashore but fell into the water from the floating plank. Heavy showers followed throughout the day, with sometimes a gleam of sunshine when the rain ceased. Sadie hailed from the bank, a sodden figure in a long, weatherbeaten coat, smoking a cigarette. She said the river would go to 70 feet tomorrow, rising now .4 foot an hour. She was worried about their lines, whether they would be sufficient.

I talked with them later, all standing on the deck like wet chickens and about as disconsolate. Sadie came down again to say that the Wittes were moving out of the store and advised us to go now if we needed anything. So I went, walking along the track with the water close up, only the tips of the tall waterside willows showing. Little driftwood remains along this shore, many old familiar pieces floated away. Still a few extensive fields of it. At times, one comes floating by us, set on its way by the rising water. Witte's store was in a commotion, with more confusion than normal. Mr. Witte was on a ladder packing goods into cartons ready to move out. The daughter was filling other boxes with notions and various loose articles. Mrs. W patiently served the customers—Sadie, who was buying everything she could think of, with Donald waiting to carry it home—the two of them are always off on some excursion together, like picking up coal along the tracks; a boy with a note which called for sugar, and Mrs. W divided her last 5 pounds between him and Sadie. Mrs. Harry Smith, an old campaigner, veteran of many floods, now already packed. I went back to the store late in the afternoon. A truck was backed up to the door, and the neighborhood men were loading the furniture to haul to the McDonalds', where upstairs the Wittes plan to carry on their business. The store room was desolate.

Coming back down the track, I saw dark clouds in the north, and expecting wind and rain began to run. The Detisches had seen this weather too, and were heaving on the lines, at which I helped, in the rain that was now falling. The wind blew hard upstream. We were headed almost into the bank, with small locust trees on each side. These held us in position. Astern we are still fast to the wire cable which runs down to the first trees.

There were strange goings-on along the railroad this afternoon. They seemed to be moving equipment out of the yards soon to be under water. A string of cabooses on one train, and a line of 12 engines, all different, each with steam up and crew in the cab passed by in a stately parade, with 12 plumes of smoke. An N. and W. passenger train came down. At 4:30 the Chippy made its last trip. It seemed to carry many women and children. All these last trains used the inside track, away from the river. No. 7 came through on time and later an engine with 3 passenger cars went up, returning in a few minutes backwards. Now the railroad was out and the boats can tie to the rails. Other ties were getting scarce and flimsy. We worked by lantern light. Donald came down to borrow a line. With 2 lines on the head and the other cable pieced on, all our lines are out now, no spares.

March 7 The river asserts itself now, casting a spell over the land. No wheels move there. Men feel its power and are subdued. On the shores it is peaceful and quiet, somewhat as it was before men came with all their disturbance and change. The river itself has retained even in this day much of its primeval character, and now the shores regain something they have lost.

March 8   I thought the river had fallen a trifle last night before bedtime, and this morning the drop was evident, possibly 6 inches. Today it fell very little. The crest was 69.2 feet.

Today was cool, clearing before dark with a light north wind. We saw the evening star bright over the hill, a cheering sight after the dark nights without moon or stars. . . .

Whenever I get away from here these days I am amazed at the extent of the flood. This afternoon Anna and I rowed up to Winter's Lane, then across the river and up the backwater on the other side up to Coney Island. Then across on a long slant to our landing. This was our first crossing, the longest row in the new johnboat, which seemed satisfactory.

There was very little drift running today, but yesterday it was quite heavy and I was busy getting in some that seemed valuable. Going out to investigate a large box, I found it contained 4 oil cans, three of which were full. This got away from the railroad. Also they lost a lot of 8x8 timbers, one of which, about 12 feet long of oak creosoted, I got in and tied up. Several more lodged below, and Donald towed one in, too. They are fine timbers and should be put to use.

March 10   Another fair sunrise, and warmer this morning. The river ebbs slowly, but I see Sadie and Donald removing their lines from the track rail, ready for their descent down the bank grasping at bushes as they go, for there isn't much to tie to for aways. So I will shift our lines, too. There is a small stout sycamore at the top of the bank in a favorable position which makes a fine tie for the headline. For a straight-in line, I will try to make a stake hole in the railroad bed, mostly cinders. There is so much water it seems that it never could run away and get as low as it was, with a bank thick with trees now covered. . . .

Yesterday was a fine day. I was out in the johnboat in the morning, crossing to California, back to this side almost down to the Water Works, looking into driftpiles, observing the budding trees. The elms and maples are way out, the box elders and poplars swelling. There never seems time enough for this. All one's time could be given to watching the swelling buds and plants coming up, birds arriving and changing their song, and the time could not be better appropriated. The spring steals up almost unnoticed and slips away unobserved. It is summer before we are awake.

March 12   We were roused from bed this morning by the familiar whistle of a passenger engine, and sure enough, No. 8 came through.

This evening the river stood at 64 feet, fallen 5 feet, with a drop of up to 3 feet forecast for tonight.

Early this morning I went up on the open hillside between the railroad and highway. . . . Planted a little garden there, asking no questions of anyone, merely scratching the ground with a little spade, cutting up the green things growing and making the surface fine and smooth. There I planted a little lettuce, beets, carrots and sugar peas, all in a very small place.

March 13   In the woods now the buckeye buds are swelling, and the little white flowers with red stems and centers, leaves like hands, are in bloom. The elms and soft maples along the river are in full flower, I should say.

This year I feel less strongly the regret and sadness, the frustration and failure of my aspirations, that go with the early spring. It must be because I am outside more, away from town, on the river and living in a manner I have long desired.

I plant more garden this morning—spinach. The entire space is probably 60 square feet. With weather like this, clear, warm sun, not a cloud, after a misty morning with heavy frost, even ice, I would be unhappy without a place to plant some seed.

I drift down in the johnboat to the intake pier and below, scratching up against the strong current, examining the driftpiles, not finding much of value, but some good boards and blocks. I have gathered quite a lot, and at first glance our landing looks like it has the usual collection of junk. However, there is little but firewood and good boards, nothing to hold us here if we want to move.

Old Bill Edwards was alongside when I returned, talking through the open door to Anna. He did not conceal his admiration for my johnboat. I noticed he was building a small one in his shed. He sold the flat he had made during the summer to someone who needed it during the flood, receiving, he said, $25. It seemed worth more, to the buyer and to the maker, for even if the material cost no money, there was much labor getting it out of the driftpiles and putting it together.

I watch Sadie's flock of chickens in the sun by the track, shaded by the canvas over my bicycle, scratching and fluffing their feathers in the cinders, pecking and preening.

March 14 Cars seem to be using the highway now, though Three-Mile Bridge is still under water. We are told the store has moved back into its own home. The river is falling fast now and will probably go below flood stage tomorrow.

I shoved way out this evening, running a line out to the top of a small elm which is above water. We need the johnboat to get ashore. Again I find that the shore seems a strange one, though the river was exactly at this stage when rising. All seems unfamiliar now.

We plant more garden on the hill today, burning a brush pile. The days are sunny, the stars bright at night. . . .

The *Sam P. Suit* is passing, close to the Ohio shore, both search lights on. When it whistles I discover it is the *Catherine Davis*.

These are full busy days.

March 15 Bees find the little flowers scattered in the woods called salt-and-pepper. What can they extract from these tiny blossoms?

I rise early this morning and break up more ground. Before breakfast we plant more peas and carrots, spinach. This garden is exciting.

It is a fine morning. I wander through the woods and hillside fields and gather some dandelions for dinner. . . .

Yesterday we heard something crash into the window pane. Looking out I saw a cardinal struggling in the water like a wounded duck. He kept afloat until he drifted into some twigs, dazed and bedraggled. Soon, however, he hopped onto a low branch, sitting quite still for awhile, then hopped up higher. I looked out occasionally and saw him there, then he was gone, perhaps having flown away when he dried out and regained full consciousness.

It began to rain at midday suddenly and hard, continuing most of the afternoon. It ceased before night and stars shone through broken clouds. The river fell below 52 feet, flood stage, today and traffic began crossing Three-Mile Bridge.

March 16   So warm a morning I build no fire until we want to cook breakfast. The sun burns, I take off my shirt. . . .

March 17   This is the first summer day. A new adjustment must be made for the coming season, more in our case, for we are closer to the earth. Weather and temperature affect us more directly, because we are out in it so much. Yet cold and heat, rain and wind, as we experience them are not hardships. They just make an adventure out of everyday living. Most of the complaining about the weather is done by people farthest removed from out of doors.

March 18   These evenings, clear, a new moon in the west and bright Venus, and in the dark east, Jupiter shines. . . . The river falls steadily, 4 or 5 feet a night. Now we are out of the little clearing and over the stony shore.

These are summer days. The tension of winter is relaxed, and its peace and simplicity are disturbed. Spring comes late to the river and summer remains longer there. . . .

Company and going abroad are dissipations. Only on occasion can we have visitors or go to town. Both take a lot out of us. Yet such variety to our life is necessary. We see ourselves through the eyes of others and in the end appreciate more our life here, and are thankful for our opportunities. The lives of most people are drab, full of frustrations and longing that cannot even be known plainly, let alone realized.

March 20   I do not put the important observations and happenings in this log. The view up the river between dark hills this evening as I walked up the track. The eastern sky at sunset, barred with silver and copper. The woods now above us on the steep hillside. The terrible rain last night, with a feeling almost of despair, the swift, foul water, rising up the muddy bank.

March 21   The desolation of last evening, and now the clear sky and fresh wind from the N.W., the shining moon and stars. . . .

We try to be ready for either a rise or fall and do not depend on forecasts from the weatherman. However, we usually get these from Donald or Sadie. Their boat is just above the water, the waves slapping up against the bottom. It is well so, for their houseboat is old and ill fitted to stand rough water. Donald paid us a visit this evening, bringing half a dozen eggs as a gift. He said I had helped him.

> *Though not a word was said and nothing intimated, the few Brent families, the store people, the solitary men and women who lived in the little houses, squatters' shacks, and shantyboats accepted us as one of them. Brent itself became as a new place to us. At the time we did not grasp the meaning of all this, but it was the beginning of a deep and permanent alteration in us. The river would leave its mark.*

March 22 The river is set apart. It is separated from the rest of the world by two invisible walls which run along the outside of the fringe of trees which line the banks. Above this wall is country, below it, river. The difference is felt at all seasons. The river even has its own climate and seasons. Now, for instance, when the countryside is in bloom, buds bursting and flowers opening, the pastures green, the riverbank is dead. Not a blade of grass or opening bud.

March 23 Rising water last night and today, with a stage of 50 feet predicted. So we go back into our clearing, surrounded on three sides by small trees. Again I feel a strangeness about it, even though this is the third rise, the third time we climbed up this bank. . . .

We work in the garden a little, though the ground is almost too wet. We plant a few beans. The first seed we planted is up now. These days we enjoy dandelion salads.

March 24 Last evening we visited the Detisches, whose boat is now afloat for the third time this year, so far. Last year, only once. It was nine o'clock when we arrived. But we had just finished our supper and chores, showing how long our day is. The sun rises about seven in the morning now, I believe, and I am always up when No. 8 goes by, often long before. The trains are our clock.

Quite early, before six o'clock, a passenger train goes west. Then No. 8. About 7:40 the Chippy, going to the yards. About 11:15 is an eastbound passenger train, and at 5:15 or 5:30, another. These are convenient for telling the time. . . .

March 26 Yesterday in the warm almost hot sun at midday, we trailed along with Sadie and Donald when they went out after greens. We walked along the open hillside above the tracks, while Andy sauntered along the smooth, level way. I was pleased at the opportunity of going with someone as well versed in the art of gathering wild greens as Sadie, who seems to have a real country background. Early as it was, we found each of us a mess, and when I got home I counted nine kinds in our sack. There were dandelion, the only one I was familiar with, and I did not know until told which was the sweetest kind—the fine lacy variety. Sadie pointed out wild beet, white top, narrow dock, shepherd's sprout. She picked 2 or 3 leaves of bloodroot which she called "p'coon." It seemed to have more medicinal than food value. Then we found squaw cabbage and rock lettuce which is highly esteemed. Sadie then led us into the woods for some deer tongue, with turned out to be dog-toothed violet or adder's tongue, as Mary Bias called it. She is the top authority in this neighborhood on wild greens, and even Sadie takes specimens to her for positive identification and is pleased when the old lady goes with her. We must get acquainted with Mary Bias. Sadie took one kind to her yesterday, a large leafy plant spotted green and white. It was wooly breeches, a good green but evidently not one of the best. Sadie said her mother used to say that every other weed was good to eat. Probably so. She said that if milk flowed from the cut stem, it was edible. The shepherd's sprout was referred to Mary, too, who said it was also called hen pepper. In the woods where the deer tongue grew, Sadie was delighted to find shawny, which she was seeking all along, but was afraid it was too early for that. It was a tender leafy woods plant, very mild in the cooked greens. It can be eaten alone, while most of them are too strong for this. We enjoyed the greens for dinner, cooking them in two waters and serving them with butter and sliced boiled egg. . . .

Today we made a trip to the city. . . . We went over on the

10:30 a.m. bus from Brent. Sadie and Dellie Grissom were passengers, too, and sitting in the same part of the bus, we held conversation all the way. About greens, garden, falling into the river from a houseboat and other related topics. Sadie was after a pair of shoes for herself and did not return until around 5 o'clock, while we were home two or three hours earlier. We rode the bus to Fort Thomas and walked down Altamont Road. The walk along the river was unbelievably fair. In the sun now after the showery morning, with the greening woods above on one hand, the sweep of the river and hills ahead of us and off to the east.

When we come back here down the bank to the water's level, we reach solid bottom. One can go no farther, nor is there a desire to. Looking back on the city, it seems a bad dream, an unreal, impossible place inhabited by creatures of fiction. We ourselves do not manage well there. A change has come, living here. We are more shantyboat than we realize, and perhaps it would be better to be so wholly. . . .

The moon is bright tonight. I build a little fire on the shore to heat water for soaking the clothes. We work on the deck in the bright night.

March 27   This could be called a perfect day. The sun rose clear, not a cloud all day. A bright moon almost full, no wind, the sun not too hot. Everyone responds to it in the same way, I am sure. It was a fine wash day, too, and all the clothes were dry early in the afternoon. I said there was no wind, but I remember the clothes flapping in the wind from the south. . . . As we worked in the garden, Donald said the clothes made a sound like horses running.

He had some onions to set out, carrots and beets to plant. I am glad they have an interest in the garden. It gives it more standing in the neighborhood, and they can watch it more closely when the river is down. After planting the onions and the seeds, we went up into the woods and picked some shawny, or milkweed, which grew there in abundance. It was pleasant to get some of our food in the woods, where it grew with the yellow violet and trillium. Our mess was all shawny, and we boiled it not too long, a very delicious dish.
. . .

50

The *Verity* was up at twilight. This was a remarkable time today. As we walked up the tracks to the store then, it was very light. The air was filled with light, though darkness had fallen, the moon was bright and Venus in the west, Jupiter in the east, gleamed like suns.

Now the redbuds are in bloom, the first dark hue is past. The pear trees whiten on the hills, and soon will look like candle flames.

March 28   Late in the afternoon we went up to our garden on the hillside, in the shade now of the wooded hill above it to the west. The ground was getting dry, and a gentle rain would be welcomed by the young plants, and the weeds, too, for they are springing up. We carried our bucket to get water at Mrs. Grissom's, and on the railroad watched the *George Washington* eastbound. As the engine passed, the engineer heaved out a chunk of ice for us. We waved him thanks and took it to Mrs. G who was concerned about keeping the milk fresh.

The night was bright with a full moon, which had risen as we sat playing some music while the daylight lasted. I had seen the sun rise while down the shore getting firewood. I found in a driftpile a handle for a foot adze, never used and in good condition. Strangely, I had been looking for a stick to use as a handle in that tool, for I had borrowed one from Andy minus the handle. I suppose one could find anything, given time, but here I found a special article when needed, a rare coincidence.

Last night as I pulled offshore against the trees but still in the inside, I heard the peepers across the river, a spring song as fine as a bird's. That shore is flat and low, very different from this, and I hear red-winged blackbirds, killdeers and other birds not found here, besides the peepers.

We had greens again for dinner. This time shawny, or milkweed, and wild beet. Raw, cut up and served with oil, vinegar, brown sugar and salt, very good.

March 29   I called on the Detisches this afternoon, rowing up in the johnboat, carrying the adze I had put the handle in, to show Andy. They were all on their porch and I sat in the johnboat with Skipper and visited awhile. They keep track of the whole neighborhood, keenly observant, and our activities are part of their concern. They wanted to know——

March 30 Good Friday and somewhere, I suppose, they are singing the Brahms *Requiem*. . . .

I had gathered some greens in my old fields on the hill, and these I showed to Sadie for positive identification. It pleased me to find that it was really squaw cabbage and rock lettuce that I had picked, and land cress. Also the first poke. These we had for supper, a wild mess, but good. We heard many birds on our walk, more on the hilltop it seemed, although the sun shone a little when we arrived there. The first brown thrasher and in the fields a meadowlark.

Those fields, where I have wandered so many days in the confines of the town—now I have no regret from not seeing them. They are in the past, like those days which I would not want to come back. It is wonderful though, how much I found then, such a variety of growing things, because, I suppose, I knew it so well.

The river continues to fall and we inch out into the river, leaving the protection of the trees. Today I picked up a new pick handle floating by.

March 31 Considerable rain during last night. The fall of the river continues and now we are over the edge of the bank and should show a riding light tonight. I walked aways up Three-Mile and over the ridge east to Winter's Lane. All familiar ground, for some 16 or 18 years ago I had the studio on Winter's Lane, and wandered over every foot of these hills and hollows. Those must have been dark, lonely days, for these views always seem to be under lowering clouds, in chill winds.

April 1 Steady, gentle rain without wind coming on at nightfall, after a cloudy afternoon. I think of the plants in the woods, the wild flowers we saw and the tender plants we gathered for our dinner. I think of the tender slip with a tiny leaf or else a grass blade, the sprouting plants in our garden. Ring is asleep in a barrel somewhere. All the drowsy world of people hears the rain on roofs. Our roof is so close. The rain falls softly into the river which is under us, too.

April 2 We rowed the boat across the river, looking at the fair hillside bright with new green and redbud and white bloom of pear, under which we live. . . .

Darkness falls, with a misty rain. I sit by the fire, my sweet wife preparing supper by candlelight. The little dog sleeps on her bed, belly full and weary after the day's running. I look through the open door at the familiar view downstream, different though, as often as I look that way. Now I can hardly believe the hills were blue and purple, the near mass of trees brown. The hills are fresh green now, even the trees along the water, at least their tops, for the falling water leaves them bare and muddy. The rain falls harder, tapping on the roof. The lights downstream shine out in their familiar pattern.

April 4   A showery morning, a flash of lightning, a roll of thunder, the sweep of rain across the river. I was out in the johnboat in the driftpiles below, and picking up two 4x4s 8' long, highway posts thrown off in the mud, over the bank where they would never be recovered. These I had spotted yesterday. I also found 3 good apples in a paper bag, and in the driftpile, several good pieces of timber. Quite wet and muddy when I made the boat again.

People have a fear that freezing weather will come. The trees and plants have no thought of that.

Being on the river seems to bring one closer to the sky. You can see it better without foreground all around, and nothing overhead. Then the water is closer to air than solid earth. Also, the sky is so often reflected in the water that we sometimes seem to live in the air. Even when the water's surface is disturbed and clouds are overhead, there is much light. Only seldom is the air heavy and dark.

This country is all familiar to me, but now it is like having a new territory.

April 5   These long days are good. I arise at sun up, rather just before. We still have our supper after dark, and in between there is time for work and leisure. Really no distinction can be made between the two. There is no pressure about any of it, except when I get in a hurry, or we must meet an engagement at a certain time. We enjoy our playing together these days, after a bath, before dusk.

April 8   Yesterday we worked in the garden on the hillside above the tracks, breaking up another patch of ground, planting more peas and beans and a little corn. . . .

Skipper is eager to go in the johnboat with me, insists on it, but is anxious to get on shore, especially when her friends range along. This morning there were 4 dogs with me, all of a size.

A sign of spring, the first Sunday excursion of the *Island Queen.*

April 9   After breakfast and the chores we go up the hill. . . . Then down over the hill by no path and again the wide span of the river valley, the sweeps of the bend, all in a slanting sunlight, which made the sloping hillsides into a single flat shadow. Always the uplift in spirit when town is left behind and this expanse opens to us.

April 11   The *Arthur Hider* up at noon with only a loaded fuel flat. It was followed by the *Verity.* The sight of both coming toward us, close to the far shore, had a lot of steamboat in it. Often the boats seen close have not. Their charm is glimpsed as they round a bend, away, or approach in mid-river, a pillar of smoke arising.

April 12   Yesterday in the evening light we ate our supper out on the forward deck, using the covered tub, in which river water settles clear, for a table. It was a novel experience, with the river coming toward us. We felt that we were moving through the water.

This morning, as the sun rose red, we dropped down the river in the johnboat. . . and went up to the clearing where the log-roll house used to stand. Here Mrs. Grissom had made a garden last year, but she not wanting it now, we planned a garden of our own.

April 13   Our new garden and the season and weather demand our time and attention. . . . There is considerable ground to break up in our four gardens.

The river continues to fall. Now we are down the steep bank and over the rocky shore, with two spars out, as far as they can hold us from shore. The water is getting more clear and warmer, though still cold, as I found when I bathed on the gangplank at midday.

April 14   The *Omar* came in after dark, searchlights blazing, slacking headway to land her tow. . . . As she passed here the deck hands were loading a line into the yawl from the barges in the glare of a searchlight; an empty oil barge was being shifted from one side to the other around the head of the tow. A strange, monstrous animal, casting her eyes about.

April 16 This evening I thought I heard a thrush warbling in the far distance, as one might hear the song in a dream. I had walked down the track gathering greens and we had a good mess for supper, mostly poke.

The rain pelts down as I write this, Anna asleep in the bed where I shall go presently. Skipper asleep curled up on a cushion atop the two chairs. She is delighted when she can have a chair and a cushion for herself, which is rarely possible here. I write by lantern light and think of the river flowing past, the rain beating on the wet hillsides where the green growth is already knee-deep and the leafy trees close us in from the sky.

April 18 At day-break this morning, under a clear sky, the thrush sang and the catbird. Now it can be summer.

This cool evening, clear, the slanting sun lighting up the far shore across the dark river, where the trees waved in the strong wind which turned them almost white as it passed. The petty affairs we are concerned with on this wild earth!

April 19 The hickory buds are opening now, the gaunt, spare tree, its thick twigs with those great, tender expanding buds.

The river rises steadily, gradually mounting the steps I made up the bank, like an uninvited guest.

No gardening today. In fact, no work, in that sense, all day almost I might have worn my good clothes.

April 21 The railroad motorcar, with a crew of laborers aboard, stopped just below the garden, and one of the men dashed up the hill with a pick and a piece of newspaper. I could not see what he did, but when they started up and passed me I saw that he carried a wild larkspur, its roots wrapped in the paper.

April 22 Yesterday was a rough day on this stretch of water, with a high wind from the north. An extra stern line was run out, and the boat pitched considerably. As the afternoon wore, the wind dropped and by night the river was smooth. It began to fall immediately on reaching 29 feet, having mounted our steps half way, gently and with even pace, as the sun descended Hawthorne's steeple.

I worked 5 or 6 hours on the *Bozo* with the Detisch family. It had beached out with a list toward the river, and Andy wanted it more level so that the water would spread over the entire bottom to keep it from drying out and cracking. The importance of this I did not realize at first. It was a heavy job in the soft mud and sand underneath. Now this morning there is a fresh breeze downstream and the lines ahead are taut. . . .

In the afternoon we rowed, or drifted, down to our garden, planted some lettuce, carrots and beans, and had supper there, rowing home in the first shine of the half moon.

April 23 Yesterday I was quite surprised to find a fish on a line I had put in from the stern—a tiny catfish which we put back in the river. This morning we caught 4 little chubs and another little catfish. The chubs we ate for dinner. It was food as innocent and clean as the poke we gather, and I feel the same about cutting a fine growing stalk as I did about taking the fish from the water. The worms have the worst of it.

April 24 Our fish line with the tiny hooks was out today. For perhaps half an hour morning and evening the small fish were biting in this shallow water. We caught a catfish as long as the pail was wide, two other fish neither of which I knew and 2 or 3 chubs. This is getting serious. I suppose we must get a license and lines and tackle. Fried for supper they were very good.

April 25 The little fish were biting again this morning for a short time, and I quickly caught a dozen. One was a catfish, a beautiful slender one, bluish. Another was unknown to me, slender and round with a pointed head, a green or golden color, barred along the back, lighter underneath. These we cooked for dinner with boiled greens and baked potatoes. Coming back from the store where I went to mail letters, I picked up a fishbox in the driftpile that will serve, with a little repair. Perhaps we can catch fish to sell this summer, have a sign out on the road.

Our garden above the railroad track is flourishing. Lettuce and spinach are big enough to eat, so we will have some in a salad for supper with the little carrots I thinned out and young lamb's quarter. Late in the afternoon we rowed down to the other garden and set out some tomato plants that were languishing here in a box.

The river is falling and suggests pool stage. Perhaps dams are being raised above. Anna was reading about Rouault, I was whittling a wood block, water heating on the stove for the washing. I went out on deck every few minutes to take off little fish or put worms on hooks.

Summer comes closer every day.

April 26   Coming home tonight, the almost full moon casting a veiled light through the broken clouds, a chill wind blowing from the N. W., late it was, we found the river had risen and Skipper was unable to come ashore to meet us. We managed to get on board and pull the boat in, set up a footboard to the gangplank and walk on board with dry feet. The cello to carry, too. Then a fire and a few paragraphs of Thoreau's journal. We settle back on our own level, and all seems very right again after the dissipation of going about.

Our meal today was charming. A mess of tender young spinach from the garden, boiled a little, and the delicious juice we drank, too; a pan of tiny fish fried brown, caught just this morning. This was Gulliver eating Lilliputian food.

The river rises and falls without changing much either way. This morning I had to get out and shove out a log that had drifted against us. Under a cloudy sky I was unable to decide whether the dim light was from the moon or daybreak. The birds seemed not to be sure either, and I would hear a few notes from a song sparrow or cardinal eager to begin the day.

April 27   In the morning, not very early, but without breakfast, I walked up Three-Mile Valley. I believe it is the best around here, mostly because there is no road and the water is clean and abundant. I came back along the ridge to the east through fields and pastures, filling my sack with poke, asparagus, rhubarb, the first daisies. I heard the chat and red-eyed vireo, birds of summer. . . .

April 28   This roaming the fields and woods, gathering the wild or neglected fruits of the earth appeals to me, and is I think in no way trivial. Rather than to farmer or nomad, it relates to the Garden of Eden.

April 29 We had several visitors today, seeming to come one after another. We may have to drop down the river aways, if this place is too available and well known. Yet so far we have enjoyed our company.

April 30 Now we have a fishbox floating by our boat and more character has been added to our outfit.

May 1 Donald had supper with us last evening, and today began work at Coney Island. He came down after work a little alarmed at some gossip about us leaving. We hear strange things about ourselves, too. The other evening, when we took our instruments to Covington to play, we waited in the store for the bus. Next day I was asked what radio station we played over. A certain picture I painted when the water was high was seen by Donald and little Roy, and now is one of the features of Brent gossip. If the natives were to hear us play or see the picture, their opinion of us would drop, and we would be considered almost as frauds, although we have made no claims at all.

May 2 Sometimes it seems that I dissipate the days into little fragments and accomplish little, but looking back over the days, each has some production or achievement, whatever its value. Today, a wash day too, and in spite of the cloudy morning, all was dry in the wind and faint sun by midafternoon. There was also some painting, that is, a sketch or two, watercolor, and woodblocks printed, a few more good ones of the old block and a trial of the new one. Also we did some reading which was profitable, bearing on our life, and work. I am proud that we can read Emerson and Thoreau with our heads up.

May 3 I go around Grand Avenue almost down to Newport, and pick asparagus along the roadside. I know where to look for it, yet continually find it in new places. This is hunting game for me. It is good to get back to the boat again by the fire and have a warm bath. I use the Altamont Road for bicycle trips now. It is a shorter route, but steeper, so that I walk the last stretch. But the way appeals more to the imagination, this private way through the woods, where other vehicles cannot go and no one is met.

May 5   These are cool wet days with frequent showers and wind. One cannot work in the ground, and all growing things need warm sunshine. They are cheerful days on board, though, with fires blazing.

The river has been falling slowly. . . . We are no longer in the gap of our little clearing, and cannot see the railroad. We feel much closer to our neighbors the Detisches, who can look down on us from their porch. From this, we seem nearer to all people and towns. With a boat, though, each anchorage is temporary, for a longer or shorter period. Just one night, if one desires it so.

May 7   When I have been in the hills I come back to the river feeling that I have escaped from a sort of confinement, and find more freedom here. There the land is all owned, one is a trespasser. The roadways are open to all, but so narrow and traveled compared with the broad river. Also I am disturbed now in the country, though I believe never before, because there is so much up-and-down and unevenness. There is lacking the feeling of repose and balance. Yet how wonderful, unbelievably fair, is the countryside now. The song of birds is everywhere. I came back with my sack filled with asparagus, rhubarb and poke. Blackberries bloom now.

This morning early the *Arthur Hider* was down with the third tow of houses we have seen, 19 this time on 4 lengths of barges or sand flats. Dan McTamney was here when I returned, on the after deck with his feet hanging over, playing his mouth harp. He went down the river with us to the garden where we had dinner. . . .

A hard rain after dark, a prospect of a rainy night. The river rising slowly and I must move the lines up the bank.

It makes little difference to us here and now, whether the river rises or falls. Yet when it comes up, we have an uneasy feeling about it and a release of tension when it begins to fall. This is not strongly felt, we are hardly conscious of it, but nevertheless it is definite. Dwellers along the shore and in beached boats think they feel this way because the rising water might reach them, but it is partly from this other cause.

May 8   Far off this morning, in the direction of the city, we heard the whistles and sirens, and surmised that warfare had ceased and victory was being celebrated.

It was rough weather last night. The hard rain seemed continuous and the wind was strong. We were tossed about. The johnboat took the worst of it. I lay awake listening to the noises. The footboard splashed into the water, loosened by the waves and rising river. Yet the morning was calm, cool and the sun rose clear. It shone all day, fortunately, as Anna washed the clothes.

May 9 I visited with Andy and Sadie this morning in their small, littered kitchen, not clean but with a certain air of home and welcome to visitors. They told of Patsy the cat who had kittens a week ago. It seems she had chosen the kindling box, a small wooden box just large enough for her, with a few sticks in the bottom, an uncomfortable bed but the folks let her have her way, merely carrying box and kittens outside. Sadie told all this nearly in tears, her hard face even more set. Some stranger had looked at the kittens and taken out the sticks. Because of this handling, Patsy had killed the kittens, biting their throats and dragging the bodies away. This is all quite in character for cats, as they impress me. Other news was about Dellie Grissom, who is to be married and move away. In fact, is moving now. She is to marry Warner Cunningham, Sadie's brother. His former wife, Rosie, was the mother of Sadie's son-in-law, John Garlander. She died some five weeks ago. Sadie's sister, Josephine Harris, who lives in a little house up the railroad, close to the tracks, is scheduled to move into Mrs. Grissom's house. All the conversation I heard was so rich, had so much character and drama, that it would be worth writing down word for word. A cold summary of what they said has not near the worth.

May 13 A summer day, strangers about, down to walk along the river, motor boats on the water. The cottonwood casts loose its seeds, like wisps of cotton. They swirl past our window like falling snow. The river rises slowly, 26 feet now or more. The water stays clear and there is little drift so each hour we expect it to stop rising. This morning early a yellow-billed cuckoo, his familiar notes heard close by.

May 14 I walked the track as the red sun rose clear over the Ohio hills, down to the garden where I chopped the weeds now growing tall and broke up the crisp, moist ground. A summer morning, warm and still, the song of birds everywhere.

Yesterday we had guests, all in their Sunday clothes, awkwardly making their way along the tracks. Older people almost lose their power of handling themselves, after a life of riding, or walking only on pavements. Even poor people in the cities and towns live a life of external luxury and softness. It was a problem to get these people down our path and into the boat, and we were relieved to get them out again, dry, and whole. Now we wonder if they have ivy poisoning. Yet we are pleased when anyone comes, even if curiosity is their principal motive. Yet I believe there is a deeper reason, a real interest in our way of life.

May 16 These are rainy days, warm and sultry between heavy showers, thunder and lightning, driving rain veiling the distance, then bright sun, the weather of June. We washed today and hung out the clothes in the midday sun, but they were rinsed again and again by the rain. Sadie, fishing from the steps below the boat, smoking her pipe. A boy was there, fishing too, earlier, and Donald after work. He works at Coney Island, rowing across about 7 in the morning, returning in the afternoon. He brought us a card this evening which was addressed to us, "Houseboat on river, Brent, Kentucky."

May 17 A rainy morning, though not so hard downpours. I tinker with windows and screens. . . . After a day or two, or more, with no painting, all my activity and busyness seem empty and trivial.

May 18 Terns floating down on driftwood, four of them on a short piece close together, balancing themselves to the pitching of their craft which was barely long enough for them.

River rising, up over the bank now. I row past the place where we were tied up yesterday, and it is difficult to recognize any trace of us; it might have been years since anyone used that path, and in the higher water hardly a tree or a rock is familiar. We vanish more

61

completely than a dweller in a tent, for the water leaves no trace.

May 19   It was a busy day, with the excitement and tension of rising water, gardening. . . . Drift has been heavy all day, and when we returned from the garden, a snag was caught alongside our boat. It was the waterworn remnant of a large tree, oak probably, the trunk, root and stumps of branches at least six feet longer than our boat. . . . We floated down to the garden late in the afternoon and worked almost until dark. . . . We rowed home in the pale moonlight, a fine evening. Boat at a different angle, headed partly into the bank, and all the world is turned around a few notches.

May 20   A great event occurred today. By the calendar it was time for Skipper's puppies and sure enough she stayed close today, not following me as she did even yesterday. She was very restless, sometimes crawling into a nest under some sheets of metal, then coming into the cabin. I went down to the garden alone in the boat late in the afternoon and when I returned an hour or an hour and a half later I heard a squalling inside. Three pups had come out. By evening there were five, all in the corner behind the stove, a favorite hideaway of Skipper's. When we started the supper fire she became too hot, so we moved them all to a pen near the other stove where Skipper usually slept at night. Much squirming and whimpering. Skipper very quiet and wise through it all.

Detisches' boat came afloat yesterday, with great concern at first as to leaks. There were no serious ones, but considerable pumping. Now that they are floating safely, with only the ordinary pumping to do, the tension has relaxed.

May 21   We moved Skipper and her family, all doing well, to a house and yard on the shady bank. She comes to the water to drink and once followed me to the garden. There she suddenly remembered her youngsters and hurried back. . . .

It is a big garden we see now, and if it turns out well will produce a year's supply for us. The view is splendid there, of the river both up and down, and the little town across lies in the afternoon sunlight.

May 25   Yesterday the *Ferry Queen,* motorboat that carries passengers to and from Coney Island, came from down the river towing a landing flat. Now she is tied up above Detisches' and we have a neighbor afloat.

The river falls steadily, 29 feet this morning. Soon the rocks will show at the bottom of the bank and we will think of pool stage.

May 26   We see so much out of our windows, and miss much too, no doubt. A solitary bird floating down on a log, black and white and brown, curious marking, which we identified as a ruddy turnstone. The *Omar,* shifting barges as she passes slowly. The mate calls from the tow and the slow, pounding wheel stops.

May 27   The full moon rose copper-colored above the pale lights of man. . . .

A summer day in every aspect. Everything seems relaxed a little, less aspiring. This morning I put some legs under the Detisches' boat, in the middle, so that Sadie can walk about in safety. She helps me, tells me how to do all of it, hands me tools and blocks as I work in the mud underneath. She trudges through the mud, wearing enormous overshoes, sweating away, patient in all. . . .

Skipper's pups are a week old now, and grown larger and stronger. We derive much entertainment from watching them, and her, for she is a painstaking and sagacious mother. She has her own life too, and goes off with us or on expeditions of her own.

May 29   The affairs of the world are revealed to us by visible evidence, not beaten into us by radio and newspaper. We see the Chippy making regular trips all day, and surmise that something is wrong with the buses. Sure enough, a strike has stopped their operation. It makes little difference to us, nor would it to most people if such news was not made important by its way of presentation. This is true to a large extent. Perhaps there would be no wars if they were given no publicity.

May 30   Very conveniently for us at the end of our lines to shore, the river has been at an even level for 36 hours, falling very slightly. I guess the stage is about 18-19 feet. The water is clearing, current slackening. The river goes into summer like the countryside. The early swimmers splash into the water on the far shore. . . .

I chop weeds in the garden across the tracks this bright morning. All grows fast now. I pull out a carrot big enough to eat. The weeds surrounding the little space of tended earth are high and rank. Except for our efforts the whole hillside would be an unbroken growth, a miniature Amazon forest.

June 2   A clear sunrise, but clouds in the west and in the earliest morning thunder and rain. I went to the garden before the rain, walking all the way along the shore now that the river has fallen. However, I must come home without accomplishing much. But the rain is good and needed.

Gardening is a battle. The earth would rather have horseweeds and wild sunflowers than beans and sweet potatoes. The insects and rabbits feed on our tender plants. A constant struggle is called for to bring in a crop, and losses must be counted on, rather than gain.

This life that we lead makes demands on us that we would not have to meet in the prevailing mode of living nowadays.

Yesterday, the first day of June, we saw a lightning bug. That was summer.

I think of the days I used to spend on the river, paddling about rather aimlessly. All is so different now. When I take out the johnboat, it is for a definite purpose—a trip to the garden or across the river or for wood or drift.

Late in the afternoon there was a hard rainstorm, straight down, the heavy drops seeming to bounce from the water. The storm passed off to the east and the sun shone, low in the sky. There was a beautiful rainbow, very distinct, one end springing from the water just outside our window. For once we were at the rainbow's end. It receded across the river still in front of the glistening trees, the green band of the rainbow giving them an unearthly look. The distant ridge was still veiled by the rain. All this moved off into the eastern sky and we went about our business.

June 5   This doesn't seem like June. Winter had more reality. Then there was less distraction. No people and pleasure boats, amusement park or ferry, yet above all is the serenity and unconcern of the river.

June 6 Another trip up the hill yesterday, occasioned by strawberries mostly. We picked about 4 quarts of fine ones. Perhaps only
3, but we have an abundance of excellent fruit, such as few people
can enjoy this year. . . . In the afternoon, after a good dinner, and
reading and hulling strawberries at the same time and some playing,
we rowed down to the garden, spraying, hoeing, planting. . . .

These mornings Andy and Donald go across the river and Andy
rows back very slowly, backwards part way. It is hard on him and
climbing the bank, too. I stopped to chat a while at dusk this evening. Sadie, tired from extra chores and climbing the bank, sitting
there, heavy and well-braced, smoking her pipe. Yet she is high-
strung, sensitive and imaginative.

This morning I made a short excursion into the hills, up to
Dodsworth Lane, then Duck Creek to Winter's Lane. It is good to
get into the hills and hear the crickets and smell the new-cut grass.

June 8 Now it is summer, and cool days and a fire for warmth
seem far back, though it was but yesterday, even this morning.

Yesterday I ferried Donald across, but today Andy made the
trip. I always bring back something. Driftwood, perhaps a good board
or two, firewood anyway; a black-crowned night heron on the end
of the dike where the shallow water swept over; a sketch or a picture.

June 9 I was wakened in the night by a boat, either by the
noise of its engines, or lights or its nearness. For when I looked out
it was just ahead of us, perhaps no more than three rods, propellers
turning slowly, a big diesel. It had swung way inshore to get lined
up to go ahead, and suddenly it went full speed ahead, apparently.
It sent a great wash against us, the strong current flooding over our
gangplank and footboard. I was dressed, ready to slack off the headline if necessary, but the towboat, which had loaded oil barges ahead,
moved slowly away. The stern spar was carried away. I reset this,
and as the towboat had crossed the river and was waiting behind
the dike for a downbound boat, I went back to bed and was asleep
before the other boat passed us.

Sometimes, the good times, and quite often, I feel the river strongly, its course through the green valley and all the life it flows by. . . . The green hills of June and the summer evening sky, these and the river are part of the earth on which I live, a stranger and traveler here at Brent as much as if I were passing by never to see it except this once, on this day at sunset.

3

The Spell of the River

Through the metamorphosis of all things caused by our coming to live on the river, Brent had taken on a new meaning. We were content within its limits, and felt no longing to visit distant fields. . . .

Our original plan was to begin our voyage down the river that first winter, completing the boat on the way. Now that we were actually living on the water, we felt no desire to set ourselves adrift. It was a strange new world we had entered. . . .

The spell of the river was upon us.

June 10, 1945 A fine dawdling day, rain threatened and finally coming in hard showers toward evening. I had a morning bath, diving into the water from the after deck, climbing into the johnboat, soaping myself and diving in again. After all the years of swimming in the river under many circumstances, this is a new experience, and brought out strongly the conditions of our life here. We really have our house afloat.

Today we put out a sort of a trot line, tying one end to the boat, the other to a rock as anchor, with a few hooks baited with worms. It is fine to go out on the water on business.

June 11 After a fair dawn, with a swim soon after sunrise, it became cloudy and rained steadily, gently and warm. I had engaged myself away but the rain kept me here, and the morning was a gift which made me very happy.

June 12 I find that I spend more time than I realize in visiting. I talk with people all along the way: with Andy and Sadie at their porch; with the Wilmers, sprouting potatoes at the door of their root cellar in the shade, when I go for milk; I pass a few words with the storekeepers and customers at the store; and we have occasional visitors on board, invited or accidental.

Today a young artist with two friends, making holiday, somewhat out of place, compared to us living on the water, or the natives. Yet there is room for all, and these and other trappings of summer will go with the insects at frost. The artist asked me if I was "exhibiting," but that to me seems more unnatural than otherwise.

June 13 At daybreak, caring for the howling pups, I saw the gangplank was flooded by the muddy water, a rising of perhaps 16 inches overnight. I put out the lantern and went back to sleep, on this sultry, uninspiring dawn. Later a plunge into the murky water, good though, and an hour's work changing the lines and tossing wood up hill. I never carry this far, as would be foresighted, but toss it ahead of the rising water. This I did in the flood. Also, if I once set aside a piece of driftwood to save, I care for it for days and regret its loss, if that happens, even if it is the most useless piece of yellow pine.

I rode up to the Wilmers' for milk to have with our breakfast since all that we had was sour last evening. I met old Kits on the road. The years have changed her hardly at all, not weakened her frail frame or dulled her flashing spirit. It is strange to think of those old days on Winter's Lane, to be here in the same neighborhood, with visible reminders of those lonely wanderings and dark searchings, yet with flashes of brightness, and painting and thinking of a kind I will do no more.

June 15 These nights I get up to quiet the puppies who twice in the darkness, possibly at the same time of the clock, all rouse at once, yelping, trying to climb out of their pen, and some do. I put them out, they find Skipper, and after they satisfy their hunger they explore the corners of the cabin, tug at a shoe or the edge of the bedding, all by candlelight. I am back in bed now and when they quiet down I put them back in the pen, which I had cleaned before, put out the candle and all is quiet. The vision of the night stars, perhaps, makes these wakenings like a fair dream, and the second time there is a faint light in the eastern sky. Half asleep through it all, I look out at the river and the simple aspect of earth and sky, and seem close to the heart of the earth.

June 16 A showery dawn after a night of intermittent rain. Rain is always imminent nowadays. Night before last it was very heavy. Four-Mile Creek was running out and I must be up between showers with spike pole shoving the drift from the head of the boat. A good walk board drifted in, a worn plank of white pine, 18 or 20 feet long. I found an unopened tin can in some drift, and must open it to see what it could contain, of all the numerous possibilities. This I did with Anna and Skipper watching and to the disappointment of all of us, found just some thick lubricating oil.

June 18 Saturday night was a wild one on the river. The heavy rain at dusk had sent torrents down the creeks and heavy drift was running close to the bank, piling up against the boat and spars. I was up late, with a long spike pole that Andy loaned us, and before daybreak. A long, heavy log became fast under the crossways and gave me quite a tussle. The river rose three or four feet. During Sunday it lapsed as many inches but was rising slowly at evening, and this morning was on the step below the one marking 29 feet.

Contrary to custom we went up the hill on Sunday, walking up in a gentle rain. As we were to leave the studio a heavy downpour held us there, pleasantly, by a fire reading *Typee* and before that listening to a Brahms quartet. All this time, however, an alarming happening was taking place at the boat. When we looked down at our landing from the top of the path, the johnboat was gone, a bare space where it had been tied. The staple to which the chain was fast lay on the deck, and I was convicted of gross carelessness. I called to Sadie who was at her steps, but she knew nothing about it. At once I rode the bicycle down to the camp below, and from our garden, saw to my joy our red boat tied up with their green one. Later, coming back with it, I caught drifting a little pup of a johnboat less than six feet long, which now rides jauntily astern.

June 19 This morning we have fresh raspberries for breakfast. I picked them just before from some vines which grow along the track. They are specially large, comparable to the cultivated ones, and with our fresh, rich milk, make the highest kind of food. Even the most wealthy epicure could not have better, and this could be said of many of our dishes. The vegetables from our garden, for instance. . . . —peas, two kinds, carrots, turnips, beets, chard, celery, cabbage greens, broccoli, lettuce, three kinds, parsley, beans. . . .

June 20   Today I walked up Three-Mile Valley, a lovely place in all seasons. . . . Today is memorable because I identified a bird whose song has puzzled us. Now we know it is the alder flycatcher. Skipper went with me on the walk. It was a fine June day, the country fresh and green now.

June 23   Walking down the valley by the narrow road at dusk, with our cans of berries and sack containing other items gathered from the fields we passed, I heard a mockingbird in the far distance, I thought. Then a whip-poor-will. I was surprised at this for they are not here in summer. The mockingbird's song continued and as we passed some trees, pines among them by a house, we realized that the singing bird was just overhead, singing not loudly as in daytime, but in an even, sweet voice, pouring forth in the twilight the loveliest bird melody that one could ever hear. He imitated several birds, the rhythm and intervals accurately but in his own voice—a blue jay, cardinal, Carolina wren and other notes which were evidently in imitation. The whip-poor-will must have been one of these, though its song was not repeated. We listened a long time as it grew darker.

June 26   We make another excursion for dewberries on the ridge above Winter's Lane, and returned just before dark with ten quarts and some raspberries, these from a cultivated patch, or was it neglected this year? Going through Brent, everyone we met was surprised at our berries. We gave old Mrs. Witte a handful, and John Edwards some in his hat. Also a couple of quarts to Sadie, who gave us fresh eggs in return.

June 27   The dull, copper-colored moon rose tonight above the point of land where the river bends, and then sailed across the water.

June 28   These are warm dry days, and some of the abundant rain of a week or more ago would be welcome now. The wet ground is baked hard by the hot sun. . . .

We swim every day. It is good to dive overboard. One realizes more then that he is living on the water.

Night before last I was wakened by, or woke up to see, a searchlight just below us, the barges on a tow close to the shore, deckhands silhouetted against the light as they slid a plank down and carried a line ashore.

July 1 It seems to be fishing season now. This morning after we had landed Donald at the dock, Andy and I set out a trot line. . . .

July 2 Andy is a true fisherman and life flows back into him when he is out on the water, baiting hooks deftly. I enjoy his talk, which is meager enough. He mentioned the whistle of the old *J. T. Hatfield,* how it used to echo among the Kanawha mountains. Then, he said, it went on the *Mitchell,* and I remember when it had a whistle like the *Fleischmann* whose tone, Andy said, it resembled. Then it disappeared from the *Mitchell.* All this brought up by the *Charles R. Hook* whistling for the lock. It seems to have now the whistle off the *Fleischmann.*

Saturday night following the *Island Queen,* about 9:30 p.m., the *Gordon C. Greene* passed on its first trip up the river this summer. In the darkness, with its deep whistle, which has a mournful cadence at the close, it was like a real packet.

Below us on the other side another houseboat appeared a few days ago. A fine mark on the green shore. There is a landing just below us now where the Pollitts have two johnboats tied and a trot line off shore. Fishing is practiced all along now, boys on shore, boats anchored and trot lines set. . . .

This is a windy day with a secret exhilaration about it. When I look at the rough water patched with cloud shadows, the boat pitching slightly in the wind waves—all this is from a higher plane somewhere above these little affairs. Yet they are part and lead into it.

The fishing was good last night. Andy and I baited the line

with minnows after taking off three catfish. After Donald came across he and I traced the line in the still darkness, a little rain falling. There were six fish on the line, one a good-sized perch. The line had 47 hooks. This morning was rainy and everyone was sleepy, even I was up later than usual. Donald and I traced the line about 9 o'clock, with Anna in the stern. There were 9 or 10 catfish, all nice ones. So we had fish for dinner, all we could eat, and the Detisches must be full of them too, for Donald took up some ten pounds.

July 5 I recline in the stern of the johnboat, these summer evenings into the twilight, looking at the sky, water and hills, absorbing the forms and colors, the character and details, making it all part of my very bones, all while Andy is deftly baiting the trot line. Or I go out in the starry night alone, mist rising, thickening into obscuring fog. . . .

It is good to see how Andy revives when he is engaged in this work, which he does so quickly and neatly. I am no fisherman at heart, nor am I a born gardener. Such pursuits occupy the entire time and thought of some people but to me they are one of many things to do, all good, all subordinate to a greater occupation, and leading to it and supporting it.

It is natural to catch this food that swims under us as it is to raise beans and potatoes on shore. It is a good diet, too. We have an abundance of food, rare in these days, of prime quality, and the fun and adventure of procuring it for ourselves.

July 6 Anna and I traced the lines this morning and brought back 21 catfish, large, up to 2 pounds, and small ones. Most about a pound. . . . The natives come down to buy fish, 30 cents a pound strung on a string, weighed approximately with Andy's scales. We have agreed to divide the money thus taken in, and use or give away all the fish neither family wants. So far we have received for our share $1.50. This pays for our license procured yesterday for $1.00, and we will probably be able to pay for the line and staging $1.65 and hooks 30 cents.

July 7 What has made this day memorable? My walk back in the hills in the late afternoon, picking the last raspberries and dewberries, perhaps; the cornbread that Anna made for dinner, the best yet, and really what we have desired. . . . There was a sturgeon on the line this evening when Andy and I traced the first one after baiting the second, a prehistoric monster almost.

July 8 I weary sometimes of writing about the stage of the river, fishing, the Detisches and dogs. This is not the true river news. When I go out on the water at night, and as I bait hooks, watch Cassiopaeia, rising in the eastern sky, draw up her fishline, Perseus with the misty Pleiades as bait and bright Venus caught, and then all grow dim in the faint beginning light of dawn, then I feel that I am fishing with the one who made the river and set her flowing. I feel its length and sinuous flowing, fed by swift streams in the wooded eastern mountains; and somewhere, through a country unknown to me except by hearsay, past the mouths of new rivers and towns known only by name, it will at last enter an ocean and lose its identity, as I will too, at the end of my devious flowing.

July 10 Yesterday we had the first potatoes from our garden, quite a good size, the first potatoes I ever grew. . . . The fishing was good last night. Donald and I brought in 19 last night, one a skipjack, and some small ones. This morning Anna and I went out.

July 12 These are cool days with a burning sun and chilly nights. A fog last night, and a boat, the *Ashland,* tied up below. Last night in the rising fog I baited and traced the lines, the bright stars overhead. . . . We caught 28 fish last night. Morning before Anna and I brought in 30 in the morning alone. We have been selling some 10 or 12 pounds a day. . . .

July 14 Yesterday the first ear of corn from the garden. . . . Yesterday we sold 20 pounds of fish, 10 or 12 the day before, and there was still some in the box.

July 15 I was out on the line after darkness fell, baiting the rest of the hooks by lamplight. The last two evenings I baited the lines by myself, Jess Detisch rowing out with me. He is a thorough river boy, as native there as a catfish and as much at home. I went out again late in the night, and when I came in the first daylight was showing through the broken clouds. . . .

We have now collected for our share of the fish sold, over $13.

It seems an innocent way to earn money. Besides, we have eaten all we could and given many away.

July 18 This place attracts boys. Sadie uses her grandsons very cleverly so that they help her and have a good time too. One is with me often, Jess or Jerry or Chuck, and Donald Wilson, to whom we gave the puppy called Junior, spent a morning here, going down to the garden with me. . . . Jerry made a paddlewheel with a rubber band, exactly as I used to when his age. He could not tell me where he learned how, but I could, for Frank instructed me. This must be an Ohio River tradition.

July 19 Last night after midnight I rowed up along the shore, taking advantage of the eddy up to the point. The half moon was low in the sky, and of a yellow color. I rowed away from the shore now and, caught in the current, drifted down, but in the darkness this change of direction was unnoticed. The shore willows moved by against the moon, but the effect to me was of a great orange lantern being carried swiftly along the railroad track.

July 20 I was amazed to learn that Sadie is two years younger than I.

Sadie visited us on the boat recently for the first time. She has hesitated all this time, because our stage boards did not look strong enough to support her weight. She is rather sensitive on that point. Our interior and furnishings made quite an impression on her, and in a few days Andy came in to see. All our guests are surprised when they enter the door and step down into the cabin.

Fishing has not been good lately. Some would say because it is in the light of the moon. I have an idea it is the swift current. . . .

These are hot July days. When there is no wind, as today, and the afternoon sun shines in, the cabin is pretty hot. Not bad, though, and it cools off at once when the sun dips behind the high hill to the west. Hot as it was, Anna washed clothes today, more than usual. I heated water on the rocky beach and the washing was done inside. I put up some lines on the deck, trot line and we hung clothes there, giving the boat a domestic housewifely appearance.

July 22 This morning a fine excursion after blackberries. Up early, both of us, at sunrise, a plunge in the river, a getaway breakfast, this time delicious new bread. Then the lines to trace, and not much on them. We rowed now up along the shore, almost to Four-Mile Creek, and tied the boat. . . . We climbed the hill to the Wilmers', where we dropped off our cans and a bucket for milk and water. Then we walked up the road and up Dodsworth Lane, with Skipper, Ring and a strange dog. Our berrying was done on the hillside to the left, where we found them large and abundant. We picked at least 7 quarts. Returning about 10:30 we stopped for our milk and water, and a phone call; or more important, a visit with those friendly people. It was good to get down to the river again.

July 23 Mondays are quiet, coming after days of noise and strangers. I traced the line alone Saturday night with barbaric revels ashore. That is how a writer might describe it, but the sounds and actions of savages would never—

July 25 People come to the boat for longer or shorter visits but without exception they get between me and the river. Some more than others, but it is only in solitude that I am conscious of the river above all else. I escape to the dry hills and pick blackberries and listen to the field sparrow, towhee and summer tanager.

This is hot weather, as it should be. I enjoy it as I do the cold. These days are part of the year's cycle. I think of them on winter nights and it does not seem possible that they should be.

The fishing is not good now, but to be out on the river on a warm night of the full moon, to watch the late afternoon change to night, or the first grayness come to the eastern sky, dimming bright Venus,—

July 29 Last week, arriving on the noon trip of the *Island Queen* Tuesday and leaving at 4 o'clock on Thursday, Warren and Patricia Staebler were here. Possibly the first string quartet to float on the Ohio River, and in a genuine shantyboat.

July 31 The dam was lowered today, in the afternoon while I was away on a bike trip to the city. Anna was here, and single-handed moved the boat inshore as the water rose.

On the river nothing is stable, all living fluctuates like the level of the water.

Our half of the money for the sale of the fish for July amounted to $29.15. This means almost 200 pounds of fish sold. We estimate that we have eaten, the dogs and all, 50 pounds, about 40 pounds given away, so this month we took from the river say 300 pounds of fish.

August 1   Another rainy day. Into the evening, too, after a fair afternoon. The river rising at nightfall after being stationary all day. I move the boat in, tie lines farther up the bank and am minded of winter evenings, though the katydids chant in the leafy trees overhead.

August 3   The river rises slowly. It is muddy, almost without drift. The free-flowing water and clean shoreline are a joy. Even fish in the live box feel the difference.

August 4   There is an unusual excitement about today, the rising river flowing swiftly, the sparkling air and sun.

Our boat being turned around makes a change in our living. We might have drifted down to a new landing, in a strange place. Last night I heard boats on shore, trains in the river. . . .

I was wakened by a rustling noise this morning and found a complete tree had drifted into the head of the boat, the dry leaves brushing the deck. Venus had risen in the east, and just above it, no brighter, the thin old moon.

August 8   We have begun fishing again, with the river in pool again. Monday we grappled for our line, across the river, and were lucky to get hold of an end and retrieve all the line and hooks. Tuesday we set out another line a little farther downstream, out of the course of the *Island Queen,* and Andy and Sadie began their trapping of minnows. They take that upon themselves and often spend most of the day on the bank, watching lest the waves of a passing boat roll the precious glass against a stone. Yet the hours are pleasant for them, sitting by the water with nothing much to do. Sometimes they sit together, more often one or the other. Once they had a disagreement and sat almost a stone's throw apart.

We baited the line before dark and traced it after the *Island Queen's* last trip down. There were only half a dozen fish, but in the morning Anna and I did better, taking off 13, one a perch weighing two pounds, and one on our little line. Tonight Anna and I went out on the river after sunset, a fine evening, rather cool, to bait the line.

August 10   I went out in the starry night, the Pleiades arisen, light fog on the water, all quiet and dark. I fished alone.

August 11   For a few fish I take to the Wilmers we receive a gallon of milk, half a dozen eggs, and 2 pounds of lard. This is to the advantage of both parties, for each gives what he has a lot of and receives what he lacks and needs.

August 18   The war is over, now, they say, but I who aided so little cannot celebrate the victory. On the other hand I did not hinder. For my part, I feel that nothing is ended or beginning. What conditions are changed?

Now we pick the peaches from the tree by the railroad, which we watched with increasing anxiety as they ripened. They are large and juicy, of beautiful color and flavor, many of them perfect.

August 24   I am never myself when anyone is with Anna and me. If they stayed long enough, I might come to the surface again.

August 26   Bright, clear night, last night. Moon past full, the air so clear the stars shone in the moonlit sky. . . . I was wakened in the night by a steamboat whistle and went out to fish.

In modern living there is such protection from the elements that those who live in cities pay little regard to the weather unless some extreme condition causes them discomfort or inconvenience. On the river we had lost this sense of communal protection, and were on our own. Our existence tended toward the primitive. Since natural forces affected us directly, we became more alert and watchful, always scanning the face of the sky, noting all changes of wind, weather, and river. . . .

Our senses were sharpened by this continual watchfulness.

September 3   This summer, fishing, I have watched the stars and planets in their course at all times of the night. . . .

Labor Day. They tell us that the *Island Queen* can carry 4000 passengers, and that yesterday 700 were turned away at the landing. The boat was behind schedule all day. This day is the last for it and Coney Island. Everyday will be Monday now. The river has not been quite normal except on Mondays and late at night.

September 6 This and yesterday morning I went out alone at daybreak to take off the fish, and bait. To see the day come from night, the bright stars pale, the rising sun, the sound of roosters crowing when it is still dark, to see the sunlight come down the wooded hillside, all this is an experience equal to the ending of a day.

Yesterday we put out a new line, just below the boat near the old one which we will take up. The clean line, new sharp hooks, the length of the line with the staging hanging down regularly, the odd collection of sinkers from someone's junk pile, the big stones at each end—

September 7 *Annie's Birthday.* Lamb roast today, with carrots and potatoes from our garden.

Travelers and strangers come by once in a while. A houseboat this morning towed by a small motorboat, rigged for quick landing, gear piled on decks and roof, even a johnboat loaded. They came in just below us, a stout girl at the bow, a young man handling the motorboat. A plank lay across the forward deck, extending over the water. When they touched shore the man walked out on the plank, which tipped down with his weight and the girl and some dogs went ashore. There was a big white duck too.

September 10 I write dull prose. Sometimes I feel a surge of ecstasy and a desire for a deeper, more concentrated expression where not a mere statement of facts would be given.

The riverbank, this open, rocky shore, is a flower garden now. Most lovely, the small, slender trumpet of a morning glory, white, purple and scarlet. By our path the zinnias and marigolds bloom and behind them, tall sunflowers.

September 13 Today Donald and I are after minnows. First on the Kentucky shore below the dam, and when a trap was opened we crossed over to the dike. A cool, gray day, wind easterly, a sprinkle of rain. With this occupation there is plenty of time for contemplation. One looks long at the familiar landscape, listens to the sound of insects, and of water pouring over the dam.

September 14   The days seem fruitless sometimes, much waiting and time occupied with trifles, work to be done hangs over for days; much is begun and left unfinished. Yet everything important seems to be done by the time it is needed; and sitting here by the dike with the minnow trap out, Anna writing a letter, Donald fishing with the "reel pole" and "cane pole," Skipper in the boat now ready to go home—these hours are not wasted. I must just look sometimes and marvel, not thinking of pictures or painting.

September 19   Monday I visited the garden across the river in Coney Island which seems to be abandoned. There I gleaned some beans, dry, some still green, dried corn. This is perhaps my favorite gardening.

September 21   The river rose swiftly last night and this morning to perhaps 24 feet. There was heavy drift, about as much as ever in the winter, and winter drift it was, not a sign of summer in it. I suppose there is no season to driftpiles. There were heavy logs, and great trees complete. . . .

I was out shoving driftwood away from the head of the boat and the Reusches, father and son, came by close in their old johnboat, the boy rowing against the swift current. The man's remark was, "Buddy, you're payin' your rent now."

The trip down the river is much on our minds now. We try to think it into reality. . . . Now at nightfall there is little drift on the smooth river, flowing now. This current makes our drifting seem more possible. It will be a great day when we cast off.

September 22   I write now on the sandbar below the dam. . . . It is pleasant here on this limited sandbar, insular, with the 3 dogs, and a little fire rekindled from the embers of a fisherman's fire. The wet dogs crowd close to the little blaze. The towboat *American* is passing up, slow against the swift current. This old boat, small and out-of-date, is a treat to see, but it reminds me of the time not far back when there were dozens like her and better.

September 24   It is strange that during this rise in the river the weather should be springlike. Moist warm air from the south, not the humid heat of June, but the warm, caressing breath of April. This all is in harmony.

September 26   The river rises so slowly it can hardly be gauged. How much water above, we do not know for certain. Even if we were told by engineers and experts what the river would do tomorrow we would but half believe it. It is all much like the future in our lives and nothing is quite sure, so we have not much faith in predictions.

September 29   When I leave the river, as yesterday, and see the countryside there in autumn sunlight, the fields with their varied harvests, asters and goldenrod along the road, I realize that this is not all, and that one would miss a great deal by living all the time on the river. The atmosphere changes when one leaves the shore. It is a different world.

October 1   Now the trains run an hour later and our clock must be regulated. It is a complicated affair, the sky its face, the sun, moon and stars its pointers; the figures on the dial are trains, whistles and bells.

October 3   Now is the season for pears, that is, Kiefer pears. I rode out Dodsworth Lane to the top of the hill and pick up some under the trees. Walnuts too, which seem plentiful this year. The countryside is wonderful now. I see a pair of winter wrens.

October 5   A few ducks on the river now and one gull, so far, one day this week. Today a misty day with low clouds, weather of a new season. We fish across the river and do well with a line or two tied to the willows. Quantities of catfish. Today an eel, the first one we have caught. The river falls a little, then rises again. We are close to the bottom of the bank. A cool night, the one before last, but warmer now with a misty rain.

To the symphony concert this afternoon, for a change from the riverbank. In the midst of it I thought of the shore close to the willows.

October 10   The coolest night last night, 32 degrees they say, but in the heavy fog no frost. Then the usual clear day, warm sun and clear air. The school bus was late, and the youngsters roosted along the road like sparrows. "Mr. Hubbard, that bus ain't come yet."

October 14   In the night we heard geese as they passed over. Ducks on the river now. Mornings we hear the song sparrows on the shore. They are our winter companions. The cardinals sing.

October 19   The autumn colors on the hills now, seen from midriver, such a glowing to the shaggy hillside—the bare stretch of rocky shore, then the scrubby trees all in color, red of poison ivy between. Above is the steep wooded slope, where now each tree stands out distinct as in spring.

We caught another eel this morning, perhaps 30 inches long. Keeping a tight hold on him until dinner time. It was a beautiful creature in color and form, of unique grace. The flesh was good, more fishy than I expected.

October 20   The spare chirp of crickets
At night one listens for each chirp
Dry leaves fall
Trees on steep hillside
Are like painted ones
Not all the same color or shade
Darkness falls early
We swim no more in the river

Selling fish to river people and fishermen, such as Al Edwards and Harry Smith—that is noteworthy. After we had gone to bed, two men appeared on shore with a flashlight. The boat was off shore as the traps were open. After the dogs had barked long and madly I roused up. The heavy box must be towed in, but we did not disappoint our customers.

October 21   Today our fish box was cleaned out, 21 pounds being sold to two parties. They buy fish now because they like to eat fish.

We had two skipjacks for our Sunday dinner. This fish is despised by many, but skinned and baked crisp, or broiled, you might say, we thought delicious. Broccoli from the garden, mashed potatoes and pear cake. As usual a home grown or home made meal. We take this as a matter of course. It would seem strange to buy all of our food, or even most of it.

October 23   Daily in all weathers I am overcome by the earth's appearance, the colors of the hillside and river shores.

October 25   Today and the two preceding days the Detisches worked at their new bottom plank. They did not work hard at it, waiting till the threat of rain was gone, and stopping when the wind blew hard. I helped off and on, in pretty much the same fashion.

October 28   The campers below borrowed our johnboat to put out some lines last night. . . . I see them going across now, three in the boat. The johnboat is almost part of me now, like my clothes, and looks as strange when used by others.

Yesterday we finished putting on the new planks on the Detisch boat's hull. . . . The work is fun, such an odd team working together. I am pleased with myself that I can fit in so well.

October 30   We fish now for food. We have eaten no fish since Saturday. Sunday we had chicken, a gift from Andy and Sadie.

November 3   When we came down to the river last night, after a trip to the city visiting, the footboard had floated away from the shore and I had to wade on board. In the night the north wind sprang up and it was a rough time. The spars did not hold, and I must get up and take in lines, move the johnboat; then later to stop the squeaking of a spar. So we slept late this morning and I woke suddenly to find us almost aground. In fact, one corner was fast on the rocks. The boat was moved off easily. Later the trap that had been raised to make this drop in the river was lowered and in the afternoon some wickets were lowered, so now we must move inshore. All this may seem like much bother and labor, but with convenient tie-ups and good lines, it takes little time. However, one must be always alert.

November 4   Suddenly a winter morning—frozen ground and ice, white frost showing through fog, the cottage chimneys smoking.
. . .

November 5   This morning a rare sight—a drifting shantyboat.

82

It was a rather small one, painted light yellow trimmed in white. Coming down past the dam in midriver. The south wind blew it toward the Ohio shore as it rounded the bend, and we saw a man rowing in a johnboat ahead of it to keep off the lee shore. He was later either blown ashore or he landed at the Water Works, but later he continued on down the river.

November 7   A quiet overcast day, when one could not hurry. The fringe of willows, it is now really a soft colored edge to the land, displaying colors, soft greens and yellows that are no longer to be seen on the stark hills. The river's shore always has its own season.

November 8   I cross the river at sunset and see the winter sun for the first time, a band of purple light on the distant ridge, the houses gleaming white below it, the blue shadow creeping up soon to put out this last light of day. Yet still the clouds gleam in the sun, floating in a clear green sky. It is all brief, night falls quickly. In the western glow a new moon shines.

November 16   The wind sprang up Wednesday morning from the north or northwest and we tossed in the waves all day. Even as darknesss fell the wind continued to blow and we were rocked in our sleep. Next morning, though, was calm and we were glad of it.

November 17   A mouse came aboard, and Anna discovered him, or his tracks, in the food cupboard. We set a trap and soon heard it go off. There was the mouse, caught by the tail and squealing. I turned him loose on shore. . . .

We seem resigned to our dogs. They are really a lot of fun. . . . Skipper is quiet and lady-like, Whizzer a rowdy, Brownie is keen.

November 26   Today was taken up pretty much by the washing of clothes and setting out a fishline. . . . I had previously launched the johnboat which looked not familiar, all painted red and named *Annie*. . . . A sailboat with two on board, passed down yesterday or the day before, almost flying with a current and downstream wind.

November 28   We played some yesterday morning and this, a good start for any day. How we enjoyed the Brahms quartet, even two parts at a time.

November 29 I feel that I haven't yet begun my river life, that I am not yet at the kernel of it. This will come, I think, when we leave this familiar territory and also when we have drifted aways and get farther from a city than we are at present.

November 30 Time is precious now more than ever, since the days are short. These cloudy days, darkness until 7:30 in the morning and from 5:30 p.m. Yet we have time for playing, reading, leisurely meals and a bath, even though the days are full of chores and work.

A sunny day is now hard to imagine. It seems impossible, like something dreamed of.

The days are full of accomplishment.

December 1 Unexpectedly the sky cleared, and tonight is cold and starry. The river rose slightly. There is just enough bar exposed at the bottom of our crude steps to give us a tiny beach. It is composed of ballast washed down the bank here.

This morning we set out our net, just off shore beyond the boat. Our attempt to catch fish on our line across the river has failed. I suppose methods successful in summer would not work in winter. Anna and I rowed over before dark but not a minnow had even been nibbled on. We landed to look for cabbages in the Coney Island garden, second growth ones, but found only a few second-rate heads. One after another of our summer crops comes to an end. The green corn we had today is the last. I picked up the last pears when out for walnuts. After this trip to Uhl Road, which is good walnut ground, we have perhaps our winter and next summer's supply.

December 7 A warm though winter day, a hazy sun after a cloudy morning. In the evening the new moon over the western ridge after many dark nights.

December 12 The last few days have been quite cold—11 degrees this morning I was told. The river falls slowly.

All is changed when there are strangers on board, and everyone is a stranger to me. The sky and earth itself are not the same, nor am I the same. Sometimes I wonder where I am these days, where my refuge is, where I can be found by myself. I am alone so seldom, in every action I consider other people.

I am pleased that our boat, our way of living, designed for us two, can accommodate others at the same time, with little strain on ourselves or our facilities.

December 14 A good snowfall yesterday, all the ground covered now. I go out into the dim moonlight to arrange the lines and shove out the boat for the falling river.

The dogs and the fires are company for us. I can't imagine the place without them.

December 16 We shucked out ears of corn from the withered standing stalks, bare against the snow, the dim moon already giving some light. There were flurries of snow as low clouds raced across. It grew colder by the minute. A duck hunter fired two shots, and his dogs went into the swift water after the birds. We filled our three sacks and a basket with yellow corn, which we had decided the grower had abandoned. We carried it as darkness fell down to the johnboat, white banks and dark river, and rowed across in the cold wind toward our lighted windows.

December 20 Awakened in the still, cold night, long night of winter, by the crunching, grating sound of moving ice. We were unprepared for it, too, for none was in the river all day. At daybreak we were frozen in, but the ice was thin. . . .

A sunrise of red and gold and blue, the sun over southern hills, to the right of the Ohio point. The moon rose there last summer. Now the moon, and it is just a night past full, or perhaps a full moon, rises directly in the east, by casual observation.

These are busy days, printing woodblock Christmas cards, getting off packages, baking, all in a spell of cold snowy weather, clear today but no melting. The snow six inches deep. I walk up the hill to Fort Thomas, up the hollow through the snowy woods. . . .

I chop wood on the snowy shore as darkness falls. What is this harmony?

December 21 Tonight a bright moon, late, though the sky is not clear. A river full of tinkling ice. . . .

This morning the ice between boat and shore was strong enough to walk on. A solid field had built up ahead of the boat, curving out into the river, so we had a quiet night, for the floating ice did not scrape us. Another morning of white frost.

December 22 Ice conditions about the same, river almost covered with broken, floating ice. Reported frozen over up above somewhere. We live and go about our work, thinking little about the ice. . . . We are used to the cold now and pay little attention. There has not been much cold windy weather, the still cold is pleasant. How the ice changes everything! Johnboat out on the bank now. It seems strange to see the rest of the world going on as usual.

December 24 Now the boats have a hard time getting their tows through the ice, and are delayed for hours at the lock. They are gay places at night with strings of lights and searchlights on the snow.

Last night the ice was heavier, running past the boat and shaking it. We were concerned about it, but could think of no better arrangement than the present one, so went to bed. We heard no ice during the night so I slept through, except once or twice when the dogs wanted out. By morning a sleety rain was falling, freezing.

The rain this morning froze to every twig and stem, transforming the earth.

December 25 This morning after a night of rain, much ice and drift ran by out of Four Mile Creek, the ice frozen thick and smooth in large sheets. . . . The fifth day of ice.

We find that Scottish tea scones and Sadie's Old Joes are the same. A wonderful dinner tonight, a chicken stewed, with mashed potatoes, gravy, hot biscuits, string beans and Christmas trimmings.

December 26 Last night the river was rising, and cakes of ice bumping into the boat, giving us a jolt each time. In the middle of the night, looking out, I was amazed at how much the river had come up and I had to move the boat in closer at once.

This morning I took the johnboat, which was floated yesterday by the rising water, down along shore for firewood, bringing back a good load, and turnips and carrots from the garden. I had covered them in the row with grass and earth and the snow had protected them further.

The beautiful flight of gulls into the wind.

December 27   The rising river floated loose sheets of shore ice which bore down on us, but the largest ones, of an area several times that of our boat, missed us. . . .

December 28   Cakes and sheets of ice bumped into us during the night, some of the jolts so heavy that before morning I got up and rigged a boom ahead, using our long spar which I replace with the other plank. I tied the spar at the outside corner of the boat, and it was held in position by a line to the shore. It worked very well for ice and drift.

Warm today, dead calm, a pale sun for awhile in the middle of the afternoon.

A visit today from Lou Gander, who came down over the bank with a bucket of coal he had picked along the railroad, a gift for us.

Much drift today, less ice as the day passed. The river rising moderately fast. Donald and I rowed across the river to the cornfield. More ice and drift running close to that shore. . . . We soon gathered a load of corn and Donald took his back to the boat while I picked more. The three dogs had a fine chase through fields new to them. In all we gathered about 14 bushels of corn, and divided it between us.

December 30   A few notes of the redbird's spring song this rainy, warm morning. No drift or ice, no rise or fall.

December 31   A dull day, north wind and snow flurries, heavy clouds, yet now after I get wood in from the snowy deck, I see the southeast stars. . . .

Again and again I am moved deeply by the view of the river, on dark, yet clear days like this. The tawny water under the cool gray skies, the far blue hills, almost fading into the sky, the curving point across the river, related in color to both distance and warm foreground, where there is always brown weeds and yellow grass, some scrubby trees.

Some river people complain of the dreary confinement of winter,
but we find it a season of special delight. The mere joy of being
sheltered is magnified by our closeness to the elements: rain on

the roof directly overhead, snow sifting on our faces asleep, the swaying and the rolling of the boat, the wild and muddy world without. Our fires have the directness of campfires kindled in riverbank driftpiles for warmth on a winter walk. In bad weather, one can sit by the fire indoors without compunction, and not feel that he should be stirring about outside. It is then that we reap the harvest of winter, painting, writing, reading, making music.

January 1, 1946   A fine winter day, clearing and colder, after a morning of snow flurries. The river falls steadily, but not fast. . . . Not much cooking today, no wood chopping, some painting, the first in many weeks. Yet there is no interruption.

Tonight the stars are reflected in the smooth water. . . . The bright stars of winter.

January 2   A clear cold winter morning. I went down alongshore for wood and as usual enjoyed the excursion, and brought back a boatload. There is a joy about foraging along the bank, picking out the wood best for burning, that doesn't need to be chopped too much, finding pieces the right size, or a block that needs only splitting. New green locust trees torn out in the railroad grading, weatherbeaten planks of fence rail, sometimes a piece of black walnut.

January 3   Anna went to the city this afternoon, and brought back a lot of good things—a glass minnow trap, which we have been trying to buy for several months, a new carbide miner's lamp to replace the one I dropped in the river, they only cost $1.25, the three Brahms quartets in one collection, a new billfold, for my old one was falling apart, stationery and I know not what else, all this on an errand to get symphony tickets for Sunday.

These little riverbank dogs, always muddy and hungry, dashing up the bank to the railroad in full cry, Whizzer trailing, to bark at a passerby or a strange dog. Not without character, and Skipper is a superior dog. Yet they are a shantyboat lot, all our outfit is of this character, except inside.

Warm today, thawing and muddy, the sun out for a while, in

an expanse of blue sky. Then the *D. W. Wisherd* passed up, close to the far shore, red barges and white boat, the houses of the little town, all gleaming in the sunlight, the warm winter shores.

January 5 A bright starry time, new moon long gone, strange constellations passing along the horizon, Jupiter gleaming like a yellow lantern. A clear sunrise, not over the hills, but over a bank of clouds, low, with a ragged sharp silhouette, a strange range of mountains in the southeast.

Looking across to the far hills while at the evening chores, I saw the hilltop glowing with the light of the setting sun, the windows of houses seeming afire. Thus today the sun rose and set clear.

January 8 A steady rainfall this dark day. In bed I had heard the thumping of drift as it hit the boat, and sometimes rumbled under its length, sounding like a wooden bridge when a wagon goes over it. By morning the end of the stageboard was under water. The rise today has been very rapid, with swift current, moderate drift. There is no doubt this time we go over the bank.

January 9 Last night and today, the river rose swiftly, at its fastest rate, and the current poured past us. I did not have to get out during the night but spent a large part of today moving stuff up the bank, and bringing the boat single handed down to the old anchorage in the clearing. Even moving the boat a few rods, in the current and wind, must not be undertaken without foresight and preparation. Now we feel secure, out of the current and drift, not even needing a riding light.

January 10 Yesterday morning the section foreman came stomping down the hill to borrow our johnboat to raise their pump, which the rising water had covered. We were pleased to accommodate the railroad in return for many small services on its part.

This was a fine day, sunny and mild. The river rose at a slower rate. It was said to have risen yesterday at a rate of 6 inches an hour. There was a stream of heavy drift running. . . . I saw Bill Edwards out in his little skiff looking it over but when he passed he said there was nothing in it.

January 12 This morning I was rather surprised to see the river had fallen a little, leaving a tiny clean beach, even way up here.

There was not a stick of driftwood out in the river. . . . Each morning I make an excursion along the shore. Little driftwood has been left. The old driftpiles are afloat, for so long draped over the rough shore. Stage of river at crest, 47.3.

January 13 A fiery sunrise this morning, in the turbulent east, while from the dark clouds overhead wisps of a snowstorm.

I am often surprised at the sincerity of our living here. It is all of one piece. We could do things in the conventional manner, buy food from the stores, having what most people have, buy store Christmas presents, have a radio, daily newspaper, go to movies, yet all our actions seem to be in conformity with some mode of living which while it's "shanty boat" in a way, springs from ideals which no ordinary river dweller ever thought of.

A clear night, still and cold. I think I hear a screech owl.

January 16 Last night working in the bright moonlight, I shoved the boat out into the river again, outside the line of trees, where the strong current rippled past. Just a week ago was the day the river was rising so fast, and I brought the boat into the harbor among the trees. . . . A cold clear morning of winter now, a fair sunrise reflected in the smooth river.

Donald and I cross the river, each in our johnboat. We stop at the corn field just across and find there is still corn there. Then we row up to Coney Island, and each get a load of boards and junk. I come on back first, and now, at dinner, see him returning laden.

January 18 Crows spattered against the sunrise sky, flying southward in their daily migration. . . .

In just those few days of high water all trace of our activity ashore was obliterated. No sign that once there was a path of stones, bordered by flowers and garden beds.

*[The Hubbards make a visit to Anna's family
in Michigan.]*

January 26 I came back here alone last night, a dark, mild night, a skim of soft mud over the frozen ground. Off the bus I looked over the bank at Brent, and saw our lantern burning. I almost heard its voice. . . .

January 27   A quiet time, some music and painting. . . . I rowed across the river, and found good firewood in the new driftpile. . . . This starry night, most clear, I look to see where Jupiter now is. . . . The dogs sleep so soundly, there is a crackle of fire burning, a whistling noise from a pan on the stove, and the train's whistle fades away into the valley up the river.

January 28   Today the much talked-of wing net was begun. Andy, using the needle I had made, cast the first stitches, if you would call it that, and I was soon knitting away. In the evening Donald came over, had some toast and cocoa with me at supper, though he was supposed to come home to get his own. There he knit, while I washed dishes for the day. This was his first experience. Sadie asked us to leave the work with her if we went away tomorrow. There is a fascination about it and with many hands the task will not be as long continued as it first appeared to me. . . .

I saw a large owl on the shore at dusk.

January 29   Sadie said she would knit while we were gone, she really wanted to do it, and enjoyed it, proudly announcing nine rows completed. . . .

Last night I heard the sweet sound of rain on the roof.

January 31   Listening to Andy yesterday, as he explained how to make a dip net, from a certain use of words, I saw the connection between "poke," a sack, and "pocket".

I felt how strong the west wind was when I crossed the river this afternoon. I rowed up along the shore, gathering firewood. . . . Returning, a stranger walked down the bank, evidently on some purposeful end. He turned out to be the game warden, and thought I was out fishing, evidently had been waiting for my return. Such zeal and devotion to duty.

February 1   Up and awake in the earliest morning, by starlight, when they have lost some of the lustre of night, and the sky is lighter in the eastern horizon. This could be the day of a great event or high achievement. Even in midafternoon, after spending the day so far doing nothing of importance, the morning sky is still before me, and I felt its influence.

February 2   Anna arrived last night from Grand Rapids, a week after I came back.

February 7   A clear, windy day, cold but not severe. Some playing, just after breakfast, the first in some time. Yesterday we fetched the cello from Mr. Kerr's, arriving here just after dark, coming down in the johnboat from Detisches' steps, where we had left it. The banks are almost too muddy to walk along now. In the boat, Anna sat in the bow, the handiest place, with the cello between her knees, and all three dogs climbed aboard, too. They insisted on being in the bow seat, just about room for all to find a foothold.

February 9   Lou Gander appeared at the top of the bank today, and came on board carrying a paper shopping bag. It contained articles of feminine dress, which he had brought for Anna. They were clean and quite nice, strange things for him to possess. He acquires much clothing and such truck from ashcans, or as a direct gift from superior people who are throwing the things away, anyway. He is a master in this line and has that detachment. He has considerable practical knowledge of river and boats. Today, he said that a light line tied to a small elm where it would give or to a branch, would hold more than a heavier line tied to a solid trunk, for that line would snap. . . .

People like Lou Gander are on solid ground, economically, they have as much security as their neighbors who seem more prosperous without their worry and strain. He lives simply and with little expense, does a few odd jobs in the neighborhood, and receives whatever comes his way without question. He relates with gusto the list of things given him, or found in ashcans. To some extent we are in a like position. For instance in the store the other day, I asked the clerk for some leaves of cauliflower he was peeling off and discarding. I thought they would make good dog vegetable. However, it was so green and fresh that we ate part of it ourselves, and found it very good.

February 11   Our living here becomes more orderly all the time, the interior of the cabin cleaner and better arranged, if that is possible. Even the decks and storage spaces are in good shape and nowhere is space crowded or things in the way.

February 12 I try again to trap minnows up on the sandbar, but return with only a handful. Yet some firewood, a walk along the open shore, and the view of the reach of the river eastward, make the trip worthwhile. And the dogs enjoy it so.

A perfect washday, and we were through in good time. Coming back to the boat, the view from the river of the bright washing, white and various colors, the different shapes and sizes, all formed a sharp contrast to the shaggy, dun-colored hillside. Our living here somewhat represented defiance to the mud and bad weather. No giving in or lowering of standards. All this due to Anna.

February 13 Last night it rained considerably after gently beginning. A dark wet morning. . . . We had a quiet, busy day inside, dogs too. Some mending and fixing, playing, cooking, a great variety of activities. Hardly away from the boat.

Last evening we called at the Detisches'. Sadie had yelled down after dark that there was mail for us. One item was a valentine from them. Their conversation becomes animated after awhile and we enjoy hearing about their river life, and former neighbors. . . . Sadie's, or rather the family's hens are laying well, and keep us supplied with eggs.

February 15 Some rough weather, high winds, rain, snow, now cold, rising water. Night before last it came up several feet, nine feet in the 24 hours, from the bottom of the steps to the top. Yesterday morning very early, I had to get out in the snow flurry and darkness, set spars, change lines. Then back to bed.

Last night the rise was less, but I was up early to build fires, as it had cleared off cold. The wind very strong early in the night, from the west, probably, and there were strong puffs of it here. It was worse the previous night, sweeping across the deck, as if we were out at sea. We had not the least damage, nothing blown overboard. . . . When it was snowing and we sat by the fire reading, George and Elizabeth Potts came down over the bank, to our surprise.

February 16 Buds are swelling on the soft maples and hawthorns, birds are active. The daylight increases. Evenings are light, and in the morning you get up with the sun. Now we feel the urge to make great changes. . . .

I am pleased with our spars and planks. The former is a long straight oak tree, about 5" at the butt, quite heavy, with a row of bent nails on one side. Perhaps it has been used as a foot bridge, way up some creek in the hills.

The river is rising very slowly, or has stopped. No change in stageboard or lines the past 24 hours, or since last evening. A bright, sunny day, quite warm in the afternoon, with a southwest wind. We were out on the river, Anna and I, and the three dogs. First down to our garden. . . . Then we crossed over to the shantyboat settlement down toward the Water Works, the first time we have been as far down on that side since we have been on the river. Rowing up, still on the Ohio side, we felt the force of the wind, dead ahead. We stopped at a driftpile for firewood, then rowed up to the Coney Island landing, and back across with quite a load of wood. A marvelous afternoon.

February 18 A still clear day, as near spring like as February can be. . . . River falling at a good rate. The current is swift.

Yesterday Anna and I rowed up to Willison's landing in the afternoon, sunny but cool, with a breeze from the north. We walked from there to the Wilmers'. It is strange to leave the river, and walk along a highway or street, and see people doing conventional things, driving on Sunday afternoon, dressed for town and waiting for a street car. A conversation with a friend on the sidewalk. They never seem to realize they are out-of-doors. Even a street has something between it and the sky.

This time the rising river stopped just short of floating the Detisches' boat. They watched the last few inches with apprehension and stayed up nights. . . .

February 19 Today we just about completed the wing for the net, ready for tarring. I made wood floats, gathered up some scraps of lead. The Detisches finished the edges, with floats and weights. Soon we can set it in the water, and will await results eagerly.

February 22 At daybreak this morning, I rowed across the river and set out the wing and net.

February 23 Yesterday, riding through the country and over roads I have traveled so much, though now I go that way infrequently, we saw farmers in many places, plowing the hillsides. . . . This morning I chopped up a little ground in the railroad garden and planted some spinach and Bibb lettuce, a very small quantity.

Earlier, while still dark and overcast, I had rowed across the river to see about the net. I found two tiny fishes, minnows almost, imprisoned within. . . . While there still in half light, the *Taric* passed moving swiftly, brushing the willows almost. The first barge that passed, with a bone in its teeth, seemed close in, but the next tier was wider and a barge width closer, actually brushing the willows. It must be fun to steer the boat. It passed with the familiar sounds and smells of a steamboat, the *Str. Taric*, as the sign read, and was soon blowing her whistle off the lock.

February 25 Washday today, and a success—all nearly dry now at evening. Four-sheet wash. Another mark for this day was the finding of a rat in a trap I had set on the roof near our fishbox corn crib. It was a brown one, larger than I had expected. If it has been all one rat we have had many encounters, and until now he has always escaped, though it meant swimming in the icy water.

February 26 This warm morning, a stiff south or downstream wind. The sun rose behind broken clouds, red as fire. By then I had returned from a trip to the net, difficult to handle in the wind and darkness. A few fish, which later I took to the Detisches. The morning was one of those blue ones, the wind continuing, clouds becoming thicker. I went down along the shore for wood.

February 27 Heavy rains last evening and night, distant lightning. Now a slow current. The slope of the river is constantly changing.

During the heavy rain, while we were eating supper, Skipper had her second litter of puppies.

Dark and heavy sky this morning. What will come for this day?

February 28 A fine starry night, clear and mild, after a bright sunny day. I am always surprised, though, when I go up the hill, to find how rough and cold it is, compared to our sunny, sheltered harbor.

March 2   A rough night. Beginning with light rain, after a warm, calm day, we heard in the night the waves and rain. I was up twice, to ease the jolting against the spar, make fast the johnboat. River rising at a fast rate. Today is windy and clear, not a cloud now. . . .

A guest in the evening, Marian B. . . . We go all out for our guests, giving up the day mostly, beginning preparations days ahead.

March 3   A fine day, warm and sunny. All the Sunday people out, some to see us.

Our gardening is underway now, chopping and planting in the patch across the track, earlier by a week than last year.

March 4   I hear frogs, across the river, as last spring, a contented song, like the voice of the spring fields. . . . I climbed up to the woods on the hillside, where it is still winter, though under the dry leaves the spring plants are sprouting. Dandelions in our salad today.

March 6   I worked some on a woodblock, and got some odd jobs off the list. One was to put a handle in a sledge hammer the Wilmers had given me, after I had asked if they had an old one. I trimmed a suitable handle out of a piece of driftwood, and am pleased to own a new and often needed tool, and one which has more character than a store-bought one.

I looked at the net at dusk, having managed to raise it after the river had fallen a few feet, but found only 4 small fish and a waterdog. I must move it to another location but will wait to see what the river does. A trip across the river, this one especially in the rain and gathering darkness, is always worthwhile.

March 7   This week we have been hearing some spring bird song, mostly in the distance, across the river, perhaps. The seasons change slowly on the riverbank.

March 8   We have had dandelions in salad, and some dock and wild beet—all mild and tender. So this year's crop begins. . . .

Rain seemed imminent throughout the day, and about 4 o'clock it began coming down smartly. I had just started across the river.

. . . It rained hard for awhile with distant thunder, but soon began to clear, and out on the water I had a fine view of the broken sky, all dark to the south and east, breaking in the west.

March 13 A fair misty day, of early spring. Warm. We neglect fires, open windows, leave off coats. I suppose the cold of winter is past. As usual, I look back on that season as on heights I have come down from.

Another trip downriver this morning. We regard this shore as our own, and resent intrusion. In fact, this wild shore just below us, with the untended hills above, is probably the most attractive feature of our location here. It is a good one for us, in many ways, which I suppose accounts for our staying here so long.

March 14 Rain began soon after daybreak, keeping up all day, gently and without stop. . . . We had a fine day indoors, though it never seems far within where we live. . . . So our day closes, the sound of water running down the stones mingled with the raindrops on our roof, the night not dark, for the moon makes a dim light through the clouds.

March 16 In the woods I see the bloodroot in white flower, for a few days scattered over the dead leaves. The yellow and purple violet, the former in the woods, where too bloom the anemone, salt-and-pepper, spring beauty. "But what do I know of flowers and what right have I to mention their names familiarly?"—Thoreau, *Autumn*, page 181, October 31, 1850.

Yesterday morning I went down to look at the net, first thing, without making a fire. Coming back I was surprised to see our chimney smoking. Anna had built a fire in the cookstove, and it was burning well when I reached the boat. . . . There was a new fish in the net yesterday, perhaps a jack salmon. It was very delicious, the best we have eaten, when we had it for supper, with two small catfish and some chubs.

Arriving at the boat yesterday, I saw several life belts and odd pieces of cork floating near the shore ahead of us. Of course I salvaged them. Later, telling Andy about it, he laughed and said they had thrown them into the river themselves, discards from the *Bozo*, remnants of his active life.

This morning we are baking a cake for Sadie's birthday, which is tomorrow. That is a job for all hands, one with such trouble and difficulty that each time we say we will never try it again.

I found this morning that we have a new neighbor, Old Jim Edwards, one leg almost useless, so that he leans way over his cane, still he shuffles about with great poise, and is a gentleman. I offered my services and he tendered his in return. We hope he can visit our boat. His house is a tiny shack built by his brother Bill, of driftwood evidently.

A day of storm and sunshine outside. Heavy storms to the north and south, and coming suddenly over the hill, with thunder and heavy rain. Hail for a while, the size of peas, bouncing on the shore and johnboat, floating off in the current. When the sky cleared in the west, we marveled at the rainbows against the dark eastern sky, one a perfect arch springing from the water, and reflected in it.

We went up to the Detisches' in the johnboat, Anna carefully carrying the birthday cake, with its circle of 12 candles, one "S" of walnut meats in the center. Returning, the full moon rose from the eastern hills.

March 19 I was up very early this morning, so early that it was still night. In the half light of the clouded moon, I drifted down to the garden landing, alone, set out the minnow trap, looked at the net and line. Still dark when I returned, darker in fact. I built a fire and curled up in the corner of the bed, half awake, enjoying the fire. . . .

We read that the diet of the Indian varies with the changing seasons, and are pleased and amused to find that ours is quite similar.

March 20 Tonight for supper we had the first green salad of the season. . . . Mild greens—dandelion, wild beet, a little squaw cabbage, the first shawny; these mixed with celery tops and lettuce, a little cold meat, bits of cheese, herbs, oil, lemon juice. A pot of baked beans made a grand supper.

March 23 Last evening. . . I saw a little white dog run down the bank and thought of Brownie, who had been away all afternoon. But it was not she, for there was no Brownie all night. I did not go for milk yesterday, and this morning crossing the track on that errand, I found Brownie, or her remains, for her body had been cut in two by the train. I buried her by the path this morning, the first of our dogs to have a grave by the river. She was thoroughly a river dog, knowing no other home. An elfin little thing, graceful and quick as a gazelle, dainty, and a loving comfort.

This spring morning, the redbird and first chipping sparrow, the sun is warm but it is uncertain weather, and a storm may follow close. All life is uncertain, but it is good to be by the river in the sun, while it shines warm.

March 26 We awoke this morning to hear the steady falling rain. Outside a fog which wrapped us in. . . . We played some in the afternoon, and set out a line across the river with about 10 hooks, one end tied to a willow. For bait, live minnows which we caught in the trap. . . . Tonight the stars are out, very bright. We were out on the river at sunset, and watched the day fade into night.

March 27 Each day the pear trees are whiter, and now the poplar catkins make the tree an orange color. We watch spring in the distance.

March 29 Fishing may seem to take up considerable time, but there are other results besides the fish one catches. This morning I go for minnows, at the Brent landing. It is a new view, and I make some sketches, and write this as I drift back with a few minnows in the box astern.

March 30 A wind today, from the north, and colder. We toss in the waves. . . . Redbud is out now, the pears in full bloom, or merging into the green leaves.

April 1 These last days we have made an arrangement which may be significant. We give the morning to chores and work out of doors, construction, repairs, gardening, and such. The afternoon then is free for painting, music, reading, writing or whatever. Of course this arrangement is not binding. Many of our activities are hard to classify, such as wandering about after greens, with a sketch book and bird glass in our pockets, or sketching or writing while the minnow trap is set. With the time portioned out this way, I feel that I can work at whatever is to be done with complete absorption, knowing that another part of the day will be for a different pursuit.

Old Bill Edwards rowed by this afternoon, with a sack of corn he had gleaned from the fields across the river. He stopped to talk and rest, after rowing against the wind and current, holding onto the deck railing.

April 3   Today, in the morning, after breakfast and some reading on deck in the sun, I crossed the river with the dogs, passing behind the *J. T. Hatfield,* running by with 5 empties, and had some fine waves. I made the shore about where the little shantyboat is tied up, the one the boys built, and had a look at this, a word with its builders. I rowed up along the shore, looking in the driftpiles, making some sketches, tracing the line.

April 4   A strong west wind today, unusual, I think, for April— the bright sky and dry air of October. The cottonwood, or silver poplar, they may be, are in their early April color, the misty gray-green I remember so well. . . .

April 6   Across the water I heard sounds very plainly—the conversation of the section hands, a scolding voice of a woman, a rooster crowing. A difference in atmosphere, perhaps, or the quietness of the air, before a rain which did not come.

The first mess of poke today, for dinner, and swallows flying swiftly past us when we were out on the water.

I took some fish up to old Jim Edwards in his shanty on the hill, the interior exactly like his boat on the river.

The river falls steadily, and approaches pool level.

April 7   We went to the city this afternoon, to hear the St. M. Passion of Bach. The dam was raised while we were away, Donald shoved out the boat, and was lighting the lantern when we returned at dusk. He had even laid some stones and boards for us to walk on through the mud.

April 8   When I started across the stageboard first trip this morning, quite early, I saw a small duck on shore at the water's edge, near the end of the stageboard. It was not alarmed, and we watched it through the window. At length it paddled off. After some

100

searching in our two books, we identified it as an American coot. Now we would like to see it again, to observe certain peculiarities.

April 14   Last Sunday, while we were listening to the Bach, they raised the dam. This Sunday we heard the music again, returning as before at dusk. . . . Between these two Sundays we made a trip to Grand Rapids, by night trains, arriving here this morning.   All was well, except some damage to a partition inside by the fireplace where a spar has evidently poked its way in.

April 16   The rain is over, but this white sunrise is shadowed by level clouds, with a chill wind. The robin sings defiantly.

April 17   A bright morning, the sun rising over a sharp horizon, and suddenly all was in full sunlight. . . . Anna had been making a dip net, and yesterday, finishing the netting, we took it to Andy for inspection, bringing them also a mess of poke and receiving the usual four eggs. . . . For supper the first asparagus, which I brought in yesterday.

April 18   Yesterday old Bill Edwards came down, his approach advertised by his peculiar voice in conversation with someone on the railroad, very affable when he arrived, wanting to borrow our johnboat. Someone had stolen his, he said. His first procedure in building a new one was a visit to the likely driftpiles for material, so he rowed down the shore a half a mile, up the other side, and later we saw him coming down and across with a load, which, he told us, contained just the material he wanted.

April 19   A summer evening, when I crossed the river to put out a trot line. The thrush was singing on the hillside, the sky of summer, at sunset. We heard other birds today, bluegray gnat catcher, kinglet, house wren, and were struck by the curious warbling of a titmouse.

April 23   It rained this afternoon, thundershowers coming over the hill, but more severe to the north and south. We both went out to bait the line, just in time to finish before dark, and Anna sat wrapped in a piece of canvas while it rained lightly.

April 27   The wind rose early, and blew hard all day, direct from the north, and the water was as rough as any we have had here. Waves rolled along the beach, and broke in combers out in the river.

101

By turning the boat at an angle, head in, which brought the stern directly into the wind, the jolting against the spars was eased and we enjoyed the tossing of the boat, the bright water breaking into white spray.

May 1 Yesterday we printed woodblocks, the last from the current blocks. I plane them off now, for new carving. The water colors now pinned up on the boards are all sketches made back in the hills. I bring back, too, from these walks, greens, asparagus, rhubarb, wild flowers.

This morning, a steady rain and heavy mist on the river. The thrush sings.

May 2 Today, with an east wind, warm and humid, the mist-like rain drove through the air, so light it made no mark on the smooth water. . . .

The river rises slowly. The ground is soaked and thoughts of gardening set aside. We are busy with various activities. It would be a long rainy spell in which we would run out of work or play indoors.

May 7 Coming back from the garden, I stopped to pick up a board floating near shore and heard what I thought was a duck where I had just passed. Dropping down I saw it, a beautiful bird with perhaps half a dozen little ones following her. They were so tiny, not long hatched out, black and brown, carefully following her, climbing over the rocks at the water's edge. There is a rocky wall along there, with broken rocks and scrubby trees at the bottom, the river now up against it. Crossing these rocks in a little cove she finally settled down, as I watched her. Later we identified the bird as a female wood duck. I have always liked this particular spot, just the place where one would like to see a wild duck and her brood.

Since we are not fishing these days, we are not out in the johnboat as often, but today I had a lot of rowing. I went up to the Brent landing, with the two dogs, and gathered up a lot of orange crates which I flattened out and loaded in the boat. These were to be tried as fencing material, rabbit fence for the lower garden. Then I rowed across to the Coney Island dump. . . . There I picked up various articles and material I might use, some to fill a particular current need.

As I pulled away from the boat and drifted by, there it was against the leafy shore all in shadow, gently rocking on the swift water, blue woodsmoke from the chimney, lovely Anna inside busy at evening work, with a bright smile as I left—there rose in me a happy feeling of achievement and possession. Just having built the boat, and living here so successfully, in true riverbank style, fitting into the neighborhood so well, yet retaining our own standards, mostly, and our own pursuits, which are far different from those ordinarily engaged in on shantyboats, though we do fish and gather up junk like a native—all this seemed worthwhile and I was happy and proud.

> *Our zest for the river did not wane. . . . We went on in much the same way, in surroundings which had become familiar, with not even a flood to make the year memorable. Ruts, however, are worn only in traveled ways on land: a river life partakes of the freshness of the river itself. Each rise and fall affords a new outlook and gives to a well-known shore the feel of one at which you have just landed for the first time. . . .*
>
> *The voyage down the river was ever on our minds.*

May 10 Yesterday was a great day for us. In the evening, which was quiet and fair, we pulled in our gangplank and spar, cast off the lines, whistled for Skipper who was missing and set off down the river, drifting on the swift current. This was new for us, the thrill of which we could not anticipate. We made a good landing below the Whirly, almost to the old camp landing and proceeded to tie up. Not much of a journey, but a taste of a joyous experience to come, when we cast off for good.

The boy from the little shantyboat across the river arrived as we did, in his johnboat. Perhaps he thought we were bound down the river, and came out to wish us *bon voyage*. Soon Anna went about supper, which had been cooking as we came down, woodsmoke from

103

the stack in good style. I finished my chores, and we had a bath. All inside was the same as ever, but the outlook in every direction was new, though we had been here many times. . . . Even the garden seems different, and this familiar shore has a newness to it.

After supper, pork chops and asparagus and new potatoes, we rowed back to our old landing in the dim moonlight for Skipper, who was there waiting for us. What a surprise it must have been to her coming home to supper, and the shore empty. . . .

Today we observed a shantyboat drifting down towards us, a johnboat out, pulling for the other shore. What a joke if he had landed at our landing we had just left. After our experience we watched his landing across from us, below the last shantyboat, with a professional eye. . . .

We came down here to work in the garden, and spent most of the day there, though we took time to play in the afternoon. More asparagus and new potatoes, not home grown, cornbread, meal ground this morning, and eggs, a parting gift along with much advice, from Sadie. I do not think they liked our leaving, even for a few days. It is good to be on this wild shore where no one is close to us, no steps or accumulated junk, a screen of trees hiding the railroad which is farther away from us, too. Much driftwood on the shore, and best of all, new views. A fine one of Brent on the river bend, and across we cannot see a house on the shore above.

The day was cloudy, with occasional sprinkles of rain. Toward evening it rained awhile, but we had all our seeds in the ground. We just made it, though. The bicycle was loaded on the roof, along with the wire fencing, tubs, a box or two, the fishbox of wire that has been there a long time. I was pleased that we could get away so easily, not be overloaded, and yet nothing of value was left behind.

The bicycle we unloaded this evening, and I made the usual run for milk. Coming back I had a surprise, looking down the river, for there was a boat where none had been before. It was ours.

May 14   Today, this morning, arriving at noon we moved back up the river. I walked along the stony shore, in rubber boots, towing like a canal boat. It was slow progress, slower than I expected. I wonder at what pace the canal boats proceeded, for I should suppose the relation between power and weight about the same. Surely faster than we did. There was a current, being open river, and a breeze which might blow either ahead or astern. Anna was on deck, with a spike pole to keep us off shore when necessary. Donald came at the end, helped us tie up, then soon after, our being away did not seem a reality.

May 16   A fair evening of Wednesday, but during last night and today, heavy rains. The clouds move in from the S.W., at times broken, with the hot sun shining through. Then gray rain, and there is no distance. . . . An exciting day, sharp contrasts of light and dark and at evening a broken sky flushed with the color of sunset.

May 17   A chill cloudy morning. The river rose considerable during the night, and there is much drift, close in to the boat. Much boat work to do, tieing lines up higher.

May 18   I went to the Brent landing this morning, rowing up with the three dogs. There I set out the minnow trap, and gathered up a load of orange crates for rabbit fencing. The dogs, especially Buster, had a great time. I walked up the path to the railroad and looked at the store and mill and station with new eyes, such was the different approach. Got a few minnows, not the usual dark-backed kind, but lighter. Made a couple of watercolors, drifted back. . . . We are in a snug harbor now. Cooler this evening, a little fire.

May 20   I like to see the boat now, from out in the river. It is close to the leafy bank and the blue smoke rises in the foliage.

Yesterday there was great excitement about bees. While we were eating dinner, a swarm flew by the window, having apparently crossed the river at an angle from below. I went out and found them clustered on a branch of a small elm, about 10 feet above the ground, in the thicket between us and the Detisches. I went up the hill, to Highland Ave., after our beehive, and while riding back, a Fort Thomas policeman stopped me, and told me about another swarm on Lumley Ave. After some hesitation I was led to go over there and try to hive that swarm. I left the hive on the sidewalk with the bees clustered before it, after I had cut them out of a small locust tree. I came down to the river empty handed and fixed a box to receive the bees. This morning they had apparently accepted

105

it as home. . . . Tonight, just as darkness fell, we moved the hived bees from the thicket through the briars and branches, slippery footing, to our clearing, where we hope they will be happy and industrious.

We noticed that the little shantyboat at California, the one the boys built, was missing. Now Sadie tells us that it broke loose and drifted down. So far not recovered. A sad loss to the boys.

May 25   Today Coney Island opened. The flag flies. The *Island Queen* made a trip, going up along the other shore. The landing is little more than a gap in the willows. The little *Ferry Queen* runs back and forth. But it is just another day on the river. . . .

After a heavy shower, the fragrances of a summer evening, the smell of new earth.

Never before have I noticed the flower of the mock orange. Perhaps because the bloom is so heavy this year. Or perhaps it is always so, and I did not notice.

The bees are properly housed now, and seem content, flying in and out, busy as bees.

May 30   The yellow rising water sweeps along high shores, at the top of our steps, and we are shaded by trees from the afternoon sun. It has been rising fast, drift running now. I cross the river, and with difficulty take in the trot line.

June 1   This has been a rainy day. . . . We did rainy day chores—Anna cut my hair, I repaired my sandals, we printed woodblocks, played and read.

The river is rising slower now, but is within a foot of the bottom of the Detisches' houseboat. The *Bozo,* which they have sold, is afloat and will probably go out on this rise.

We went to the garden yesterday afternoon, had hardly finished our planting when the rain began. We rowed back in a heavy shower, against a stiff current and wind, Anna wrapped in a piece of canvas, and Buster inside.

June 4   We stayed at our old location as long as we could, cutting branches and crowding close in to the trees. Yesterday morning, however, when we heard that the river would go to 45 feet, we dropped down to our opening. We have enjoyed it here in this summer high water, the highest since 1909, when it was no higher. 43 feet, tomorrow, is predicted.

I went on up to the Wilmers' in the johnboat, stopping at the Brent Store, then crossed to the Coney Island dump, looking for wire fencing. The ripe mulberries hung over the water, in great abundance and I picked them from the boat.

June 5   We use the johnboat like the farmer does his wagon— for hauling, running errands, going places. Today I used it as a scaffold when washing the window glass and painting the sash. Yesterday I picked mulberries from the boat. This morning I and all the dogs went down to the lower garden, where I completed the rabbit fence.

June 6   Hot June weather now. Having painted the sash, I put in the screening on one window, and must do the other tomorrow, for we need them open. The bees are very active, day lilies bloom now, and the garden grows fast. The river falls slowly, and soon we must leave our cove. . . .

June 8   We put out another line across the river, heaved another rock overboard, tied on the hooks and baited them with minnows. A fine evening, summer twilight on the river. That is a large return from fishing, the trip across the river which otherwise we would make seldom. The nights are warmer now, dogs sleep on deck, and all our screens are in. . . .

During the recent high water—it is still way up there, but somehow, falling so fast with a prospect of lower stages it seems further down than it is—a variety of drift passed by, "floodwood." The river seemed covered with it at times, then it would run in a long line, perhaps close to either shore, or in the middle. One day the long line passed by our window, fantastic shapes of tremendous trees, or islands of wood and brush matted together. Now there is hardly a stick floating by.

We move up to our landing by the steps, the top of which is now out of water. . . . Our beehive seen from out in the river, a significant spot on the bank, giving character to our landing.

June 9   Supper last night on deck after dark, in the light of the half moon shining above the fringe of trees, our riding light hanging above like a Japanese lantern, across the water the sound of music, of a sort, and holiday. I even wore white pants.

I rebuild the steps again. Never very good steps, for people who are not able bodied seldom venture so far from pavement. If they do, we gladly help them down. Or perhaps they should be reminded of their weakness and dependence.

This morning a yawl came up the river, with a heavy outboard, and the *Bozo* was towed and drifted down the river, out of sight. It left a big hole in the bank. We hope it will have a new beginning and a long and active career.

We caught two fish on our line, one a big one, the biggest this season so far. Broiled for dinner, with turnips and greens, canned beans. We realize again and again how much of our food we produce, or get by our own efforts, how little we depend on the scanty markets in town.

June 11 The first swim today, in connection with a midday bath after some dirty work. In this instance, rebuilding the stone steps and cleaning out the hatches, or one of them. Bottom bone dry.

Anna and I baited the line yesterday at sunset, a quiet evening after a hot day. Then we ate our supper in the boat, tied to a willow over there. Our return was by moonlight, and we watched the sinking western stars, Venus bright.

We arise early these days, by the clock, but one must, to see the sunrise.

Yesterday evening the Coney Island ferry, J.D. Laughead, prop., made a rescue in midriver, of a boy who was trying to swim across. He had been shouting loudly for help, and may have had a log to hold him up, until help arrived.

These days are quite hot, summer now. Meals on deck, as few clothes as possible, shade instead of sun. The dogs feel it too, and sleep in cool places.

June 12 A large bullfrog has moved into our neighborhood, under a willow above the boat.

June 15 I went up into Three Mile Valley this morning for raspberries. This wild hollow, with a fine creek, no road, no farms, after you pass Andy Fueglein's and the next place, is the best walking to be found in the section. One would go far, up and down the river, to find a more isolated place. The creek has more water than most, fed perhaps by Cold Spring, and has many ledges, little falls and pools. I found raspberries there.

June 16   I went out to bait the line last evening in the face of a rain, which began at once and came down hard, with thunder, lightning and wind. Huddled under a canvas, I hooked on the minnows. I could hardly see. By the time I reached the boat only a light rain was falling, and soon after the moon came out. After all this not one fish was caught this morning.

June 17   Supper on the roof, last evening, at sunset, the pleasure boats homeward bound. Before dark in the red afterglow, I put on my old pants and boots, to do the chores attendant on the rising river.

June 18   The river, at the top of the steps, almost, rises slower today, but yesterday mounted quickly. The yellow flood among the green hills, and bushy shores. The days are hot and sultry, and we are glad to be close to the trees for early shade. The deck is a delightful place, all day.

June 26   Dewberries yesterday and today. I went out yesterday morning and picked enough to can 6 quarts and a pint. Also, some to eat, and a quart for Andy. This morning I went out again, later, to the same place, a washed out, neglected weedy field on the ridge between Three Mile and Pleasant Run, or Winter's Lane, as it is called now. There was enough to can 9 quarts and a pint, making 16 quarts in cans. The canning goes smoothly, but with the picking took up most of these two days. We feel it is worth it, and besides, it is good to get back in the hills, good to come to the river again, hot and thirsty and hungry.

June 29   This afternoon the river has been at a standstill that is neither falling nor rising. "Stationary" is a poor word to apply to a river.

This morning we brought the boat close in shore, pried up the side with a plank and set some stones under it. The river fell a little, and I could clean off the side below the water line, fill the rake seams, and paint the side. The boat was at this angle for a couple of hours, and living aboard was strange.

We went up the hill in the evening, riding the 7:30 bus, and later, a still summer night, we walked down the hill. When we leave the river at this season we feel how closed in the roads and streets and yards are, by trees and bushes, the houses almost hidden. On the river the sky is open as in winter.

July 3 Yesterday and today I painted some more. The cabin is all white, with red shutters, the hull red, edge of guard and deck posts black. It is all very handsome, especially when seen from the river.

Our gardens are doing well, and with the fish and corn, we need buy very little. In fact, we could live entirely on our produce.

July 5 The quiet hazy morning, hot sun of July filtering through, the yelping of the hillside chat. A quiet, low serenity, after yesterday's disturbance, a crowd of strangers everywhere, a fleet of boats in the river, their lights at night, campfires on the beach.

July 7 I went out berrypicking this morning up Three Mile, then to the ridge, east. Blackberries are just ripening, the early ones, and I gleaned about three quarts of black raspberries from an overgrown, picked over patch. They were dead ripe, sweet and mellow, like nothing else that grows.

July 10 I never know what to expect when first looking out in the morning. Day before yesterday there was a thunderstorm cruising the sky, and we had showers from its fringe. Yesterday, I found that the river had risen in the night and was muddy, with driftwood. This was not quite a surprise, though, for I had gotten up in the night to move the boat in closer. That was easy to do, just to get out of bed and wade into the water, move in the stageboard, tighten lines, then dry myself and get back into bed. Think of stormy winter nights. . . .

This morning there was fog. From the after deck, ready for a swim, I watched the driftwood floating through the mist. I saw one piece of drift that looked like a swan, and, sure enough, it moved its head. Then it rose from the water on broad wings, flying to the shore nearby, a Great Blue Heron. I slipped into the water and drifted down close to it, had a good view of it, but it was suspicious and flapped down the shore away, I following.

July 14 This last rise, not high enough to cover the rocky shore below us, left a heavy line of driftwood. We pick up a load as we come back from the garden. Last evening, Anna rowing, I walked along and tossed the good pieces into the boat.

Of the great quantity of driftwood, little is good even for firewood, yet when dry all of it makes a good fire on the beach. We do much of our cooking out there these hot days.

The fishing would probably be better on the other side, but this shore is attractive.

No *Island Queen* yesterday or today. A new peace.

July 17 Now in early night we hear the katydids. In full voice, but when we walked down the hill Friday night, we heard but a note or two. A summer sound. It is midsummer now. River low and clear. All the expected sights and sounds, but still, over all, an adventure in a new world.

July 24 This morning I was up early, the old moon shining in the east. I traced the line and went after berries. . . . Now at nightfall, I remember the concert of birds in the morning, which now seems so far away, with its dew and coolness.

July 27 The Northern Lights last night, before we went to bed, brighter and more extensive than it has ever been my experience to see them. They spread over the sky north of the zenith, and there were even lights and flashes in the south. The colors glowed almost into brilliance, red and purple, green and yellow.

Yesterday was noteworthy also because of Anna's fall from the stageboard into the river.

August 2 The song of locusts now, ironweed beginning to bloom, flap of grasshoppers in the dry field, the chirp of separate crickets. I hear now in midafternoon, a thrush singing.

August 11 We sailed the johnboat yesterday in a stiff upstream breeze. It handles very well.

August 14 I go up on the sandbar for minnows. The fish are hand to mouth nowadays.

August 22 The hawapple trees in the scrubby woods above the stony bank have a fine crop beautiful to see, more than any apple and of a wild flavor, yet not sour. They lie scattered on the ground, of a bright redness.

August 23   A cool clear morning, could be of October. Before sunrise the eastern sky was bright with the winter stars, and a low crescent moon.

I write this in the sunny doorway of the Wilmers' barn, an old affair, with all the good smells of a barn and stable. Chickens cluck about me, morning traffic passes in the road. I hear the whistle of the approaching westbound passenger train. Beyond, not misty this morning, lies the river, the sparkling sun's path, which is cut across by the dam. This trip for milk is a daily chore, made before breakfast in the summer, for then we have fresh milk all day. One of the four quarts I place on the heading of the Detisches' boat, where everyone is asleep usually. We make away with the other three, giving a little to the dogs, often having some sour to make cheese of. The Wilmer family is a mixed lot of grown, now past middle age, brothers and sisters, but they seem to be a harmonious and well balanced group. I have known Tony and Bob for years, in an acquaintance begun when I wandered over their hilly fields.

August 24   Yesterday, old Andy Fueglein made his way with difficulty down our stony path, with a sack of sugar pears on his shoulder, desiring a mess of fish. We gave him our own dinner in exchange, gladly, for this idea of barter appeals to us.

We had a fine dinner last night, without the fish—baked potatoes, corn, cornfield beans, stewed tomatoes, baked apples. The last were not whole apples, for we seem never to have one that does not need whittling into pieces. But cut up and baked with Anna's mixture of brown sugar, butter and other things, is very good. She patiently trims and pares quantities of fruit which another would throw out. Our gardens yield well now, more of everything than we can use.

August 25   Much boat work yesterday, for me. I rowed the johnboat up to the Wilmers', trying for minnows up that way. Later I trapped some at the Brent landing, making several trips there, once going up to the store. Returning I rowed down to the garden, for corn for dinner. I had taken the sail and sailed back in a fresh breeze, with a load of wood from the shore below the garden. Late in the afternoon I put out a new trot line, just below the Whirly, and made two trips down there later, to tie on hooks and bait. This morning 3 small fish. . . .

Remembering last summer, all seems different now, as if we had landed in a new place. Even the same affairs such as Coney Island, the camps across the river, the Detisches, all is in a different balance. I wonder if the people who visited us last summer were to return now, would they feel any difference?

August 27 We enjoy the Coney Island fireworks at night. They are especially impressive from out in the water, in an open boat, the flashing light, the bright colors, the reflections and reverberations from hills, as if there were a heavy round of applause.

August 28 We had eggplant for lunch today, not from our garden this time, but a gift from Sadie, who wasn't sure whether it was an eggplant or a rutabaga. She found a sack full along the road, and distributed them around the neighborhood.

The fishing has been better. Anna went out with me to bait up last night, and to see the fireworks from the water.

September 1 Two shantyboats down this morning, lashed together, towed by an outboard motor, down the river out of sight.

September 3 The *Island Queen* has made her last trip for this year. The last fireworks are shot, the fisher boys have gone back to school.

September 5 Tuesday night, past, we were awakened by unfamiliar noises, and saw the expected dredge, or her lights. In the morning we saw the *Omega,* suction dredge, steam, oil burning, towed here from Straight Creek by the *Scioto,* which went on down in the morning. The days and nights are as noisy as in a factory, and strange people pass our door as on a street. The natives pick up coal, washed clean and round and smooth as a pebble, as it comes out of the pipeline.

September 6 Sadie and Andy were down, Sadie rowing the johnboat in fine style.

September 10 At evening, the minnows rise to the water's surface, all about our boat, often leaping clear of the water. Every evening at the same time.

September 15 We sleep in our texas, these nights, and find it very satisfactory. A strange experience.

September 21 This morning our guests are on their way home, and the river is normal.

September 23 Last Friday afternoon I went after more apples, bringing home almost a bushel, as well as elderberries and wild grapes. The latter are abundant. The first walnuts, too, in green hulls. We can apples, make juice of the grapes and elderberries. The pulp and seeds of the latter went into muffins, with a curious blue-green poisonous looking result.

September 25 Last night the sharp air of autumn.

We went to the garden this morning, picked beans, and later canned them, the boiling of jars still going on now, after dark. The last canning of beans, we are sure now.

September 26 A heavy fog this morning. The *Scioto* tied up above us, supplied all the smells and sounds of a steamboat tied up in a fog.

October 2 Two ducks this morning, the first ones small, diving always, rather sinking than diving head first. In the garden, in the sunny midday, a quiet warbling in the brush, like a little hidden waterfall, and blue gray gnatcatcher is all we could think of. We were digging potatoes. . . .

The river went down to a new low level today, the lowest it's ever been in our experience here. The nights are clear, and I enjoy baiting the hooks under the stars.

October 3 Sadie speaks of the fish one buys in stores as "dead fish." Bob Wilmer tells me he saw a loon on the river, that the ducks I saw were "hell divers," or grebes.

A mess of poke for dinner, as good and as much enjoyed as in early spring. It is a fine vegetable, better than many grown in gardens, with much labor. These plants were young, probably from seed, and we found them in the rocky creek bar, washed down from up the hollow.

October 4 I rode out Four Mile and Tug Fork this warm sunny afternoon. The dry fragrant air of the hills. . . . A trip into the country affords us new sensations and experiences, sights and sounds. Formerly this was to be found on the river.

I bathe in the river, but the water is colder now.

A fine dinner tonight. We live as well as ever, and as easily. Few can say that, now.

October 7 Skipper brought forth her pups on Saturday the 5th of October. On the floor of our closet in a little space, while we sat with our guests on the deck, knowing nothing about what was going on. Six of them.

October 8 A gray unchanging day. No wind or life to air or water. But one does not expect rain. I ride up the hill after breakfast for jars—new pint jars to can fish in. The box was full, for the last few nights, especially Sunday night, there were some big ones on the line. I clean 13 fish, possibly 25 lbs., say 20 to 25 lbs., they go into 9 pint jars, with a pan of backbones for soup, livers for our supper, a kettle of heads and trimmings for the dogs. Also some fat which we will render out for an experiment. Quite a lot of time and labor goes into this, time is what I consider most valuable; but when you see the way other people get their food, such as it is, nowadays, this seems easy. At least it is pleasant and honorable.

Yesterday I finished the hand rail, along one side and around the corner for the ladder just above the gutter, so I will not have to hold to that when going along the outside of the boat. I can think of no more construction on the boat now, for the first time. Perhaps it is complete.

October 10 Shooting stars last night. We had a good view of them from our bed in the texas, before we went to sleep.

October 11 We awoke this morning in our bed, I called it, falling asleep the other night our "unleavened" bed in the texas, hearing light rain on the tin roof close to our heads, and looked out on a gray world. Yet in the east there were streaks of sunrise, which spread over the whole southern sky, bringing out a rainbow in the stormy northwest. I saw it when out on the line, but it soon faded,

115

and the rain set in which continued until afternoon. We went to town, to hear the first symphony concert.

October 13   A cool night, still and clear, with a morning fog, white frost, close to freezing surely in some places. I have kept up river bathing, the last time being yesterday morning, right out of bed. . . . Evenings the blackbirds, grackles are they?, flock into the willows along the river. An occasional duck and the sound of the song sparrow. This is new.

October 15   The fine weather continues, warmer after the frost. I beach out the johnboat today, after washing it, intending to paint when dry enough. It is still in good shape, after all the battering and scraping on rocks, and needs no repairs.

We think much of leaving now, and consider what must be done to get ready. This shore and the river bends look so fair this evening, that one hesitates to go elsewhere. For what reason?

October 16   The water is getting colder, and swimming now is in and out. . . .

Darkness coming on in the steady falling rain. The still misty river, a few blurred lights. So warm and cheery inside, after a warm bath, supper underway. . . .

Luckily I could get the johnboat painted before the rain began, inside and out, the familiar red color. I considered replacing some bottom boards, but the present ones will do, I think. Yet the johnboat must be strong and seaworthy, to stand winter and rough usage.

October 18   Launched the johnboat this afternoon, and glad to have it in the water again.

A large gull circling over the water.

Hard rain last night, and a gray, heavy day, though the sun broke through this morning. . . .

The sound of geese flying overhead in the darkness.

October 20   We sailed down to the garden this morning, with a good breeze. . . . We came back swiftly with the wind "like a motorboat," Sadie described it.

October 23   Visitors from the outside yesterday. Their life seems unreal, something from a book. The time when I associated with them must be from another life.

I sit in the warm sun, waiting for minnows to go into the trap I have out for them. Old Bill Edwards rows across the river, on one of his many expeditions.

October 24   From the river now I see lights before hidden by the leaves. Soon the trees will be bare, and I look forward to this aspect as eagerly as any one ever longed for the green of spring.

November 2   The sun rose and passed through a narrow band of clear sky, shining forth and lighting the underside of the clouds with a red light.

More ducks on the river now, and a few flights of geese. A robin singing today in the warm sun.

A bath in the river this afternoon. The water not too cold, but swimming is no longer a pleasure.

November 4   Last night we walked down the hill, down Altamont Road in the dark, but we could see well enough by the veiled moonlight. This was our return from hearing the Brahms *Requiem*. First we must pass through the unsightly city, noisy even on Sunday. Then a visit, with bright lights and empty conversation. Then the dark walk to the river.

November 14   The fringe of trees along the river, willows, even the soft maples and sycamores, have almost a spring look. Sparse foliage, yellow green at the end of the branches, so that it outlines the tree. The river shores are spring-like now, contrasting with the bare hills and trees.

November 19   Each day we do something which makes us more nearly ready to depart. I went to Grimm's this afternoon and brought back the rope which was left there for us. Now, for the first time, we have enough lines.

This warm afternoon, after a night of heavy frost, however, we went to the garden, an infrequent trip now. There we dug the last of the potatoes, late ones, and were surprised to find half a bushel. Digging potatoes is fun. Also we brought back some beets, carrots and parsnips.

The river is so smooth and peaceful now. Water, sky and earth are in such perfect harmony.

November 20   Put out our new stern line this evening, a piece

117

of 3/4" Manilla rope 100 feet long. It is so satisfactory, gives such a feeling of confidence. No more wire lines to handle, for with our other new one, we have three spare lines.

November 23 Quite cold, last night, and this was a winter day, though quiet and warmer. We canned pears, again caught a catfish, perhaps 2 pounds on the line behind the point above us. This is worth recording, since it has been a rare happening lately. I baited the line at sunset today. Fishing, especially baiting the line, sitting there in the midst of the waters, is so consonant with the landscape and out of doors that it causes no interruption.

We can play after dark, now, for I rigged a carbide miner's lamp on each stand.

November 25 A foggy night, with a drizzling rain, after a rainy day. We are working on a hoop net. The length of netting hanging on the door jamb is an appropriate decoration.

November 26 We awoke to a rainy morning, the river roily, drift running out of Four Mile Creek. The river rose so that we could not walk ashore. I must shift lines and spars for the first time in many weeks. Planking of all kinds to toss up the bank, trash left to float off, a clean shore when the river should go down. I pull up two drift bolts, the stakes for the stern line, as we will probably leave before the river goes down again. At least it is likely.

November 27 A bright clear morning, and a sunny day. The darkness and rain of yesterday almost cannot be believed. Fishing is good now, some big ones taken today.

The river is falling. . . . So this isn't the rise after all.

In Sadie's kitchen, the range oven does not function, for baking, at least, so they use it for drying wood. A greater and more constant use.

November 29 When we got off the bus at Brent, darkness falling, the riverbank seemed a bleak and chill place, with a chill damp wind from the north. After fires were made, I went out to tend the fishline, and out on the river, under the stars, I felt again the earth's charms, the warmth and joy of the outside. Returning, the cabin was a cheery place, lights and fire, supper cooking, dogs all asleep.

December 2 A high wind from the north last night, in the first watch. The strongest we have felt here, I believe. The waves tripped the stern spar, and I could not get the boat far off shore in the wind. It was quiet toward morning, clear as only winter can be. Arcturus and Spica shone in the east, Corvus to the south, and before sunrise, the morning star.

December 10 We trim and mount cards for Christmas, print more. Last night, in the light of the moon past full, I gathered firewood with the johnboat down along the shore. These days I am using the one-man saw that I brought down recently, sawing logs and splitting the blocks. I went up the hill yesterday afternoon carrying 10 packages to mail, Christmas presents. Nine of them were little wooden boxes, each containing a smoked fish wrapped in silver paper and tied with a red ribbon.

December 11 I climbed the wooded hillside this morning, first time since spring.

Sweeps for the boat are on my mind, and it makes our departure real.

December 15 The dam was lowered Saturday after 5 months of pool stage. This seems unbelievable. With the open river, our departure is a possibility and we hasten our preparations.

December 18 A cold morning. The bright stars of winter, growing pale before the sunrise. The old moon, above the two morning stars, close together now, a large dim star on the horizon, another farther north.

This day we went to town, in Jim's car, and bought all the things we had listed, some from way back. Fiddle and cello strings, anchor, rough weather clothing, a new bird book, tarpaulin, fog horn, colors and paper, food for reserve.

Back to the riverbank at dusk. A falling river, and the dam was raised, leaving a very muddy shore. Donald had to shove the boat out, three times. The usual flurry on arriving, hungry dogs, fires to build, lamps to light, then return the car, a swift bicycle ride back through the darkness. Supper by candlelight—smoked fish, the last broccoli. Then after chores are done, moving out the boat again, a quiet time by the fire, the dogs asleep, Anna working at the net.

December 20 The first snow today. . . . We continue prepa-

A River Way of Life

rations for leaving. . . . Before daylight this morning, I put our new tarpaulin over the deck load. The sweeps are nearly finished.

This was the long dreamed-of moment. . . .
We were stirred with a vague sense that a new world was opening before us. It was river never before known.

December 22   This day at 11 a.m. we left our mooring at Brent, and drifted down around the bend. . . . There were many new sensations. . . . Boat swinging around as we drifted, tossing free in the waves. . . . The familiar hills were new and strange country. . . . As we rounded the bend to the west we had light head winds, and at times must row from a lee shore. . . . The weather cleared, and we had a wonderful view, as we drifted toward the city. . . .

We tied up at sunset on the Kentucky shore. . . .

We had a quiet evening, all things the same within, but a new view through the windows, the city lights on the hillside, the western stars.

December 23   With some difficulty we pulled away from the lee shore, and crossed the river, drifting down slowly. We have much to learn about handling this heavy boat with so little power, about what you can do in wind and current, and making these forces aid you as much as possible. But we feel we are learning fast.

December 24   We had fine drifting this morning. . . . We find the current is swift enough. In fact, it does not seem like slow traveling at all.

December 25   Christmas Day. We lay over at mile 479.7, above the daymark. A clear windy day, after a most clear night.

December 26   I was up with the morning stars. . . . Anna was up early and we cast off when there was but a faint glow in the east. . . . Perfect conditions for drifting. Even a downstream breeze.

December 30   A quiet day, perfect for drifting. . . .

December 31   Tonight we have the dark river again, the hills rising against a sky in which there is no light of cities. . . . Last night, for the first time, we felt the dark peacefulness of the river.
. . .

120

We are now tied up against the willows which extend above and below for a long ways. The island above, the hills of Big Bone behind it. Across, an uninhabited shore, rough and steep.

I rowed up to the island. . . . The fascination of an island, the sand, one feels that few come there. A bird nest there, or a chicka-dee, seem wonderful. I found a walnut log, and came back with a boatload.

Looking down at our boat against the unbroken shore, it was a part of the river.

At mile 517.6, we are 55.6 miles below Brent.

The days go on like the river,
Time does not stop with this one,
Around another bend
Is a new prospect, reaching far into the sunlight,
And we will go on, drifting with the steady current.

II

Shantyboat Drifting: The Ohio

January 1, 1947 – November 30, 1948

Harlan Hubbard

4

Driftwood

The pure delight of drifting. Each time, it was a thrill to shove out into the current, to feel the life and power of the river, whose beginning and end were so remote. We became part of it, like the driftwood. . . .

The tension and excitement, the near ecstasy of drifting. We had to stop often and take it in small doses.

January 1, 1947. Big Bone Island. Light snow during the night, freezing rain this morning. We can stay in and be snug as a rabbit in his nest.

We are closed in with mist. The rain freezes, though later in the day it seems warmer, and rains harder. It is a satisfaction to know that I need not go out, but I do so anyway at intervals, because I enjoy it. I gather 2 bushel of corn from the field above.

Anna writes letters, I take care of some odd chores. The dogs are feasting on the mess we prepared from the bones the butcher gave us at Rising Sun. We add cornmeal and vegetables, this time greens from the river bank, wild beet, narrow dock, hen pepper.

Our woodbox is filled with walnut now, and its fragrance when burning hangs about the outside of the boat. Good firewood, too, and a joy to split.

January 2 A week ago today was that rare sunny day, only a few in a winter, when we drifted down to Petersburg, through the lock and past North Bend. Today was far removed, dark and rainy, a mist closing in before dark, after a rainy night. The river is rising quite fast, drift passing our windows. We are in a safe harbor behind the first willows, lines tied way up the bank. . . . Will it ever be sunny weather again, like that day? It seems impossible. Yet we are content, and enjoy life as usual.

This morning I came upon a man bailing out the skiff above us, and found he was the farmer who owned, or rented, it seemed, the land where we are anchored. He came down to visit us, aboard with his muddy boots. A muddy day, surely, but now we are all cleaned up, inside and out, writing away, both of us, by candlelight, the fog thickening outside.

After dinner we went up to the farmhouse to telephone, and found an open, grassy country along a highway. The country and the dwellings of men are always more attractive when seen from the river than when entered and observed closely, the inhabitants met. So with the towns.

We heard a steamboat heaving away below us, and the old *Kenova* passed, close to us, for she took the Indiana side of the island. She was making slow progress, but it was a fine sight, and a rare one nowadays.

January 3 The mist vanished in the night, and we saw a sky full of stars. . . . Rise continues, and we are almost at the top of the bank, and look at the next row of trees, sycamores and elms now, instead of willows. Reading after breakfast.

The farmer came down to get my assistance in untying his skiff, which he could not reach from shore. He said they might come down this evening, to "chat us" awhile. Thus we soon find a place for us in life ashore.

Anna washed some clothes this morning, I cut wood on the bank, walked down the shore aways. Much corn is left in the fields which have been harvested by machine. Thus it is a boon to shantyboaters. . . .

This afternoon I explored a little, rowed up this shore, crossed at the head of the island, landed on the far side, crossed the main channel to the Kentucky shore. Then back past the foot of the island.

A raw day, with a strong wind blowing over there, which we hardly feel on this side. A strong current, especially at the head of the island. That is a wild place. The other shore is fine, steep and rocky, wooded, a fine grove of straight sycamores. A little road goes along, higher up.

When I looked across at our boat, against a long unbroken line of willows, a desolate shore, it was hard to believe that inside it could be so warm and cheery. So dry and clean. What marvels these modest fires and lamps can produce. And Anna working away inside or writing a letter, not bothered at all by the wind and mud outside. In really congenial circumstances.

We played before dark, cello and viola parts of Brahms' Sextet 18.

The days are longer now, I do believe.

January 4   This day is my birthday, and I will record the meals of the day. Not that meals on ordinary days are inferior, but these were a little more elaborate. For breakfast, buckwheat pancakes, which were set the night before with yeast, and baked as eaten at the fireplace. With these, bacon, and canned apples, the first of these we have opened. Fresh oranges, to begin with. Late in the morning, a cup of cocoa, fresh brown bread and cheese. For dinner, early in the afternoon, fish hash, buttered beets, broccoli au gratin, celery, cornbread and pear salad. The hash was made from our canned fish, the beets gotten out of a box of earth on the upper deck, the broccoli of our own canning. In the afternoon Anna iced the cake, which we will have for supper, with wild grape juice, a dish of vegetable soup, and popcorn. The cake was made to my specifications, a yellow layer cake, with chocolate frosting. It has little white candles on it. The Christmas tree is flourishing, and has been left standing for this day, according to custom.

All this for us alone, hardly a soul in sight all day. Some duck hunters on their fruitless quest. A pair in a johnboat, an elderly couple, a bearded man fussing with an outboard motor which would run a minute, then stop. His wife kept her seat at the oars, and she would row when the motor failed. But for her efforts they would not have advanced all day.

The current is still swift, the river rising but slowly, little drift. Quite cold, last night, but milder tonight. Still cloudy, with never a glimpse of sun or moon.

January 5   Snow began to fall this afternoon. One realized that air and earth had been prepared for it for days. It fell thick and fast, from the southwest, or directly upriver, blowing out straight in the wind. In a few minutes the landscape was transformed. One thing we noticed was the number of roofs of buildings we could not see until the snow brought them out. The snowfall lasted perhaps an hour, then there was a break in the western sky, and the sun appeared for a brief time. A wonderful sight, before the clouds rolled in again. . . .

While we ate dinner today, a rather elaborate meal, for we had prepared for company, a song sparrow was picking up his dinner from the floating drift outside the window, not concerned with us at all.

The upbound boats run close to this shore now. The *Jim Martin* was up at dusk, with 6 loaded barges in two rows. I guessed there was 50 feet of water between our boat and the barges. The other night we saw the upbound Greene Line boat outside the window, it seemed, looming as large as a city building.

January 6   A full moon tonight, directly upriver, over the island. Not clear, but in a nebula of light, the circle of its edge nearly lost. It was a fine sunny day, though cold, and we devoted it to washing clothes, pleased to have an opportunity at last. . . .

Duck hunters out again, almost more of them than ducks, pursuing their sport with intense earnestness. I feel a little ashamed when I admit that we do not hunt.

For supper tonight we had fish cakes made of our dried salt catfish. We had been using it for dog food, and not attracted by the smell of it cooking, so were surprised to find it delicious, in this form.

January 7   Today I made an excursion across the river, and climbed the hill through the little hollow. . . . The house in the hollow was deserted. On the windy hilltop above, a little burying ground fenced in. An old thin stone rounded on top, marked the grave of Lucetta P., wife of E.C. Edwards. A carved rose quite finely done. I climbed another hill beyond and had a good view of Big Bone valley, as far up as the spring, if I could recognize landmarks. For I walked that way one hot July day, at least 20 years ago. The light snow revealed all the details of this rough country, the creek with its green water winding back, the rough fields and small farms, little roads leading back. The farmer chopping logs with a double bitted axe. He turned out to be a fisherman, the same who passed our boat with the balky outboard on Saturday. The creek is at his back door, his lane leading to the river. This country is poor and rough, mountain country, in contrast to the treeless bottom land across, rich and fertile. There is always this opposition along the river, shifting from side to side. . . .

We plan to leave here tomorrow, and have taken in wood and water. That will make 8 nights here. The river began falling today, as slowly as it has been rising.

> *Our progress down the river continued in this manner, drifting by easy stages. . . . There was no hurry, no desire to be farther on our way. We drifted a few miles, around a bend or a different kind of shore, and there had a new outlook, new banks, and new inhabitants to become acquainted with. . . .*

January 8 A bright, cold morning. We got away at sunrise, with an upstream wind. Wonderful view of the island and background of hills in the morning light. We drifted into the mouth of Wade's Creek, about a mile below, at the upper end of Patriot. The wind was quite strong, so we tied up there, a line to a tree on either side of the creek. This was still not late in the morning, and we had breakfast there, sun through the windows. . . .

Patriot is a country town, making no other pretense. A horse and buggy on the road. Country stores. A homelike place. . . . . I wandered about. Once to the cemetery above the town, a fine view of it, after sunset, the dark hills a background for the white houses. . . . Across the river, the beginning of bottom land on the bend, the mouth of a creek called Steele's, where we see the walls of an old brick farmhouse, roofless now, and on the other side of the creek, a log house.

Skipper roams these new fields all day.

January 9   Still tied up in the mouth of Wade's creek, Patriot. I moved the boat in farther, head in, to have a gangplank ashore. Four lines out to trees, some small ones, so we swing back and forth in the wind and waves.

A wonderful day. Before sunrise, the morning stars across, the waning moon still shining. The sun rose clear over the distant Kentucky hills, and shone all day, with white clouds in the west wind. I stayed close today, painting a little morning and afternoon.

After dark I walked up to the P.O. and store. What we buy is mainly for fun, as we have enough supplies on board to furnish us good meals for a long time. Three lighted stores, I believe, a pool room, filling station, the lights of a passing towboat, lights in the houses. A few steps and these are left behind, and one is in the darkness, the constellations bright overhead.

Most memorable today was the other shore, at sunset, the rays striking up river, a new angle for us. The old roofless house across, in the warm sun, its doorway having sidelights, the big barn, curved roof and streaked with rust. Every tree was brought out by the cross light, warm against the distant blue hills.

January 10   Another clear morning. I was up early, Venus is near Scorpius now, Jupiter farther away. I snaked the boat out of the creek mouth and we were under way, doing the morning chores as we drifted past Patriot. A beautiful river town.

Fast going, in the swift current, no wind. Breakfast as we approached Sugar Creek. We saw barges coming around the sharp bend. I went on deck and began pulling for the Indiana shore, thinking he would cross over. However he gave us two short blasts, and all hands pulled in the other direction. First I answered 2 blasts with our fish horn, but doubt if he heard it. He cleared us easily, and crossed over above. The *Sohio Fleetwing*. Just behind, our old friend the *J.T. Hatfield*, up with a few empties.

Below at Sugar Creek we saw the boat waves breaking on a shoal and must row out to clear that. We pulled into an eddy a mile below, to let the dogs on shore, and relax. The highway just above us now. After half or 3/4 of an hour Skipper came aboard and we pulled out into the stream, talking of passing Warsaw, and of where we would tie up for the night. But a crosswind caught us, and we could not keep off the lee shore, that is, the Indiana shore, for the wind was south. I dropped anchor offshore, the other end swung around against a stump. We got out a line ahead, pulled upstream a little, so the anchor was our stern line. Some small poplar trees held us offshore.

The wind blew fresh, and we had dinner, read and worked on the net. I painted in the afternoon, while Anna wrote. Some wood chopping and mopping before dark, our customary bath, supper.

I explored the shore a little when we first landed. It is uninhabited, rather open and sandy. The first bottom is not cultivated. Then another bank, with a border of locust and elm. Behind that, level bottom, corn land, the hills far back. It seemed a tremendous stretch of open level country, houses and road back against the hills, above and below us, perhaps half a mile. A farmhouse out close to the river. A round barn, painted white, standing on a hilltop, caught the eye, ranging the farmland back toward the hills. Its roof was not a perfect cone, but had a swell in it, like a gambrel roof. If we leave in the morning, this might be my only view of this stretch, but most likely it will remain in my inner vision. . . .

A splendid sunset, the whole sky open to us.

January 12 Yesterday we remained at our anchorage above Rail Landing Light, 2 miles above Warsaw. The wind was blowing from the south at daybreak, and continued until almost sunset, with considerable force, from a clear sky, until it became cloudy in the late afternoon. We kept busy, of course. I worked on the new chest, cluttering the place with tools, boards and shavings. Cut up a 4x12 oak plank for firewood.

I have heard a variety of birds lately. Goldfinches singing, when we tied up for a while the morning of the tenth. The woodpecker which I called the red bellied, Carolina wrens, titmice, song sparrows heard along the shores, robins and bluebirds, every few days. Occasionally an unfamiliar note or cry.

131

I remember yesterday's early morning, I sat working at the net as day broke, the blazing fire lighting the cabin, the fire in the stove crackling away, the dogs contentedly sleeping after a run ashore. Anna still in peaceful sleep. Outside the moon, stars and sky changed. Bright as they were, it was no longer night.

Late in the afternoon, as I was painting and Anna writing, the wind dropped and we decided to get away, though there was but an hour to travel. Under way we discovered the wind still blew enough to prevent our crossing to the other side. It began to rain gently and grow dark, so we prepared to tie up in the first available spot. At the mouth of a creek, a man in a johnboat hailed me, asking if we had any nets to sell, or "skift" oars. We felt complimented to be taken for true shantyboaters. Past Wiley's Creek, there was a shallow cover and we decided to anchor there. But before we could get close in, we had drifted by. Having tied to a willow below, we decided to pull ourselves back, perhaps 75 yards to an opening in the trees where the bank was stony. It took some time and labor, in the light rain, and we will do as little of this as we can. The hard bank was desirable, however, for in the falling river, the mud is deep and soft. . . .

After a bath, I went to telephone while Anna prepared supper. First a rough climb to the road, then inquiries about a telephone. All in the darkness, a half mile walk down the road to an unlighted gas station. Inside 3 men and a woman playing cards, a rough sort of place, but no more accommodating people could be found. While the man put the call through with much cranking and shouting, I played his hand at euchre.

We lay over here today, with no thought of moving on. . . . Our meals today deserve mention. The hominy for breakfast was quite raw, so we had popcorn in hot milk, seasoned with nutmeg and sugar. Delicious, and with canned milk, too. For dinner, one baked dish, made up of corn, which was fresh hominy ground, ground dried catfish, chopped celery and cabbage, seasoning of herbs and peppers. This too, was a success.

January 13   We had breakfast and were away soon after. Below, a hail from the gas station man who helped us telephone on Saturday night. . . . A heavy sky today, the sad hills stretched forever into the distance. . . .

Drifting is serious business with us. So much to see, gear to keep in order, charts to study and landmarks to identify. . . .

The variations of current in different stretches, and in various distances from shore, are noticeable. Also, in almost no wind, just a breath astern, we moved a little faster than the drift, about as fast as I could move the boat in still water. So it is not surprising that we can make no headway against the wind. . . .

We saw a steep stony shore ahead and along there, upriver from a daymark (533.8, or six miles from Wiley's Landing), we dropped anchor. While eating dinner, the *Sohio Fleetwing* came down, with a big tow of empties, swinging around the bend, quite close in. We thought perhaps this was not such a good place after all, but since we would have some protection from wind behind the point below us, and the stony bank was a relief from the mud of a falling river, and because we liked the view and the place in general, we decided to stay. . . .

Just after we had anchored, a native walked up along the shore, Skipper barking. He was curious to see who we were, saying he "thought this might be Clark's boat." He bought junk, and sold crockery. Said he had not seen him for 3 or 4 years. Commented favorably on our boat, dogs and johnboat. The johnboat always receives a good word.

I rowed back aways, to a patch of turnips in the lower bottom, almost washed out by the rise. Also picked up half a dozen apples, stranded along the shore.

January 14 I hear the spring whistle of a redbird this morning. The bees insisted on getting out, and flew around the deck, even in the rain. We hope they are doing well. The thunder seemed to arouse them. It is good to carry this summer sound with us.

The man from down the road was here again this morning. He turns out to be a professional fisherman in the summer, and I ac-quired some points from him. . . . Later in the day a man walked down the shore from Markland way. He was a trapper, hunted mink, possum, skunk at night with a varmint dog. He asked if we had any hounds to sell. We will learn all the articles a shantyboater might deal in after a while.

January 15   A high wind last night, and a lee shore. Before the wind began, the Greene Line boat had tripped our spar. It was downbound, late, I guess on account of the fog, and we were already in bed. The wind came up later, apparently from the southeast, from across the river, slightly downstream. Not having a long sweep, the waves were not high, but the force of the wind was great. I expected to hear our deck load of tubs and bicycle go overboard, and wished I had used new pieces of line to lash down the tarpaulin. I got up and dressed and set our spar, the thin locust pole I cut last week.

I stayed up quite awhile, built a fire, and worked at the net, listening to the wind. Everything held, the wind quieted down, and toward morning I went back to bed.

> *The evening after a day of drifting is a busy time. Now Anna can take her mind from navigating and watching the passing shores, and attend to household chores, mopping the floor, preparing supper. I tie up the boat securely, get a gangplank out to shore if possible, pick up loose ends. . . . On a new shore, I always reconnoiter to get some idea of the lay of the land. I cut firewood if the daylight allows it. Then we have a bath by lamplight and supper before the fire.*

January 16   We decided to leave later in the day, and I was ready to set out on a walk to Markland, when we noticed an upriver wind. So we cast off at once, and then happened that serious accident to Skipper, for which I am to blame. Our drifting was out of control for awhile, Skipper to care for, a mess inside to clean up, lines scattered about, gangplank floating alongside. First we skirted the shore, and I had to push us off with a pole. Then the current and wind carried us out, and I worked steadily to close in with the Indiana shore. Making no headway, and a buoy at the upper end of Vevay bar approaching, all hands were called. We cleared the buoy, and pulled in shore close enough to drop anchor at the mouth of

Plum Creek. We worked into the creek mouth, and tied up in the upper side, below the towhead, which was still connected with the mainland.

After lunch I made a trip to Vevay, first rowing up the creek, about a mile I guess, then walking down the highway a mile. Thumbed a ride part way there and back, and got some drinking water before leaving the road. Some current up the creek. Quite a stream. I saw a green growth on the bank, and found what must be a canebrake. The leaves were large, like willow leaves.

This is a wild, isolated spot, the nearest houses are in Kentucky.

January 17 Stars shone dimly last night, and this morning the old moon, just as high as the brighter morning star, was veiled by mist.

We were very busy this morning after an unhurried breakfast of rice cakes, and another section of *Art as Experience*. Anna washed out some clothes. I did various odd jobs, replaced the broken glass, finished the chest.

After dinner I poked into the various drift piles near us, some huge ones. At a time of flood, this point must be a wild place. Even now the steep bank on the lower side of the creek is caving into the rising water. This morning the water covered the narrow neck of land, and our towhead is an island.

Our harbor remains quiet. Last night our sleep was not broken by boatwaves or wind.

January 18 We pulled out into the stream about sunrise, after breakfast, and rowed for the left bank, which we made easily, for the river was narrow there, and there was no wind. Passed Ghent close in, the ferryboat *Martha Graham*. The courthouse clock in Vevay tolled 8 bells. . . . Wonderful drifting, and fine country. The Indiana side was hilly and wooded. The hills seem of different shape, and the rocks are not like those in Campbell County hills, often ledges near the top. Vevay makes a fine appearance from the river, and there were old farmhouses at the foot of the hills as we went farther down. . . .

We decided to tie up near Carrollton, above the town, and,

liking the open gravel shore, with huge sycamores against a steep bank, we dropped anchor. . . . A marvelous anchorage. Big trees out in the water, a gravel shore, much drift. . . .

After dinner, a flurry of cleaning up and getting all in order. I put in 3 panes of glass, to replace cracked ones, and did other odd jobs. Some reading while Anna ironed. Before dark I climbed the bank, finding a level field where tobacco had been cut. The highway close, but hardly to be heard from the river, the bank is so steep. A very fancy countryside, wide landscaped highway, estates. . . . What a strange experience, coming from the river to the highway, noise, lights, cars, busy people. Rather, hurrying breathless people. I realized that we were not that way, busy as we kept ourselves. We do stop our activity often, and have quiet times without tension.

January 21   This day we will remember as the day of the great blow. That is, until we meet with a stronger wind. But the waves today were about as much as we could take. It blew all of last night, but today shifted to the west and northwest, and in the middle of the morning was at its worst here. We watched the muddy whitecaps out in the river, not choppy waves, but long swells. Soon they were rolling along shore, even in the trees where we were anchored. We shipped no water but were in danger of being driven against the steep bank, where the waves broke with great force. There was a sycamore about 6 feet from the upstream quarter, inside, which seemed too close at times. The stageboard and spars were washed out last night. No spar would even have held now. I got out extra lines. Our inch line I had tied to a great sycamore ahead of us, and now I carried the other end of it out to the small poplar, from which I ran another line to the stern, to ease the strain on the anchor. I was busy every minute. Our planks were adrift and I went in with the johnboat and hauled them on the bank. The johnboat was filled with water by the waves. I managed to get back to the boat and bail out the johnboat from the after deck with a bucket. All was in good shape now.

The waves seemed to diminish, I think because the wind shifted more to the N.W., making it more of a crossriver wind. We had a fine dinner, roast beef and all that, and read some in the afternoon, with interruptions. At sundown the wind diminished still more. I went ashore to cut wood. Anna cleaned and mopped the cabin, we had a bath, which we had missed for 2 days. The temperature dropped steadily all day. Lines are stiff as wire cables.

The wind still blows, but in force not to be compared with that of this morning. We have blazing fires, shutters closed. Bees all wrapped up, for they are on an exposed corner. I wonder how they are.

January 22 A clear night, still, stars shining, very cold, and I keep up the fire.

January 23 We never know what will happen next. Last night, about midnight, I guess, I went on deck to see what was pounding. It was a still cold night, clear. The river had risen a little, and waves from a boat, probably the Greene Line steamer, had loosened the gangplank from the bottom, and it rose and fell, jarring the boat each time. I went down the gangplank, untied the running board, and tied it to a nearby line. Turning to go back to the deck, I slipped on the frosty board, and went into the river, head and all, not touching bottom. I swam a few strokes to the boat, tried to climb to the deck but first had to remove one of my slippers, which was coming off in the water. This I placed on deck, and then climbed up. All the while I held the lighted flashlight in my hand. Now I untied the line holding the stageboard, shoved the plank in the water, and tied it so it wouldn't float away. Then back to bed.

January 24 Another day in our snug harbor. . . . We see the Carrollton ferry slowly making its way across below us. Another feature of this town is the carillon, which plays tunes 2 or 3 times a day. A pleasant sound over the water. . . .

January 27 A fair morning, frosty, up early, breakfast, and we cast off about 8. Very calm, current still swift. Passed Carrollton 8:25 by the courthouse clock. Sternwheel ferry *Indiana*, a similar boat, *Ohio*, tied up on Indiana side. Slight breeze astern, but as the river turned toward the north we were carried close to the Kentucky shore. Rugged hills at Notch Lick Creek. We rounded the point at Locust Creek close in, and below pulled to shore and tied up. Dogs ashore, dinner, rest.

Now below Indian Kentucky River, Brooksburg, opposite Firth Hollow daymark, 7 miles drifted. Underway again, breeze stronger, and must use the sweeps or be blown ashore before reaching Madison. Rowed almost steadily while we drifted 41/2 miles to upper Madison. Bottom land on left, fine old houses. Steep wooded hills on right, often with rocky crest, evergreens on top. These are our castles. . . .

We intended to land above Madison, but the shore was bad, flood willows and muddy cornfields. Hard pulling to keep off. No place desirable, so we pulled out into the stream to clear the bridge pier. Fairly into Madison now, barge and 2 coaldiggers on landing. *Kenova* having tied up her tow, delivered a barge of coal to one digger. We drifted below them and pulled in as close below the lower barges as we could. A good landing. . . .

All through this people were watching from the bank, from what seemed a parkway. When I went ashore at 5 o'clock, I found we were just below a riverside parkway, at the foot of Broadway Street, in an elegant neighborhood. . . . This is a strange situation for us, street lights shining down, shutters closed for privacy, strange lights, barges tied up above us. Quiet, though, as usual. 14 miles today.

January 28 Colder today, with a downstream wind, east or northeast. We lay at Madison. Went uptown this morning, two trips, and were delighted with the place, so clean and prosperous looking, friendly, energetic people. A great contrast to Carrollton, probably the difference between a midwestern and southern city, though Carrollton is much smaller, of course. One of our stops was the Irwin Feed Store and Mill, where we bought 25 lbs. of wheat ($1.00) and some soybeans, found that we could get our corn ground there. They were grinding it by the wagonload, 15 cents per hundred pounds up to 1000 pounds, 10 cents a hundred over that. There are many old buildings on the streets, brick mostly, used as residences or places of business, in good condition though seeming old.

A chat this evening with the elderly man whose shantyboat is above ours, in behind the barges.

January 30 Still at Madison. . . . Listened to Arthur Moore for a long time, when I rowed down the river in the morning, past the float where he has his cabin. He is caretaker for the boat club, but has spent all his life on the river, traveling from Wheeling to the Saline river. He came up in the evening, and stayed to supper, without any coaxing, quite at ease. . . .

Some good playing in the late afternoon, interrupted by the arrival of the Coast Guard cutter *Fern*, which tied up for the night below us, running its barge up to the tree where our stern line was tied.

It rained in the night, very hard, driven against the windows by a high wind from across the river. Lightning and thunder, the wind eases, rain pours down. River had risen a little by morning, coming up all day. Rain ceased before noon, wind veering to west. By midafternoon was blowing hard, and tonight we toss and creak in the howling wind.

February 1   Two more days at Madison. Tonight the wind is coming again from the west and we rock in the long swells. . . . A clear, cold night, ragged clouds racing past the moon.

Some painting this morning.

A. Moore came in while we were eating dinner. Not at all shy or backward, he comes in without hesitation, is quite at ease, and talks freely. Yesterday our neighbor Jocko Davis, who is seldom on his boat, came by in his narrow johnboat. In the bow was a red coffee bag, which he told me to take. It contained six fresh, as he said, eggs. I did not quite understand where they came from, but they were a gift to us. . . .

We went shopping this afternoon, and found the stores crowded. Many country people buying. We were delighted with a harness and hardware store, which changed into a harness shop in the rear with two old men working away. I saw many things I would like to buy, mostly because it was so honestly made, and evidently very useful. . . .

The shore is clear except for some big willows. At the top of the bank, say 12 feet out of water now, is the parkway. It doesn't seem like Ohio river shore, has a suggestion of a river in France, as I know them from pictures.

We are really living in town now, and do not feel as close to the river, as much a part of it, as when we were out on the open shores and lonely reaches. It is remarkably quiet here, though. Now the upbound Greene boat is passing close to the Kentucky shore. I must go out on deck, see that all is well, put out the riding light, then to bed, where Anna has been for some time.

February 2 This morning the *R. W. Turner*, down with its empty barge, landed close below us, still headed downstream. Some difficulty about tying up, and the captain, R. W. Turner himself, told us we were on his landing place, that he would pull up there, and we must take the consequences. I made ready to move, but he turned around and anchored close below us. He lives in Madison, spent Sunday at home, and they will leave at midnight. About sunset, the engineer, Mr. Singer, called on us, chatting awhile.

This afternoon, still cold and clear, we went for a walk, calling on Arthur Moore first. He took us out on the float, and into his cabin, which was truly a shantyboat interior. Then we went to the Lanier house, from squalor to grandeur, enjoying each in its way.

Some playing when we returned. This attracted the attention of all the passers-by above us. . . .

The *R. W. Turner* passed us regularly at Brent. So often that I did not think it possible to go so far below—5 miles below Louisville to the Standard Terminal, and as far up as Ashland. She carried a crew of four, pilot and engineer on each watch, the engineer doing the decking. Mr. Singer was an old riverman, having run small packets of his own between Madison and Louisville, the last being the *New Hanover*, which I think I remember.

February 3 Underway this morning, not early, for we had breakfast and I took a walk before leaving. About 9 a.m. As we cast off, a crosswind that we had not noticed, or that just sprang up, held us against the shore, and we thought our day's run would end at the Madison Boat Club. However, by both rowing, we worked off shore and passed the Marine Ways. A steel sand flat under construction, a pleasure boat blocked up, the steam towboat *Bob Tresler* on the ways, far gone toward ruination. Now a light breeze sprang up ahead, and increased quickly. We began to think of shelter, passed by Crooked Creek, and, wind increasing, looked for the mouth of Clifty Creek. It was suddenly ahead of us, but we were close in, and I got a line around a willow, holding the boat in the current at the creek's mouth which was swift over a rocky bar. We worked into the creek, and were glad to have shelter from the wind, which roared through the tremendous trees, and made breakers on the bar, deep as it was. The creek water was very clear, green, and had a skim of ice, farther up. So 2 miles is all we made today, but it took us as far from Madison as a long day's run would do. . . .

Tonight the wind is still, the moon shines through the clouds. . . . What a contrast to our anchorage at Madison, how good it is to get into a retired place, really on the river again.

February 4 We noticed a creek called on the chart Cold Friday Creek. This one might be called "Cold Tuesday" for today was the coldest day in a long time. Last night the wind shifted to the west or north of west, and blew hard, with snow, which I felt on my face, in bed.

February 5 The west wind still blows today, roaring through the treetops, the boat rocking gently. In the still night ice formed about us, and up the creek it is frozen over. Icicles hang from the branches close to the water, long festoons of them, 16 inches, and growing with the falling river. . . .

Many times through the day and night we congratulate our-selves on being in this sheltered place. Our open anchorage at Madison or above Carrollton must be cold and rough now. Here it is really warm, with the sun shining in on its first rising. There are many birds about. A list of those we have seen here would include almost all we have seen this winter: Crows, ducks, gull, cardinal, goldfinch, titmouse, chickadee, sparrows, junco (slate colored and white-winged), towhee, hairy woodpecker, red bellied blackbird, jay, Carolina wren, robin, kingfisher.

One night at Madison I got up to see what was bumping us so heavily and found a piece of timber 14 or 16 inches across with a line around it. I tied it up, but not finding a claimant, next day I cast it off. No one claimed the line, which we brought with us. Last night we worked an eye splice in one end, practicing that again, and found we had a piece of new line perhaps 7/8" thick, 30 feet long. Lines mean so much to us now, when our safety depends on a single one, often. . . .

We have much to do in the way of upkeep and repair. The viola sound post fell out of position, and I had to devise a sound post setter. Always something on my shelf, or on my mind, to be repaired or made.

One has a good selection of wood in these driftpiles. The main deck is piled with it, as we have the stageboard at the other end here—pine stumps, railroad ties (a new one), locust, chestnut, fir for quick burning, some black walnut.

A full moon last night, and tonight, soon as it was dark, the moon rose again, a bright coin on the horizon. A happy coincidence, the bright moon, on any clear night, but in this cold winter air it is brightest of all.

The river is never quiet here. Always a steady sound of waves, like that of a waterfall. It is the wind, and the current sweeping over the creek's rocky bar. Tonight it is almost calm, here, yet the sound of waves is continuous. The moonlit sky through the tall trees, stars spaced among their gigantic branches.

February 6 A still, cloudy morning. We decided to leave Clifty Creek. Took on board all the cut wood, slung the gangplanks under the guards, had our breakfast of hominy, took in the lines, luckily the ends and knots had been kept dry during the cold weather. We ran a line to the outside tree on the upper side of the creek, pulled the boat out there, cast off and were at once slipping past the willows, and the creek mouth was lost.

A fine morning for drifting, and we were glad to be underway again. Skirted the Indiana shore, the river curving southward in a long bend, Madison soon closed in. Hanover College seen on the hilltop, camps at Hanover beach. Then a head wind sprang up, suddenly, and we considered anchoring, but instead rowed across the river. It took us 2 miles of drifting, and we just made Gilmore Creek, for which we were aiming. The mouth was narrow, evidently a small creek, but we pulled into it, into clear green water, where the white boat with its red hull and shutters made a good appearance.

A sharp line between the creek water, clear and green, and the muddy river water, which billowed like clouds. We were welcomed by a coot, who paid no attention to our coming, however. At Clifty a pair of robins saw us off. The coot swam around the boat, catching fish and taking them to shore to eat. Snow was falling now. We tied up, put out a plank.

February 7 Whenever we tie up in a creek, or along a stretch of shore where no boats have been, it makes a new light for pilots, and they usually turn their search lights on us when passing. I wonder if they recognize us as the same boat they saw up at Big Bone, or some point above?

A cold day today, with a strong west wind, which died down at sunset. We puttered about various jobs this morning, mostly in the kitchen. Experiments are always under way—bean sprouts, toasted hominy grits, ice cream. . . .

Some good playing this afternoon.

At sunset, a winter sunset over snow.

The coot is still about, fishing, walking along the shore, preening himself in the sun, as if we were not here. How solitary he is, how contented.

The wind is blowing again, now little waves slapping against the rake. They formed icicles today, and the boat wore a beard of them. Knots in lines are frozen hard, tied in a wet snowfall as they were.

My walk today was the most satisfactory since we have been travelling. The country makes a fit shore for the river.

> *We had listed the requirements for our summer location. First, it must be far enough below Madison to be completely in the country. . . . It was strange to be thinking of summer gardens in zero weather and snow storms, but we got out our warmest clothing and explored the shores and back country, with a garden in mind.*

February 8 A very cold night. Kept the fire burning all through the night. A cold windy day. Now after dark the wind is quiet. Our creek, shrinking steadily, has a polar look, with fantastic formations of ice, and snowy banks.

February 9 Kept a blazing fire all night, and all of us very comfortable.

February 10 Yesterday we noticed the shad swimming in the clear, sunny water of the creek, and I made a cast with a seine made of a mesh cabbage sack on two sticks. To my surprise, I scooped out all the seine would hold, and made several more hauls, catching perhaps a tubful. They are still on deck, frozen solid, food for the dogs, and for us too, for we toast them over the coals.

Yesterday afternoon in the cold wind, all of us walked back to the nearest house, with our empty bucket. Two men were there, evidently repairing the house, and we talked with them. They live on farms south of the house and told us about the bottom, which was first called Trout's Bottom, from the name of the owner, who lived in a large brick house. This I had seen in my walk yesterday. . . . These men had taken shad out of Gilmore's Creek, enough to fill a wagon, feeding them to hogs. . . .

A hunter came along, and we talked awhile. He is a native, living on a hilltop farm, but comes to the river to hunt and fish. Part Indian, he said, and his appearance seemed to carry it out. He gave us a rabbit he had just shot. Very friendly, as were the two men yesterday, leading one to think that the whole valley might be so.

A wonderful view here, up and down and across. The river wider than above. Coming down, the steep hills on the Indiana side were cut by two openings, sharp clefts in the rock. One was Hart's Falls Creek, the other above Big Six Landing, where we saw two shantyboats beached out. The hawk along here we identified as a marsh hawk. In spite of the fine view of the distant hills and river, this is an unattractive place. The bank was very muddy in the warm sun today, the bottom shallow. . . .

Quiet tonight, not so cold. The fire can go out, after blazing for a week, day and night.

February 11 After breakfast we cast off, making all shipshape, though we did not intend to go far. We had seen floating ice toward the other side, and now it filled the river, in thin sheets scattered about. We drifted slowly with it in the warm sunshine. Past the Spring Creek Light, which is an oil lamp. So the one at Hart's Creek was too, as we suspected, though we never could see it being lighted or put out in the morning. Below the light an old steamboat landing, Moreland's, with a store building still standing at the top of the bank, the faded sign, "Groceries and Dry Goods". Another house, with a row of children watching us. The johnboat which had passed us before we cast off had come from here. There was a pump near the water, on a pipe driven into the ground.

We anchored 1/4 mile below, just above Moreland's Creek. This creek is against a steep hill, which continues down the river, sloping sharply down to the water. It is at mile 566.5, 104.5 miles below Brent, 9 miles below Madison, 37 miles above Louisville. Our first impressions were favorable. It is strange how at once one place will attract. The same shore half a mile up, we did not like.

After a while I went back to the pump for water, but found it broken. A man came down, one of those in the johnboat this morning, very friendly, explained about the pump, got a hoe and dug out a spring back on Moreland's Creek. The man lives in the old store building, his brother in the other house. His father, 80, lives there, and owns the farm, 140 acres. The name, as I made it out, is Fresh. His father is an old river man, pilot I believe on the *Hanover*, and his son said he had taught Jess Singer, the engineer of the *R.W. Turner*, our visitor at Madison, to be a pilot. The man I talked to was as open as day, and we soon had a garden made and a crop of watermelons planted on shares. We could have our boat near and watch them, he said.

February 12 It was cloudy this morning, warm and still, so we abandoned our plan to wash clothes. Other things to be done, too, enough to fill more than one day. I cut a sycamore for a spar, putting our "traveling spar" out on the bank, until needed. Shifted lines, ran out our long inch line astern. Out in deeper water now, ready for wind and waves. . . .

Floating ice covered half the river, fortunately for us the far half, a sharp line dividing it from the open water. It moves slowly.

I walked to the mail box again at sunset, clear after an overcast day. The scrubby valley of bottom, a background of wooded hills, steep and rocky in places, with many cedars across the wide river, the sun setting over the level line of hills. Conversation on the way with Cleo, Wilmer, and a Marshall boy. The latter, about 18, keen and healthy, very friendly, said they had just moved here from near Louisville. He liked the place, the people were friendly, and it was near town. I wonder how far back he lived before coming here.

February 13   Colder last night, and a starry morning. This was our washday, the first since January 6, at Big Bone. It is after dark now, and Anna is just putting away, all folded neatly and in piles of varying size. . . .

Three natives went down the river in a johnboat today, as they did yesterday. We learned they were dynamiting fish down at Payne Hollow. Had not much success, for the drastic means used. . . .

This was a warm day, quiet and sunny. The redbirds sang their spring song this morning, and so did the chickadees.

February 15   I took a walk back into the narrow valley, and up the hilltop directly above us, following an abandoned road. At one time a road to the river was important to the farmers. Cleo said they used to haul peaches down to the landing. Now there is a blacktop road leading the other way, and all is hauled by truck.

February 16   A week ago was the cold windy Sunday at Gilmore's Creek, when we caught the shad and took a walk in the afternoon, talking to the men at the house nearby. Today is mild and cloudy, apparently clearing. Shores are muddy. In fact, we haven't been inspired by this place, after my enthusiasm of the first day. It is that way with the different spots we anchor, some have an attraction for us, some we don't take to, all for reasons under the surface.

The hunter, whose name is Jess Powell, happened along this morning and gave us a mallard duck he had shot. We looked in our books and identified it as a red-legged black duck. I think the hunters call them black mallards. Powell came on deck and talked awhile, very friendly and helpful, encouraging. He, as well as Cleo and

Wilmer, give the impression that they want us to stay in this neighborhood.

This morning I rowed around the rocky point below us for the first time, and down to Payne Hollow, about half a mile, or a third. I was much taken with the place. There is a big spring up the creek aways. Very likely we will move down there as soon as we can for a trial period, perhaps coming back here, or exploring farther down, into the Corn Creek bottom.

February 17 We moved down to Payne Hollow, towing with the johnboat most of the way, for the current was slow. . . . We took a walk late in the afternoon, back up the hollow, pondered the chimney and fireplace of an old house standing in a level field, and a barn against the hill. The hills about the narrow valley are steep and rocky, covered with quite a forest. I look forward to learning the country about. The view up the river is even better than from our recent anchorage at Moreland's.

> *We landed at Payne Hollow with great expectations. How good it was to have a sandy beach, and solitude!*
>
> *We explored our new territory with the eagerness of castaways on their desert island. The freedom of the river was still with us. We occupied the shore as naturally as the driftwood and river sand. . . .*

5

Payne Hollow

When I left the road and began the descent to the river, glimpses of which, far below, could be had through the budding trees, it seemed that we lived at the end of the world, more remote even than the last farm up Corn Creek; yet I approached with an inward lifting and when home again, our little Hollow seemed the center of the world.

February 18, 1947 Yesterday for dinner we had the wild duck that Powell gave us. Roasted in the oven. We found it delicious, rich and juicy, somewhat tough, especially the first serving, but we left it in the oven while eating, and had all degrees, from rare to well done. Duck soup from the bones.

This morning after breakfast and some reading and a trip to the spring for water, I made a short excursion down the shore. I came back with favorable reports, and a bucket of shad for dinner.

February 20 Yesterday afternoon in the sun and cold north wind, with the two dogs, I walked down the shore, past the re- markable root cellar across the creek, where there is an old founda- tion, too, and followed an indistinct footpath along the steep face of the hill. Half a mile down was Preston Hollow, not much of a creek, just a dry rocky ravine from a notch in the hills. Apparently this is the beginning of the bottom land which extends down to Corn Creek. A deserted house and barn, hayfields. Then up the steep hill and back a short distance through fields to a road which I fol- lowed north through farming country. It joined a blacktop road, possibly one from Corn Creek to Milton. Much country to explore. Down through Payne Hollow, a rough way where it opens out into a level, narrow meadow is an old chimney, a barn still used.

February 22 Today we made a new lamp shade, proud of our handiwork. The material came from our own stores, which pleased us, too. It seems that whatever we want to make, some adequate raw material can be found. Recently we dipped some candles, successfully.

Today I fixed a better footwalk ashore, using some driftwood planks. Our dock is a large poplar tree, uprooted and level with the bank but still growing.

I made a trip to the landing above, but found no one at home, the johnboat gone. I walked on to the mailbox, where I found nothing. Still, somehow, the row against the wind, and the walk, were profitable.

The days continue cold and windy. We enjoy the sunny afternoons, it is so warm and bright in the cabin.

February 23 I walk to the hill and ridge down river from us. The fields reach to the edge, there—cedar trees, a crest of rock in thick layers, a sheer drop through the woods. The light at Spring Creek, Wilmer's light, is just hidden by the wooded point at the narrows. From the outside corner of the boat, by leaning over, one can see it. At night it shines through the trees. . . .

A bright young moon in the clear western sky now, a very cold night coming on.

February 24 Winter clamped down on us last night. We knew it would be cold and got in chunks of hardwood to keep the fire burning all night. We were waked from sleep by the ominous sound of ice grinding and cracking against the hull, about 2 feet away from our heads. After a while I got up and dressed, but there wasn't much I could do. The ice was thin, in large sheets. A dark night. I longed for daylight. After a while the ice piled up ahead of the boat, and formed a boom so it ran farther out. I went back to bed and slept till daylight.

The weather moderated during the day. Snow fell lightly, driven by the west wind. A solid sheet of ice extended about 50 yards beyond the boat, but not far up, or down, as we could see. We seemed to be in the thickest of it, but were not concerned today, but went about our usual activities. A beautiful winter day. Wood-chopping, painting, reading, playing, meals, breaking ice away from the boat. Could not get into the creek for shad.

Last night, when we went to bed, not expecting ice, or anything unusual, we remarked how little we considered our remote situation, far from towns or even people, on a shore almost uninhabited, the wind blowing a winter gale, yet we went to sleep with easy minds.

February 26 A long walk this morning, over the high, wind-swept countryside. Beginning up Payne Hollow to the road, where I stopped to talk with the Hammonds, owners of this riverfront. Then north on the empty road, stopping at 3 farmhouses for eggs, but each place was deserted except for the watchdogs. They were all friendly, and a varied race. At the fourth place, a lady directed me to Oakleys, half a mile farther, where I did get eggs, 2 dozen, at 38¢. Now I was close to the Spring Creek road, I thought, and turned off where directed. But I got into a maze of lanes, and so took off across the fields toward the river, going down into a steep hollow, a beautiful place, which turned out to be Moreland's Creek. This, of course, led me to Fresh's landing, where Cleo welcomed me. Even had me come in his rats' nest, where Wilmer and the Marshall boy soon joined us. When I left, after adding a package that had come in the mail to my load, I climbed the steep hill to Marshall's and along the ridge south, a striking view. I have seen places hereabouts which are not Ohio river country at all, being more rugged and on a larger scale. Mountain country, almost, not what one would expect.

February 27 A cold night past. We were frozen in hard this morning, and even after a day of sunshine, it took a lot of pounding to break up the ice around the boat.

This morning, cold out, but warm and sunny inside, we worked at fixing things, my heavy shoes and the battered volume of Shakespeare. Everything in one volume, condensed reading for us. It was a gift to my mother on her 21st birthday, from Uncle Cal and Aunt Zylph. What strange quarters for it to come to, but at last it is being read.

February 28   Last night a boat went by, broke up the ice, and the banging against the boat woke us up. Surprised to see the river almost open out from us. In the morning most of the ice along this shore was gone, as suddenly as it had come, though much floated by all day. It was good to put the oarlocks in the johnboat and row around a bit. . . .

This afternoon Powell came by, without his gun, talked. We went to the creek, dipped out shad. The number was amazing, even to him. He says they disappear when the water gets warmer, often earlier than this. He took with him the dip net that Anna netted for him.

Buds opening, on vines on the hillside. Trumpet vines? Soon a great bursting forth, and new birds coming.

Now at bedtime, a light snow sifts down through the veiled moonlight. Johnboat and stageboard are white.

March 1   After breakfast I went to Fresh's landing. Good to be out on the open water, green and clear now. Only a little floating ice, close to the Indiana shore now. I went past Cleo's house. Little Lucille happened to open the door just then, a cigarette in her mouth, which she tried to hide when she saw me. Cleo came to the door barefooted, talking away without introduction or pause. Quoted his father about the ice, and sound advice it was. As long as the ice was moving, says he, there is no danger even if you are frozen in the shore ice. Keep it out away from the boat, and when the channel clears, the shore ice will move out. But if the river fills up, the ice stops moving and freezes up solid, then you had better get your boat out of it, for when it does break up it will grind along the shore, taking boats with it. The moral is, when winter sets in and it gets cold, and the river is low, anchor your boat on a bar, where it can be pulled out on skids. It would be well, too, to have trees near by to cut for skids and to tie your block and tackle to. Sycamore is best, the old man says, being straight and slippery, and strong.

After leaving Cleo, which meant stopping his speech, he is a cheerful, good hearted fellow, though, kind and considerate, too, I walked along the snowy lane to the mailbox, stopping to talk to the Marshall boys who were shucking corn, working at it with a will. The mailman hadn't come and perhaps would not, over the snowy, rutted road, a steep hill to climb. A word with the Boulders, or Boldery, I believe it is, and a short walk north on the road. One turns off up Spring Creek, a little way farther a country school, typical of 50 years ago, I suppose, old benches, blackboard, potbellied iron stove in the middle of everything. Returning, more conversation with the Marshalls, watching their bantam chickens. A word with Wilmer, all bundled up against the cold, and the row downstream, which is a mile by the river book.

A long afternoon inside, after dinner, some painting, playing, repairing my heavy shoes. Wood cutting in the winter dusk, a new snow covered world, the sound of the axe.

March 2   A cold night, with a west wind, snow flurries. It blew all the ice over to this side.

The *Gordon C. Greene* down this morning, bound for New Orleans.

I walked up the snowy ridge to Marshalls this morning, for milk, carrying to them a bucket of shad. They had two baby chicks hatched out by a hen who had stolen a nest in the barn. The winter weather is more severe on the ridge, as on a mountain top.

I see robins nearly every day.

A rough, blustery day, flurries of snow, the west wind slapping waves at the side of the boat, breaking up the soft ice.

A good afternoon, playing, reading, a stint of wood chopping before dark, bath and supper by the fire, little shad broiled, eaten with bread.

March 3   Another cold night, and windy day. Skim ice formed on the river in extensive sheets. These bore down on us, and crashed with a great noise, but, of course, no damage to the boat. Clearing at noon, warmer, a windy March day.

Pancakes for breakfast, with our abundance of sour milk. I cut firewood, then made another trip to Marshalls, returning with a gallon of sweet skim milk, and a steak, and a piece of fresh pork. Country meat, country generosity.

March 4   Today we decided to stay here for the summer, hoping to have a garden. . . .

We tapped two maple trees up at the narrows. . . . This evening, I noticed that the sap was running, but slowly. Another project current is smoking fish. I prepared the large shad we picked out of the river yesterday, and will try to make a smoker out of an oil drum, half buried in the frozen ground. With all this to do, we keep up our playing, reading and painting, and leisurely meals.

A moonlit night, quiet and still.

March 5   A light snow during the night. Very still this morning. What will come from the sky? Our fireplace has blazed, more or less brightly, day and night for more than a week. . . .

Much accomplished today. 7 more maple trees tapped, making 9 in all. We went up together this afternoon and were pleased with the sight of the buckets hanging on the light gray trees standing straight on the steep hillside. The dripping of sap into the bucket. . . . A fine dinner of fishhash and cornbread, a wonderful salad of tomatoes, soybean sprouts, cottage cheese and toasted sunflower seeds.

March 6   Today is marked by the passing of Brent. An end to his suffering, and a grave on this strange shore. Yet his life, until the last few days, was as happy and eventful as any dog could wish.

A busy day. Fish smoking to get under way and tend. A trip to the Marshalls' for milk and eggs, taking them a bucket of shad. Coming back I came down the hill from the log cabin. There, just under the highest layer of rock, is a spring. Looking down the steep hillside through the trees, I saw a wooden trough which once carried the spring water down to the farm on the hillside. It was made of halves of trees, 6 or 7 inches in diameter, roughly hollowed out with an adze, I think, one lapping over the lower one. Perhaps 100 yards from the spring, this aqueduct empties into a big wooden trough, made of a hollow log. With some repair the trickle of water could be made to run down through the woods again. A novel and pleasant sight. . . .

Among the trees I found what might turn out to be a corn grinder, an old-fashioned coffee mill such as was once used in stores, apparently in good condition, though I haven't yet examined it. I could not have been more surprised to find a pot of gold, or more pleased.

March 8   Yesterday for the first time since we have been washing clothes on the river, we rinsed them in the stream directly. I took the sheets into the johnboat and managed to accomplish it with no difficulty, in spite of misgivings.

This afternoon I rowed up to Fresh's, against the wind, had a talk with Cleo, who seems now like an old friend. . . .

Last night for supper we had some of our smoked fish. The large shad, in spite of their many bones, were delicious. Our supply of green vegetables now comes from soybean sprouts. Anna has them coming on all the time, and has developed a fine specimen of sprout, served in many ways and combinations.

I am sure the elms and soft maples at Moreland Creek, against the hill, showed a change in color. It is time.

March 9   I heard a dove singing this morning from across the river. Later in the day, one on this side. A wonderful clear morning, the fading moon in the western sky. . . . Tonight is perfectly still and clear, the bright stars before moonrise.

This morning various chores about the boat, maple fire to keep going, a visit from Powell. We took our dinner to the maple camp, and baked potatoes, broiled shad, and made corn pone in the ashes, while the sap boiled. The syrup was finished, sap gathered from the buckets, another batch begun. We rowed back to the boat, then left at once for a walk back the hollow, as far as the Corn Creek road. Then a visit with the Owen Hammonds, which we all enjoyed.

March 10   Up before sunrise, and to the camp. A cold morning, ground frozen hard. The red bird and Carolina wren and titmouse sing as if it were spring air, instead of winter. There is something new. Winter is past, though signs of spring are few. . . .

Yesterday was significant for us. A definite understanding with the owner of this land, we can take some definite action that we hesitated about. We can unload stuff on shore, begin the garden, settle other questions that depended on our staying here, such as a mail box, and trips to town.

I never feel that the river bank belongs to anyone, though. In fact, I think it by right belongs to us as much as anyone. They have land rights, a sort of distant ownership, but we have an inherent right and interest by being there, as naturally as the driftwood along shore.

Yesterday, too, I made another trip to the Marshalls', returning with 3 quarts of skim milk, which they gave us, a dozen eggs, 35¢, and a white rooster, for which we paid a dollar, and found he weighed 61/2 pounds. I put him under a tub on the roof, and he crowed as naturally as if in his own barnyard. A pleasing sound, much in harmony with our living.

An important day for us. This morning, when the ground was yet frozen, we put the bees on shore. We slipped a pair of carrying poles under the hive, with cleats to prevent its sliding. We worked the hive from the deck to the johnboat, then on to the shore. We had to carry them about 50 yards through the old cornfield to the higher field where our garden is to be. Later there were many bees out in the warm sunshine about the hive. From its weight there must be both bees and honey inside. We are eager to see conditions within.

With the maple syrup making there was not time for gardening, but with the other decisive steps, we feel located here.

These were special days. It was a joy to be working in the winter woods, above the river, building huge fires.

March 11   This afternoon I broke up a corner of our new garden, first raking down onto it leaves and mold from the steep wooded hill above. The soil seems excellent. There is a splendid view from the garden which is higher above the river than it appears from below. Time to plant some early things now.

I expected the sap to run more freely today, but we gathered only the usual boiler full. It dripped a little after dark last night, the jars and cans were nearly empty, and various tones and rhythms of dripping could be heard from the dark hillside, a fairy-like sound.

March 13 This morning I was waked by a patter of rain. I went at once to the maple camp, started a fire under the half finished batch of syrup, put up a canvas shelter and windbreak for the fire, got dry wood under cover. Now after breakfast I sit there, warmed, scorched rather by the fire, the south wind blowing the rain through the woods. . . .

Yesterday was an eventful day. Another kettle of syrup was finished, the fifth. I raised the net, and found a dozen large shad, nothing else. After dinner, I rowed across the river. . . . A wonderful view, down, and across, to our hills and hollow. I felt that a more desirable place could not be imagined.

One feels strongly the difference between the contrasting shores, trees, birds, even the air is different. . . .

I saw a large flock of grackles and red wings. Just now a phoebe sat on a twig a few feet away. I had remarked this morning that he was due.

More work in the garden yesterday, and the first planting, lettuce, peas, parsley, carrots, the only early seed we have, so far. An unrivaled experience, putting seeds in the ground, intensified by the strangeness of our situation, an adventure compared to a long migration to rich country afar.

March 14 Last evening, very thick fog and rain. In the night the wind shifted to westward, and this morning appears to be clearing. Did not hear the rat last night as we did before in the stillness. Then I saw him scamper down the plank when he heard me. He should go on our list of visitors.

Today we made the much-talked-of trip to Madison. In a haphazard way, after all our planning. We crossed the river about 10 a.m., pulled the boat out and locked it to a tree, left the oars and Anna's galoshes at the first house, Joe Montgomery's. Harry Schirmer, in the second house, was not at home. We waited at the corner, encouraged by a milk can. The milk truck came by shortly and carried us up the river road to Madison. We were pleased to see the hills and farms that we had passed coming down. . . .

Reached Madison about 1 o'clock, and hurried with our buying, as the milk truck driver, we learned later his name was Jim Bruce, told us of another truck that would go out toward Saluda school leaving about 12:30. We found the driver of this truck, he was having lunch in a hamburger joint, and he agreed to take us. So we loaded our stuff in the back. It amounted to a considerable pile, a hundred-pound sack of seed potatoes, much more than I realized I was getting, a fifty-pound sack of potatoes for current use, two cartons of groceries and meat, a sack of green stuff. Anna and I sat in the cab of the truck, eating our lunch of smoked fish, cheese and rye bread, with handfulls of lettuce.

It was after 2 before the boyish driver came, and in a short time, over narrow country roads, through a surprising, wooded, swampy country, dropped us at the Saluda Township School, having come out of his way to accommodate us. Soon Harry Schirmer arrived with his bus, but seeing all our plunder said he would come back later with his pickup truck. We stood in the hallway of the school, enjoyed the dismissal. Harry came, and carried us and our stuff as near to the river as he could, and we ferried it across.

Arrived at the boat at sundown, quite pleased with ourselves for having managed to get to Madison and return with 200 pounds of freight in one day.

We were appalled by prices of food, especially meat, in town. Who buys it at that price? Bacon 75¢ a pound. We are thankful for our fish and cornmeal.

March 17 So truly March, the thin sunshine, great white clouds rolling against a blue sky. Last night the bright stars, yet the ground was white with snow this morning. In the first sun it vanished.

Sap is running again and we have a log fire under the boiler. I am glad to have more of it to do, this working in the woods is so pleasant, building fires, sitting by in their warmth for awhile. The rising river is more seasonable, too, current and roily water.

J. Powell came by yesterday, with his rifle and dog. This time he came in, and sat by the fire for an hour, at least, telling fish yarns in his quiet, full voice. Anna picked over bean sprouts, meanwhile, and at last I got out our new mop, out of which I took half the strands, making a smaller one, just the desired size. Enough cotton to make another mop. I feel that it was quite an achievement.

Made a mail box this morning of unique design and construction. Planted 100 hills of potatoes yesterday, in the snowfall, putting shad in the row for fertilizer.

March 18   This was a red-letter day for us, as Anna said. For we put out our own mailbox with "Harlan Hubbard" painted in red on its side. The box is made of a square 5 gallon tin can, but is complete with door and flag. I rowed across this morning, cut a locust post over there, and set it up next to Montgomery's box, at the turn in the road. The carrier came along and I introduced ourselves to him, received our first piece of mail, addressed to "Boxholder."

March 19   After the wind and frost, the sap began running again with the sun. We finished a batch yesterday and have another coming on this morning, the eighth one, which we can figure at 2 gallons. It goes by a system now that requires little thought, but I still enjoy the trips to the woods, the fires, nights and early morning. Yesterday we took our dessert and book there after dinner, to take care of the syrup. . . .

Now as darkness gathers, writing this by the maple fire, I think I hear far off, yes, I am sure of it, the peeping of frogs. What more earthy, springlike sound than their tiny whistle?

March 20   We awoke to a gray day, mist closing in, soon rain, light and steady. I had time to stretch a canvas over the maple fire, get the fire going, get in wood. Then an easy restful morning. A special breakfast, bacon, hominy, fried apples. I tended the fire under the boiler, sheltered from the rain, writing two letters. All this a welcome change after the bright, busy days. We feel a satisfaction, having planted the garden seeds, the gentle rain falling on them.

We wonder who the early inhabitants of this hollow were. No doubt there were many. Several families at one time, perhaps. And we are the latest.

March 21   More March weather of the lion-like kind. Cold and cloudy, high, variable winds, snow, rain, sleet and snow. Now and then a ray of sun through a hole in the clouds. It is good to be indoors, yet good to be out, too. The air is like cold water to the thirsty.

March 22 Today was quiet and sunny, the storms of yesterday seem far in the past. I crossed the river this morning with our first outgoing mail, 14 letters and 6 post cards addressed to Maine and California, Texas and Michigan.

March 23 I hear a phoebe. His song marks a point in the slowly turning seasons.

Powell comes by, after our late breakfast. We go to look at the line I put out last evening, and take off two nice catfish. The net is stocked with shad, a pound sucker. So fishing is under way, at the same date it was last year.

Powell had been to see Art Moore yesterday. What a pair. Powell tells me his great grandfather was a Mohawk Indian. He asked me if I were not part Indian. Perhaps I am.

March 24 As darkness falls, there is a gale of wind from the west, or south of west. It comes in waves, at its height shaking the boat as it whistles by. The dead poplar at the creek mouth was blown down. We are thankful not to be in a westerly reach. This follows a thunderstorm and a mild threatening day. We saw a little rainbow of our own in the cornfield, arching against the woods.

We forego our bath this eve, the boat pitches so, and I do not like to be unready for action.

For dinner, creamed smoked fish with baked potatoes, and the first mess of wild greens. An event.

I paint some this afternoon in the changing light and tossing boat.

Sunday when I was at the Marshalls', inside the old house, I saw several shelves of books in an inset bookcase. The entire series of Harvard Classics, a set of Thackeray, and others. Where did they come from? I like to think that the old house was once clean and sweet. The brick part must be very old. What sort of a man would build there, the brow of the hill, with so much of the world at his feet?

March 25 The gale from the west last night was as bad as any we have come through. Rain drove through the windows and down into the cupboards. I had to get up and retie the johnboat. No other trouble and this morning was quieter. Soon, however, the wind was blowing hard as ever from the N.W., almost. The short waves shook the boat, splashed over the deck. . . .

Evening. Wind still blowing, not so violent, but one does not know whether it will increase or go down. We go about our living, Anna busy sewing and ironing. I putter about, play the viola a little. A walk through the woods, the hollow is a roaring tunnel. Quite heavy snowfall at times. I gather a few tiny dandelions in the pasture about the barn.

March 26 Last night and this morning were downright cold. The sun thawed the frozen earth by afternoon, but it was a winter day. Wind not so strong, but steady from the same point, north of west. This evening is calm, and probably tomorrow will bring a change. It is good weather, though, the air so clean and fresh, and this coldness now may mean a good growing season next month. . . .

A good portion of reading and playing today.

March 27 A wonderful, wintry day today. Snow began to fall early, a fine, thick, windless snowstorm. We are so closed in. Surely no one lives in those far, shrouded hills, and the country back in is unbroken forest.

Skipper has a friend, the old hound from the Marshalls' who howls a serenade from the bank.

I traced our fish line this morning, and found two catfish and a little waterdog. The bait was put on Sunday, and nothing was on the hooks Monday morning. I raised the net, too, and took in quite a haul. A good sized blue cat, with a square tail, several suckers, and a tubful of shad, of all sizes. We broiled some of the small ones at the fireplace for dinner.

A quiet day for us.

March 28 Fog this morning after a cold night. Frost work on the trees which this condition brings about. A most beautiful feature of winter, unbelievably fair, unearthlike. As the fog dispersed, the far shore came forth, trees with white winter foliage, like a floating

160

land, the earth they stood in being hidden as well as the distant hills.

March 30 I went to Marshalls' for milk, taking some fish, but brought back the fish and an empty jug, as they were not home. I looked at the gravestones near their house, evidently in a private or neighborhood burying ground. The name Moreland. The creek below a more lasting memorial. . . .

A still evening, the sun going down in a clear sky, with little color attending. A cow lowing, somewhere in the shadows across the river. The warm sun, warmth from the fire, where the remnant of sap, almost syrup, boils with a low roaring. The steep hillside behind me, the straight sunlit trees like arrows against the blue sky.

April 1 All our senses feel the new season. A different quality to the air, sounds and smells of spring.

I noticed another spring up the creek, near the one I cleaned out, and when the leaves were cleared away, there was a fine stream of water pouring out from the rocks at the base of the hill. Almost as free flowing as the one near the boat. I enjoy going up into the hollow for water.

The game warden was by here yesterday. Two men in a skiff with outboard motor and box of a cabin. They saw our trot line, stopped, and raised it. I went to talk to them. They asked if I had a fishing license and were good enough to excuse me, on my promise to get one at once. These men were looking for nets, but passed ours without seeing it.

We brought the garden up to date yesterday, planting peas, lettuce, parsley and various seeds in beds to transplant—cabbage, red cabbage, broccoli, kohlrabi, Brussells sprouts.

April 3 An expedition to Bedford today, for path finding and a fishing license. I carried and shoved the bicycle up to the Hammonds', taking them a mess of catfish, four, weighing perhaps 7 pounds. Then I rode down the hill into Corn Creek valley, having enjoyed the view from the hillside, a long sweep down the valley to the river. The blacktop ends at the foot of the hill, where I turned left, following a muddy, rough road, fording creeks, walking much of the way.

Where the road crosses Corn Creek is the end of the mail route. The carrier came along in his jeep, and was met by a strange figure on horseback, a little old woman, bundled up in a long black coat and stocking hat, just her nose out in the air. She gravely took the mail from the carrier, several newspapers, small packages and letters, which she put into a canvas bag such as newsboys carry their papers in. Then she proceeded up the valley on her shaggy red pony, I suppose delivering the mail on the way. . . .

A long climb, afoot, to the top of the hills, then a level, smoother road into Bedford, 4 or 5 miles. 81/2 miles from Hammond's. A store at a corner, a tattered local school, in operation, scholars visible through the open, sagging, door. A little box of a house with a sign in the window: "Lending Library, Light and Life. Books Free." Near a church, of which there were many, mostly well kept up. Bedford 11:30 a.m. Completed errands and shopping, ate some crackers and cheese, watching the stream of traffic on the Louisville road. 43 miles to Louisville. . . . 10 miles out of Bedford, I turned south and it was 6 miles to Hammonds'.

When I saw this hollow, and the river as I started down the steep path, I had a feeling of attachment, that this remote spot was after all the center of things, the river the true highway.

April 6   Easter, I think. Yesterday was bad. A warm, threatening air, foreboding storm, high wind from S.W., sweeping the ragged clouds across the sky. The river became very rough, and the long swells rolled in. I got out extra line, and the anchor. We spent most of the day on shore, cooking a little lunch, reading. Toward evening, the clouds became heavy and dark, there was thunder and lightning. We embarked in the johnboat, which we had landed in the creek, it was impossible on the open shore, and got on board before a driving rain. After that the wind went down and the night was clear. . . .

The river rose in the night and this morning I turned the boat head into the bank. Thus the wind and waves do not hit us broadside. A new prospect all around too, sun coming in at different windows.

Powell was here again, bringing a piece of country ham he had promised. He took another mess of fish with him. They are biting on the line now.

Two strangers came down from up the hollow. They turned out to be Bruce Adams, Owen's brother-in-law, and a neighbor boy. They said they had come for small water maples to set out in their yards. They live on upper Corn Creek. They did get the trees, using our grubbing hoe, but we think they came for fish, in their indirect way. We gave them a mess, which they really wanted to pay for, but on our refusing, said they would bring us some eggs next time. This suits us much better.

April 7 Every undertaking of ours requires first of all a list, and this is the one we made of requirements for a place to tie up for the summer. We made it when we were drifting.

> view—outside of curve?
> country to explore and paint in
> purity of river water
> some protection from winds
> some protection from boats
> accessibility?
> drinking water
>> well?
> farmer
> milk
> mail-box?
> telephone
> garden
> quality of shore
>> no ledges of rock
>> no mud
>> place for clothes line
>> tie up
> neighbors
>> no bad neighbors
> fuel supply
> groceries

Considering this today, we thought most of the conditions had been met. Payne Hollow has some evident weaknesses, but they can be worked around.

We decided that if you like a new place from the first impression, even for no evident reasons, it would turn out to be a pleasant and convenient place to live.

Last night we watched the moon rise in the notch of the hills. First the glowing light, increasing, then the sudden appearance of the moon, and the transformation of the landscape.

April 8 Considering today, it does not seem possible that one could live so richly. Yet this was not an exceptional day. We rose early, and I was out on the river at sunrise, watching the first light on the far hills, red, picking out the notes of spring as it moved down, shining through this notch on the shore. Only one fish on the line, five yesterday.

After breakfast, rice cakes and maple syrup, there was a threat of rain in the clouding sky, so we were active out of doors. I went up the creek for clear water, a new and enjoyable chore. Then we worked some in the garden, planting potatoes and a little corn. Next I made a trip up the hollow for drinking water, my attention divided between birds and plants. A new bird, the Louisiana water thrush, which we had heard from the garden. Familiar, nameless flowers in the woods. Shawny of a good size, with narrow dock, wild beet and some others making a mess of greens which I washed in the creek. Anna cooked groundnuts with it. At the foot of the hill, across the creek from the spring, I found the remains of another house, two piles of stone, the foundations of chimneys, but no relic of the house that was between them. An indistinct trace of a road, a little walled-up well near the creek. How many residents has this hollow had, how many at one time? Powell told me there had been a murder committed at the house in the clearing, the chimney of which is standing.

Returning, wood to cut, fish to clean. The rain began as we were ready to eat our dinner, and we were glad that our outside work was done.

164

A little reading after dinner, then painting for me while Anna washed dishes and wrote letters. . . . I went out on the river to raise the net and bait the line. Five nice ones in the net. The misty river, mist on the hills bringing out new valleys and hollows.

> *On some days we deserted the boat and rambled through the country. . . . We explored the hills and valleys, marked the location of crops to be gathered in their season—raspberry and blackberry patches, wild and untended fruit trees. We stopped to talk with farmers as they worked in the fields, became so well acquainted with some that they invited us to spend a day with them. . . . The change was good for us, the society and conversation, the dry air of the hilltops, the smell of pines and hay. Then, too, we are ever curious about the way other people live.*

April 10   We dug in the garden today, spurred by a threat of rain, and planted the potatoes. A little rain fell while we ate dinner, and, in place of a sunset, there was a spectacular electric storm in the west, which moved away north as darkness fell. . . . A warm day. I worked with no shirt on my back.

April 11   We rest this morning, after the hard work and storms. It was a rough night, south wind rolling in long swells, rain following. The rising river scours away all the loose soil. We rejoice that our potatoes are in the ground. . . .

A quiet evening with a promise of a fair day tomorrow. The wind and storms pass on, leaving a clear sky. So our minds clear, the clouds are forgotten, and one feels they will never come again.

April 13   A host of visitors today. Jesse Powell and his neighbor's dog, in the morning. The young Marshall boy, with his dogs and gun, after groundhogs, he said, but we think he came down to see us. Leaving with his string of fish he met the young Bolderys in the woods path above us. They came aboard, too, lively and interested in our boat and river life. We gave them fish. Everyone wants to pay for them. If you mention their services to you, they say they want no pay for them. . . .

165

We find many groundnuts along the Indiana shore, back in behind the willows. They are washed out by the rising water, strings of them, and have turned out to be delicious food.

April 14 What would we do without fish? Yesterday we gave away 14 fair sized fish, ate 3. Today we gave away 7, to Marshalls and Schirmers. Still 10 in the box. . . .

This is the time for poplar trees, the rich red and yellow of their flowering. Red buds next. In a few days they will change the landscape.

April 16 A wet chill morning, heavy clouds, light breaking through, then very dark. . . . Now we can take on some of the inside chores that we have saved for a rainy day.

April 17 Set up the smoker, and began smoking 12 catfish, which I cleaned last night after supper. Catfish liver for dinner, today, and greens from the hill. I rowed up to the maple camp, for wood to smoke the fish with. Now, with green plants on the hillside, and flowers, trees budding, how far back do those days and nights of sap making seem.

Anna baked bread this afternoon, using whole wheat flour that I ground in our grinder. . . . The bread is good, and we are pleased to know that we can grind our own flour.

Yesterday, as we were finishing our dinner, Anna glanced out of the window, and said "Look who is there." I expected to see Boss, the Marshalls' dog, but there was Wilmer, with his long overcoat, boots, gloves and all his winter outfit except the red bandanna around his face. He had come down to get some fish, walking along the brushy hillside by no path. He came aboard, cautiously, sideways, balancing himself like a rope walker. He had a cup of tea, a dish of berries. A friendly, honest fellow.

April 18 A fair day, perfect for our washday. All out on the line before dinner time, which was not late. We used creek water, perfectly clean for the entire washing.

April 19 We sold 22 pounds of fish today, or 20 pounds by the way I figured the price. Four Marshalls came down this morning from Trout Bottom, having struggled down along the steep river hill. They came aboard, and were much taken with our life afloat.

After dinner we were hailed from across the river. I could not hear what was wanted, but we guessed fish. As I had a trip to the mail box I went across, taking some catfish, which were just what the young man wanted.

April 20   Now in the dark evening the rain falls. No wind. Drips and trickles coming in the cabin. I must make a job of it, and be a little more watertight. After days and weeks here alone, we suddenly have many visitors.

April 21   We served our guests marvelous food yesterday. Small catfish, dressed just before frying, mashed potatoes, kale just brought in, salad of choice tomatoes, cottage cheese and bean sprouts, hot biscuits made of our own grind of wheat flour, and containing toasted sunflower seeds, with maple syrup, wild strawberry jam. Just before they left, we cut the cake Anna had made day before, nut cake, white, with white maple icing. This with wild grape juice to drink. Rare food anywhere, but, after all, our daily fare.

April 22   This evening, the fairest of the past few days, as I was out on the quiet river, baiting the line, a new moon in the western sky, there suddenly began the singing notes of a whip-poor-will, from up the hollow. The earth was transformed and it was summer.

Also today I found some poke shoots, and heard the red-eyed vireo. A good day on several counts. We did some satisfactory playing this morning. In the afternoon, Anna cut my hair as I read about the tortured years of Tolstoy. A walk up the hollow in the slanting sunlight.

April 23   We looked out today, and saw a man and woman standing on the bank, the man with a rifle, the woman with a paper poke of greens. I went out, and we had the usual round-about conversation. He was out looking for bee trees and had found three. He wanted to transfer them to gums in his yard. They lived on Corn Creek, William Abbott. At an invitation, Mrs. Abbott, with no hesitation, walked across the gang plank to the tossing boat. Anna was sitting there, mending a blue work shirt, a very domestic rural picture. . . .

A new warbler this morning, bright yellow head and breast,

dark back and wings. The prothonotary. The book says he lives along quiet streams, in willows, and we were pleased to see him here. A bobwhite across the river, and a thrush singing in the hills.

April 24 It is exciting to see the hills from out in the river. Every day makes a difference. . . . The new colors are reflected in my paints and it is an exciting part of spring to use new ones, bright yellow and strong green. . . .

We saw a catbird along the shore this morning, and a thrush sang in full voice.

April 25 The young moon shines amid the low winter constellations. A cozy, indoor day, fire burning.

April 26 This is the time of redbud.

April 28 A summer sunset, fair and golden sky, north of west, while the south was gray and cloudy. New birds arrive every day, the crested fly-catcher today, scarlet tanager yesterday. Their songs are new notes in the hollow. The increase in bird song corresponds with the leafing trees. At sunset, a whip-poor-will sounding across the river.

We work in the garden today, planting a large patch of beans. Yesterday we had tiny lettuce leaves in our salad. Our guests were delighted with the dinner that Anna served to them, as well they should be. Catfish fillets, fried, mashed potatoes, greens, poke and others, tomato salad, fresh bread, from our own mill and our raspberries with cream, wild grape jelly. Our guests are always amazed at the quality of our food, its abundance, and so well served. On a shantyboat.

April 29 This morning we read the short chapter from Emerson's *Nature* called "Spirit." It came very close to me, especially when he said such ideas could not be expressed in words.

April 30 A splendid rainbow up in Payne Hollow. . . . We heard the peewee in our woods for the first time. Evenings we can hear the whip-poor-will, off in Indiana. . . . Is our red flower a Shooting Star?

May 1 A true May morning with a great concert of bird song. Not robins and cardinals who awake the villagers, but wood birds, warblers, peewee, vireos, thrushes and cardinals, too, but I have not seen a robin in the hollow. A Kentucky warbler this morning.

May 2   As fair a morning as one could see, air and earth washed by the rains, swept by a cool breeze. . . .

I made a trip down to the narrows, where I cut down a sizable oak, split a piece of the trunk, and brought it back, intending to rive out slats. As I worked in the woods near the water I thought of Ulysses hewing out the planks for his boat.

May 4   Yesterday we canned poke, 11 quarts. Gathered in the morning, on the hill south of us, a pleasant walk up there and back, both of us this time, through the flowering woods, and blossoming apple trees in the old orchard. . . . Dogwood in bloom now, and wild strawberries.

May 6   This is perhaps the first summer day. We did our washing on the deck, with the tubs lined up on the high bench. No fire in the cabin, either for breakfast or dinner. We cooked our mush on the fire which heated the washwater, and baked beans in our iron kettle oven alongside the same fire. From the bottom land across the river comes the sound of tractors running. The farmers make the most of the time they have to work the soil.

May 8   Yesterday I walked up the hollow with a sack of catfish on my shoulder, about 15 pounds of them. No one had come after fish lately, and the box was too full. I returned with no fish, but produce of the country, a piece of ham shoulder, a slab of bacon, 18 eggs, and, as an exotic note, two huge grapefruit which Mrs. O. Hammond gave us from a crate Owen had bought. I also made a new acquaintance, Ansel McCord, who bought fish, giving eggs as part payment. We are to get milk there, too and he offered us a job picking strawberries. . . .

In arranging to get milk from Mr. McCord he said he preferred it otherwise when I suggested coming on Sunday. For my part, I dislike handling money on any day, particularly taking it from another. I would rather give a mess of fish for a dozen eggs, even if I could get enough money for them to buy 3 dozen eggs. Or I would prefer to give them away for nothing. . . .

I return from the farm country to the woods and river bank with an inward lifting. A different air seems to hang over the shorn

169

fields and straight roads. The same difference between that soil, heavy and lifeless, and the earth on the hillside where our garden is, which is forest mold. . . .

Trees are of summer, now, even the willows are putting out leaves. The redbud have faded into the green hillside. Yet the dogwood is blooming, so very white, and formal. Sassafras sprays, lilacs in the dooryards. . . .

We have such country food, more rural and earthy than farm cooking. Tonight we have poke and ground nuts. The latter could be one of our winter foods. Now it stretches our supply of potatoes, perhaps until our new ones come in. The crop is promising, though the Hammonds said theirs was rotting in the wet ground. The subject of new foods is fascinating. Very likely we work hard to raise difficult crops, with wild ones equally good still unrecognized.

May 10   We were considering a design for a flag on our boat. It might be a man carrying a sack of catfish on his back.

May 11   I walked over to Spring Creek, by road and across fields, coming down the steep hillside at Mr. John Fresh's back door. A good visit with these two old people. He is 81, a riverman in his younger days, on small packets running between Madison and Louisville, and between Bethlehem and Louisville. They made a round trip daily to Bethlehem, sometimes two, if there was freight to pick up. They went up to Madison one day, down the next. He was pilot and part owner, I believe, of the *Hanover*, the boat Mr. Singer told us about at Madison. Mr. Singer was a youngster learning the river on Mr. Fresh's boat. John Fresh left the river, bought a farm on Patton's Creek at the lowest corner of Trimble County, and then bought the 140 acre place where Cleo and Wilmer now live. He says they don't tend it well, which is evident. Cleo often speaks of his father with an apology for his old time ways. With all his years, he needs little help on his farm, though he raises no crops himself. They were pleased to have the fish, and gave us 2 dozen eggs. We feast on eggs and ham and bacon these days.

May 13   Yesterday afternoon I turned the boat parallel to the bank. From this new angle, we feel like we had just tied up in a strange place.

Heavy thunderstorms coming over the western hills before sunset. They pass over and we see a double rainbow against the dark sky up the hollow. Later, to the south, the clouds piled high, lighted by the golden sun.

May 16 I sit out a shower in the McCords' barn, waiting for them to get up and milk. A delicious feeling of shelter and comfort. I have some toasted wheat grains and walnuts for a snack, and the white spitz dog keeps me company, chews the nutshells. Now the rain has stopped, dripping from the roof still. Outside the birds begin again their morning song, doves, field sparrows, Bewick wren, robin, thrasher, an orchard oriole, unfamiliar sounds up here, a rooster crows, and English sparrows, which we never hear down the hollow. The barn is open to the road. Across from the house, a tobacco barn is in season, farm machinery in the driveway. A new tractor. Loft overhead, a dusty framework of beams poles and strips, which will carry the tobacco. . . .

I spend considerable time going for milk and waiting for it, but I always, or almost always, feel that the time is well spent. Each trip a new experience. The difference in farms and people, how they live and do their work, what is revealed of them, such I take as I go, along with the sounds and smells and what I see.

May 17 We went to town, Madison, this sultry, showery day. Such trips are about a month apart. We walked up the hollow after breakfast, left our overshoes and Anna's long brown stocking tops in the Hammonds' shed, slowly walked along the road, north. Within a mile we were picked up by Mr. & Mrs. Jesse McMahan, whose car was the first that came along. They were going to Carrollton, then Madison, so they left us at Milton, which place delighted us, and we walked across the bridge. Madison about 11 a.m. We did our "trading." Met more people we knew than we would have in Cincinnati or perhaps even Fort Thomas. Dressed in their town clothes, we hardly recognized Jesse Powell, and the young man who had been at the boat for fish, named Watson. Met Art Moore, and we had a little reunion. Strange how glad we were to see one another.

May 18 I woke up in the night to hear rain on the roof.

171

We observe Sunday, to some extent, more, I believe, than at Brent. This afternoon, I changed my clothes and did nothing that might be called work, unless it was some woodcutting. Powell and Wilmer came down this morning, in Wilmer's johnboat. Rather, Uncle Charlie Fresh's, on loan until Wilmer and Cleo get theirs out of the mud. Wilmer brought us half a gallon of milk, and Powell a squirrel he had just shot. Each took a mess of fish. The three of us sat on the bank in a row, and talked a while. I begin to feel like a native.

Anna and I took a walk in the garden at sunset, marvelling at the growth of things.

May 19 I saw a muskrat playing in the water in the creek backwater this morning. The first bobwhite in the hollow. And a house wren, his first day here. A showery uncertain morning. I row across for mail.

May 20 Still rainy weather. It seems normal, now, and a dry sunny day cannot be even imagined.

May 21 Last night, toward morning, the rain came down in a deluge continuing so after daybreak. We lay snug in bed, listening.

May 22 A heavy fog this morning, and a summer day. As the fog lifted, the far shore was revealed, but not the hills. Only a line of trees was visible, and with no background, they appeared closer. Drift passing close to us. The crows ride the islands of trash, one coasting past just outside our door. We play after breakfast, much interested just now in our arrangements of the simple Bach prelude. The *Island Queen* hove in sight from below, and passed with her familiar sounds. . . .

A sharp rise in the river last night. Is this the June rise?

Groundnuts with our fish and spinach for dinner. These are the last of those I picked up across the river, perhaps 6 weeks ago, buried in the sand meanwhile. Two had sprouted above ground, so I planted them. Could we raise them in the garden? They replace the Irish potatoes.

A bright cool evening, the clear moon in the western sky. I sit watching the stars, and suddenly see a lightning bug over the water like a flying star.

172

May 24   I made an early trip to the ridge for milk yesterday morning, climbing out of the fog to a clear sunrise. No one was stirring, and I had a quiet half hour in the barn with the dogs. The golden sunlight, slanting upwards, lighted the old barn timber.

Owen Hammond has been plowing this bottom. We take pleasure in the sight of his white horses against the dark green trees. He is a team with them, soft voiced, he and they moving in rhythm.

May 25   We adapt our living to the hotter weather, go barefoot and bathe from the stageboard. . . .

I went way up the creek for clear water yesterday. That is a pleasant chore, and the clear water, with such a muddy river, is a satisfaction. . . .

We had visitors today. Wilmer and young Marshall rowed down after the rain, each one bringing a can of milk. No fish to spare today, so they had a long row back, and nothing to bring home. This afternoon O. Hammond brought his father down, and his son. They sat around our fire and talked freely, especially the older man. We learn about former days here.

May 30   Owen plowed the bottom near the boat this evening, inviting us to plant as much as we wanted to.

June 1   The first swim today, water not cold.

June 2   A tremendous storm last night, wind and rain and bolts of lightning, one striking at the creek mouth, we thought. . . . In the quiet intervals the moonlight filtered through the clouds, and the fireflies streaked through the darkness.

June 5   A summer day. Warm nights now. I pick strawberries on the hill for Marvin Barnes.

June 7   Berry picking again, yesterday 54 quarts, 12 this morning, for McCord.

June 9   Even after the chores I had to do here, I was up on the road early, the first berry picker in the patch. Anna came up about noon, with a basket of lunch, and we had a picnic in the pasture. Then we picked ripe berries in the old patch overgrown with grass, like wild strawberries, and it is likely that they develop this way. Down in the heat of the afternoon. A bath in the river, berries to look over and hull. We brought 12 quarts down with us. Bacon and

173

eggs, new potatoes and peas creamed, lettuce salad, with nuts and maple syrup. Strawberries and cream for dessert. All products of our garden or our neighbors' farms.

> *These were full and busy days. . . .*
>
> *This busy life is quite different from the shiftless leisure that shantyboaters are supposed to enjoy. We became industrious and respected members of the community. I even cut corn in the fall to get our winter's supply. On Sundays we prepared for visitors. I kept myself presentable, and did not become involved in any work which could not be dropped instantly.*
>
> *This placed us in a new position with regard to the river. Watching it from the shore, almost as a landsman, we might have felt a longing to drift with it again and, ever passing new shores, make only brief stops along the way. Yet we did not regret our present shore-bound life, rather we made the most of it; for the autumn and our departure would come soon enough.*

June 10 Saturday night last, a violent williwaw from the north. Anna heard the wind, woke me in time to close the shutters. The critical line held. It was tied to a small willow, which gave a spring to the line.

Yesterday in the berry patch, I was asked by a stranger, if there are any such in this country, if I painted. He was a preacher, as I had guessed he was, and had brought his son to pick berries, was helping a little himself. It turned out that he wanted a picture in his church, the Mt. Byrd Christian Church, which we have passed on our way to Milton. The picture was to be behind the pulpit, a river stretching into the distance, "a baptismal scene," though figures were not essential. Anna and I were taken with the idea, and will go to the church to see about it. The preacher, McConnell, had heard that I "painted" from A. Yaeger, the young farmer I had talked to in the field, the only man in the country to whom I had confessed that I was an artist. . . .

One of the rewards of berrypicking is the conversation overheard between the country people. In M. Barnes' patch the other day there was some singing, of hymns.

June 12 Washday, and a record breaker. Like 9 sheets, 9 pillowcases, I believe 11 shorts for me. Yet as we worked at an easy pace, and the deck was shady and cool, we enjoyed the day. . . . We used clear water from the creek, difficult to obtain now for the river has backed far up into the creek, and only a trickle of water comes down. I always enjoy the trip, pretending to be a longboat going ashore from a ship anchored off shore, with empty casks for fresh water. The creek is dark and cool, and to go into it from the bright sunlight is like going down into a cellar.

June 15 We were up early this morning and after a dish of strawberries, we climbed the hill and along the ridge to the Marshalls'. While they finished their breakfast, we sat in the front yard, looking down into the valley below us, reading about Cortez. Then we visited a while in the house, had a glass of milk and a piece of Johnny's birthday cake, got our milk and cream, returned to the boat.

June 17 Strawberry shortcake, now brought to perfection by Anna.

June 19 A houseboat passed yesterday, a nice trim one with a cabin motorboat for towing. We were impressed by its shipshape appearance, no gear cluttering the decks. When they drifted close to shore, he started the motor, towed out in mid-stream, then drifted again.

June 21 The longest day, and I was up this morning at daybreak. I had the groundhogs on my mind. They are seriously damaging our upper garden, and Owen loaned us his gun.

June 22 The last strawberries of this season, the last of a long line of shortcakes, and thick cream. Now the black raspberries are ripening. How much more satisfactory to pick this wild fruit which belongs to us than the tame berries in someone's field, which are a commercial crop. Yet how we have enjoyed the strawberries.

A visit from the Hammonds last evening. Owen and Daisy,

Allen, Barbara, Catherine, and the older boy, Norman, came down after finishing the discing of the field across the creek. Visiting is serious business in these parts.

June 23   In the woods above the garden at noon time, gun in my lap, watching for the groundhog. Not much chance of seeing him, with old Boss rummaging around on the hillside. A siege of varmints lately. A whole colony of mice between decks, so we cleared out that space, scrubbed it, and repacked the plunder in good order. A rat on board the other evening but he escaped. . . .

Yesterday was Sunday on the river, motor boats passing, one hailing us to ask for fish. Three young fellows were by in their small craft, seeming to have no destination or knowledge of where they were.

June 24   This was an unusual day, though we did not plan it so. I went up the hollow in the early fog for milk and eggs. Returning past the chimney, I heard a strange whistle and Art Moore appeared from ambush. He had been watching for a groundhog. He and his two friends, Jack and Evelyn Sturgeon, I think their last name is, had come down from Madison in a motorboat, one that Art is taking care of, arriving here quite early, so early that Anna was still abed. They woke her by firing shots and then went off hunting. Anna fixed breakfast for them, bacon, eggs, cornbread, coffee . . . . Art took us all for a ride and in a few minutes we were passing Preston Hollow, Corn Creek, Marble Hill, Squaw Creek, Saluda, places which were only strange names before. A wonderful view up the river into the rainy north, our familiar hills taking strange shapes.

June 27   Yesterday we went to Madison in the johnboat. Left not very early, were eating lunch within sight of the lower end of town at noon, arrived at 1 o'clock. Considerable trading, leaving at 4, reaching the boat just as darkness fell. A most pleasant trip, not as hard as we had expected. . . . All our meals on the way, breakfast above Lee's Creek, in the boat, lunch on a little gravel bar across from Crooked Creek. Supper while drifting above Hanover. The trip opened new possibilities. It was fine to read aloud, write. I even dictated a couple of letters. . . . We spent a week on this stretch of river when we drifted down, and now it was thrilling to follow the course in one day, coming down in the middle of the river, watching the hills unfold, familiar to us now.

June 28　These are hot days. This is a hot place on still afternoons. Yet a breeze is usually stirring and we could go down to the spring where it is always cool. . . .

I killed the ground hog about noon. Skipper cornered it in under a willow root, at the water's edge, 2 or 3 rods from the boat, quite far from any den we know of. I discovered a dead one in the garden, and we remembered the dogs had made a fuss there a few days ago. That kill belongs to Skipper, Boss and his friend. . . .

The wasps are making nests in various corners of the boat, and Anna has made a study of their activities. One made repeated trips from the water's edge to his construction inside the cupboard. A marvelous mason.

June 29　A traveller went by today, moving slowly along the shore up river, rowing an old johnboat, the same shabby fellow who went down some weeks ago, I believe. He did not speak then, nor did he notice Powell and me today. Yet when he passed the boat he asked Anna how far it was to Madison, with all possible courtesy. He was towing another johnboat, ahead of him like a barge, this one covered with a rude cabin of sacking. . . .

For dinner we had fried rabbit, a young one that Powell had brought to us. He brought us a live chicken, too. Then we had the groundhog cooked. No lack of meat, and fresh and smoked fish. Bacon for breakfast. Peas and new potatoes, black raspberries.

July 1　Raspberry picking yesterday and today. We now have 13 pints canned. I found more than expected on the hillside across the creek, below the woods. A steep, rough place. I take pleasure in berry picking, and find the same interest and excitement in it that other men do in fishing.

July 4　I dammed up the creek at the mouth, to have an available supply of clear water. The entire stream appears to be the overflow of our spring. The dam washed out, but just now I have built it up again.

July 11　Elderberry pancakes for breakfast, an Elysian food. Out

on the bank over a smoky fire, the two pups playing in the sand. . . .
Fishing is at a standstill. No minnows, no action on the other bait I
try. Fish of all kinds seem to have left this part of the river. Yet the
natives come down to fish, with pole and line and great hopes,
taking advantage of the rainy weather, probably using it as an excuse to leave the farm. . . .

We have a quantity of new apples, and Anna's season for whittling has commenced.

July 13 We hear today the golden swamp warbler. In the spring
this prothonotary warbler was seen and heard all day long.

July 18 So much that I see and hear, worthy of record yet it
leaves no mark, except its effect on my mind and thought. Hardly
any important happenings, but sometimes the passing details seem
very significant. When I went out to bait the line in the early night,
a dark cloud moved down from the north, across the clear sky. Suddenly the wind blew, the cloud passed, the wind dropped, and no
rain fell.

July 19 We made an excursion to Corn Creek. First rowing up
to Fresh's landing, where we found Millie and all the children washing clothes. Then we walked back through their pasture and up the
"middle hill," as Wilmer calls it. At the top, after some rough going,
we came into open fields, and followed a lane out to the road. Passed
a small, deserted farm house, an attractive place. A drink at the
well and some yellow transparents to eat. We went on out to Chan
Watson's, where we left the sack of fish. These friendly people invited
us to eat dinner with them, which we did, enjoying the fried chicken,
mashed potatoes, beans, fresh bread and lemon pie. . . . Our relations
with these country people are an important part of our living here.
This was all unexpected, and unsought.

Yesterday two boys came down to put out a trot line. They
hardly asked to use the boat, expecting to use any one here as a
matter of course. I let them have our boat, with hesitation and
reservations, and it was well that I did. The boys were Buddy Hall
and Junior Wilson from Corn Creek. Later they returned with Milton
Hall. The Halls lived on the hillside above us, having built the house

and barn, cleared the woods. That must have required great labor. Milton told me they bought a house at Charlestown, knocked it down, hauled it to the river, rafted it across and packed it up the hill. We learn about Payne Hollow. We went through the Willis farm on our way to Corn Creek. Mr. Willis' wife was of the Stevenson family, who lived here in a house below the creek, until it was washed away in the flood of 1937. The landing is called Stevenson's and they built the root cellar.

The boys yesterday were much impressed with our boat and river life. They had a bite to eat sitting on the after deck, while we ate dinner. We gave them some broiled fish and cornbread, tea. Buddy Hall spoke of the "itchweeds" by the path to the spring. Nettles. Art Moore, when he landed his boat by a fallen tree across the river, said he guessed we could "coon out" on the log.

Yesterday we canned beets, 7 quarts, and 2 quarts of broccoli, the first cutting. What a satisfaction it is just to raise and harvest these garden crops.

July 21   Walter P. Dolle up today with about 10 empties. The boats that passed us at Brent are like old friends suddenly met in strange places. . . .

We picked blackberries yesterday evening up the hollow. After we had returned and were getting supper, almost dark, some folks trooped down through the bottoms. The two boys coming back to look at their line, Milton Hall and his wife, Marilyn, their 9 month old baby. They stayed quite a while. We are always complimented whenever anyone comes down this long rough walk to see us, whatever their motives might be.

July 27 We are canning beans today, Sunday though it is. Blackberries yesterday, and likely tomorrow. We pick splendid ones up in McCord's pasture, large and of an unusual spicy flavor. The usual number of Sunday visitors. Owen came down to get the yellow cat for Bruce Adams. Later he sent Norman down for fish for their dinner. Evidently they had unexpected company. Wilmer was down yesterday for a mess to serve to Millie's father and mother from Pineville. I took some to the Marshalls this morning. We give away more than we sell, but how much have we received from these people.

A terrific storm just past, the second one which came at sunset on a Sunday. I was down the shore aways on a fishing chore. When I saw the storm coming down out of the north, I raced back to the boat but did not reach it before the storm. Not able to make head-way against the wind, I tied the boat to shore and ran across the creek. At the boat I found the head line had parted, the waves driving us into the shore. A driving rain, darkness. We got the boat offshore, and waited. The rain slackened, but before I could go down to the johnboat, the creek was running out so heavily that I could not cross. The spring was under water, and our milk and cold lamb. Luckily this was safe. I waded down to the johnboat, retrieved the minnow traps, and foot planks which had washed out. Before long we had the processing under way again, supper.

July 31 We took honey from the bees yesterday, one section from the super, not completely filled or capped over, perhaps 4 pounds, comb and all. It is of good flavor and color and we are as proud of it as if we had produced it ourselves. This completes the story of the bees, their acquisition, voyage, and now the first fruits of the venture.

August 1 The run-out of the creek Sunday cut a deep channel through the mud, deep enough for a johnboat and too wide to cross. Our bridges were carried out, but I found them floating outside. Luckily we did not lose our milk and meat cooling in the spring. The cold lamb was covered with mud.

August 3 The brightest, most perfect rainbow we ever saw. It rose a perfect arch, from the river, against the sunlit Indiana hills.

August 5 The *Greenbriar* has just passed this afternoon, upbound, making stops at all the lights. A long and three shorts is the whistle signal for a landing, and at its sound I suppose Wilmer is awakened into action. What a fine trip that would be!

I had a river trip of my own yesterday, rowing up to Madison. . . . I followed the Indiana shore down, and most of it was new. The clean, open gravel shore below Hanover was a joy. Nothing like it have I seen below the Kentucky. A tremendous drift pile on the bar at Hart's Falls Creek, looking like the funeral pyre of a giant ready for lighting. Powell, who was here today, said there is a shelf out from shore and a sheer drop of 80 feet at its edge. Below there I got into the grateful shade of the hills at Big Six. Found Bill Shadrick sitting in the end of his johnboat, cooling his feet, and talked with him quite awhile, about himself, mostly, and fishing. An enjoyable and instructive conversation, some strange tie of sympathy underneath. He lives in a little boat 6 feet wide, beached out close to the water.

August 7 Stormy weather again, after 4 very hot days. Yesterday afternoon we took refuge in the creek bottom, by the spring. We seemed to be in the cellar of the world. Suddenly overhead, on the wrong side of the creek, appeared three men. They turned out to be Rev. McConnell of the Mt. Byrd Christian Church, his son Russell and Ray Green, whoever he might be. We went down to the boat, where it was very hot, looked at a few pictures. Meanwhile, a party from the Corn Creek bottoms below had appeared, asking for fish, of which we had nary a one. They stayed a while after the others left, sitting on the bank, talking. One was a Mahoney, but the others I know not. What a contrast in conversation, theirs and the reverend's.

August 8 Hot August weather, the noisy cackling of katydids in the night.

August 10 When I return to the boat, I can expect to find almost anyone, or any kind of a group, waiting for me. This morning, coming back from the hill with cream, milk and blackberries, I saw quite a party of men, women, children and dogs under the willow tree. There was Powell with a live chicken for us and his fishing poles. The Milton Hall family was there complete, with 4 children and a dog. They wanted across the river, where they were to spend the day with her kinfolks. Their car was out of service, so they all trooped down here, taking it for granted that I would be here to set them across.

August 15 A rainy night, last, welcomed after the hot, dry days.

181

More rain today in scattered showers. Our spring runs freely again. What a blessing that cold, clean water, in abundance, has been these past days.

August 21 The nights are the glory of the season, they are so mild and bright. The concerts of locust and katydid merge together at evening. The only quiet time is at daybreak, when the night singers have stopped, and it is not quite warm enough, or dry enough, for the locusts to begin their long chant.

August 24 Another trip to Madison yesterday. . . . On the streets of Madison we meet our friends and talk a little, in the manner of the natives. Home at sunset, so glad that the river is so far away, and that we are so cut off from the towns and roads.

Our first lima beans for dinner, an event in the garden. A little ripe watermelon last week.

J. Powell down this morning, having missed last week. He brought us a chicken, got a mess of fish. No doubt he feels a longing for the river, during a week of work, and this is gratified somewhat by coming down here and being out on the river in the johnboat.

August 25 Everyone rejoices in the rain of yesterday evening. . . .

We think this must have been Labor Day, for a good many motor boats passed. There were visitors to the Hollow who arrived in deepest night, in a johnboat. I heard their voices, looked out and hailed them. The sleepy watchdogs did not bark. One of the men knew this landing but was surprised to find a boat here. They were paddling then, and I did not know they had a motor until later. In answer to my hail, they said they had come down to squirrel hunt, and they landed below the creek. Later in the morning I met a man and boy, with guns, walking through our garden. The man was Thurmond Moore, Art's brother, and we held conversation. He has a special liking for this place which is felt by Art and J. Powell. It must spoil it a little to find a boat here, garden and washing on the bank.

September 3 This morning before daybreak, I woke Anna to hear a whip-poor-will, far off in the distance. The green heron who lives at the creek mouth does not mind us now, and often perches on our lines. He is very amusing to watch, at his toilette, for instance.

September 5   A stormy daybreak, as was yesterday. A rainy morning then after a spectacle of sunrise, with storm in the N.W., the dark clouds tinged red with the sun. In the south a strong yellow light. The rising sun, breaking through in the east, lit the crest of the western hills, above which, a fragment of a rainbow.

September 7   Several bad tossings by boat waves. *The Gordon C. Greene*, bound for St. Paul, passed this morning, running full speed. The *Pioneer*, a big diesel running light, was up, the two boats passing above. In the turmoil we were baking Anna's birthday cake. No wonder it was uneven. Very good, though.

September 10   Warm weather. A hard rainstorm, which was soon over. At the time, we were sewing with our sewing machine. It is so much in keeping with our boat, so toylike, yet efficient. Perhaps the boat's name should be "Multum in parvo" ["Much in little"].

September 12   One storm after another rises in the west. Dark sky, wind and heavy rain, then breaking clouds and sun. I was up in the half-light of night and morning, a thin moon just over the hill in the lightening day, when Sirius shone. I had baited a string of hooks yesterday on three lines, but caught only 10 fish even so. The *Robert F. Brandt* passed down, lights still burning, fires of the furnace lighting up the fireman and coal passers. A steamboat is a rare sight now. This boat is one of the best left to us. . . .

The Hammonds were in the bottom yesterday, working in the tobacco. Mrs. H. and the older girl came to the boat, to warm a tin of coffee. We gave them melons for their dinner. We have a quantity of them now. Our river bottom is producing its crops.

September 22   A windy time of it. From the south yesterday, beginning in the night. . . . Wind died down some late in the afternoon, cloudy. Then we saw rain blotting out the hills upriver, and soon a squall hit us from the NW, or thereabouts. As strong a wind as we have ever felt. Driving rain, wind waves breaking over the deck. It settled down to a steady rain, without wind, which continued most of the night. This morning windy and clearing, and now we are tossing in the waves.

September 23 A fair cool day. A sharpness at sunset, even in the looks of things. What could there be in the appearance of the hills at sunset which would make us feel the coming of cold and death?

October 2 In the garden, we go about gathering up various crops, and remnants, a few dried beans, a fine mess of broccoli, half ripe tomatoes, a sunflower head. We dug some of our peanuts, hung the vines on a wire. The garden is a peaceful place now, the weeds are beautiful flowers in it, and we have made a truce with the bugs. . . .

Dinner on deck, the sun and air of autumn, but windless and warm, reflections almost perfect. In the afternoon I bathed in the river, from the floating johnboat. The water is cooler now, and every swim may be the last.

October 3 A mild evening, and the katydids give a concert. We crossed the river in the afternoon, to meet the rolling store. Waiting for him, we visited with the Montgomerys, to whom we took a watermelon, and sat in the sun, reading. We bought margarine from the truck, bread for minnow bait, white flour. The margarine was the only needed item. Before crossing back, we picked almost a bushel of wild grapes from a vine in the willows, at the water's edge.

October 4 A mild day, south wind. We have dinner on the bank, cooking on a fire we built for our wild grape juice. . . .

The cows were out again, but I did not disturb them today, and Owen had to go to the far end of the cornfield for them. Once the seven of them came down for a drink, and we enjoyed the sight of them on the sand bar. It made a different river of it. . . .

Yesterday when we returned to the boat, we learned by the signs that the green heron had visited our deck.

October 7 Each day we marvel at the approach of autumn on the hillside.

October 12 The weather continues warm and dry, day after day. The nights are mild, and the wind gentle.

October 15 I have been going off to work these three days, or part of each one. Monday afternoon I went over to Jim Hammond's, Owen's father, to help strip cane for sorghum. Johnboat to Trout bottom, and up the trail to the head of Moreland's Creek. The farm is just at the top of the hill, an old saggy place, part log. Dark when I returned home. Yesterday I cut corn for A. McCord, from 7:30 to 11:30 o'clock. Both these jobs were new to me.

Last evening, after dark, we climbed the hill to the McCords', where we met a delegation from the Mt. Byrd Church, to discuss the proposed picture for the church. We enjoyed the meeting. There were the preacher, A. V. McConnell, and four or five ladies, of different ages, all farmers' wives.

October 16 A slender new moon in the clear western sky, soon after sunset. Just under the evening star, which we call Jupiter. Starry nights. . . .

Late in the afternoon Anna and I went up to the McCords' for the 4 x 8 panel on which the picture for the church is to be painted. We carried it on two poles, left it in the barn in the hollow.

October 17 I primed the panel we carried down. The barn is a delightful place, in the rain. One corner has no tobacco in it, the open ventilator, shutter, gives a good light.

October 23 Geese. This was yesterday, a long wedge, of perhaps 50 birds, flying high, a course due south, down the river. Many killdeers on the wet bar, having a good time. Geese again tonight, flying south in the moonlight.

October 28 The creek is flowing again, and the spring gushes forth. Each morning I paint a little up in the barn. It is all quite pleasant.

October 30 Anna canned the first pears today. We had persimmons with our dinner, mashed, strained, served with cream and walnuts. A full moon last night. Harvest moon. I went up the hill yesterday after sunset. The moon rose as I gained the hill top. It was just the color of a persimmon.

November 1 We harvest our crops from the garden.

November 3 The peanuts are finally stripped from the vines.

We learn how much time and labor goes into a crop, before it is ready to eat. So much, often, that just the picking and preparing are not worth the results. The machine production, harvesting and processing of main crops, such as grain, potatoes, dried beans, makes the price so low that it does not pay to raise such food "by hand". Yet most of our living, and more of it as we learn new ways, is gotten the latter way. This is from choice, after due experience.

November 9   Ducks flying now. Flock after flock down the river, high overhead. . . .

Powell was here with his gun. Brought us two coots, or water hens he called them. Shot another above the boat, which he gave us.

November 10   We had the coots for dinner today, boiled, and found them very good. Dark, with a decided flavor, but tender and not strong.

An outboard with 3 men passed us early in the morning. They ran into a flock of birds on the water above us, coots they turned out to be, and blasted away. Later I saw what appeared to be ducks floating down, and went out and retrieved 6 birds, coots, one alive but wounded. I do not believe the hunters picked up any of those they shot.

November 11   I worked in the barn this morning. We played after dinner. These dark days are short. Chores must be done and the unused daylight is precious.

November 14   After dark I went up to the McCords', to call the preacher about the picture, which is almost ready to mount. Took them some fish, brought back milk, most welcome. . . . I walked over to C. Watson's by devious ways, and came back with a sack of pears, hickory nuts and rye.

November 17   Today we set in place the picture of the river, painted in the barn up the hollow.

November 20   Last night we went to a supper at the Pleasant Retreat Community House, which was once the local school. We were the guests of honor, and to our surprise found 75 or 100 people there, all but a handful members of the Mt. Byrd church, most of them friends or known to us.

We were amazed to find that all this was in our honor, an appreciation of the painting. . . .

As we walked down the dark road to the river we were a little dazed by our rise to such high estate from our humble beginnings there.

After the painting was completed we could give all our time and attention to the business of getting under way. We had arrived at Payne Hollow self-contained and unattached. After spreading out on shore and almost taking root there, we must again make ourselves compact and movable.

November 22   The first jar of tomatoes. A new season begins.

November 25   Today we decided to cast off as soon as we could be ready.

November 27   We did much today besides celebrating Thanksgiving. Anna canned pears in the morning. I worked all day at loading our plunder from the bank, part on the roof, part in the hold. Now the tarpaulin is stretched over the deck load, all the potatoes, carrots and squash are in the middle hatch. Not much more to do before we can cast off.

November 28   Tomorrow noon is the time set for our departure. Yet when will we go?

I made what might be the last trip up the hill this afternoon, picked up a few hickory nuts, persimmons, a jug of milk from the McCords, who have been most kind in this matter. I left a jar of our best honey for Mrs. Adams, who is ailing. Anna had a most busy day, pickling beets on the side.

November 29   An important date, for we set sail from Payne Hollow. A light steady downstream wind moved us faster than the current, I think. We did not get away at noon but more nearly 3 o'clock. There was much to do, and a trip across the river to settle with the mail carrier, and say farewell to the Montgomerys and Schirmers. We had loaded the bees on board with no difficulty early in the morning. I reassembled and mounted the sweeps, put aboard the anchor and firewood, while Anna carried water from the spring.

We took in all lines but the head line, lashed the planks under the guards. Then pulled up on the head line, cast off, and rowed out into the stream, just clearing the bar. I looked back at the dark hillside, only the oaks with leaves, dark red colored. . . .

The sun set behind clouds, and we anchored below Wildwood Landing, less than a mile and a half below Payne Hollow. . . . The shore where we tied up was sandy and open against a steep bank, with a cornfield on top. We had our supper soon after, quite welcome after a distant lunch. It was good to light the lantern again.

6

The River in Winter

*The winter weather was glorious. The river of ice spar-
kled under the bright sun and moon. . . . The river became a new
creation. . . .*

December 1, 1947   Up before daybreak, casting off in the bright
moonlight.

December 2   Again I arose in the frosty tail of night, no sign of
dawn, but the night stars low, the moon paler. I cast off, and at
once the boat slips away, in the slow current and a like current of
air moving down the river. So still and quiet, a rooster crowing
inland. We seem to be drifting through the air. . . .

We had fine drifting to Bethlehem yesterday, past steep hills
and then a gravel shore with sycamores. Anchored off town and
went ashore. Post office, Sanford B. Smith, postmaster, a riverman
with pictures of the *New Hanover* on the walls, and his pilot license.
Just as we cast off, a light breeze sprang up ahead, so we pulled
back to shore and anchored off shantytown. Dinner, one of our
three live fish.

Underway again, not long before sunset, towing across to the
steep rocky shore above Jobson's Light. Tied up in the dusk. Tired
and sleepy, both of us. However, I was up in the moonlight again
this morning, and Anna soon after. Patton's creek, a narrow, shaggy
valley, the finest place we saw so far. The sun is behind it, the sun

189

finally getting over the ridge. Some rowing to keep us to the Kentucky shore. A fine breakfast of pancakes. Warm sun this morning. I write in the johnboat, between spells of rowing.

We met head winds below Bell's Branch, pulled in to shore and anchored. An old man went by in a johnboat with a load of logs for firewood, "for my drum stove." He lives in a mountain cabin on the hillside just below us. We passed most of the rest of the day here, quite a breeze blowing upriver. Near sunset it lay, and we cast off. Made little progress in the slow current against the dying breeze and swells. Pulled in below the cabin, banging into a rock while anchoring. Found a small leak in the hull, a fine crack in the end of the shoe gunwale.

A light breeze continues at night. Clear and starry. We are across from Camp Creek, above Fulton light, which is green, Mile 578. Two miles today.

December 3　I awoke to find the moon shining, the air still, so I dressed in warm clothing, and cast off. About 1:30 a.m., I guess. Perfect drifting, a wonderful experience so close to the night, moon, stars and clouds. . . .

After breakfast tried cordelling the boat down along the willows. Hard, unrewarding work. The wind increased and we anchored off shore, tossing about in the wind waves for awhile. . . . Toward evening we tried to continue our voyage, but there was no current and a little wind ahead, so we tied up after rowing 1/2 mile, just above the Westport Light, red.

December 4　This cloudy morning we were not up so early, but our departure was in the nick of time. A light downstream breeze sprang up as we cast off. I towed across the river while Anna made the bed. We had breakfast by candlelight while sailing past the sand-digger, the *Kentucky*, which was just getting up steam. The breeze freshened. The boat sails well, sideways keeping her broadside to the wind, and does not spin. Must claw off the shore around the bend. . . . Sailing swiftly now, on a long west reach.

December 5　Rather a windy night, and today a steady breeze from the west. So we remained at our anchorage in the lee of Twelve Mile Island all day. Both of us busy, of course. The dogs had a shore leave. . . . I walked down the island, found an immense corn field, where I picked up a bushel or two of corn. We were both a little tired after yesterday's long run. It was 4 a.m. when we began, and dark when we tied up here.

December 6 Yesterday I picked wild grapes, large ones, from the johnboat. We pressed and strained them, added a little water and sugar. This is our breakfast drink.

A cloudy night. We cast off at daybreak, very still, a breath from the west. Slow drifting down along island. . . . In the slow current, we would have been stationary, so I rowed with the sweeps off and on all morning.

At dinner time we anchored off the Kentucky shore, in front of some fancy summer homes. A spell of rowing for both of us took us to the mouth of Harrod's Creek. I went up in the johnboat to investigate while the boat lay off shore. We decided to lay here tonight, and pulled into the mouth of the creek, tying up to the north shore, putting out a stageboard. Both of us rowed up the creek to the settlement of Harrod's Creek, store, post office, taverns, etc. Boat harbors and camps along the south bank, several, outboards coming and going past us.

December 7 A rainy day, rain beginning in the night, continuing steadily through the night, continuing steadily through the dark day, but never a hard downpour. We lay tied to the bank at the creek mouth, from where we could look out on the windswept river.
. . .

I did not go abroad much today. Up the creek for a word with the harbormasters, Frances and Jim Meade. Out into the river before dark for clean water. A fine prospect up and down this long reach, low shores, tall trees, an island each way, the town of Utica across.

December 9 These two days in port, with various activities. Two sessions of printing wood blocks yesterday, for Christmas cards.

December 10 Yesterday for dinner we had muskrat stew. The animal was a gift of a local hunter and trapper, and was one whose skin was useless, having been chewed by a mink, as the hunter said.

December 11 "Uncle Jim" Meade came aboard today. He is care-taker of the boat harbor up the creek, and lives on a big steel hull houseboat. He is an old shanty boater, very shrewd about all that concerns boats and rivers. He was familiar with the Mississippi as far down as Memphis, at least. He enjoyed our fireplace, into which he could spit.

December 12 Saw a great blue heron today. It flew past the creek mouth, landed on the lower side, but soon took off again. The weather cleared today, after a dark cloudy spell. Much traffic of johnboats and outboards past our door. Many are duckhunters from the city. We have never seen so many well designed and well built johnboats, in good condition. A few good yawls and skiffs, too. One today, a long narrow bottomed skiff, which the owner said was 50 or 60 years old.

December 14 Today we moved from our berth at the mouth of the creek to one of the slips of the OK Harbor. We did it very neatly, I thought. Took in the lines, lashed the stageboards under the guards and rowed with the sweeps. There was a crosswind so I made a line fast to Meade's boat when near it. We pulled in to the head of their boat so Mrs. Meade could come aboard, as Uncle Jim wanted her to see our boat, particularly the fireplace. Then I took a long line down the dock, the wind holding the boat off as it tacked up the creek. It was an easy matter to pull it into the slip and make fast, but I would feel more secure tied to some trees on the open river bank. This is almost like being beached out, the roadway about level with the decks. . . .

The feature of yesterday was the reading in the evening of "A Winter Walk," in the volume of Thoreau's called *Excursions*.

December 21 Dull sunshine of winter, air cold. We came in at midnight last night, returning from our trip to Grand Rapids. . . . The experience of living the way other people do is valuable to us. Thus we get a detached, distant view of our life here. It seems almost like a life on a frontier, far from the refinements and luxu-ries of the cities close to the elements of living. I can never get out of doors in the city.

December 23 Today we left the harbor of Harrod's Creek, about

1 p.m. The wind was from the north, quite fresh earlier but light at our departure. We had arisen at daybreak, made preparations, and after breakfast we moved out of our slip and down to the creek mouth. Thin ice had formed again and we found it not so thin as we had judged it. It must be broken as we went. . . .

Out of the creek mouth we stayed close to shore, going inside the sanddigger just below. Then we pulled out and the wind and current took us down at a good rate. As we approached Six Mile Island, the wind freshened, and we could not hold the boat off shore. I dropped the anchor below the Goose Island buoy, above the light. We tossed considerably, in the waves, which often washed over the deck. Yet we could think of no improvement to make, so we had a bath and supper. A very civilized meal, of roast beef and cauliflower. . . .

No list of requirements for our summer location this year. We had decided that a favorable quiet impression was more important— "if you liked a place from the first, even for no easily explained reasons, it would turn out to be a pleasant and convenient place to live."

December 24 We are lying at the entrance to the Louisville canal, just outside of the riverward wall. A good harbor for a craft of our size. We were glad to spot it as we approached the canal at sunset, for it might be a long pull to another. Below the locks probably.

This was a hard day. After our windy evening, we had some quiet rest, but I awoke to find a light, downstream breeze, and the moon shining through broken clouds. About midnight, I guess. We decided to travel, so we dressed in warm clothes and cast off. Now instead of clawing off the Kentucky shore we must pull toward it, occasionally, or land in Indiana. We moved swiftly. After awhile, Anna went back to bed, but I kept watch as we sailed down, past tree lined shores, the darkness of night broken at intervals by lights on the highway. Past the waterworks, close in, sign telling that 50 feet of wickets were down at Dam 41. The flashing light on Towhead Island ahead, a fresh breeze. I wanted to keep close to the island, planning to be up at the foot. We sailed by at a great rate. I

193

rowed hard to keep off. The tumult woke Anna who manned the sweeps. We rounded the end of the island and anchored in its lee. Close to daybreak but we slept an hour.

December 25 We liked Towhead Island, as wild as Big Bone, though within the city. Skipper caught a rabbit, which we cooked for the dogs' dinner. There was a shantyboat inside, above us. The man hailed me, "What you got to swap?" We were underway at sunrise, still with a downstream breeze. We ate breakfast as we drifted past the sand fleets, barges, diggers, boats and unloading apparatus, great piles on shore. Then past the Greene Line wharfboat, the *Tom* and *Chris* tied up there. At the Coast Guard boat just below, we warped in and tied up. Soon we were up town, buying groceries and rope and other boat supplies. . . .

December 26 A clear sunrise this morning, except for the smoke in the air. The city itself is a fascinating place, the waterfront its most interesting aspect. I like to watch the trains and study the bridges. Yet the filth of it, in the air, in and on the water, along the shore. One feels contaminated always. The lights and noises disturb our nights. Yet the city takes up but a very little part of the river, and a small part of our time. Soon we will drift away, and be in the lonely reaches. . . .

December 29 This morning, at sunrise, we got under way. A long tow down the canal almost two miles. . . . When outside we met the current of the river, quite swift between the lock wall and sand island. We had to row hard to miss the abutment, but were soon adrift on the open river. . . .

This is a remote stretch of country, not a house to be seen from the top of the bank. The hills came in to the river below Knob Creek, steep and knobby, like the country above the mouth of the Kentucky. A lovely shore here, a steep sandy bank clothed in soft gray and shiny grass, some trees, a sandy shore. Good drifting today, not fast, but it required little attention. At that we made 9 miles.

Now came one of the surprises of our voyage. In our minds we had pictured the unknown river ahead as a wide stream flow-

*ing in long curves through a country of diminishing hills. In-
stead, at the bend below Salt River, the Ohio was contracted by
steep, bold shores which rose into palisades of rock. The current
was faster than ever as it swept around the sharp bends. We
partook of the enthusiasm of explorers to whom an undreamed-of
discovery was being revealed.*

January 1, 1948   Heavy rain last night, beginning with showers from the north. I was awakened by the bumping of the johnboat
and found a warm moist wind from the south. Today the winds
have been high. . . . Grand effects in the sky, and in the sharp
contrast of light and shades. We can see the surrounding country
for the first time.

January 2   A rough time of it yesterday and last night. The
wind continued to blow after dark, and we went to bed early, as it
was uncomfortable to sit up. . . .

January 3   A long, exciting day. I was a "sooner" this morning,
starting much too early. But it was light enough, probably moonlight filtered through the clouds, to see to take in the lines, plank
and spar without a light. What a peaceful place the cabin is then,
what remote thoughts the watcher has, with all the inmates asleep,
fire crackling, the dim shores moving by. . . .

River narrow and swift. Buzzards on the ridge. I heard Carolina wrens today. . . . We drifted 181/2 miles today.

January 4   This day we remained tied up against the steep
wooded bank below Falling Spring Light. Current and drift went by
almost unnoticed and for a day, we were permanent dwellers here.
. . .

We feasted today [*Harlan's birthday*]. A splendid dinner, after a
breakfast of pancakes by the fire. Anna baked a chocolate cake this
morning, the best made on board so far. In fact, it could not be
improved. . . .

This day we did all the things we like to do. Read Van Wyck
Brooks and Jefferson, *Notes on Virginia*, out of which, to our disgust,
the description of the Ohio was deleted; played music, two parts of
a Beethoven quartet, 127; I walked on shore, along a railroad for a

change, and cut wood, dry locust and oak. I was showered with kindness, but this was not unusual.

January 5 A quiet, gray morning. We cast off at daylight. The same swift current. Breakfast while drifting. A light wind and the set of the current carried us to the right bank. We pulled all the way across to be able to land at Brandenburg. . . . The town was attractive, most of it on the hill. Not until right then did we see the one street coming almost down to the river, through a gap, with a beautiful old brick courthouse and stores with permanent awnings over the sidewalk to the curb. . . .

Evening, Potato Run, 21 1/2 miles of drifting today. Ideal conditions, swift current, almost no wind, exciting new country. Stars all over the sky tonight.

January 6 Tater Run. We lay in the creek mouth today, while a west wind stirred up the waves outside. . . . The trapper returned today, gave us a possum, and we talked. He is a retired shantyboater.

January 8 Tater Run. . . . Yesterday was washday, the first since Payne Hollow, perhaps 7 weeks ago. So it was large, and we worked from dark to dark. All went well, a good drying day, and we enjoyed it. Fresh, clear water from up the creek, though I had to break ice to get it. Possum for dinner. We would prefer squirrel, muskrat or groundhog. The trapper gave us a rabbit yesterday, which we will have for dinner. He pulls out of the creek every morning, is gone on his trap line for an hour. Has been fishing for 50 years on the river.

January 9 Another day in the mouth of Tater Run, another fair, mild day, another washday, too, and now every article we can think of is clean. Other odd jobs, too, a new locust spar, the leak in the johnboat stopped, I hope, for I beached it out up the creek. While eating dinner we were visited by three conservation officers, Ellis, McCutcheon, and Engles. In spite of all their badges, uniforms, and weapons, they were mild enough, rather dull, but quite taken with our life on a boat. Fowler, the trapper, was in and out again, gave us another possum.

January 10 Potato Run. Another fine day, fairest of them all.

January 11 We were up early, and under way soon after sunrise. . . . At Blue River, tied up at the mouth on the lower side. . . . Another boat is just above us, on the upper side. A whole fleet, small houseboat, sternwheel, motorboats and johnboats.

January 13 We went to town, in the raw weather, rain falling on the way back. It was a longer walk than we expected, for Leavenworth had moved to the top of the hill, after the 1937 flood. We keep finding changes which this occurrence of nature has made in life along the river, both private and commercial. Some of the old town survives, old people living there most likely, and the contrast is sharp between the two parts, one with a river town atmosphere, tattered and dingy, aimless as an old man, the other out in the wind and sunlight, like an ugly, new house on the highway that hasn't been lived in long. Yet we were well treated. Found a button factory in operation, in a corner of a garage, perhaps 6 or 8 operators. Later we learned that musseling is a thriving business for river people in summer. Harvey Alcorn, who visited us with his wife and little boy in the evening, said that they paid $50 a ton for shells, that in a good week, he could get out a ton, even a ton and a half. I remember hearing of musseling at Leavenworth, from someone long back, although I could not remember, until I had seen the button factory, the significance the name of the town had for me.

I rowed up Blue River a short ways before dark. . . .When I got back to the boat I found a johnboat tied up and candles ablaze, the Alcorns aboard. They are rather young, have been on the river since 1939, in this neighborhood lately. In summer they lay across from town, have a garden, fish and mussel. Winters they lay in this creek. The boy goes to school, third grade, and Harvey takes him in the johnboat every morning. In this season he works in his machine shop, aboard the sternwheeler, repairing guns, etc. It is for working at night there that he has the lights and generator. For themselves they have oil lamps. They were very talkative, probably being alone much with no neighbors, and we enjoyed listening and found it profitable. We eagerly listen to all river experiences, especially of the river here and below, new to us.

January 14 A cold morning. Last night about 7:30 p.m. we rowed up the creek to call on our neighbors, the Alcorns. They entertained us well, Harvey playing his guitar. We pulled out of Blue River this morning, about half an hour after sunrise.

January 15 There is more activity on the river down here than we expect in winter. Above we hardly saw a johnboat in commission. Here they are numerous, and large yawls with outboards, hunters, fishers, and trappers are busy. They are friendly to talk to, and we meet no suspicion. I conversed with three today. A man from Leavenworth who was down here to raise a net. He pulled his johnboat alongside on his way back. Had a little fire in a bucket to warm his hands. He told me of a spring up the hollow. Hunting for it, I met a young man from the farm above, the only one below Leavenworth, I think. He told me this was all state land, and he sees deer about. When I was chopping firewood below Indian Hollow, I met the light tender in his long yawl. He lives at Schooner Point, 4 miles below, and cares for 5 lights on a five mile stretch all on this bend, all oil lamps. He visits them every other day, has done so in all seasons for 21 years.

January 16 Today we ran from Indian Hollow, mile 665, to Little Blue River, 678.5, or 13 1/2 miles. This distance we made without a stop, leaving before sunrise, and entering the creek early in the afternoon. Breakfast on the way, and dinner after we arrived. It was a beautiful and exciting run, around one sharp, short bend after another. . . . A swift current. Some lovely country. I remember especially Cedar Hollow, Kentucky, a lovely place with a little old farmhouse. An uninhabited hollow above. Bull Point, the last bend before Little Blue, was the sharpest bend we have seen. . . . This is a remote country, inaccessible by land. Towns, even farms are far apart. The roads cut off the river bends.

January 17 We got away from Little Blue River about 10 a.m., had a head wind down past the Alton bar to the bend. Then we had an exciting run around one bend after another, the wind with us at such an angle that we just cleared the points. I stayed on deck, enjoying the sun and winter air. . . .

We went down the back channel of Flint's Island, after some hesitation, and had an exciting ride on the narrow, swift water.

Closed all shutters but nearly had the stacks carried away by over-hanging branches. Finally tied up in good time near the foot of the island, against its shore. It is an extensive island, with a large corn-field. We passed a ferry flat the farmer uses, but the only inhabit-ant we saw was a pig. As usual, cut wood until dark. Mile 689.5, 11 miles below Little Blue.

January 18 Another cold night, even colder than last, we thought. Our situation last night was unusual. The back channel was like a small wilderness river, flowing swift in the pale moon-light.

We cast off at sunrise, the clearest of mornings. . . . The little town of Derby, below Oil Creek, was fair in the morning sun, and was built part way up the hill, with a white church and steeple highest up. One of the loveliest towns. Below on the Kentucky shore, a group of old, weatherbeaten houses, Chenault landing perhaps, dignified, spacious, of a large past. Another place we liked was the old double log house on the shoulder of a hill, in a little hollow, called Pate's Hollow. Stephensport, Kentucky, made a fine showing from the river. The country around Dam 45 seemed more familiar to us. Rolling hills.

At Towhead Island—"Where you going?" "New Orleans." "What have you got to swap?" "Nothing." "What will you take to trade?" "Nothing." "How much do you want for it, dad?" "I don't want to sell." "All right."

January 19 We wonder at the absence of shantyboats down here. Not one beached out have we seen below New Albany, nor any afloat except the Alcorns' in Blue River. We expected to see ferries, too, since there are no bridges between Louisville and Owensboro. But the only one we saw, not counting the motorboat passenger ferries at Stephensport and Cloverport, was at Branden-burg, and it was busy.

January 20 12.5 miles today. We started off in a quiet time before sunrise, a clear morning after another cold night. Ice frozen around the boat, and we drifted with sheets of thin ice. . . . Light snow began to fall. We tied up on the curve which gave us some protection from the reach above and below; all fast at 4 o'clock, which was intoned by a beautiful deep bell in Troy. Still light, so we played some.

Troy is a pleasant faced neighbor, after Tell City with its forbidding floodwall, and Cannellton with its factories and smoke. The lights across the water are cheering to see, and no doubt our light sets the Trojans to wondering.

January 21 A clear dawn and sunrise. Not quite daylight when we cast off. At that uncertain time, when even light does not seem probable, it takes an amount of faith to shove off. More than ever when you know that around the bend is a long reach into what might be rough weather. Yet the day was quiet and sunny.

On land one would hardly have noticed a breeze, but light as it was, we were almost stopped. We crowded close into the Indiana shore, and in its lee, where luckily there was some current, we drifted along the clay bank, with a sandy beach at the water's edge. A delightful place, littered with drift and wreckage. . . .

This was a day when we had time for writing letters. I worked on the sunny deck making a new cavil. Navigation required not much time today, until late in the afternoon when I rowed against the light breeze to reach Blackford Creek. The weather was uncertain, clouds had filled the sky, and the north and west were dark. We wanted some kind of shelter and were pleased to find the creek large and deep enough.

Our course of action was never the most prudent. If safety and comfort were to be considered first, we should never have left Blue River in the face of winter. As it turned out, much strain and discomfort, even danger, might have been avoided had we remained in that safe harbor. Yet we would have missed some glorious winter drifting, and an experience which, rough as it was, revealed to us new aspects of the river and of the people who live on its shores.

January 23 I did not write in the log yesterday, January 22, because I had enough of the river by the time it was over, and did not care to write about it. The night previous we had stayed in Blackford creek. It was a rough night, cold with a N wind and clearing sky. Next morning the wind lay, the sky became heavy and snow fell, which continued all day. I considered laying over, but the momentum of travelling, and the lack of wind, led me to propose casting off. The current was slow, and we had gone but a little ways before trouble began. Sheets of ice were blown over to this side, and most of the open water was slush, caused by the falling snow. Sweeps and oars could not be used. I kept us off shore with a pole, and the quartering wind carried us down. We had not started early, taking a slow breakfast of pancakes by the fire. We could not make any distance, and decided to tie up when we reached the sand bar marked on the chart opposite Honey Creek. We picked out the widest open shore we could see and tied up in the running ice, about halfway between Honey Creek and the light, less than 3 miles below Blackford Creek I was busy until almost dark, getting into the best shape possible, and then we had supper, having been too busy to eat our dinner. Ice was bad, large sheets sailing into us with the crosswind, which was stronger now and colder. I put our longest gangplank in position to take the grinding, carried the anchor out on shore for another head line. The boat shuddered when the ice rubbed by. There in the quiet we went on reading. To bed about the usual time, and that was about the last of the ice, for it froze fast overnight, several rods off shore.

January 24 We studied what to name this, and decided on Cape Horn Landing. Last night was Cape Horn weather. The east wind of the afternoon continued and was a gale all night, with fine snow. The river has been rising very slowly, and I was forced to get out last night and carry the anchor and line from the sand, where the water was about to cover it, to the higher shore. Then I broke up the ice all around the boat and tried to move it in, but it would not start. So I went back to bed, not long before daybreak. We slept late and had a leisurely breakfast of rice cakes by the fire, read quite a long time. Our favorite morning reading now is Chaucer. Then I went out, broke up the ice again, and moved the boat 6 feet in-shore. Snow has ceased now at midday and blue sky appears, wind down.

Night. Almost a full moon, no wind, ice sparkling, the open water dark.

At dinner today we had a visitor, who, however, came only to the top of the bank. Hailed us, had come over to see how we were making out. Quite dismal about our prospects, but kind of him to come and offer advice and help. We played some after dinner, and I spent the rest of the afternoon until the end of the light working outside.

January 25 What exhilaration there is in work out of doors in this keen air. One is not cold at all, the air is like cold clear water to drink.

Word has gotten around the country that a houseboat was caught in the ice, and we had 17 visitors today, several more looking down over the bank, and one yesterday. All concerned about us, not giving us much hope. All willing to help. We will no doubt call on them, as we have about decided, moved by their doleful stories, to pull out the boat.

January 26 Night. Our evenings are quiet time, all at rest and snug and in good order. . . .

Last night was cold, cold. This morning every twig was coated with all the frost it could carry. A dull sun shone in the sky, giving little warmth or light. No wind. A light snowfall at times, now. Water froze harder in the cabin last night than ever before. . . .

I was busy on the bank, clearing a space for us to rise into with the river. After the visit from Mr. Lawson Green yesterday, we had decided to try to haul the boat up the bank on skids, though not entirely behind the idea. This afternoon I walked down the road to call on Mr. Mattingly, who lives in the house with the windmill. He was our first visitor, though he did not come down the bank. A farmer, with considerable ground, and has had river experience. His brother, and himself, operated a ferry at Tell City. He thought we would do as well to stay where we were, rise with the river and keep crowding into the bank. If the ice was soft and the run-out not too severe, we could make it. If the ice was hard, the river against the steep bank, nothing we could do now would save us. We prefer this plan to that of trying to raise the boat, which would be difficult with our equipment and perhaps damage the boat as much as the ice. But who knows what is best? . . .

Last night a full moon. Tonight its light is felt through the clouds.

January 28 Six men and boys came down the bank to help us as they could. We cut the ice and shoved off the bottom. Yet the boat was heeling over when I awoke in the night and it meant either blocking up, or cutting the ice and shoving out again. One does not know what to do, one does the best he can. . . .

I built some steps up the steep bank yesterday. We went up to Murray Estes' in the afternoon, and enjoyed our visit with Mrs. Estes, her mother and aunt, Mrs. Carl Green, in the homelike kitchen. Kitchen and living room combined. A large room, with range and heating stove. The amazing kindness of these people, and they do not make us feel like refugees or unfortunates. . . .

We will remember last evening's sunset, the sky so finely threaded with yellow and orange, the red ball of the sun dropping. A good fire burning all last night and the cabin not so cold. Boat at the same list, not bad. Somehow, our mood is changed since yesterday, at the end of which we were tired, uncertain and doubtful. This morning we are living on the river again.

January 29 Another cold morning but not as cold as yesterday when it was -10° at Owensboro. I get little done here, interrupted continually by visitors. All afternoon yesterday, beginning with Uncle Bill Mattingly. Today the men are to help us move into the big empty farmhouse between Estes and Mattingly. . . .

This evening we are in the house, tumbled in with all our gear and plunder and what a load of it there was, several trailer loads, many, many trips up the bank. When I left the boat at dusk, how desolate it was, dirty and littered like a tenantless house. On the slanting, ice covered bank, fires out, no one to care for it.

January 30 How different sleeping in a house, already farther removed from out of doors. Strange smells.

The picture of this room at present: Fire burning in the stove, seen only through some chinks in the fire door. Anna asleep, under a golden coverlet. Floor space not taken up by the bed is covered with our stuff, and it is a large room, perhaps 16 feet square. Only a narrow pathway is left. The canned stuff covers a quarter of the floor. We were embarrassed with it yesterday, yet it is so good to see, so valuable to us, and represents hidden virtues, too.

January 31 On Friday, January 30, we pulled the boat out of the water. First time the bottom has had air under it since the boat floated at the end of 1943, a little more than 4 years. It was a day of stress for us. I was at the boat at daybreak, down the road with Murray Estes to Carl Green's, for cables and jacks. He came up later, and we fastened cables to each end. Meantime, 3 of the Smothers cleaned off the bank. Just time for dinner before the winch truck appeared. It belongs to Ford Sacra of Maceo. He has a sawmill and lumber yard there. Brought 2 men with him, cables, several 3 x 10's and 6 x 6's, new timber. They shoved 3 of these under the near side of the boat which rested in mud. Then they hooked onto the cable, and after some difficulty in anchoring the truck hauled the boat up the bank, placing timbers under it. A rough, jerky ride for the boat, but it seems to be unhurt. A crowd of 40 or 50 people were on the bank to watch; strangely, no children. Nearly everyone had his own plan, but no one would listen to the other fellow's. Lines attached to each end of the boat were snubbed around trees as it moved up. Anna stood at the top of the steps, I was moving about down below doing nothing much. A great relief to have the boat at rest, 15 or 20 feet above the water and everyone gone home. I have not been able to pay anyone for their service. . . .

> The crowd departed and left us alone with the boat. It lay like a wreck, at a sharp angle on the snowy bank, but it was unharmed and out of the ice. Only in the most extreme conditions could it suffer damage now. We were relieved of strain, and thankful, and tired, tired.
>
> Murray Estes and the others had offered their services so freely that I knew they would accept no money in payment. I asked

Uncle Bill what to do. He said country people are accustomed to turning out and helping one another, so we must thank them heartily, and when the opportunity came, help them or another, a stranger perhaps, and expect no reward. His philosophy might have come from someone's Utopia, yet here it was, practiced in Daviess County, Kentucky in the year 1948.

February 2 A fair, still morning, after days of heavy skies and winds. We are well organized here now, and feel that this is our base of operations. Yesterday we called on the Mattinglys in the afternoon, and were back in time for a good session of playing. . . .

Today I worked at the boat, leaving Anna here alone. I raised up the lower side with jacks, but not to a level position. It was good to be working on the bank again, and to be working alone. While I was gone Anna did some good work in our house, mopping both floors, perfecting the arrangement of things.

February 4 A dreary, drizzly day, slush and fog. The snow and ice melt. I tinker about the boat in the morning. After dinner some music and painting. . . . Yesterday we were both at the boat in the morning when Anna gave it a good going over and cleaning. Visitors in the afternoon—Cecil Mattingly, our landlord, and J. W., Marian's brother. Later Marian came and stayed most of the afternoon. We hadn't had our dinner and finally ate with a spectator. I think all our doings are amusing to the natives, here as everywhere.

February 6 The snow ceased during the night but 7 or 8 inches has fallen, the deepest snow we have had in several years. This cloudy and still morning it was plastered on everything.

We both went to the boat this morning. Anna began the task of cleaning the ceiling and walls, and I continued making tieplates and cavils. It was so light and cheerful there. The boat has a gay spirit that no sedate house ever has. We had our midday meal by the fire there. It was a lunch that ended by being a dinner. Baked potatoes, from the ashes.

A strange fog is rising from the snow this evening. Earth and sky are all one, with the bright evening star shining above.

February 9 The sunset last evening, and the sunrise this morning, the stars in the night, such a sweep of sky in this flat country.

When I went down to the boat the other morning stomping on deck, I routed out an owl which had settled in between decks, a good sized reddish brown bird.

To Owensboro today with Murray and Marian Estes arriving there about 10 a.m., leaving about 1:45 p.m. For us, a strange approach to a town by land in a car on the highway. You feel how little connection the town has with the river. Even for us the river had little meaning. When you approach by water there is always some remnant of the days when the town faced the river. You enter through a ruined gate, but you understand that at one time life flowed that way.

Yet we enjoyed being in town, buying some things we needed, the first real shopping since Louisville at Christmas. A town of that size can be taken in at once, whereas in a large city, one can see only part at a time. The mechanics of a city, the various stores, warehouses and businesses lined up along the streets, the inhabitants engaged in their trades and jobs of selling and handling or producing goods, the buyers crowding the streets, all this is fascinating and one can understand Whitman's interest. The sad and ugly part is the way people live there, how it changes their natures, a fact easily seen when one has been with country people. Aesthetically it is bad, downright ugly. The houses and farm plants in the country are so, too, but there they are engulfed in the sweep of the landscape and one sees old buildings and barns and roads which are in harmony. But the city is a dead waste.

February 13   I was at the boat most of the day making ready for our move back aboard. Once I looked out and the river, which was nearly open the last time I looked at it, was suddenly filled with floating ice, sheets and piles and cakes, grinding against the shore. Then I was thankful that we were not in it. . . .

I heard this morning in the rain the song of the towhee. Also the cardinal sang, the titmouse, and song sparrow. Meadowlarks we hear now, too.

February 17   Skipper's puppies came last night, five of them this morning, all doing well. . . .

Now we are afloat again. The swiftly rising river reached the boat about Sunday noon, February 15. I finished the painting and caulking that morning. . . . River still rising slower now and our roof is even with the top of the bank. The johnboat is perched up there, painted yesterday. We hauled it up the steep bank Sunday using our blocks, and having some timely assistance from Uncle Bill. We borrowed his team of mules and platform wagon and made two trips. The wagon bed is about 8 x 15, and we loaded on all it would hold. The boat floated off the blocks while we were moving on. Between trips the river filled with ice, reaching almost to this shore and we began to doubt our decision to move back on board. Yet the ice soon decreased. . . .

The mule driving was a pleasant experience for me. Years since I have driven a team.

Yesterday we finished loading, doing some cleaning as we worked and taking our time. All decks scrubbed, hatches and between decks in good order. . . .

A heavy fog closed in this morning about sunrise, forcing all boats to the bank. Walking along the road I saw a perfect fog bow, the two ends close by, and perhaps 200 yards apart. The arc was whitish, lighter than the fog with just a trace of iridescent color, stronger near the ground where the fog was thickest. . . .

Launched the johnboat this afternoon and now we feel complete.

February 18 A warm, sunny morning, like a spring morning, the birds singing. I heard a dove and flicker. We cast off about 8 a.m. and were soon drifting swiftly past the willows. What a contrast to our landing, in the ice and snow, zero weather, low water and little current. We marvel at our good fortune, how the breaks are with us. We really enjoyed our layover. Yet it might have been a disaster. . . .

We kept close to shore, perpared to tie up at Carl Green's a mile below. He met us in his outboard, but we made the landing alone. It was a tight place, but we managed neatly.

February 19 Heard this morning a robin in full voice. Yesterday a dove and flicker. A grand washing of clothes today. We put everything to soak, even stripping off the clothes we were wearing.

February 20   Carl Green makes serious work of catching drift. He goes out in his yawl and outboard equipped like a whaleboat. He caught two long mooring docks, and yesterday afternoon, in the rough water, he came from across loaded with the wreckage of a boat cabin. It is good to see such a man in the active years of his life. We have known several old timers who would tell us of their early adventures and this is the material of which they were made.

February 21   We had it in our minds to leave this morning for downriver points, but there is a stiff wind and snow from the north. Luckily had time to get in wood before the snow began. Last night we paid a visit to Carl Green in his house which we found clean and rather elegant. . . . Day before I gave Mr. Smothers, Sr. a pair of old oars. He walked off with them, saying nothing much, but yesterday handed me a paper sack containing a quart of sweet milk and a pound of country butter, with as little comment. So for supper last night we had the butter and milk with fresh baked bread.

February 22   Today we really cast off and drifted away from our ice harbor, away from people we know. Just a month after our first landing in the ice. . . . Had some trouble getting through the driftwood which had collected between us and open river. Carl helped us, probably his last service to us. He said he did not like to see us leave.

We drifted in the swiftest current we had yet experienced and were pushed along by the light wind, too. On a level with the countryside, we could look over a wide expanse of flooded fields, with houses and barns barely keeping their feet dry on the higher places. The first flock of grackles. . . . At the head of Yellow Bank Island we pulled into the chute, and had a delightful passage down the tree lined corridor. The island just about awash. We tied up to the mainland above the Owensboro bridge. . . .

We enjoy the view of the city through the great trees on the island, the graceful bridge arching its way across. At night the lights of the city and on the bridge, reflected in the smooth water, make a fair prospect. Looking up the chute, it is as wild as the back channel of Flint Island, the moon shining now as it was then.

February 25 Evansville. We drifted into shantyboat town and tied up at the head of a line of 4 boats. Ahead of us are two sand unloading outfits. Below the boats is Pigeon Creek. . . . Train whistles and switch engines, puffing and banging cars about. A busy street, too, along the bank here, a truck route. What a contrast to last night, in the quiet empty chute of French Island. . . .

The approach to Evansville was something to see. As we rounded the bend the stacks and smoke below the city were first seen, then the buildings, they seemed part of a modern Venice, the land across all flooded. . . . All this day's trip was exciting. We felt somewhat like Noah afloat on the flooded earth, even had enough livestock aboard to carry on the suggestion. Yet the dogs, not ashore from early morning until afternoon, were patient and quiet. The pups, in a crate placed as much out of the way as possible, cause no disturbance. Their little chirping is pleasant to hear. . . .

We watch with interest our neighbors on the bank. A darky who lived all winter in a tent now under water, and a white man whose shanty was just emerging near our boat. He was elated to see the door knob today. This morning he appeared carrying a packing box which once contained a refrigerator. This he set up, covered the top with some roofing, extending this for a porch. He made a salamander and all day in the rain and tonight he and the darky, apparently by turns, sat in the box with the fire blazing before them.

Anna stayed within all day but this afternoon I did some walking about Evansville. The creek, Pigeon Creek, above the bridge is a great harbor for shantyboats. I never saw so many, of all sizes and design. At low water they must make a solid line along the banks.

February 26 This morning was as dark and foggy as yesterday was, but a light west wind cleared the air and the afternoon was mostly sunny. People came out who had taken shelter in the rain. The man in the refrigerator box had company. We finally decided that they were his wife and family, all waiting for their house to come out of water.

We had dinner early and cast off about 1:30 p.m. Drifted past the terminals and power plant, and were soon in the country river.

We could look across the flat land to the bridge up toward Green River and see its hills. Evansville lay fair in the afternoon sun, as impressive as when we approached. . . .

We found swift current again, and in what seemed a short time were passing Henderson Towhead. We were surprised and alarmed by the appearance coming up around the bend of an empty clipper, but he swung out as he passed. It would be bad to drift around a point, close in, and suddenly meet an upbound tow. . . . We pulled within the outer fringe of trees, almost taking down our smoke stacks, but found a snug harbor tied between the trees.

February 27   Fog almost closes us in. . . . I heard killdeers last evening for the first time that I was sure of. Listen every day for redwings.

February 29   I must mention the splendid rainbow on the 27th. We were playing late in the afternoon of that stormy day when the sun broke through the western clouds low to the earth. In the dark eastern sky the arch of the rainbow sprang, high, a great span, but not reaching quite to the earth. Segments gleamed more brightly in the purest colors. . . .

Yesterday we went to Henderson in the johnboat. We were favorably impressed with the city. I believe I like it best of all the places we have seen on the way down. . . . The waterfront at Henderson is open and clean, the buildings facing the river being used and kept up. The courthouse is a fine one, on a little hill. We found good stores, and a Saturday crowd on the streets. Bought some soybeans at last and a new lantern, a little one which pleases us much. . . .

Who knows just when the water maple buds begin to redden and open? Suddenly we see them. And today we heard peepers and red wing blackbirds.

At midday we pulled into a small cove, tied up. We put the dogs ashore, cut wood, ate our dinner. The last one of our smoked fish from Payne Hollow as good as ever after more than three months.

This afternoon we drifted until about sunset, around the sharp bend at Cypress Bay, then pulling across to the bluff shore above

West Franklin. Looking for a harbor we drifted on, through the right channel at Diamond Island almost to the end of it, where we found a very good anchorage against a bank which had a grove of locust trees on top. . . . Our two landings today were in such pleasant places and having passed attractive country that now we feel more hopeful about the river ahead of us.

March 2 More wind and we remain at the locust grove. A short gale from the east last night. I had to get up and set a spar at the upper end of the boat. The bank is steep here, but not sand. Still there is danger of caving, in an onshore wind, as the river falls.

March 3 We travelled 11 or 12 miles today. . . . The wind was with us below and carried us down the back channel of Slim Island. We tied up to eat our dinner. Shortly after taking off again the wind carried us into the bank regardless of my pulling through and over the small trees to the shore. We are still there tonight.

March 4 This evening we are tied up on the Illinois side of the river, even if not actually to the Illinois shore. Above Shawneetown, across from, slightly above, the J. C. Crossing light, below the Raleigh light. Mile 854.7, a good 20 miles from our anchorage behind Slim Island. We had breakfast there and read a little, finishing with delight the prologue to the *Canterbury Tales*.

A cloudy morning, wind blowing out of the north which was down along our shore. So we cast our lot on the windy waters and were soon sailing past Slim Island towhead. The direction of the wind allowed us to make about 10 miles, cutting close to Cottonwood Point on the Indiana side, so close we almost scraped it. We seemed to be making 10 miles an hour. Then we were carried over to Poker Point, oil wells near the river and past Uniontown. We were in close to the sharp point below and across, and pulled in to the willows, tied up in the lee below the Uniontown ferry. . . .

In making our landing here Anna's foot was caught in the line which tightened around it with the pull of the current and we were fortunate to escape a serious injury. That is a critical time, for you must work fast. Our procedure usually is for me to be in the johnboat with lines ready, and when in position Anna casts me loose and I row quickly to the tree I have selected, making the line fast. Then Anna snubs it around the boat's cavil, checking its motion. Another time I was nearly swept overboard from the johnboat when I was on the wrong side of the line.

March 5   The mouth of the Wabash was a remote place. The land was low and flooded. Trees rose from the water in thick clumps. Thick woods on the island, it had the appearance of a partially cleared country. . . .

We were looking for a harbor now and ran close to Brown's Island but we could find no way inside of it and swept by in the wind and current, pulling hard to avoid the trees. Below, we let the wind take us behind a point of low trees under water and tied up among some large trees well behind the line of river shore but still nearly 100 yards from land. . . .

We were delighted with the view, having a long reach of river to look at. The sun set behind the tall trees between us and shore. Deep water back in there, some low, cleared land, meadow, and farther back trees and water in the distance. It was a clear, cold night. The wind, a little east of north when I sighted the Pole Star, roared through the tree tops and we swung back and forth.

March 6   We stayed at Belle Isle, the wind blowing fresh from about NNE downstream. A visitor was a shantyboater in an outboard, a true man of the river. I feel so much like a novice talking to such a man, and he knows my inexperience. Yet we do things they do not. My weakness is that I do not engage in the accepted shantyboat activities, catching fish to sell, trapping, junking, trading. This man came from Pittsburgh 44 years ago and made his way slowly down. Yet he wants to go back, even though he has been told the fishing is no good above Louisville now. He evidently was many years on the way down, for he had laid over in many places, Brent for one. We learned much about the river here and below. . . .

We are beginning to see more attractive country now, woods and islands and sloughs, fine trees, some hills and farms, not so much of cornfields and cottonwoods.

The man had a book in his pocket which he offered to loan when I mentioned it, *Scarlet Sister Mary*. He said he "flopped" in a barn back in the slough somewhere. His boat sank recently. . . .

Late in the afternoon we decided to drop down to Millrace Slough above Shawneetown, which the old man said was a better place to lay. The wind still blew and we sailed and drifted the two miles in a short time and pulled into the slough just above daymark 856.9. The only land we saw was back in and up, so we cordelled several hundred feet, pulled through a line of trees, rowed across another channel and into a grove of large trees. It was dark now, so I tied up in the best manner I could, with a hard clean shore close by. A quiet night. . . .

I rowed down to the upper end of Shawneetown, climbed the levee and was surprised to look down on the old town. It is a walled town. A block of old buildings of true steamboat architecture, but about all that is left pertains to the waterfront—fishermen, boats, taverns. I never saw Ohio River fishing on such a scale, nets, seines, mussel bails, boats everywhere. A powerful ferry, *Margaret J.*, towing a huge flat. Another sternwheeler tied up, *Guy L.* Our being here was known probably soon after our arrival. At Logsdon's hardware store the man told me "they" owned this stretch of river bank and the fishermen going up and down report any newcomers. Even the man who tied up and talked yesterday, Joe Henderson I found his name was, was a henchman of the Logsdons'. It was their barn he slept in.

March 7 Millrace Slough. At nightfall we hear a chorus of owls. Before, at sundown, an immense flock of crows gathers in the woods. We see unfamiliar trees. One huge one near the boat, with catkins opening in the top, we deduced was a cypress, and as we rowed up the ravine we saw more. Some birch, too. Pecans are numerous. . . .

The gnawing heard last night turned out to have been made by a rat. We heard him between decks today. I began taking the stuff out and soon found the rat dead from poison. Lucky for us. How and when did he come aboard? They were numerous at Evansville but we had no plank ashore there, no line tied to shore.

March 8 Up early and cast off, pulled out of the trees and down the slough as the sun rose across the river. . . . A fine day for drifting, sunny and still. Swift current, though the river is falling fast now. Wonderful reaches of river and distant hills. A long bend, the Shawneetown bend. . . . Close to shore, we pull into the mouth of Saline river, Illinois, tie up for dinner. A steep, rocky bluff makes the lower shore of the river. More rocks and hills below, along by Battery Rock towhead, and Caseyville, Kentucky, is built on a hill. We are delighted. . . .

We entered Crooked Creek at Ford's Ferry, and finding it open and wide we made it our harbor. . . . A gone down place, only 2 or 3 families where once there was a town, stores, post office, ferry. We read that in early days it was an important crossing for settlers moving into the Northwest country, a ferry here being operated by a man named Ford.

March 9 Drifted down past the head of Cave-in-Rock Island. We tied up to the mainland at the foot of the island in a swift eddy against a steep sandy bank. Got out a plank and the dogs had a holiday ashore. . . . After dinner we decided to cross over to the town. We rowed through the end of the island up aways on the outside and crossing over, landed directly at the mouth of the robbers' cave, which we could see plainly as we approached, an opening in the rocky cliff, which at this high stage of the river rose straight from the water. It was a surprise to us, and we were impressed with the beautiful shore, the steep rocks crowned with cedars, and with the cave, inside and out.

March 11 Yesterday and today we have been held to the bank behind Cave-in-Rock Island by a wind from the N. Quite cold this morning, freezing hard, with a skift of snow on the ground.

Nothing memorable about yesterday except that I fell in the river from the johnboat while reaching for a piece of driftwood, just after making the boat fast to the cavil.

March 13 Passing Dam 51 about 10:30 a.m. . . . Good drifting below, keeping on the outside of the islands to Big Hurricane Island where we took the left channel. The sailing line is now to the Illinois side. A glimpse of the village of Tolu.

Now we marvel at the colors of budding trees. At what other season are the trees fairer?

We are pleased with this river.

We found ourselves examining the shores with more than a passing interest. The idea of making an end to this season of drifting and laying over for the summer became more and more insistent. . . . Drifting was as fascinating as ever, but we might have been getting a little weary. Looking back, it seemed to us a long time ago that we left Payne Hollow and made our way past Louisville; then after a long stop at Blue River came the strain and excitement of ice, and flood. A quiet harbor for summer began to have its appeal.

March 15 Bayou Creek. Today we have been thanking our lucky stars for the break in the wind at dark yesterday during which we were able to make this harbor. The south wind boomed all night and all this day, making the open river a rough place to be. I must even get up in the night to make fast the johnboat and get out another line to check our swinging about. This morning I moved the boat into the bank, made a path through the mud by shoveling it aside and uncovering the hard ground. I was minded of shoveling snow. Now we have out our gangplank and feel that we are in harbor for a few days.

I found a dead chicken floating in the creek. It seemed to be in good condition. I plucked and cleaned it and Anna cooked it for the dogs. It was the fattest bird I ever saw and we are tempted to share it with the dogs. . . .

Now at evening the wind has ceased and rain falls. A coot has been swimming about the boat today. The *Gordon C. Greene* passed down the river today, making not a sound which could be heard above the roar of wind and water.

March 16 Bayou Creek. . . . This morning we walked to the town of Bayou, a quarter of a mile down the road. Found a handful of houses, a little store and post office. The people seem not very friendly.

After dinner I and the dogs drifted and sailed in the johnboat down to Stewart's Island. Then over to the main at Phelps Creek. I left the boat here and walked down to Birdsville, another such place as Bayou only on a hill. A hard row back against wind and current.

215

When I come on board after such a trip on the muddy, inhospitable shore, I find the boat so neat and clean within.

March 17 After breakfast we rowed across the river, explored the shore a little ways, and rowed on up to Bay City. A misleading name for there is no bay unless the gap between the bluff hills could be called such. Certainly it is not a city, with half a dozen houses, some of which turned out to be used for chickens and storage. The store, no post office, is a good one, clean, well stocked and arranged, with a friendly woman to deal with. All much better than the store at Bayou.

March 18 A terrific wind today. It began last night, blowing hard from the south, and continued so until midday. We rocked considerably and the direct force of the wind was as strong as we have ever felt. It shifted to west this afternoon, blowing just as hard but not rolling waves as high. This evening is perfectly quiet, and the frogs are heard again.

I made a scouting trip by bicycle down the river shore through Bayou and Birdsville to Smithland. . . . An uncertain, threatening day, warm and windy. Found Anna playing cello when I returned.

March 22 After some hesitation we pulled out of Bayou Creek in the face of bad weather. Good to be out in the open again, running the long reaches with ranges of blue hills far off. Looking back, the section we were leaving was an enticing country.

Head wind came up but we drifted into it past Stewart's and Dog Islands. As we entered the left channel at Cumberland Island we had a last look down the river, the flat shore on the left curving into the distance but not opening up a new reach. Reached the point above the Cumberland, towed in, taking advantage of the eddy, and found a snug harbor at the old ferry landing, not far above the mouth.

Dinner and exploring trip ashore. Found river people living in an old farmhouse nearby, above us, where they had a little houseboat. The afternoon was taken up by a trip to Smithland for all of us and further tying up of the boat, getting out a gangplank, rigging up the net and placing it. We are delighted with our situation, and more pleased with our prospects than we have been for weeks.

7

Bizzle's Bluff

It was in this setting and among these people that we spent the second summer after leaving Brent. This particular bend of the Cumberland soon became as well known to us as Payne Hollow. Indeed, home was wherever our boat was tied, since our lares and penates were always aboard, and no essential left behind.

March 27, 1948 I made a bicycle expedition back into the country through Iuka and up the Cumberland, to the Kentucky dam on the Tennessee. . . . I found a place that I took to at first sight and it seems to meet most of our requirements. . . . A beautiful old house there, the Barrett quarries above, then Bizzle's Bluff and Bizzle's Creek.

March 28 A bright, cool Easter Day after a night which froze ice. We had Sunday visitors coming afoot down the old ferry road and by water. We liked especially old Mr. Hedgepath, our neighbor. He was raised near Birdsville, worked in timber all his life, now fishes a little, makes johnboats, repairs guns. He goes to the woods, cuts walnut trees out of which he makes gun stocks. Later in the day we had a drove come down from the various houses on this big farm—tenants and squatters. . . . We liked too Mr. McCandless who runs the farm, a superior man above the others in character as well as in position. We haven't been able so far to figure out the relations between the different people. . . . Great interest shown in our pups or they use that as an excuse to come aboard. The boat meets general approval.

March 29 One of our visitors yesterday used an expression I have been trying to recall since. I heard it from Harvey Alcorn—"driftwrack," meaning, I think, a tangled mass of driftwood either floating as an island or left onshore by the falling river.

March 30 Today we made our voyage up the Cumberland, to the upper end of Bizzle's Bluff, 7 miles above Smithland. We were towed by a motorboat. . . . Two young fellows working for the owner of the boat, who used it as a ferry to Cumberland Island, which he farmed, operated the boat. We arrived about midday 3 1/2 or 4 hours after leaving Smithland. The boys had dinner with us. . . . We enjoyed the trip up the river, a novel experience for us, and a fine river. . . .

It is good to be in the country again. After the town is left behind one feels how close it has been.

Seldom we have guests for a meal, and Anna got up an excellent dinner, or rather lunch, with some flourishes. Our long table, an array of china and silverware which probably startled the boys. The food was strange to them, or part of it was. They ate the baked beans and fried potatoes, tasted the brown bread, drank several cups of coffee but passed up the tomatoes with herbs, cabbage and peanut salad, canned blackberries. That is, they ate the food they might have had at home, failed to try the new things. So prejudices are formed early.

April 1 Yesterday, a warm day, we made an excursion down the river. First we rowed to the quarry where we talked with the Howards, elder. Then walked down the river road and through the fields to Moody's mine. Returned the same way, got water, buttermilk and butter from Mrs. Whorton at one of the quarry houses. Also got two carp from Isaac Jones, the fisherman who lives in a boat beached out along the road below the quarry. . . . He has a string of nets across from us, behind the willows. Today he baited some lines in the backwater up Bizzle's Creek, and one right near our boat. A more friendly or helpful neighbor one could not have, and I will no doubt depend on him for fishing lore. . . .

We have about decided to remain here, thinking that the advantages outweigh the objections by a sufficient margin. . . . I walked up to the top of the hill yesterday afternoon, finding one of the best views of all I have seen. . . . I walked up that way again this afternoon, and down the ridge to talk to Mr. James A. Joiner, who owns this ground. Agreed to rent the cabin for 50¢ a week, garden to be included, although we may bargain for more land when he comes down, possibly this Sunday. In the 2 1/2 days we have been here we have become marvelously well acquainted with the lay of the land and the inhabitants.

April 2   Began the garden in front and to the west of the cabin, finding rich virgin soil among the rocks. We feel the thrill anew of beginning to plant in the early spring, and a new place with different surroundings adds to the excitement.

Ike Jones was by twice on fishing business. This morning I watched him raise some of his nets in the backwater across the river. He caught a good many carp, and gave us a bass and a jack salmon he had caught up the river. These we had for dinner and they were very good.

April 3   This day should be marked with a circle on our calendar. First thing this morning we put the bees ashore, carrying the hive, which did not feel very heavy, up the path to the cabin, in front of which we placed it. A good location, we think, facing the south, open to the morning and afternoon sun, under a little peach tree which will cast some shade at noon.

This day too we did our first planting for our 1948 garden, planting early things in a little patch, unused before, near the cabin. A fair, warm day. Late in the afternoon we climbed the hill, were both struck by the magnificent view. . . . Heard the first mockingbird singing far in the distance.

This evening we realized one of the hazards of being on a small river. The *Frances M. Hoagland*, travelling fast downstream with 2 empties, swung far to this side on the curve to pass the *Mary Jane* coming up on the other side. The waves were bad, washing over the afterdeck.

April 4 This morning, just before daybreak, I heard, and woke Anna to hear, the call of the whip-poor-will. Loud and vigorous, but I heard this one call only.

A little gardening this morning. Early in the afternoon Mr. Joiner came down. A most agreeable landlord. Now we have possession of the cabin until October and a large garden, all I care to work, in rich ground. We to pay $15.00. The rent of the cabin at 50¢ per week would be $12.00.

Late this afternoon I climbed the hill in search of milk, which I found at the Mitchell's. First I went to Ellis Lytton's, then to the Mitchells', from here directed to his brother. Now I have visited all the farms on top the bluff. Almost dark when I returned.

April 6 A week ago we were towed up here. We marvel at how much we have accomplished. Our location picked out after scouting up and down. Considerable exploring of the countryside, except across the river, which is cut off by the backwater. Acquaintance made with nearly all the natives, it seems. A good start on planting the garden. Besides we have kept up our reading, playing, and painting.

April 7 Ike Jones comes up the river in his outboard, singing and whistling loudly, the sound rising above the buzz of the motor, though he probably thinks he is below it.

April 8 We opened our canning season today with a flourish— 15 pints of carp. Having a fire on shore for heating jars and processing, we cooked breakfast there, and also dinner, which was mostly carp hash. Even tonight we used the embers to cook dog food and our carp soup. Also baked a rice pudding in the outdoor oven, heated bath water and dishwater on the same fire. And Anna steamed the soybean sprouts there, too.

April 9 After planting the last of our potatoes early this morning, we rowed down to the quarry, put up our mailbox.

April 11 Yesterday we finished planting our early garden, knocked off in midafternoon, had a bath and a real Saturday evening. We are still reading our winter's mail. From every part of the country a cold and severe winter is reported. Who has been exposed to the weather as much as we? The dread of cold is partly due to the shortage of fuel, its high price. Also from newspaper reports, which fix public opinion more than actual contact with the elements. Everyone has heard alarming reports of ice in the river and our nervous friends were worried about us.

April 12   First exploration across river this morning. Talked to Mrs. Champion. Visitors yesterday, Mr. Joiner and his son Harmon, who is engineer on Federal Barge Line towboat, *St. Louis*, out of New Orleans. . . . Mr. Joiner told us a yarn of buried treasure years ago. A man came down the Cumberland in a canoe, took sick here and died, attended by neighbors. He told them of money he had buried under this bluff, but no one has been able to locate it. The stranger's name was Bizzle, and the bluff and creek are named after him.

Anna spotted a prothonotary warbler this morning.

April 14   We went down to the quarry this morning to put a dozen letters in the mail. Received a notice from the Burna P.O. that our box not being an approved one, could not be used. So a man can't make his own mailbox.

April 15   Before sunset we climbed the hill and walked through the level fields to the Mitchells'. Took them 3 of Ike's carp and brought back a jug of milk. Everyone satisfied.

April 17   It is but 3 weeks ago today that I first came into this valley, yet we are well acquainted with the inhabitants. We call them by first names and know some of the relationships.

This sunny afternoon we wandered over road and path after drifting down to the quarry. . . . We walked out the road past the white church to the highway, up to Uncle Bud Lloyd's little store. We found it filled with people, nearly the whole neighborhood sitting in there, mostly Lyttons. This is their Saturday evening diversion I guess, sitting there in silence. Anna caused a little excitement by asking for tapioca. After saying he did not have it and pondering a while, Uncle Bud said, "What is it, anyway?"

We walked from there past the Dyer Hill Baptist Church and along the wood path, noting new flowers. . . . Down the road to the river. As we approached it, we could still feel the same excitement I had on my first trip here. A conversation with Ike Jones, who had been at Smithland today, and another with Mrs. Howard. After exchanging mailboxes, more talk with the Whortons, while getting buttermilk and butter. As usual, it was a relief to get on the river again, and we were home at sunset.

April 19 The first lightning bugs this warm, still evening. Their appearance is as important in our calendar as the spring peepers or the first snow.

April 22 I must record what Ike Jones told me this evening when he stopped by to leave the carcasses of fish for the dogs. He said that a few years ago, early in May, the fisherman down below here had raised a net with 984 pounds of fish in it. There were 98 head, as Ike says, all buffalo. The total taken from the nets that one day was over 3,000 pounds. . . .

These warm, sunny days we get into the odd corners of the boat, and there are many of them, and clean them out with Dutch thoroughness. Yesterday Anna washed woolens. I find time to work in the garden each day, breaking up ground. We have time enough for all our activities, including painting. The little cabin is my studio.

Again the ground was prepared, the crops tended, by hand labor. We ate our bread in the sweat of our brows, entirely happy with our choice, and thankful to be free from that voluntary slavery which most accept in order to earn a living. . . . Here again we were earning our living in the most delightful and interesting way we could imagine.

April 24 Full summer today. Locust in bloom over the boat. Song of chat and thrush.

May 4 Yesterday we cast off from our anchorage, but did not drift far, tying up about 200 yards below. The mud got to be too much for us, with the swiftly falling river getting down over the bank. This place is in deep water, with the current flowing by, against a very steep bank which was formed by small stones and clay from quarrying operations above. It is as steep as a bank could be, rising from the water to a level strip perhaps 30 feet above. A few trees still remain on the bank. I cut some notches for a toe hold and now we are out of the mud. . . . It is strange to us, having come here in high water and we look to see what shores will be revealed to us, to what levels the river will fall.

We are catching more fish than we can eat.

May 5 We cooked the turtles today. They were small, soft shelled ones, looking like rubber toys. A gift from Ike. We boiled them first, then picked out the meat. Found it very good with no fishy taste.

May 6 More new flowers blooming in the woods, one we call Shooting Star. A spray of vertical red flowers, the tip of each one opening into a yellow five-pointed star. We have seen two wisteria vines blooming in the woods.

May 8 A new boat came down the river today, the *Scott Chotin*, fresh from the shipyards at Nashville. A fine looking craft. It made a tremendous wave, but our boats rode it out. However, due to my carelessness we lost our aluminum dog pan. Add this to the list of things I have lost lately, the minnow box, a washrag I poured out the drain. I suppose the river takes about as much as it brings us. . . . Late in the afternoon, another boat passed, a far contrast from the modern powerful *Chotin*—it was the *Stanley Petter*, a home made sternwheeler, popping along up the river.

May 16 This is a rainy moon, say the old timers. The river is muddy, a little higher, with some driftwood moving on a faster current, but so far there is no sign of a runout. A long quiet day for us, some reading, playing, woodblock printing. The cotton from the trees covers the floating drift like a light snow.

May 17 We are enjoying our lettuce now, and the first salad of garden greens—spinach, little beets and carrots. . . . Ike came by with a 15 pound catfish, dead, having strangled itself on the line. I made steaks of it, and Ike took half. We found the meat as mild and tender as in the small fish.

May 19 Yesterday we made a trip to Smithland with Walter Berry in his outboard. We were struck by the change in season.

When we came up here first of April, the trees were nearly bare, wintry looking to think of now. Now it is full summer. . . . The glimpses we had of the long reaches on the Ohio stirred us deeply.

May 20   This morning we moved back up the river to our old stand. I began cordelling the boat up along the shore, but Ike Jones, who was passing, offered to tow us up. . . . Heard a chuck-will's-widow this evening in the distance, and soon after, a whip-poor-will.

May 22   These are great days. The summer weather is not too hot or dry. The earth is unbelievably green. . . .

Today Uncle Jim was here with his mule, Kate, discing. He was down yesterday for a visit. He said he heard that I played the violin and asked to see my instrument. Anna and I played a little piece or two. Found out that Uncle Jim was an old time fiddler, and after gradually working into it, played us some of the old dances—*Arkansas Traveller, Soldier's Joy, Eighth of January*. It would have been difficult to connect Old Jim with a violin, his rough clothes, and scrubby appearance, yet he tucked it under his chin naturally enough, and played with freedom and command. He remarked about the pictures in the cabin, asking Anna if she was the painter. Most everyone takes that for granted. Uncle Jim is a mild, gentle person, with a trace of an artist's sensitivity in him.

When we went down to the quarry this evening for mail and water, we talked to John Whorton, and he surprised us by telling about the violin he had made. He is an old time fiddler, too.

May 26   At last there came a day when all conditions could be met, and we washed clothes.

June 1   We have now turned the boat parallel to the bank, the main deck upstream so we can enjoy the long reach in that direction when we have dinner out there.

A guest for dinner today, Ike Jones, who is preparing to leave for his summer work at shelling. Anna got up a splendid dinner. . . . He was an admirable guest, arriving in his outboard at 11 o'clock, in neat, clean work clothes. Shelled the peas for dinner. His talk was worth listening to, and he made no demands. . . .

Some gardening each day, quite a lot yesterday, but time for our reading and playing almost every day, as well as some work in the studio.

We had visitors on Sunday. Kenneth Whorton came up with his guitar, and we attempted to play with him. Old Jim dropped in, and the two of them played together—"hillbilly music," Kenneth said. . . .

Mrs. Whorton gave us a sack of lettuce when we told her that the groundhog had eaten all of ours.

June 2 I sit up here atop the shed roof, from which point I can overlook the garden and see the groundhog on his daily raid, I hope. A chat is surprised and I watch a spotted brown lizard, with a long tail, a tiny dinosaur. So far we have not been able to stop the groundhog, and we consider drastic measures. Have some of Ellis's steel traps set now, and we talk of a gun. What would gardening be like if there were no varmints or insects or plant diseases? Sometimes I consider abandoning the weak and tender crops that need so much care, and planting only wild and tough things like purslane, poke, sunflowers and ground nuts.

June 3 A day full of happenings. The bird which has been sitting on the nest in the corner of the cabin was out picking up worms. Looking in the nest, I saw the mouth of at least one little bird, the beginning of a carolina wren. . . .

Anna ironed both morning and afternoon, a tough job, with the stove burning at full speed. Yet the cabin was not too uncomfortable.

A fine dinner on deck, of smoked fish, noodles, and poke, which is a choice vegetable. If grown in a garden with cultivation and spraying, it would be esteemed highly. We enjoy at its best the view up the river.

Another event today was the capture of a groundhog. I saw it, early in the afternoon, come out of the garden, and after taking a good look at me, enter a hole in the stone wall. I dug out the burrow, tearing down the wall, but found nothing at the end. I abandoned the hunt, but Skipper kept at it and she grew excited over it. Going back I found she had trapped the animal in the burrow. . . . Between us we captured the animal and are cooking it, though the natives won't eat old ones, considering only young cornfed ones to be good.

Also today I looked into the beehive. Found many more bees than before, and both sections occupied by brood, some new honey, capped over partly. A few queen cells which I did not destroy. Much brood about ready to hatch out, but few larvae. Are they ready for swarming?

June 4   Another chore that I worked at yesterday was grinding flour and meal, working on deck. Whole wheat and soy flour, white cornmeal, dog cornmeal, minnow bait, breakfast cereal. . . .

> *Our landing and our boat attracted nearly everyone who lived on the bluff. . . . We often heard voices in the woods above and made hasty preparations to receive visitors. . . . Because of this intimacy with the people who lived about us, we felt no longer that we were drifters, but settled residents.*

June 7   We were visited yesterday by Ernest Joiner, out squirrel hunting. He is the true habitant of this place but seems to take kindly to our residence here. He showed me the location of a spring down the shore.

June 11   Uncle Jim Joiner has been down here today and yesterday with his mule Kate, working the ground, getting it ready to plant corn in. He had dinner with us each day. We enjoyed his company and conversation, and he had a good time and good dinner, surely.

June 13   We cook and eat breakfast on shore these days. Have planted and transplanted flowers there, made paths, a cooling well, fireplace. Keep plunder out of sight, so the shore is quite nice.

June 14   Each day has its novelty. Today we worked and ate supper on the bank in the twilight. We were pleased to find not a mosquito. Today also, a new salad, made of ground fresh beets and a new kind of rice cakes, made with cold rice flour and elderberry blossoms.

June 16   Yesterday we shipped our instruments to the Howards' and played trios.

June 18 All sorts of company lately. Yesterday evening the Howards, Ray, Lucille, she calls herself Lucel, and Phil. Today Uncle Jim Joiner ate dinner with us, for he was working in his field. In the afternoon Walter Berry brought his guests down this way, Mr. and Mrs. Harvey Broome, Knoxville. . . . Uncle Jim used a nice word today, "play-pretty," meaning toy. We enjoyed his company as usual and Anna had a splendid dinner—fried fish, fiddlers and carp, new potatoes, new beets and greens, fresh light rolls, canned pears.

June 19 Supper on shore this evening, begun in the twilight. As we sat there, the darkness came in, the light of the moon and the stars appeared. Swarms of willow flies left their branches and blew over the water.

June 20 Yesterday we went down to the Howards' in the afternoon and played for two hours. As I walked with Anna up their walk, carrying our instruments, and expected and welcomed, I thought of the short time it was since I came here a stranger, keeping out of the way of people, as an intruder.

June 24 We are eating groundhog today. Skipper detected one in the stone wall, and I moved enough stones away to get at it—a young one, half grown, and delicious to eat.

June 26 Yesterday the first corn from the garden, Golden Bantam. And in the evening I heard the first katydid, a solitary one which we heard this evening. Blackberry picking again, along the fence rows across the river. Shortcake for supper and a bucketful for the Howards.

June 29 On Sunday, about dark, W. Berry took us up to his place, to sit around the campfire, and talk with his friends.

June 30 I had picked blackberries in the morning, 11 quarts, which we canned in the afternoon, the first batch of the season. The blackberry season is a month ahead of last year's at Payne Hollow. . . . We went up to the Mitchells' to begin Martha Ann's picture. A rain while there. We were invited to supper, and returned to the boat about dark, with milk, eggs, some native pecans and a few old magazines. They are generous, hospitable people.

July 2 Canning every day lately. Beans and beets today, blackberries yesterday, probably tomorrow. The nights are cool, 56° Thursday morning, Mr. Howard said. During the day the sun burns with a heat we are not used to.

July 5 These are hot days, even when cloudy. Yet we picked blackberries this morning, along the fence rows across the river, also bringing in some passable apples. Canned the berries this afternoon. On days between canning I pick all we can eat.

July 7 Blackberry picking again this morning, alone this time, up on the hill. . . . Beside the berries, which we canned this afternoon, I brought down the hill about 1/3 bushel of plums, from the tree by the back door of the old Joiner place. . . . The plums are beautiful, airy globes of color from yellow to a purple red, plum color. I climb up among the tough branches to pick some of the fruit, and was minded of a Christmas tree decorated with colored balls.

July 10 It might be safe to record the fact that our life here is running smoothly, at present.

July 17 On Wednesday last week we played sonatas, violin, at the Howards' and a joy it was. . . .

All crops are growing well. River is at a higher stage, some drift and current, water opaque.

Uncle Jim's country speech is very descriptive. He told T. Mitchell that he had a bush field that made steamboat men of 3 of his boys.

July 19 I looked eastward up the river when the sun was setting. There suddenly the nearly full moon had appeared through the heavy clouds whose tops caught the red glare of the sun. On another day recently, the setting sun shone through the western clouds, lighting up the river and hills at the end of the long reach, though the nearer shores were in dark shadow.

July 22 Last night we were wakened by a sound we have not heard for a long time. I looked out in the moonlight, and saw a steamboat going up the river. Not a towboat, evidently a small excursion steamer. We tossed on its swells for a long time.

Caught yesterday morning our largest blue cat, eight pounds.

August 1 Here we were as comfortable as one could be. Nights and mornings have been delightful. We swam often, and had shady places on the bank for different positions of the sun. We are particularly grateful for the maple near the boat. It is bushy higher up, but no branches close to the ground. It shades the top of the bank in the middle part of the day, and we seldom feel the heat there.

August 4 I helped make hay at Ted Mitchell's, working all day, and intended to do so today. I mind it so, giving up a day, but always find it worthwhile, if only to test myself by working with others. At the end, I felt that I had had an easier day than usual. . . .

It is a joy to see green locust trees all summer.

August 8 We have an abundance of apples. I pick them off the ground, mostly, at the old orchard across the river.

August 23 The hottest weather of the season. Air and water without motion, sun very hot, the locusts sound from sunrise to dark. Ground very dry, our garden withering.

August 27 Caught a young groundhog today, in the river. It was swimming across when I saw it. Pretty tired, it lay in the boat, panting, after I had dipped it out.

August 30 A feeling of autumn in the storm which came in at sundown from the east. This morning I crossed the river, walked back through the shorn fields to the old orchard. Made two trips to the boat, carrying a sack of apples each time. Good shantyboat fruit.

September 4 On September 1 I helped E. Lytton get in his hay, in the afternoon, 4 or 5 loads of lespedeza. That morning we played trios at the Howards', again this morning. Wherever I go, someone quotes Jim Joiner. About elections, he had remarked to Ellis, "No matter who is elected, all we will have is beans and overalls." The haying was pleasant, working on the little hilltop farm, with mules and by hand.

September 5 We were awakened this morning at first daybreak by a familiar, expected sound, the squealing of puppies. Skipper had her seventh litter, of five, on deck, with no mishaps. Unexpectedly there were two brown ones, two black ones, and the fifth almost white with the traditional Skipper markings.

September 11 A trip to Paducah, with all the country people on this Saturday. . . . The river is stirred up a little, and its color shows at its mouth. The Ohio is very clear, the Tennessee a shade

229

less so. . . . Great Blue Herons in the river again. We hear them squawking at night. A few egrets.

On September 7, we caught the largest catfish yet, a blue cat, perhaps 15 pounds. Gave most of it to Walter Berry the same day, to share with his guests.

That day, Anna's birthday, rainy off and on, we had a picnic dinner up at the cabin. A delightful experience.

September 16   These days we prepare for winter and for our voyage.

September 26   Visitors yesterday evening, just as it was getting dark. Ellis and Bethel Lytton, their three children, of whom Pauline is a gem, and Marjorie and Kenneth Mitchell. We were just about to eat supper before the fire. We popped corn for all. . . . The Mitchells invited us over there for dinner one day. We did some playing and reading, talking. I dipped up a groundhog which was swimming across the river and it made one dinner for us. W. Berry happened along, and helped us eat it. Another day we had a chicken, given us by the Mitchells.

September 28   An autumn rain, from the NE, beginning at day-break. Now we realize that the season is changing. . . . We make a mat, of rope yarn, after Walter Berry. A little painting in the cabin on the hillside.

September 30   A left handed day, with Anna lying in bed for the first time in these five years.

October 1   I walked eastward along the foot of the bluff. An autumn landscape now, but I am surprised at the greenness of the trees. I found no persimmons up that way. Those I brought in from the hilltop on Monday were the finest we ever had. Anna puts them through a sieve to remove seeds and skin. Then we sprinkle walnuts on them, eat with cream.

October 5   We still bathe in the river daily.

October 6   Late this afternoon I climbed the hill. . . . A thin new moon lighted me down the hill. The trees let in more light now. Two katydids answered back and forth and I thought of the tremendous antiphonal choir of the summer nights.

October 21   A small flock of geese, perhaps 15 or 20, was hereabouts yesterday and this morning. . . . The country is getting down to its winter birds now.

October 24 The colors of autumn at their best now. I have been digging peanuts, which have turned out well. Today the Howards took us for a drive, north. . . . It was strange to see the Ohio river, now blue, with extensive sandbars out, at a place we drifted by in the spring.

October 25 Yesterday, on a lonely place along the road, we saw a platform on piles, in a grove covered with withered branches of trees. Underneath, a rudely made pulpit and benches. We were told that there had been a "brush meeting" there.

October 29 We have excellent greens now, a mess of turnip greens, poke, wild beet, narrow dock and swiss chard. Wednesday we saw in Ike's boat a yellow cat which he estimated at 55 pounds. Looking into his mouth one could understand the story of Jonah.

October 31 A steady, windless rain began last night and continued this morning. In the afternoon a light suddenly appeared low in the western sky and the rain clouds were rolled back eastward like a curtain, revealing the blue sky and fair weather clouds which were above it all the time.

Visitors yesterday afternoon, the ladies from on the ridge down in the bottoms for pumpkins for their Halloween party. They invited us.

November 3 Possum for dinner today, given to us alive by W. Berry. He and Earl Champion caught 3 the other evening. . . . Busy yesterday and today loading and preparing to leave.

November 5 We worked all yesterday digging carrots, parsnips, turnips, loading all our plunder, pumpkins, sweet potatoes, honey, a hive section with 8 filled frames. . . . We considered leaving yesterday but remained at our anchorage on account of the wind. By this morning the wind had ceased, though the rain fell copiously. So we decided to cast off, thinking that clearing weather would bring wind. Last chores—picking greens and broccoli, parsley and lettuce. We regret leaving our garden even now.

About 8:30 we cast loose, blowing two blasts from our horn as we entered the stream. A slight current, but I rowed with the new sweeps. Down the left shore, tying up at the Champions'. A joy to be under way again.

November 8 We left the Barrett Quarry landing at sunrise. We had laid there the past two days visiting our friends and entertaining them on board, almost constantly. It was good to put all that around the bend. . . .

We felt like a flatboat which had drifted down from the mountains, dogs barking, myself cracking walnuts on deck, a groundhog skin tacked on the cabin, corn and pumpkins stowed away on the roof.

We approached the bridge and closed behind the bend our last view up the Cumberland. It seems as far back as the time we spent there. It is difficult to believe that all the people we became acquainted with, even knew somewhat intimately, still exist there.

It was with regret that we saw these good people for the last time. . . . Next morning, before anyone was up to see us, we were gone. The current was slower now. . . . We could not imagine that this slow movement was the beginning of the longest and fastest voyage we were to make.

8

To the River's Mouth

The Ohio was a wide river for the remaining course of twenty-tree miles to its mouth. Its width appeared even greater because of the low shores. The moon rose as out of the ocean.

November 11, 1948 We worked by starlight preparing to leave, and drifted out of the Cumberland, and past Smithland before sunrise. The Ohio's current in the chute was swift. Looking back, the view was impressive. The Cumberland, with its hills as a background, seemed the main river.

We passed outside the towhead below the island and then pulled to the Kentucky shore, for a wind sprung up from the SW, which was quartering, ahead and offshore. Rowing more or less steadily all morning, but good drifting. I put the mule overboard, found time for some work on the gear. Anna wrote a letter. But our attention was on the river and our progress.

We were surprised to find the water of the Tennessee clear with no current. A light wind was blowing out into the Ohio, so even with hard pulling we could not make it inside of the island. Landed in swift current which was flowing into the Ohio against a rocky revetment. Decided to try to pull around the head of the island. Made it in three hitches, the current decreasing then flowing the other way. When we expected to drift away we ran on a submerged rock, but managed to shove off, and had a fine trip down the narrow channel.

The mainland was lined with fleets of barges and oil docks. . . . Drifting past the Walker Boat Yard we finally tied up to their fleet, after talking with the owners. Our berth was next to the *J. S. McKee*, McKee Button Co., Muscatine, Iowa, with a barge ahead of us.

November 13 Paducah. A stiff west wind this morning kept us in port. We were ready to sail, having spent yesterday taking in supplies. Yesterday was a good day for drifting, with a downstream breeze and good current. . . .

Eel for dinner again, the second of three given us by a fisherman at Smithland. I saw him tracing his line, knocking the eels against the side of his boat. I yelled to him, and he said, come out and get them. . . .

A bright moon tonight, still, with a mist on the water. We intend to shove off early tomorrow.

I still have in mind the view down the river street at Smithland, the other evening after sunset. A November evening, the huge bare trees on one side of the unpaved street, the old brick houses on the other side, facing the river.

November 14 We cast off our lines at daybreak. . . . A light breeze from the south carried us out into the river, and we drifted slowly down, the breeze helping a little in that direction. We rowed and ate breakfast by turns, as the sun rose. . . .

November 15 We left our anchorage at dawn and were in the lock at Dam 52 at sunrise. We went through the lock neatly, rowing up to the guide wall with the sweeps, and towing out to the end of the lower guide wall. . . .

We were surprised to find here as well, as much of the shores below, not open fields but thick woods. Close in to shore when we drifted by Fort Massac and Metropolis. Several large tows up and down. Under the bridge without touching an oar, ideal drifting, with a good current and a fair, windless day. . . . Landed early in the afternoon at the gauge at mile 950, talked with some rivermen and decided to go on below to reach a bayou for a harbor, as they informed us we could get in some below Joppa. Steady rowing now, to keep off shore. . . . After drifting past several creeks we could not enter, we tied up at sunset at Hillerman Landing. It became cloudy, and in the night we heard rain.

November 16 The morning was dark and rainy, light wind from SE. We decided to cast off, to reach a harbor, at least, for our location here was exposed. It took steady rowing to keep offshore. We landed on shore across from Sharp's Bar to rest. . . .

We had landed not far above Post Creek Cutoff, and after shoving off, failed to clear the bar and were carried into shallow water by the wind and current. Mid morning perhaps. After working till almost noon, with poles and anchor, even wading in the water and shoving, we could not move the boat.

If a tow had passed, its waves would have lifted us. One did go by, the *National*—a boat we liked because it made no waves. After dinner we got out block and tackle, but the boat was fast aground. The river had fallen slightly, so we gave up and rested and did other things.

Late in the afternoon rain, mist and wind, now south, continuing, the river rose to cover our marks and we made another try, this time successful. We pulled out into deep water, where we had set our anchor. It was dark now, wind had suddenly shifted to west, with a violent rain storm. I got a line, a long one made of several pieces, to a snag on the bar, and with this we pulled into the creek mouth, slacking off on the anchor line at the same time. Retrieved anchor, made all snug and shipshape. Fire, supper and rest.

November 17 Post Creek Cutoff. The fairest of mornings, unbelievable after the rain and mist and east wind of yesterday. . . .

We decided to leave our harbor after dinner not sure of a sufficient depth of water, for the river seemed to be falling slightly. We moved out of the creek carefully, to avoid the gravel bar on the lower side. I took the anchor out into deep water above the creek mouth and as we pulled out we slacked off on the other line, which ran to a snag. Good drifting, but a light breeze from the south made it necessary to row against it.

Passed two boats coming up neck and neck, *National* and *Casablanca*. The channel is narrow, for this is Grand Chain. Dam

53 lowered, gage 15.9. They were apparently ready to raise the dam. We ran aways below the first light. This was an oil lamp, a rarity down here, I believe. Our anchorage was against a steep wooded bank, in deep water, for we must be ready for a drop if the dam is raised.

Not a sign of human life near the boat. The moon, full yesterday, rose as out of the ocean.

November 18 In the night we saw white clouds sailing fast from the west. . . . After some hesitation we shoved off, rowing to keep offshore, eating breakfast by turns. Passed a fishing village, New Caledonia, and what might have been a large mine. Close up to America Point, mile 968, the wind freshened and shifted to a point ahead of us, and at the same time rain. We dropped anchor off a gravel bar, in 6 feet of water, to ride out the squall. . . .

I haul in the fishbox, dress the two remaining carp, and put the last eel in a minnow bucket. Then I take the fishbox on shore, leave it there, with some regret. But it has been troublesome. One of our trials when drifting is the heavy fishbox, which is almost as much as one man can tow and which is always in the way.

The Paducah floating fish market and store passed down, towed by a little sternwheeler.

The dogs were on shore several hours, and I found a cornfield, not a good one, but got a sack of dog corn.

November 19 A violent storm last night, rain and wind, which blew across the river. . . . Luckily for us, the river is narrower here, and the waves were not high, though the boat was tossed and swung about, being held only by the anchor. Yet we slept most of the night, and at daybreak the wind shifted more to the south. Great combers running in midstream, but we are protected from their direct force by America Point, below us. This afternoon is dark, heavy clouds rolling across the sky.

November 20 America Point. Wind still blows, 48 hours now, and more from west. The sky cleared at sunrise. River rising, for 24 hours now, up to drift left by previous rise. . . .

We are busy with jobs saved for a layover, baking, cutting hair, sewing shoes, and the like. Today the last of the Cumberland River fish.

November 21   A fair, quiet morning. Cold, with some slivers of ice on the waterbucket on deck. We gauge our time by the light of the morning star, and prepare for departure.

Well down on America Point at sunrise, 6:39 a.m. Bar under water now, river still rising. What a windy place this was the past two days.

On the run to Mound City, we pull out and drift between the thrashing buoys, a narrow channel. We intend to land below the marine ways for drinking water. A man in a long low motor scow comes alongside, and after some conversation, we accept his offer of a tow into Cache river, below the town, where we had planned to tie up. His tow up beyond the mouth saved us a hard pull on the lines. . . .

We are tied on the right, a narrow neck of land like Livingston Point. An early dinner, much enjoyed, of baked sweet potatoes and blackeyed peas.

November 22   We are busy at various harbor chores. Yesterday, while being towed that short distance, we saw a strange duck on shore, large as a barnyard duck, slowly walking along shore. He had a white head and yellow feet. Anna identified it as a blue goose, a bird which migrates along the Mississippi river.

Removed the window screens, rolled them up and stowed them away. Where will we be when it is time to put them up again?

After dinner, I walk down the track, with the dogs, about a mile. Climbing over the levee, I am struck by the change of scenery, from the desert-like, uninhabited, except for a few driftwood shanties, river bank, to the cultivated, peopled land beyond the levee. It is almost like going indoors. I buy a cabbage and milk at a country store, pick up a gallon of soybeans from the edge of a field where they are combining, cut some choice greens. It is good to get back to the river again.

November 23   We made a washday of this, not the best, but no rain at least. Now, at dark, the clothes are all inside, some put away and the damp ones hanging about. Yet we are quite pleased, for it is a difficult and hazardous job. We do enjoy it, and are proud of our system. Now the line is taken down, all the gear stowed away on the roof until some unknown time and place when we will wash again. A splendid area for drying clothes, here on the point of land between the Ohio and the Cache, high up and open and level, with a wide view of the Ohio.

November 25 Thanksgiving Day. Cache river. We were ready to leave today but a high wind has been blowing from the south, last night and all day, and this night promises to be windier. We are thankful for our haven. . . .

To mark the holiday, Anna baked a magnificent sweet potato pie. A pleasant sunny day, and while Anna was busy all morning, I worked at various projects, firewood, a Christmas woodblock, putting my tools in order. . . . We tuned our instruments, the first time since leaving Bizzle's Bluff, I think, and it was good to play some 16th century music.

In the evening, as Anna was preparing supper, our neighbors from the boat above came to visit us, Bud and Flossie Helms, and two of their three children. She seems out of her element on a boat, but he is thoroughly shantyboat.

November 26 Threatening weather. After some hesitation and waiting, we cast loose and pulled out of Cache river late in the morning, with some doubts as we left the snug harbor. . . . The mule towed us along and kept us close to shore. Passed under the bridge and by the car terminal. Landed on riprap shore between inclines and Coast Guard landing, probably where a wharfboat once was.

We could see, in the misty weather, Cairo Point and the Missouri shore. An explorer coming down the river, from here would never suspect that this river would empty into a larger one, for there is no indication of it. . . . This is Mile 979 and the Mississippi is a little more than two miles farther.

November 27 Cairo. Up the bank in the morning, and again after a quick lunch, hunting for stores in the strange city, for we had various needs, line, groceries, some clothing, hip boots, post office. A list of our purchases would be a strange mixture. We bought mounts for our Christmas cards at a printing shop, finding just what we wanted, cut to size by an obliging old fellow, not at all busy this Saturday afternoon. The line we bought at a harness-maker named Oehler, who had nearly everything a farmer would want. Even had a machete, but I selected a corn knife at less than half the price, as a more suitable implement. Also bought an 8 x 10 tarpaulin, mainly to use as a wind and rain protection on our main deck. Bought a blue wool cap for me, oilcloth for cushion covers and experimental rain catchers and many items too numerous to mention, all of which have a use and place to be stowed away. We liked Cairo.

November 28 A tumult of waters tonight, waves breaking on this rocky shore, water gurgling about the boat. A November gale from the NE, driving a cold, fine rain through the air. It does not blow as hard now as it did through the day, when the waves, dashing against the side of the boat, splashed the windows, and came up through the drains. I pumped out, using a bilge pump for the first time in more than a year.

Anna was within all day except to the cupboard on deck, and I made but two excursions for water at the taxi stand. We kept a good fire burning all day, fishing likely pieces of wood out of the drift in our lee. It is surprising how well it burns. Pancakes for breakfast, a noble stew for dinner.

We take down the Ohio river charts, post the first ones of the Mississippi.

November 29 A quiet, starry night, cold enough to freeze. Again the unbelievable contrast, such a stormy night last night was. Wind from NE increased, tossed and jolted us about, driving the fine rain, even some snow. We were awake for a spell. I had to bail out the johnboat, shove driftwood away from the boat. Then the wind decreased and we slept again. This morning was clear and cool, only a breath left of the wind.

I made a trip to the post office early, and was busy about the boat, arranging and stowing. After an early dinner, we made a final trip uptown, carried down enough water to fill all jars and buckets, and cast off in mid-afternoon.

We floated past the unimpressive, almost unseen town. River bulletin said 23.75 feet, rising. Considerable drift. We stayed close in, past the Barrett landing, the Big Four incline and tied up below that, above the bridge. Several shantyboats, beached among the cottonwoods, now afloat. We watch traffic on the bridge, and the lights of boats at Cairo Point.

November 30 A great day in our travelling, for we entered the Mississippi river. After a cold night at Cottonwood, between the Big Four Incline and the highway bridge, we were up in the gray dawn. Made all shipshape, had breakfast, and shoved off before the sun cleared the bridge. The Ohio still rising. The point, Cairo Point, is a busy harbor for barges. We drifted close by them, and out into the Mississippi.

A fine view up, under the bridge. At first there seemed to be no more current. When we began to drift down, we pulled toward Missouri and then we felt the Mississippi's current. It seemed to us about as fast as the Ohio's at flood.

Wickliffe, Kentucky, on a hill, was attractive, but we could see little in the morning mist, against the sun. The day was warm and clear, no wind. A light upstream breeze, we set the sail.

Looking up from my work, whatever it was, I saw a large bird in a tree which we identified as a bald eagle. Saw another later. Ducks and geese, a blue heron or two.

We are thrilled by the river. I had thought that the lower Ohio would prepare us for it, but the Mississippi is a different river, a new experience for us.

> *We shot out into the Mississippi River, a large chunk in the long line of drift pouring out of the Ohio. . . . The Ohio did not end, nor did the Mississippi, at first, seem to be different. It was all water merging and making its way down to the sea, carrying us along with it. . . . We had a sensation of being in a land new to us.*

240

III

Shantyboat Drifting: The Mississippi

December 1, 1948 – April 15, 1950

9

Wild River

This river was not the familiar Ohio. The current had a new force to it, almost a willfulness and driving purpose. A piece of driftwood floating in the swiftest water—for the stream is made up of many currents of different velocity—seemed to move under power, as if towed in some unknown manner. . . . It has a wildness compared with which the Ohio's flow is a sedate rounding of smooth curves.

December 1, 1948 A nice run through the dredged channel, seeing nothing of the notorious whirlpool at Chalk Bluff. . . . At Island No. 6 we considered going behind, but the strong current carried us into the wind and around the point, just missing a black buoy. The *Commercial Clipper*, upbound, passed us here and we rocked in its waves a long time, a bad stretch, very narrow, the waves breaking on a reef extending from the Kentucky shore.

We had glimpses of Hickman on our way by, and it was the most attractive town we have seen in a long time. On a sharp bend, with a bluff behind, which was spotted with houses. Apparently two ferries, one from the town, another from a landing below, and opposite the Missouri landing they both used, below the Island. A houseboat or two, fish docks, a block of square brick buildings surrounded by a floodwall.

December 3 We had a splendid run yesterday. . . . The sandy shores of the Mississippi remind me more of ocean than river. . . .

After some investigation and an inspection of us by a man who had a cabin in the woods, we pulled down the chute a ways and tied up. Dark now, and we were very hungry. Had drifted 25 miles. . . . After supper we were surprised by a visit from the man and his wife. He fishes in summer, has a launch and johnboat. Their new cabin was built on a raft of cypress logs, to float in high water. Said they rode out the '37 flood that way in this location. Leonard and Ethel Haycraft. She pronounced it Hycraft. She seemed to be a shantyboater, a native of the Cumberland.

December 4 Yesterday we lay at the head of the chute of Morrison TH. Visited the Haycrafts in the afternoon. A fair, still day after the thick morning. We saw large flocks of grackles. This morning at sunrise we cast off and drifted down the chute, eating breakfast on the way. Anchored offshore, above New Madrid. The Haycrafts came along, bound for town, so we towed after them and they showed us the town. We liked the place, mailed two letters, bought some fresh milk, got a bucket of water.

December 7 Beautiful shores, banks of willow and cottonwood and miles of sandbar gleaming in the sun. The last view of Kentucky.

December 8 Very quiet now, after the tumult of yesterday evening. . . . Just as we approached Reelfoot Point, where we had been told was a dangerous whirlpool, as we were pulling to the right bank to stay away from it, a wind sprang up from N, directly offshore. We made it past the eddy, which seemed nothing to be alarmed about. A bad bend, though, and the towboat *Jimmy Cone* had to wiggle to get through. Wind increased below, and we gradually neared the lee shore in spite of our steady pulling. We sighted this cove and pulled into it. We could not have gone 100 yards farther. We were alarmed, picturing ourselves in this open shore in a gale. Got the anchor out, pulled *Driftwood* offshore. To our relief the wind abated, the night was calm. . . .

After the wind of last evening it is very calm this morning but we lay in our little harbor, resting and catching up on our chores. This is one of them. Anna is baking bread. I cut wood and had a walk on shore. . . . A cold day, mostly cloudy, with a wind from N. of E. It bothered us not at all.

December 9 Devilsticker Cove. Second day. . . . We printed the first of the 1948 woodblocks today. A short walk together after sunset. This could be the shore of a desert island. In the miles of river we see not a mark of man, except the navigation lights.

December 11 A long reach E of S past Cottonwood Point. Looking down, the low shores faded into the sky. It seemed that we might be reaching the sea. . . .

We passed the Missouri-Arkansas state line. Trying for a landing on a beach on the upper end of the island, dropped the anchor. The current had seemed slow there, but it was like a millrace, when we were held against it. After this bad judgement on my part, I handled myself and the lines so awkwardly that we were close to disaster. As it was, *Driftwood* must be sent adrift, and I raised the anchor from the johnboat, difficult and hazardous in that current. Farther down we pulled into the island shore again and after sunset tied up against a ledge of willow switches. Deep water and a sand beach behind the willows. . . . A comfortable evening and night but in bed we heard the wind and waves. . . .

We printed Christmas woodblocks after dinner. Walking down the shore I found among the willows a cedar about 4 feet high. First one we have seen since leaving the Ohio, perhaps the Cumberland. We went back and dug it up, put it in a bucket, for our Christmas tree.

December 12 Last night was mostly windy, and all morning. Two nights and a day and a half of it. Yet we were not bothered by it, enjoyed our short span of living on Island 21. . . .

We will always remember the view up towards Island 21 and the towhead below it, sun breaking through the clouds above.

December 13 Obion river. A warm, close day. Mostly sunny, though. Our neighbor is Ted Leaman of Monterey, California. He built a boat, a jerry-built 8 x 20 affair, light, with canvas sides, at Bismarck, North Dakota. Came down the Missouri and the Mississippi as far as Cottonwood Point, where he landed in October 1946. That was 2 or 3 months before we left Brent.

December 17 Obion river for 4 days and 5 nights. This morning we drifted out about sunrise, a clear, cool morning, the full moon still in the sky. Said farewell to Ted Leaman, who, I think, longed to go out too. . . .

Two of the Burrows boys were on board our boat one evening. There are 8 boys, 1 girl in the family. Mr. Burrows tends 18 lights, upriver one day, down the next. 3rd day the lights take care of themselves.

A fine sail along the sandy shore, but soon the Arkansas shore was in our lee, and more pulling was necessary. We weathered that point and pulled to the bank at the head of Island 26 at noon. Dinner, dogs ashore, firewood, and under way, all hands pulling offshore. The sand bar stretched for miles, gradually turning off from the wind, until we were sailing with the wind astern. . . . We opened a long reach past Ashport, Tennessee. The wind could have a sweep of 17 miles. Now it was blowing easily downstream and we made fast time. *Driftwood* required no handling, we caught up on our chores, got our Christmas mail ready, watched the shores go by. . . . Darkness fell and the navigation lights gleamed. Hunting for the chute of Island 30 we coasted the sandbars, and were finally in swift water in a narrow channel. Tied up the boat, walked down the beach, hailed a light on the other side of the channel. A man came to the top of the bank with a lantern, said it was alright to come in. So we drifted in to where he still stood with his light and, with his help moored our boat against a steep wet bank, astern of his gas boat. Swift current. The man visited us later. 30 miles today.

December 18   Some conversation with the owner of the island, who made us welcome. In his younger days he was a log-rafter, hand rafter, I believe he said, on the Mississippi. I asked if he ever had any trouble. He said he always managed to make his landing, "by sheer luck." His eyes lighted up when he saw our rig. Then he at once took hold of himself, said we should have some power. . . .

After Anna finished the cards, we walked to town to mail them, buy a little fresh food. Dreary weather, a perfect time to see the flat cotton fields, negro houses, poor whites among them, the tawdry tinsel of Christmas. Almost a 5 mile walk.

246

December 19 Talked with the man who lived in the boat near which we were yesterday, at the upper end of Osceola. He turned out to be the man who operated the Coney Island-Brent ferry in 1944, the year that J. Laughead was in the navy. He built, or rebuilt, a houseboat above Detisches' that summer, and left for down river just before we came to the river to build our boat. . . .

I was busy all day reorganizing our deckload and the between-deck section. The idea was to rout the mice which we were hearing at night. Found one, which dove overboard, and I made it drown. Later another one jumped out of a can of corn and went overboard, but his fate is unknown. Probably we will hear him tonight. One chore we both had on our hands was to cut the honey from the frames and get it into jars. After all this was done, decks and cabin cleaned up, I walked over the levee to Osceola through the streets returning about dark with water, coal oil and turnip greens. The dogs enjoyed this walk.

December 20 Breakfast while drifting down the chute of Island 30. Rounding Craighead point, a sharp bend, I let *Driftwood* sail too far out and we were unable to pull back into the current. We were blown and carried into the large eddy under First Chickasaw Bluff. After failing to pull out we made a last try and were overhauled by a little diesel pusher with a steel flat loaded with gravel. We had seen it at the lower end of the eddy and supposed that they were in trouble, too. But they said they were waiting to help us. They towed us close in to the Arkansas side and then turned us loose. We had no further trouble. The boat had no name, the men went on their way, strangers.

December 21 Each day we marvel at the beauty of this river.

December 22 Loosahatchie River. As usual after a spell of drifting, we had a busy day in port. . . . Made an acquaintance with neighbors and vicinity. A man named Boggs, his wife and little girl, Beverly, live on a boat above us. A man named Irby, I think, lives on the bank nearby in a tent on stilts, a new combination to me.

December 26 I think this was our coldest morning. . . . A visit from Chester Boggs, his wife, and little girl, Beverly. He is a good natured fellow, and seems capable and lazy. The mother shiftless.

The little girl sharp and dirty. They have lived on the boat only about 3 months, having lived in the ramshackle cabin across the river for the seven years they have been here. They have chickens, cattle, pigs, goats and dogs. Gave us a jug of milk yesterday.

December 31 We pulled out of Loosahatchie river this morning. . . . A short run to Memphis. We pulled in at the tip of Mud Island, on the outside, and tied up. . . . We cast off about noon and had a rough trip down under the bridges. . . . Pulled into the mouth of Nonconnah Creek, unexpectedly. A large, new houseboat here, friendly reception from its owner. Dinner at last. . . . In the evening we called on the Storys, after Martha Ann, age 7, had delivered an invitation. Henry Story and Louise, 4 small children. Their boat, 14 x 45, was built at Walker's, Paducah, a year ago.

> *New Year's Day. . . . The day was a vignette from the past inserted among our present days of constant change, of making new friends and at once leaving them behind, bound for shores we had never seen.*

January 4, 1949 Nonconnah Creek, below Memphis, in Tennessee chute, since December 31st. . . . Social life in this creek mouth, with the Storys and Sloans for neighbors. A fine day today. A little of many things, painting, some good playing, then tinkering about. Two saws to file for Henry Story. "Are you a hand-saw man?" he called.

January 7 Today we continued our voyage down the river after laying over in the Memphis district December 22 to January 7, 16 days. We cast off at Nonconnah Creek before sunrise. . . . We felt again the power of the current, as it carried us from one side to another. . . .

We learned much of the Story family, visiting them by invitation, again last night. Henry seems to have come from Joppa, on the river all his life. Peggy said his mother said he was "born in a johnboat with the catfish." Louise came from Metropolis, or was it the other way? Both were married before. They have four children now, from 2 months to 7 years, and other children by their first marriages. Henry is the father of 16, Louise the mother of 14. Henry, age 60, according to Peggy, is a grandfather. Louise, from the same source, is 40. Henry is a handsome fellow, usually appears to be a young man. He has owned several houseboats, never built one himself. Has travelled several times between Memphis, never above or below, always using motorboats to shove his fleet up and down.

January 8   We did not venture out of Cow Island chute. . . .

This place is just what I would expect for the Mississippi. The chute is bordered by a willow forest, the trees straight and tall, with no branches. On the island side the bank is low and flat, and will be covered by the rising river in 2 or 3 days. Eastward is a low ridge of land, narrow, with swamp and slough behind it. Perhaps 1/4 mile farther, a high levee. Beyond some flat, unkempt farming country.

January 9   After breakfast, and some debate about the weather, we ventured out of our harbor. Another day and the land, on the island side of the chute, would be covered. Outside we soon felt a light breeze from S, and it held so all day. Clearing, though, and the afternoon was warm and sunny. We first had a short run to the S, then rounded a bend into a long reach to the S.W., 15 miles. We looked down river, one point after another, lower and fainter as they receded, until the distance was lost in the sky. We could be approaching the edge of the earth, or at least the ocean. . . .

Drifting slowly past the long line of willow forest below the bar on Mhoon bend, Arkansas side, the late afternoon sun shining on the varied ranks of trees, the sound of ducks and geese and little frogs and bluebirds from deep in the swamp. . . . A splendid view of the sunset, and the long bend of the river southward. . . . The warmest day since we left the Cumberland, a mild, fair night. Moonlight and a low star in the SW.

January 10   This morning the bare trees dripped with dew. Up early by starlight, and pulled out of the chute, either Old Walnut bend or Whiskey chute, before breakfast. Light fog on water. At sunrise we were pulling off the revetment at Walnut bend. Some bad eddies. The fog, instead of disappearing, became thicker, though close to the water. Current took us to midstream, and we went through the short Hardin cutoff without seeing the old river. We felt like we were at sea out of sight of land, and when a distant rim of trees showed above the fog we wondered which direction we were going and which way the river would turn below. Current very swift. Luckily, no boats or buoys. When we finally got our bearings, we were much farther down river than we thought we were. . . .

Many cypress trees now and in the warm, springlike morning the song of birds. . . .

The worst boils we have seen at Helena bend, on the inside, a continuous sound of water, like a cataract. On the outside of the bend, a bad reef and eddy.

As we approached Helena, we saw the steam ferry, the big car ferry, and other boats, a steamboat tied up used as a landing boat. It turned out to be our friend the *Wacouta*, still apparently in good shape. A long pull across the slack water at the end of the bar, and we tied up off the town to look for a harbor. About noon now, 20 miles in half a day. We decided to enter the bayou. . . . Another boat here, a little box of a thing. Warm, summer afternoon.

January 15 We walked through the town in the afternoon visiting the barge terminal, library, stores. In the evening when we were about to turn in, our neighbor in the little boat, Gillis, brought his radio over to entertain us. . . . Anna cooked a small possum which the dogs had treed while we were away. Gillis captured it, gave it to us.

January 17 Helena. . . . Swift current in the chute and we are sideways against the bank, which is now a short narrow ridge. I broke an oar early this morning, when I fouled it with the piling across the stream. Yesterday I took over the cabin, framed five pictures. Today made a crate and packed them.

January 18 I thought this morning as I was cutting wood at the foot of the levee, how much I looked like a poor white to the negroes walking along the railroad. Wood is scarce here, compared to the river in most places, but we make out very well. With a little dry wood the green water maple or green ironwood burns well and makes a hot fire.

January 19 We remained in port. . . . We are watched by the trainmen and boat crew, as they go by on the incline, and probably more people than we realize will notice our being gone.

January 20 Cold, clear morning, ice on the water buckets outside. N wind still blew, but not so hard. After breakfast we dropped down the chute. *Pelican* ferryboat came in, we hung on Gillis' boat until the transfer boat had made fast. As we passed, her captain, to whom we had spoken the day we entered, came out of the pilot house with a megaphone, gave us some advice about the river below, the river forecast, and wished us good luck. . . .

We were soon in the Mississippi current. . . . Wind abated, air became warmer, and we had easy drifting. Passed Friar Point, the town unseen from the river, except for a water tank. Had a leisurely dinner while drifting past Kangaroo Point, but must pull offshore at the sharp Old Town bend. A bad eddy at Alderson Upper Light. A point projects, the river piles up against it. We were conscious of the different levels of water. All hands here. We thought we might go down a chute at Island 62, but there was no opening. Above, on the advice of a woodcutter, shouted as we passed, we went down the chute behind Montezuma Towhead. A delightful and exciting trip, saving a bend and a mile or two. . . .

As the sun approached the horizon, we rowed toward Arkansas, came close to going down the old river at Jackson cutoff. We ran down close to the shore, caught on to a snag at the lower end of the cutoff to reconnoiter, finally tying up at sunset against a six-foot caving bank in a little cove. Heavy log drift above and below, but we felt secure.

January 21 Stars shone faintly when we turned in last night, but we awoke early in the night to hear a gentle rain, which continued till daybreak.

Yesterday approaching Modoc Landing and Fair Landing we saw an extensive fleet of Engineer equipment on the Arkansas side, towboats, quarterboats, barges, derricks and various machinery. A barge was being loaded with sand by a steam shovel on the left bank as we passed. As usual the crew stared at us as we passed, pulling at the sweeps. No doubt we are a rare sight these days. . . .

We decided to drop down to the next bend which promised a harbor behind a towhead. Thick weather, light breeze from somewhere SE. Drifted close to Arkansas shore, past the old river, first Jackson then Sunflower cut-off. Almost down to the bend, a motorboat with a cabin crossed over to us, offered to tow us in. This he did, leaving us at the entrance to the chute. We were saved a long row.

January 22 A year ago today we made our last run, out of Blackford's creek, before being frozen in the ice above Grandview. This was an exciting day, though so different. The weather was warm and uncertain, no wind, a glimpse of the sun at midday. After breakfast we cast off, drifting down the narrow chute on a good current. The chute turned left before entering the river which it did at almost a right angle. A bad eddy below the end of the chute, and I could not keep out of it, and *Driftwood* went whirling around with some big logs. One try and we decided we could not pull out. Got out our long, light line, tied it to the top of a springy sycamore which was just in the right place, and with some hard pulling and hitches we got into the regular current, after an hour's delay. We found it effective, following Anna's suggestion, to have a line at each corner. In this way we could pull on one or another as the boat swung and see-saw ourselves ahead. . . .

After about 3 miles of the river, we entered the chute of Cessions Towhead, very wide at this stage and a swift current. As we passed swiftly along the shore, all shutters closed, Anna inside and I on deck pulling off shore, I saw a little earth, perhaps a wheelbarrow full, fall from the bank near a tall cottonwood, one of the largest size. Looking up, I saw it lean toward the river, then fall with a crash about 100 feet astern of us, its top twice as far from shore as we were. A great splash and waves, the current pulled the tree around along the bank. . . .

We were keeping close to the shore so as not to miss the entrance of the chute of Island 69. This was narrow, turning off at less than a right angle, but we made it in fine style. Tied up just below, for dinner, against an abrupt sandbank, with very small willows growing thickly an top. Then the dogs barked and I found they had cornered a possum in a driftpile. Between the three of us the animal was caught, so we will have fresh meat for dinner tomorrow.

After dinner, baked lima beans, stewed tomatoes, cabbage and peanut salad, with orange and coconut for dessert, I explored a little, finding some needed firewood in the big driftwrack which was caught on the sandbar above us. Late in the afternoon we decided to go farther down the chute, hoping to find a better shore. We drifted almost all the way through, nearly carrying away a chimney when I tried unsuccessfully to make a landing at a likely place. We finally pulled into the willows of the mainland above the last bend, where the channel seemed to be divided by an island. The shore was a swampy jungle but it was land, accessible and safe. . . . Today we heard the birds of early spring, chickadee, titmouse, gold finch, and the first song of a dove. The carolina wrens called back and forth across the narrow water. Several great blue herons, ducks and geese. We felt almost like it was a canoe trip on a small river flowing through a forest.

January 24 Another morning of spring, the sound of peepers and birds, a warm wind from the south. . . . In spite of the fresh wind and uncertain weather, we let go and drifted down the narrow chute, to the right of the island, riding down the tops of saplings which were above water in the narrow pass. Good shore for laying by before entering the river. . . . We both rowed from the first, and could just about keep off the lee shore. The towboat *Reliance* came up, close to the bank, we passed inside, thankful it was a boat that made but small waves. Wind freshened, and we pulled hard to clear a point. . . . A bad eddy below the revetment, we shot along the edge of the boiling, whirling water. The next point unexpectedly was open with sandy, caving banks. A sandbar below, the channel crossing over, and we had an easier time. Still a fresh wind, and we ran in behind the bar, Henrico bar, about 8 miles below the chute. It was open for miles about us, water and sand, not a tree or bank. We found a harbor, though, a small inlet in a low part of the bar where the current had washed through. Not much larger than *Driftwood*, yet quite deep.

We had dinner here, finishing the possum. Soon after the dogs discovered another one under a driftwood stump half buried in the sand. A small one, but it will make a dinner for us tomorrow. What a strange place to find one. What becomes of them when the bar is covered with water?

It was good to walk again in the open, to look into the distance in all directions, to see all of the sky. . . .

A little cooler tonight, after a warm day. Some stars scattered about the cloudy sky, and the mellow lights along the river. . . . A strange light in the north, like the moon rising behind the clouds. The searchlight of a boat flashing above the horizon.

January 26 The boats passing close in to the other shore, Smith point, can hardly be seen. The upbound boats seem to be standing still, those going down shoot by, so swift the current must be. . . .

Much wild beet grows here among the grass, fresh, young plants, at present our only source of fresh greens now. It makes a fine mess of greens when mixed with our canned poke and we are experimenting with it eaten raw.

January 27 At daybreak this day the wind still light, was blowing from the east, rain was falling as it had all night. Later in the morning a dark formless cloud appeared in the S. It swept across the water, with a blast of wind and heavy rain. After that the clouds gradually broke up, the rain eased off, and in the afternoon the sun came out. It set in a clear sky and the stars shone. It is almost a miracle in the remembrance of the past heavy dark days. We have been snug and comfortable, busy and happy.

January 28 A cold, windy, wintry day. Wind shifted from SW to NW, and dashed waves on the beach among the snags and logs. We were thankful for our quiet harbor. However, the rising water is almost to the level of the land now. We are tempted to sandbag a breakwater for us.

January 30 This is the day of the great snow, for this year. Beginning well after daybreak this morning, it is still snowing after nightfall, 6 or 8 inches on the ground. Wind N, sometimes shifting a little. The land about the boat is going under now, yet the water is not deep enough to float our boat and so reach the higher sandbar. So we are offshore and the dogs must be ferried back and forth. Cutting wood in the snow.

The feature of the day has been the birds about the boat. We saw our first lapland longspurs, walking about in the slush, apparently picking up seeds of grass and weeds.
They were many, and about the boat all day. A large flock of killdeers, too, in beautiful flight.

Yesterday we had a visit from the lamplighters. They did not come by on Friday which was their regular day. When I saw them approaching I went to the light to give them a letter to mail. They were so cold that they gladly accepted my invitation to come over to the boat and get warm. They stayed quite a while, talking of the river.

> *We were thrilled anew by the expanse of swift water that was the Mississippi. Drifting was becoming a passion. Though there was nothing new, nothing changed, we looked around each succeeding bend with undiminished interest. No prospect was quite like any we had seen before; no landing was like another, each afforded new problems handling the boat; and when on shore, we climbed the bank or threaded the woods with keen expectation— of what, we could not say, but our zest for new shores and reaches of river was sharp as ever. The details of drifting and landing, of each shore we explored, of towns, boats, people, even of the weather, remain vivid in our minds.*

January 31 I felt that this was our day for traveling, the first in a week, and I was up at earliest daybreak. Still cloudy, N wind, but not strong. About 6 inches of snow. The wind went down, and well into the morning we towed out of our harbor. . . . Did not have a good current until past Little Red lower light. A fine run all morning, almost no wind. . . . A leisurely dinner while drifting.

While rounding the sharp bend above the Arkansas river, a motorboat came across to us, said they thought our boat was adrift since they saw no one, and no smoke. They pulled us out away from the bad shore, gave us advice about the river below. . . .

A short, hard pull to keep in the current at Catfish point. The towboat *Midwest Cities*, up with one barge, swung out to give us a wide berth. So far all pilots of towboats have been considerate to us; never passing as close as they might, going out of their way to keep clear.

February 2 Yesterday we made the run from Choctaw bar to the entrance to the old river at Greenville, about 25 miles. . . . It was sunny and quiet when we dropped down the chute behind the bar, the current flowing in a narrow channel through still water. When we were caught by the Mississippi's current, we tore along, grazing a tree or two at Huntington Point. . . . Two more cutoffs above Greenville, which was formerly on the main river. I regret the cutoffs, and look down the lonely, attractive bend of the old river as we pass.

Saw redwinged blackbirds for the first time, and buzzards, in a flock farther down. Several great blue herons. Heard a towhee. We saw geese at Choctaw bar, and ducks. . . .

We could not make out the entrance to Greenville harbor. It was farther down than we expected. Even so, we had to pull hard to reach the willows, to which we tied, on the upper point. Dinner now very late, and I scouted around. Before dark we cordelled up to a sheltered harbor among the willows.

A visit from a pleasant young man who paddled across to see why we remained in that exposed position. He spoke of the johnboat as a bateau, a term I heard again today. . . .

The night was cold and clear, with a light wind from the north, unexpected by us. It is very pleasant here among the willow tops.

About midafternoon a man came across in a launch to look after a small log raft near *Driftwood*. After some conversation, offering to tow us to the other side, we cast loose in a minute and were soon across. Our new harbor is farther up in an open shore, where we see the ruins of an old sawmill, charred logs and timbers, a half burned sawdust pile. A wonderful view down the river, sun setting at the end of the reach.

The man who towed us over lives in a little boat on top of the bank, which we could see from our first station. He called a certain boat a pirogue.

February 4   Heavy rains yesterday, wind veering from NE to S. We caught a quantity of good sweet water from our roof, filled all our containers and buckets. All these years we have neglected this source, carried inferior water with difficulty, limited our use of it, made experiments with a separate rain catcher. Yet the roof being always too sooty at Brent from the trains, the idea was not practical there, and ever later when we tried it the water was dark and tainted. Yet we find, by cleaning the gutters, letting the first rain wash the roof, and not using the water until it settles, that the water thus handled is fresh and sweet.

February 5   Our landing is unique. The boat is in deep water but it is now over the level shore in front of us. I put a plank from the deck to a huge saw log, spiking the end so it would be a spar as well as walk plank. . . .

Yesterday I went to Greenville, alone. Had a fine walk through the town and out back along the levee which makes a wall around the city. We were visited in the morning by a man named Floyd, owner and farmer of this ground. He raises truck for the city and offered us the vegetables now in the ground which will no doubt be flooded. So we have a quantity of beets, spinach, turnips, turnip greens and collards. The spinach is like the familiar kind in appearance, but has a sweet, mild flavor, very good but surprising. Yesterday I bought fresh eggs and buttermilk from the Huffmans, who have a farm over the old levee. . . . Mr. Floyd spoke of "sallet" and a "mess of robins." Of the two miles of old levee on his place as an asset, valuable as pasture. In high water?

February 6   This morning we called on Mrs. Huffman, got some milk. Our friend, the lamplighter from Henrico bar, in town for his sister's funeral, came down to see us, or to see if we were here. In all our conversation with these people, which is mostly listening on our part, we learn about the country, climate and growing things, fishing, river, local history.

February 9   We are getting acquainted in this neighborhood, at least speaking to everyone, knowing where they live and some of the relationships. . . . The people who live outside the levee and on the riverbank here are mostly fishermen and drifters. No negroes near us, but some on the old road to Greenville, near the city dump. Mr. Floyd, who farms this land, lives on the concrete road and apparently his land extends from there to the river. Next to him, on the corner where the gravel road turns off, lives an old man who has stands of bees. On the gravel road, inside the old levee, which is useless, being washed out farther down, lives Joe Huffman and his wife. He is mostly fisherman. Across the road from him, a family, said to live in with the goats and cows. Either they live in the stable, or the animals live in the house, I do not know which. Near them a tent, with smoke coming out of a chimney in the peak. On top of the old levee, where the road crosses it, a drifter has his trailer. Farther down, on the side of the levee, a little cabin with a woodpile almost its size. The grades where the roads cross levees are the only suggestion of hills in this country. On the road before you reach the river, a lane leads off to the left. There Sam lives, in his little boat, under a pecan tree, surrounded by his gear and dogs. Next, the white trailer house of Howard, or Snap, Huffman, Joe's nephew. These are all northern people. Snap has a young wife and baby, and is fisherman. Farther down, a tent where Mrs. Snap's mother lives, with another lady, and no doubt a man or two, though I haven't seen them. At the end of the lane, on the bank of the Mississippi river, is a collection of shacks, old cars, junk, dogs, children, boats, and at least one man, for I talked with him the first day we pulled in here.

Today we cooked the last of our 1948 pumpkins. They were collected along the way from Bizzle's Bluff to Obion river and have been a main ingredient of the dogfood. We still have carrots and parsnips from our garden, and now have a supply of fresh beets, turnips, and greens from this place. The cows have trampled or eaten the beets but we have gathered perhaps two bushel. Made 12 quarts of pickled beets, our first 1949 canning. Also today, we cooked almost the last of the smoked fish from Cumberland river. These have furnished most of the dogfood this winter.

February 11   Today we left the Greenville lake, after laying there 9 days. Remarkable how familiar we became with the place and people, yet once offshore in the current it seems as remote as Big Bone Island. . . .

Wind carried us out into current as we ate our breakfast, and soon we were shooting past Warfield point. . . . Around the bend we could see the Greenville bridge, against one of whose piers the towboat *Natchez* was smashed and sunk, not long ago. I was told the boat was ascending along the Mississippi side. In fact Joe Huffman drew diagrams of it in the sand with his foot, when I visited him yesterday evening. . . . Swift current as we neared the bridge, and a U.S.E.D. work boat, *Wailes*, put out from shore above us, ran down to see if we were going to make it safely. We cleared the piers easily, one of which was about on the shore line. Water piled up against the other. Very rough below, with bad whirls. Nothing we could do, and soon we were in easier water below. Wind was fresh, due upstream, but we made good speed. A winding course we must run, crossings, sandbars, dead water and buoys to miss, but *Driftwood* made it with little help from us. We really had an easy time of it, eating dinner quietly as we rounded Kentucky Bend. . . .

February 13   Goodrich Light, 460.1, Goodrich revetment, Alsatia bend, Louisiana. We pulled into this harbor at dark yesterday, after a hard, trying day. First we spent 2 or 3 hours cordelling *Driftwood* out of the chute we had entered the previous afternoon, working against a slow current which set in there, and a light S wind, running foul of trees and drift, finally rowing out into the river in a calm spell. Soon we were drifting down in the swift current. As we rounded the bend toward Lake Providence we met head winds, and lowered our mud sail. Passed gauge and open landing, oil dock, at Homochitto, Mississippi. Wind increased, but we made good headway, and managed to stay in the current. The river was wide here and to be blown into slack water would mean a long sail back into slack water. A splendid view looking back this reach, with a wooded point extending out from each side, flecks of sandy shore, land and water checquered by sun and shadow. . . .

The current increased, with an offshore wind. We decided to try for a landing before rounding another bend into the wind. Dead water along the Mississippi side. The mud sail kept us in the current. I raised it when nearly to Fitler bend, where we saw a houseboat back in the trees. At once the wind carried us out of the current, and to our dismay, we went sailing up the river, with a drowned shore in our lee. A hard pull carried us into the current again and we drifted down below the harbor we were aiming at, on an open shore close to a levee. Fitler bend. . . . We pulled into an eddy here but could not make it back to the inlet, so we cast off again, trying ineffectually to get through the whirls below, to reach shore. Suddenly saw trees draped with Spanish moss. Lowered sail again. Quite rough. An extensive submerged bar on the next bend, where the current took us to the Louisiana side, but we rounded the bend. On the stretch below into the SE, with wind slightly offshore, we tried for a landing since the sun was down. Could not get through. . . . We pulled hard, breaking through into the eddy at this point. Dark now, though the full moon shone through the broken clouds. We tied between two trees. . . .

A pleasant evening now, in a safe harbor after a weary day. Yet it was one of the finest days on the river, and now we hear the sound of frogs inshore and the lashing of the current out in the river. Broken clouds racing past the moon, soft and quiet, the sky all pale.

Several notes from the day:
The incense of dry sycamore twigs burning.
Cutoffs in the river make it like an express highway, the old bend ways as enticing as the old winding road.
Driftwood was contrary and stubborn as a mule.

It had been a good day after all. This is what we were on the river for—to feel the power of it, to see it in action, to be near to it with as little as possible between us and it, to know it as an elemental force stripped of names and associations. The hard work and aggravation, the unwieldy boat, stubborn as a mule, water like glue, all this was good, too. What true understanding of the river could one acquire by a fast trip in ease and comfort? And now, after such a day as this, it was good to be at rest, sheltered where wind and current could not reach us.

February 15 The balmy, southwind weather gave way last night, and today has been cold and rainy. We notice the river still rises slightly. The fishermen tell us it has not come to a stand here. They are friendly fellows, and have given us several fish. They are catching quite some buffalo, gave us one weighing about 3 pounds, besides the suckers and shad for the dogs. They call the suckers "coldwaters," the perch as near as I can understand it, "gaspagoule." Something like that. These fellows have a box of a scow with a powerful outboard, which takes them along at a fast rate. They work hard and have few words or minutes to spare with us, friendly as they are. They catch logs and tend the light too, I believe, possibly a string of them.

February 17 Today we made the run to Vicksburg, arriving there early in the afternoon. After weeks with nothing higher than a levee on shore, nothing overhead but treetops and sky, we are overhung by the steep bluff of Vicksburg, crested by a highway and old battlements, and almost under the bridge, which carries highway and railroad across the river. . . . The insistent roar of water against the bridge piers is louder than the sound of traffic. On one of the piers is a smudge of oil where, we were told an upbound DPC with 12 barges lost control of her tow and broke it up.

We had intended to make the mouth of the Yazoo river, 11/2 miles above here, were well in to shore above the river, but drifted down with the slow current since there was slack water between us and shore. When I did try to pull in, the current had swung in from mid river and we were caught in the whirls at the edge, and could not break through. A small motorboat was going up along shore. I waved to it, the man came out to us, just off the mouth of the Yazoo. Having trouble starting his engine, a little, old slow speed affair and not much power when started. We did not make the shore until too far below the Yazoo, even with Anna and I rowing.

He pulled us into a cove above the bridge, against the steep bank, and after some talk, went back up the river. His name was Johnson, fisherman, living in a cabin at the mouth of the Yazoo. This was his "line boat," and he was out to fish some lines. He said he was on the *Natchez*, fireman, I believe, when that boat was sunk at the Greenville bridge. Later I went down below this bridge, became acquainted with two fishermen-loggers, named Wilson and Bowles. They live in small boats there.

We made an early start this frosty morning, pulling out of our harbor with no difficulty and into the main current at sunrise. . . . All hands pulling to clear the oil docks at the bend, where the *Ashland* was tied up. A man was waiting for us on the head of the tow, and a workboat put out to help us, the *Buckhorn Sun*. However, we cleared the barges, and drifted past in the increasing current. The *Buckhorn Sun* shoved us, sideways out into the current, saving us some hard pulling, for the wind was on shore. . . . After a rather long reach, we made a bend to right where we pulled over to the Mississippi side, the wind being slack then. Rounded the point at "My Wife's" Island and pulled back to left, at edge of current, the wind helping now, for we were going almost east. Little current at Light 634, but slack water along shore, so we drifted on, but if we wanted to make Yazoo, we should have pulled in there, rowed down to the river. In the end, we are as well off, or better here.

February 20 Yesterday we made a trip into Vicksburg, and were pleased to find such an interesting city. The streets and buildings on a steep hillside were unexpected in this country. Much to see on the waterfront, which is the Yazoo canal. Found the *Sprague* tied up there, with the Vicksburg Yacht Club's sign on it. We looked at it as we might at a lion in captivity. How different it would be to meet it on the river, especially in a narrow place. The railroad runs along the Yazoo, and there were various terminals and small boats; fish boats, and a houseboat or two. A big sawmill at the mouth of the Yazoo. This place suggested steamboat days more than any we have seen.

February 22 Heavy fog. At midday it still lies close to the water. All morning a flock of geese, lost in the fog it seemed, flew and cackled and swam about, sometimes within view, and even when concealed by the fog, the noise of them seemed at hand.

February 23   We left Vicksburg this morning after a layover there of 5 days and 6 nights. . . . A long reach SW below Vicksburg, we could see the bridge after a long time of drifting. More high ground than we expected, on both sides, the range of low hills extending below Vicksburg, back from the river now. Green appearing on the willows, due both to the advancing season and a more southerly latitude. Much mistletoe and Spanish moss on the trees. Easy drifting. . . . Several houseboats in this vicinity, which is near Grand Gulf and the bluff. Some old boats beached out or rather left to settle on rough ground in the woods. Such places seem little changed from the descriptions of river bank clearings and wood yards in the early days of steamboats, seen by Charles Dickens or Mrs. Trollope. . . .

We drifted about 38 miles today, one of the easiest and most pleasant days we have had.

February 24   We made a washday of this, a mild day, very bright in the morning, but gradually becoming cloudy. A good breeze all day and now at bedtime all the clothes are dry and stowed away. . . . This was the first time this year that we could wash on deck and delightful it was. A hard rain yesterday morning. We took advantage of it by catching water enough to fill all our empty containers and a tubful or two for the washing of clothes. For the rest we used swamp water, which was clear but contained wigglers.

After the rain yesterday, I explored the chute and in the latter part of the afternoon, when it was still and sunny, we cast off from Bondurant Towhead and drifted down here, about a mile below and on the mainland. This is a splendid station. An open level shore little higher than the deck of the boat. A swamp farther inland where we hear the frogs night and day. Some large trees here, Spanish moss and mistletoe. A long vista up the chute and into the river above.

February 27   This is the most solitary shore we have tied up to. No one has appeared since we came, nor do we see any recent traces of man or beast on the shore. Yet we can hear boats on the river, can see them above the towhead. . . . Occasionally a dog barks far off and our dogs answer. The dogs' sole pastime is digging for varmints, mostly rats, it seems. I cleaned one today, cooked it for the dogs. It appeared to be good meat. Standing in the woods this morning, watching some white throated sparrows, I was startled by a loud splashing in the shallow water among the trees and had a glimpse of deer running through. Saw at least three before they disappeared among the trees, which was in a short time.

Much color in the sprouting willows now, and the air has the feel of spring.

February 28   Our first mess of poke today. It seems in advance of its customary position but perhaps, away from the river bank, other plants are farther along than we realize. We took advantage of wind and sun to air some blankets and bedding, and Anna washed some woolens. Painting and playing together has been done the past days.

10

Bisland Bayou

Magnolia Bayou—this we called it at first, because of Magnolia Bluff which rose above it. . . . The real name of the little stream in which we anchored is Bisland Bayou. . . . The place had an immediate appeal, but there were serious objections to it. While making up our minds, we became used to living there and lost the momentum of traveling. . . . Our thoughts turned to the land which was blossoming into spring.

March 2, 1949 Magnolia Bayou, 6 miles above Natchez. A name we have given it. We pulled in here yesterday, early in the afternoon, having that morning made the stretch from Bayou Pierre. . . .

The few houses at Ashland made a great show. It is remarkable how few towns, even houses, we see. . . . Below Waterproof cutoff, we were carried out in midstream and all hands were called to close in with the Mississippi shore. Passed Cole's creek, with a houseboat in the entrance, quite a wide place. Below, a motor scow with cabin, we knew he was a lamplighter, put out to us, offered to tow us in. We were making it easily but were glad of the lift and a chance to get information about the shore below. He turned us loose, and we drifted slowly down, watching for a bayou the light tender had told us about. Heard the noon whistles blow at Natchez. Finally pulled into a small bayou, where the trees were close on both sides, at the beginning of the Natchez bluff, about mile 366. Tied between the willows, where we remained all night The lamplighter stopped on his way back. His name is Nottingham, he has a farm on the old bendway, the island above Natchez.

After dinner I went down the shore a mile to Magnolia Bluff light and the aerial crossings, climbed the bluff and walked back aways. Redbud blooming, another mess of poke. A stiff pull back to the boat but I was towed part way by a motor scow belonging to Alfred Smith, fisherman, at present in Cole's Creek with his houseboat. He stopped to talk awhile.

March 4 We explore the surrounding country. Yesterday we went down to Natchez by river with Alfred Smith, who was taking in a load of fish. Today I walked back to the Pine Ridge road, with the dogs, and made the acquaintance of Tomcat, the colored man who farms these fields.

March 6 There has been a week of fine weather, during which we could have drifted far. We seem quite definitely stopped, however.

We were visited yesterday by Mr. Nottingham, Red. He brought us a small buffalo, for bait, before he left to run his lights up the river. Alfred Smith pulled into the bayou, with his mother, wife and two children in his boat, to see if we wanted to go to town, and offered to bring out anything needed. His mother seemed to take an active part in all river work.

March 7 A fair, cool day of early spring. I took the bicycle off the roof this afternoon, ferried it across the bayou, pumped up tires and rode over to Pine Ridge. On the way I passed Tomcat, grading and ditching the road through the woods. On the Pine Ridge road passed the house of Dr. G. Shields on whose ground we have decided to make our garden. . . .

Yesterday we ate the last of our Bizzle's Bluff parsnips, day before the last carrots. Both delicious to the end. Still have besides all the canned and dried stuff, white and sweet potatoes, the sweets in perfect shape, and not one lost all winter.

Alfred Smith and his mother stopped in passing. Gave us a catfish and a buffalo.

March 9 Today began our second week at Bisland bayou, Magnolia Bluff. Suddenly we are settled here and make plans for the summer. Even have a garden started. It is remarkable how we have become acquainted with people and countryside. We considered whether to stay here or go farther on, for this place has disadvantages. The matter was settled yesterday when Tomcat came down, bearing Dr. Shields' permission to lay here. I think we would have been disappointed if his report had been otherwise. . . .

Yesterday afternoon we began gardening, digging up a patch of the rich sandy loam under the bluff and planting the earliest seed. It was a rite for the establishing of ourselves in this new place, almost like planting ourselves.

March 10 Another important day for us. We moved across the bayou (Bisland bayou) to what seems our own land. . . . We laced hoops on our net, selected 30 watercolors to send to Richmond, chopped more ground in the garden.

March 12 A white frost yesterday morning, and a fine, clear day. I went down to Natchez with Alfred Smith and his Aunt Minnie, to mail the packet of watercolors.

March 13 Caught our first Mississippi river fish today, a 15 pound blue cat, on a hook baited with cut buffalo. The line was in the river below the bayou, on the river bottom. In the net this evening was small white perch, "goule." I saw a sign in a side street Natchez fish market, "Fresh goo." Also "FRESH GAR."

Emptying the woodbox now as firewood can now be kept on the bank, and the space can be put to summer uses. The wood was seldom used during the winter, but kept as a reserve for bad weather and times when good wood would be hard to find. Yet these conditions were seldom met and some of the wood was brought in far up the river. In fact the box was full of souvenir pieces of wood, and I can remember where most of it came from, to the very tree or driftpile.

March 14 Cold rain today. Dogwood in bloom.

March 15 Tonight we have the pleasant thought that all our clothes are washed, dried in the sun and put neatly away. Our clothes yard deserves mention, a sloping open place under the bank with convenient small trees to tie the line to. Very like a real yard with a fence on one side.

Every one we knew called on us today. Mr. Nottingham, Alfred

Smith and his family and Tomcat. He came down after sunset with a sack on his shoulder. The dogs did not bark.

March 18   Yesterday was nearly summer, with south wind. On Wednesday we saw the *Delta Queen* pass, bound for New Orleans, we supposed. It whistled for a landing at Natchez. Caught another catfish yesterday. Alfred took the first one we caught to market with his. We meant to repay him for the fish he had given us, but he insisted on giving us the two dollars. They think we are a little destitute, because we have no motor, I believe.

Our feeble attempts at fishing, compared with the grand scale of theirs, must seem pathetic. We met with this condition before. At Alsatia, the fishermen gave us fish, offered us work knitting nets, though they were making their own, and much faster than we could do it.

Saw a parula warbler Wednesday, when working in the garden.

March 19   Yesterday afternoon I explored the bayou, or "ditch," above us. Found it narrow and brushy, and the land there farther back from the river. We were lucky to choose this one. I landed on the upper side and had a wonderful walk through the forest, for so it seemed. Much dogwood and redbud. Alfred set out 6 more nets along here today, making 12 now. River falls steadily and we shove out into the deep water of the ditch.

March 22   An exciting day yesterday. High wind from the south, a warm gulf wind. I worked in the garden, planting potatoes, against an almost certain rain. Then Tomcat appeared, with his mule to plant the potatoes for us. Also Alfred Smith from up the river. We had not expected him this windy day. So I left the potatoes and the boat to Anna and Tom, put on oilskins and went to Natchez. A rough river, wind, and a terrible rainstorm the last mile. They had the same at Bisland Bayou. Anna fed Tom, listened to his talk. I walked through the flooded streets of Natchez. Rain over, calm weather on our return, and a starry night.

March 24   I see more than one lightning bug this evening. Saw the first one a few nights ago, perhaps a week ago, though with the first one I believed I had been mistaken. Flashes of lightning in the sky too, this sultry evening. . . . I dig in the fertile ground near the cottonwood stumps, grubbing out vines and stumps. They were tremendous trees, only a rod apart. Much went on in their shade, in past days, for I dig up scraps of iron, brickbats, rusty remains of tools and utensils. Most interesting is the skeleton of an old Model T Ford, which found its way to this remote spot. It brings forth as many speculations and reflections as Hamlet's skull.

March 27   Rain all day, but not the tropical downpour of last night, when the earth seemed dissolving. A happy day within, a haircut this morning, some good playing. Caught two catfish today, big ones, one in the bayou, the first one there. . . . Quite a landslide into the bayou above us, making a strange, continued sound and a series of waves. A flock of coots, about a dozen, among the trees along the river. A single small duck swims past the boat. . . . Set out our net. How little it seems now.

March 30   After rising a day or two, the river began to fall but it seems unlikely that it will go on down. We are in a good position for high water, really a better condition than a low stage. Yet always the same feeling of uneasiness about rising water, security about a falling river. . . .

The day closed in heavy rain, thunder and lightning. Warm and windless. Yet this storm began with hail, scattered about like stones thrown down on us, lumps of ice as big as walnuts at least. They seemed even larger as they splashed into the water or rattled on the roof.

I managed to complete and launch our new fish box. The largest we have built. . . .

We had a visitor today. An old darky suddenly made his appearance, coming into the bayou in a bright red, small bateau. He rowed with roughly made oars, his boat loaded with 2 boxes, a metal drum, some net hoops. He said the wooden box contained tools, about 75 pounds in weight, the other box had jump lines in it, the drum had knit nets. His name was Steve Mosso, or something like that, and he was from up the river, Grand Gulf, Ashland, his rambling story was hard to follow. He knew this place as a boy, seemed to know the fine points of fishing. He had been bucking the wind and waves from Ashland, asked about the river below, distance, eddies, wind and such questions, but I felt he knew more about it than I did. After a short visit, during which he talked steadily, like a man who is alone most of the time, he pulled out into the river.

Baked eel for dinner today, very good, and poke, for the fourth day running, and it was good, too.

March 31 Last evening after supper, while we were washing and drying the few dishes, our supper had been cakes of toasted wheat and soy flour, cooked on the fireplace fire, and a salad of carrots and cabbage and sunflower seed, and while I was attempting to recite *Les Deux Pigeons*, I saw, in the lamplight shining through the window on the water, that it was not water at all but something solid. The rain still was pouring down. Looking out, we were amazed to find that we were surrounded by driftwood, logs and trash, it filled the ditch from bank to bank. My first thought was of the bateau. It was swung around to the side of the boat, safe, though full of water. I bailed it out, moved the boat closer in to the bank, got out an extra line. The rain stopped, and we heard, towards the bluff, and up the bayou, the sound of crashing trees and roaring water. It was an uneasy time, the lightning of the storm still flashing. Yet no current came down the bayou, and this morning, the drift was still the same, packed tight above the boat and for a few rods below, then open water. I towed some trees and logs out of the way, and navigation was open again. . . .

This day was quiet and serene, as fair and innocent as could be.

April 1 We washed clothes today, a cool, breezy day. It was bright to begin, but the sun set in hazy clouds. By then all was dry. We set up the tubs on deck, and remarked about our picturesque shore. The stage planks lead one between the two huge stumps of cottonwoods. Near the water is the fishbox, newly rived out of western cedar. The smoke of a fire which heated water in a black boiler.

April 3 In my walk yesterday and this evening, I realized the fury of the rainstorm. The bluff has caved and slid along its whole length, and the rush of water carried mud and trees almost across the cornfield. . . . I swept the trash and logs from the bayou around

270

the boat, making a boom of trees wired together across the stream above us and another along the other side. Now we have an open channel out to the river.

While I did this Anna baked a coconut pie. A chapter should be written about her cooking, describing the materials and equipment she has to work with, her expert manipulation of the tiny stove and the marvelous food she brings forth.

April 5 Tomcat and his very black helper were down today and yesterday. . . . I never understand the last syllable of the negroes' talk. Often there is only one—bay' pant'. This last word was supposed to be panther, one of which was reported seen in this section.

Yesterday we canned poke. I brought down a bushel basket full from the ridge, out of which we filled 11 jars, processing them on shore as customary. We hope this was the beginning of a successful canning season. We will be pleased if it turns out as well as last year's.

April 9 Suddenly it is full summer. Trees expanded into leaf, the freshest green I ever saw; frogs at night, and last night the whip-poor-wills in our bayou. . . .

The catfish are biting. Day before yesterday I went up to the ditch above, and in the swamp raked up crawfish for bait, using a newly built craw rake, a nicely made one which was very effective. It is strange, whatever is needed we seem to find material for its construction, though our source of material is scanty. . . .

Saw small white herons along the river yesterday, snowy egrets. . . . The wild grape was blooming, the air scented by the heavy flowering. Tomcat says there are alligators in Thornburg lake. . . . Planted peanuts today and will plant some melons as soon as possible.

April 11 I am fishing now in this bayou. . . . This evening caught a large turtle, and a good sized blue cat, at least 10 pounds. Anna carried on the housecleaning. I cleared more river bank.

April 12 Full moon tonight. It is quite high before we see it come over the ridge. Then it fills this narrow valley with light.

Turtle for dinner today. Alfred came by and dressed it for us, suggesting we "fry it like chicken." We found it delicious, tasting something like groundhog, not at all fishy. Turtle soup for tomorrow. Tomcat was down, bringing eggs, and taking home a catfish.

April 13   The full moon was shadowed last night by a total eclipse and the vale was thrown into darkness. Having no warning, the effect was strong. About the time the whole moon was obscured, clouds came over the sky. Waking later in the night, I saw the bright moon riding through the clear sky. . . . A beautiful, mild day. We walked to Pine Ridge, all of us. Road muddy, after yesterday's shower. Carried our lunch, and ate it when we reached the highway. Tomcat and Rosie came along, with dogs, mule and tomato plants, to do some gardening. . . . Coming back how delicious the pine woods were, how glad we were to get back on our little dirt road, how quickly we traversed the way. Yet how remote and isolated this hollow seemed, approaching it that way.

We heard summer birds, Maryland yellow-throat, Kentucky warbler, peewee. Wild roses in bloom, large white ones without fragrance. And a little flower, more purple than ironweed, along the road. Saw two deer as we returned.

April 15   How quiet on this cool night. The frogs are silent and the chuck-will's-widow. Only two little peepers are heard, their thin voices overcome by the chorus of frogs on other evenings.

April 16   I killed a large, spotted snake which we judged not poisonous. I cut off the head, dressed it and cooked it for the dogs who seemed to enjoy it. For our dinner we had baked eel.

April 19   These days are warm and sunny but the nights remain cool, and we sure enjoy a fire. A little, or sometimes more, gardening every day. Today Tomcat began plowing the bottom. He brought us a mess of green peas, early Alaska, which he planted on the last snow. Strange, when we were enjoying the snow at Henrico bar, someone was planting peas at Pine Ridge, and we would eat some of them. . . .

On the 17th, a Sunday evening, when Anna went out with me, we caught a big blue cat on the short line in the backwater. Alfred guessed it to weigh 20-22 lbs. when he took it in this morning.

The Chinaberry trees have been blooming.

April 22 Bars of red and green and gold as the sun set, after a rainy and very dark day. Sometimes it seems we have little to show for the day. Of what account is a craw rake I made to replace the one I lost yesterday? Or the scrubbing of the outside of the cabin we did?

Skipper gave birth to 7 puppies. She has done her part. The seventh litter, we figured, 42 pups.

April 24 It turned out to be a warm summer day. We bathed in the bateau, floating on the still, almost clear water of the bayou. . . .

Yesterday I did the first clearing of the bottom land, or swamp as Tom called it. At last we will have a true riverbank garden.

April 28 We canned fish yesterday, 16 pints and 5 quarts, mostly buffalo, some blue cats. The buffalo were a trade with Alfred, for the big cat we caught, in which trade Alfred was most generous. We owe much to him already. . . .

The excursion boat *Avalon* landed from below, went out in the afternoon, we were just ahead of it. This was the old *Idlewild*, we saw it on the Cumberland last summer.

Yesterday Tom and Rosie came down to see us. They brought a quart of fresh milk, we gave them some mustard. We had mustard for our dinner today, the first real crop from the garden. It is amazing how quickly some seeds come up this damp hot weather, in the rich ground near the water.

April 30 Today we moved down the bayou to the mouth, still inside against the upriver bank. . . . We made this move to be near the open river in case of a run-out, which is possible at this stage, and in this weather. . . .

I worked some on the net hoops, completing one. The wood is pecan from a tree in the swamp. Anna did some good housecleaning. Alfred stopped on his way to Natchez alone, and on his way back to get some greens, poke and mustard from our garden.

Flower buds on the magnolia now. The indigo bunting is here.

May 16 Natchez General Hospital, where I arrived about 3 o'clock in the morning of Tuesday, May 10. I had come to Natchez alone on the previous Monday, rowing and drifting to the beach above town where the fishermen tie up their boats. The trip was easy and I did not suffer at all. I was first hit by this on Saturday, May 7. . . . I suddenly felt the mild pain in my middle parts, but it seemed not worth mentioning and our evening proceeded as usual. In the night, however, I was restless with the same pain and fever. Sunday I lay around and rested, had an easier night. Monday I was feverish, but almost without pain. I worked some in the garden. However I must not have improved much, for in the afternoon I decided to see a doctor. . . . I drifted down, rowing at times against the cross wind and from the course of an upbound boat. Current, sun and wind, green hills passing. I rowed to the bank, tied up the bateau with some fishermen's boats. . . .

May 17 I picked up the oars, walked through the willows to the road, to the office of the sawmill. Mill and office were closed, but the night watchman was about—a kindly negro who gave me water to drink, and helped me to telephone for a cab. He told me how to reach George Inman by phone, which information helped later. The cab took me to Dr. Mutziger's office on Main Street. He had been recommended to us. It was 5:30 o'clock now, the doctor had left. His nurse suggested the sanatorium or Dr. Stower's clinic, so I walked the sunny street. The sanatorium was a forbidding place, but I found a doctor who said he could see me after a long wait. Before committing myself I went to Dr. Stower's clinic next door, a bright new place where a young man as neat and trim as chromium took me into his office. This was Dr. Butler. It was a relief to sit, and to stretch out on his inspection table. Yet my trek was not finished, for he advised me to stay in town overnight. My fever did not have the other symptoms which would make it malaria or typhoid or dysentery. He said it might be appendicitis, an idea which had not occurred to me. He said that the swollen appendix might have broken which would relieve any pain. If so it would flare up in the coming night. He gave me his phone number and a prescription to have filled.

I took to the streets again, headed for the Concord Hotel on Commerce Street in the SE corner of the business district. This place was suggested by Dr. Butler when I asked about a convenient place to which I might go in my river clothes. In a drug store on the way, where I had a prescription from the doctor filled, I was able to reach George Inman by phone. I explained who I was and what I wanted. He promised to get a message to Anna. . . . I had eaten nearly nothing since supper on Saturday. In the hotel, getting dark now, there was but one room left and I hesitated to pay $3.50. Yet the doctor could find me there and it might be difficult for me to direct him to a different place. It was a good decision. The room was on the street floor, it was large and clean, with private bath and telephone. I opened the one window, started the large fan overhead, took a dose of medicine, stretched out on the bed.

I did not sleep, lay quietly and without pain, burning with fever. A cracked bell tolled the hours. Loud voices came in from the street, straining to talk plainly and reasonably, but evidently drunken. Nothing bothered me. Another dose of medicine at midnight. The house all quiet now. The fan was unnecessary. I lay there, and then there was something like a great wind. I came to, dripping with sweat, the fever all gone now. Instead, a new pain was rising like a terrible storm approaching. I went into the bathroom. What I did I do not know, for I came out of unconsciousness to find myself in a knot on the floor. That settled it—I must call the doctor. This I managed without difficulty. Then I wrote out directions for reaching Anna by means of George Inman. I laid myself on the bed again, leaving the light on and the door open. I groaned with pain. The hotel clerk heard me and came in. A young fellow with red hair, gentle and sympathetic. He left me, closed the door. . . .

I heard the bell strike two, the doctor came at last, completely and carefully dressed. He went through all the forms, talking and asking questions, unhurriedly. I wished he would get through with it and take me out of this. He went out to telephone and at last we were on our way. . . . I walked down the hall after the doctor in great pain, slumped over like a gorilla. Outside, the white houses with black windows, the moon low in the sky. . . .

May 18 I found myself in a dimly lighted corridor, where there were 2 or 3 nurses. Confused, I remember following one of them

275

into a room where I was helped into bed. Rest at last, but overwhelming pain. . . .

Finally I was wheeled into the operating room. *[Harlan was operated on for a ruptured appendix.]* Daybreak showed in the sky. I could see through the skylight, a rooster was crowing. All was informal, except costumes, and there was bantering in which I joined. I was given a spinal anesthetic and a cloth put over a frame so that I could not observe, but I could feel, without pain. A young girl at my head was entranced at the spectacle. One of the nurses, perhaps she was the daughter of the lamplighter from Waterproof, Mr. Goodfellow.

The operation was soon over and I was wheeled back to bed on the second floor. I felt clear and relaxed and without pain. . . .

Soon Anna and George Inman appeared. They both looked very riverish. I have had other visitors like that, Ed Wilkinson and Alfred Smith. The list is completed by Tom and Rosie. Alfred Smith appeared again today, no one could have been more welcome. We will go out with him tomorrow.

May 20   Yesterday we came back to the boat from the Natchez hospital. . . . The trip up the river was unusual for a convalescent sitting in a hard seat without a back in the sun and wind. . . . We were thankful to find the boat just as we had left it, and are grateful to Alfred and Tom for taking care of it and the dogs.

The river has been falling steadily, and this morning we moved the boat to deeper water in the mouth of the bayou. It is good to be out on the river again, the long vista up and down, the fresh breeze.

May 22   A wind from the South yesterday and we tossed about in the swells which entered this cove. The shore caves badly, and the climb to the top is not easy. Today there is only a light breeze, still from S. We are enjoying the first green beans from our garden. The weather is hot, but not uncomfortable. Nights are cool. Rain is needed, as none has fallen this month.

May 24   Berry picking this morning, as yesterday. We row up the shore, almost to Green's bayou. The dewberries are on the sandy ridge among willows and trumpet vines and ivy.

May 27 The *Dogwood* was along yesterday, and moved the Magnolia Bluff light down the river almost a mile. Another light was set up directly across from us, as cheering as a neighbor or a light in a farmhouse. . . .

Mornings we like to work in the garden, while it is cool. There is much to do, hoeing and planting. This we do in the moist sandy ground westward of the buckshot ground we had to abandon. We were amazed to find the mustard above ground 4 or 5 days after it was planted; and beans sprouted in the same time. We have nice green beans now. Before the water became so muddy we were catching some shrimp, and look forward to that as a new food source.

May 28 River still rising, but very slowly, and very muddy. Yet I had the best luck yet with the shrimp and we are having our first ones for supper. . . . No gardening today, but Anna picked some nice beans.

June 6 Returned yesterday from Natchez after another spell in the hospital. I had rowed down alone on Tuesday, May 31. . . . Dr. Stower ordered me to the hospital, which I entered early in the afternoon after sending word to Anna. . . . Anna came to Natchez the next evening with Sonny Boy, and stayed with me. . . . I was released on Sunday. . . .

All well at the boat. River falling a little. Welcomed by the locusts, not one of which I heard at Natchez. They are past their prime here. These are hot, sunny days, full summer. In Natchez the grass was lush and green, the gardens flourishing.

This return to the hospital was a hard dose to take, at first. . . . The five days passed quickly enough. Desirous of turning them to account by producing something positive, some fruit which would never have ripened in ordinary times, I began the writing of this narrative of our river life [Shantyboat]. I had no hopes of any reward other than to be able to say, "That stretch in the hospital was good for something, after all."

June 10 Night before last we heard the first katydid. . . . We

277

are now eating our sweet corn, golden bantam. . . . When the morning air rises to a certain temperature the locusts begin their droning. . . .

This is the week of half life. I have not left the boat since we arrived last Sunday. I did manage to catch a nice yellow cat from the deck, seated in my chair.

June 11   River still falls and yesterday we moved the boat into deeper water, turning it so that it is parallel to the bayou, the main deck up the bayou. It is pleasant this way, far enough out to have a view up and down the river from our windows.

Yesterday evening as the sun shone low in the sky, after a showery afternoon, its level rays made a brilliant light in the bayou. The tree trunks gleamed in the warm light, the green of the foliage was intense, all reflected in the smooth water. The dark shadow of our boat lay on the steep shore. Farther up the bayou, where the sun did not penetrate, there was the darkness of night. The sun sank below the horizon, the color vanished. Yet for a short time, the tall stems of the willows high overhead glowed a dull red in the last rays. We listened to the last song of the thrush. It ceased and in the lowering darkness, the chuck-will's-widow sang, far off.

Perhaps for the first time we are living a shantyboat life. I sit in the sun or in the shade all day long. Anna has too much to do but still has time for rest and pleasure. I hope some of this indolence remains when I am able to be active again.

June 15   The sun is hot, the sky blue with great white clouds. A red-eyed vireo sings. . . .

Yesterday we went to Natchez with Alfred Smith, the first trip there since our coming home from the hospital 10 days ago. We are relieved from the ordeal of shots, but the doctor is still holding me down. Last week I barely set my foot on shore. Today, however, I walked over to the pecan tree garden, and have been more active on the boat, while still resting most of the time. Caught a nice blue cat this morning, which we promptly ate for dinner.

I hear a summer tanager, so much like the vireo, which has ceased. . . .

The Smiths are most generous. Yesterday Alfred brought us

berries and a turtle, after the berries on Saturday. . . . Alfred had nearly 300 pounds of catfish yesterday, the catch for 3 nights, on lines. . . .

Now the red-eyed vireo has resumed its song.

The first ripe tomatoes picked today, okra and bush limas ready.

A thrush sings now, the tanager, Maryland yellow throat. Then a chat. . . .

I listen again and the red-eye is singing alone. Then I hear a yellow-billed cuckoo, a prothonotary, a distant cardinal.

June 18   These days of rest are novel. Yesterday afternoon I spent on top of the bank, in a sandy place deeply shaded, at the edge of a thicket of small willows and cottonwood. I lay there a long time, listening to the few birds, yet they made continuous song. Some came close to me. I watched the sunlight in its changing pattern on the trees. Wrote a little. Anna came up for a short time at the end, after a busy day. Now I sit in the cabin, grinding colors, and contemplating the pictures I might work on. Anna is in the garden. . . . Each day I am a little more active. Walked to the garden day before yesterday. Anna has done well in keeping it going. She takes a real interest in it.

June 19   A stormy morning. Thunderheads rising in all quarters, fragments of rainbows. A white bird flying in a shaft of sunlight, against the storm cloud.

June 20   I put out a line off from the mouth of the bayou yesterday and have caught 2 catfish, 2 garfish and a little perch. . . . There was a parade of boats Sunday after the storm—Sonny Boy alone in his scow, Alfred, and then Bill.

June 22   I worked in the garden with Anna this morning, and am behaving somewhat like myself. Yet we keep our fingers crossed and can hardly believe that I will be able to go on with no further reverses.

June 24   We have just moved up the bayou to our old anchorage. Now we are parallel to the bank, which we find a better exposure these hot, sunny days. When we were here before we were headed into the bank. We will not have the river breeze, but more shade, more protection from high winds, and no caving banks. . . .

We have moved only a few rods within the bayou, but it seems narrow and enclosed, the river far away. The sunsets recently have been such that one might have rung the bell to call people to witness. . . .

Tom told us today that the bells we have been hearing were plantation bells, and when they ring early in the morning, at daybreak, it is to send the hands to the fields.

June 26 Many birds in the trees. A black and white warbler went up a bare trunk and just under it, following, was a downy woodpecker, female, so they were both black and white, a rare combination which one would wait long to see again. . . . At dinner we saw a Little Blue Heron, the first one we had ever seen. We had glimpses of this bird up the bayou, but never such a good view as this, when he flew by at close range. A beautiful bird. He deserves a more dignified name.

June 28 I think we have never enjoyed birds as much as we have here.

June 30 Light breeze downstream today, which we enjoyed on the high bank across the bayou. We did our stint of writing together then. This is our afternoon occupation, which we can take to the coolest place, and rest at the same time. . . . We did some good work in our garden. This has been my best day for many weeks.

July 1 Whenever Bill Smith or Sonny Boy go by here in their motorboat, they slow down on approaching our boat and run at half speed until past, so that their waves will not bother us.

July 2 Tom was down in his field, trying to mow the Johnson grass. We gave him some fish the other day, and today he brought us three eggs that Rosie had sent, saying we had better not break them together as they may be addled. He brought us too some real "White Lady" peas to plant. We were touched by his gifts.

I worked in the garden the first part of the morning, but Anna remained in the cabin, the first day she has not gone out to work. She baked bread today and now we enjoy it again.

July 4 We moved closer to the mouth of the bayou yesterday afternoon, after waiting to see what the river was up to. It fell just a little last night. . . . I caught a bullhead and a gar this morning.

The gar made us a dinner, very skillfully cooked with an original tomato sauce which contained herbs and pepper. . . . We both worked in the garden this morning, the ground wet, but we planted watermelons and mustard, the melons in the soft rich ground toward the bayou.

July 6   1 lay awake in the fading of night, waiting for the first bird song and heard a plantation bell, clearly sounding over the water, tolling evenly so that the vibration was continuous, like a vibrating string. The bell tolled 62 times.

This morning, after tracing the two short lines I have out, catching only a drowned turtle which we are having for dinner, and breakfast, I went to the garden, alone, staking beans, spraying cucumbers, untangling sweet potato vines, the rankest growth I ever saw, and picked vegetables for dinner—lima beans, tomatoes, herbs, greens. On my return to the boat I went across the bayou and cut a box full of wood. . . .

The days now are quite alike. Dinner on deck and some reading afterwards. Then while Anna does her chores inside, I write, unless there is some work that needs attention. Some days I fish through the day, always going out on the river in the evening, at least.

The spectacular skies lately. The sunsets should make this part of the world famous.

We bathe often through the day, rinsing in the bayou, and have supper in the twilight.

July 7   Yesterday as we sat in the thicket on top of the bank, a strange new bird appeared, a strong pattern of black and yellow, with dark olive wings and back. It came so close we could see every detail and easily identified it as a hooded warbler. In contrast, there is a small bird in the same thicket which we have been working on for 2 or 3 weeks. I saw it as it sang and so traced an unknown bird song to its source. We have decided the bird is Bell's vireo.

These afternoons are very hot and we are glad to retreat to the coolest place, usually the close thicket of willows at the top of the bank, where the sun never shines. The trees give the still air a coolness and freshness, in striking contrast to the air inside the boat.

Then as the sun sinks low we stir about. The half hour before and after sunset are pleasant, and we enjoy them so much after the long, hot afternoon, that the darkness comes too soon. The afternoons are good though and never wasted.

July 8 Just as we were about to go to bed, we heard Alfred's motor coming up so we lit a lamp and waited for him.

July 11 Tom appeared today, after an absence. He seemed low in spirits. From his lost battle with the Johnson grass? He brought us a small chicken, a gift. He suggested we feed it for a few days, to fatten it up. We are honored with their gifts.

Watermelon from our garden now, and today we picked two ripe muskmelons. The second crop of figs is ripening, so we have fruit again. Store fruit is not as satisfactory. Yet as we waited in the grocery Saturday and saw them carrying in huge watermelons, lining them up on the floor the length of the building, our crop seemed so paltry that I thought perhaps we were foolish to work in the garden. Why not go to the store, and get watermelons like these? . . . Yet when we went to the garden this morning, it was all so exciting and the little encouragement we had from some crop or other such a joy, and our dinner of fish, potatoes and spinach and watermelon, all of our own raising so satisfactory that I would prefer our way to the other, even if living in town did not incur the tremendous price.

Another thunderstorm off in the distance, a cool, fresh wind.

July 14 More rain this afternoon, enough to make a strong torrent of water down the creek, reaching almost to the boat. This is an unsafe harbor now, and we prepare to move out. I wonder if there is any security on this river or on any river, for that matter. Yet the Ohio had banks that were firm and trustworthy, at least. Yet lately, on the quiet summer evenings, we felt a new degree of peace and security, as if we had made friends with the river.

July 15 Another heavy rain at daybreak, the bayou putting out again. We moved down to the very mouth of the bayou, the river's current sweeping past our stern. We have a long line to a snag which is a short distance from shore above us, another line to a log which is partly sunk in the muddy bank of the bayou. With two planks we can get to fairly solid ground. . . .

I picked figs again today, perhaps or nearly, at least, a gallon, which we canned, processing them an hour on the cookstove, as it was so wet outside.

July 28 Rain has fallen every day lately. . . . River still rising, but very slowly. . . . We were in the point of leaving the bayou mouth two weeks ago, but are still here, a comfortable harbor now. . . . We can see our nearest neighbor now, the boat above the cut-off, at the beginning of the old river. He moved down there from upper Cole's creek, but until recently had been around the point of the sandbar. Sometimes we can see his light at night. He is two or three miles away.

August 2 One can never feel secure from the violence of the elements in this climate, nor can he trust this river.

August 4 The dry weather of late summer has not yet come. The river falls steadily, though, and is now almost as low as it has been. The lower stages are exciting to think about. We know not how the bars will come out, but it seems different now than it was before the last rise. The waves break on a sandbar which is much closer to us by several hundred yards. . . .

Tom brought us a bucketful of lady peas this morning. We found them delicious, the best of them all. Tom says they are not the real "white lady peas," which come later. He gave us some of those, from his own seed, to plant. He calls these "gentlemen peas."

August 6 River the lowest it has been, new snags coming out but no sandbars. A drifting tree caught below us, far out, probably on a bar.

August 7 Made an important move this morning—out into the river. We are now tied up on the shore above the mouth of the creek. Only 2 or 3 boat lengths from our previous anchorage in the creek's mouth, the outlook is so different that we might have moved miles away. . . . I walk over the strange shore, and am surprised to find the familiar landing a few steps away.

August 8 The swift current past the boat is exciting almost as if we were going somewhere ourselves. . . .

The negro woman who keeps the tiny store at the landing is

very friendly now, always asking one of us about the other, and much concerned about my health and recovery. Today she said we had been so long together that we talked alike. I said it was likely because we were both from the north.

It was a touching experience to awaken last night to see the almost full moon shining in a quiet sky, after the stormy beginning of the night. . . .

Picked the first elderberries last week, and the last of the figs.

August 11   Five fishermen on our beach yesterday, a negro lady and 4 children, the oldest about 14, the only girl. The lady knew this place, but was surprised to find us here, and our garden on the way. She had brought a hoe to clear a path to the river. They fished industriously until midafternoon, had caught by then only 3 or 4 very small fish. The lady, whether the children were all hers or not we could not tell, was kin to Rosie, lived beyond Pine Ridge. These people are difficult to understand. They looked so disreputable and untrustworthy at first, but they display such dignity and calmness. No such group of whites would be so quiet or patient. They borrowed a can to drink river water in, used our axe without asking, sat in our chair on the bank, and stared at us and our boat. She did ask if they might fish along this shore. By the time they left we felt they were our friends.

August 12   These are sweltering days. The sun is dangerous, making metal or painted surfaces, even the sand, too hot for the bare skin to touch. Yet there is usually a relief sometime during the day, when a breeze or clouds come up. Mornings and nights are delightful. . . .

Yesterday I patched up a streak of rotten wood in the hull caused probably by water from the drain. It was above the water line, but close to it. Our boat has seen its best days. Now it must be watched, and not too much expected of it. This will no doubt affect our plans.

This summer has been different, in so many ways, from the previous ones at Payne Hollow and on the Cumberland. At those places we felt settled, were bound up in the country and people. Here, long as our stay has already been, it is like a temporary stop.

We have set up no establishment on shore, and could get away on short notice. No one to say good-bye to and not much garden to leave, at the rate it is going.

Today, in contrast to yesterday's rough work, I glued up my violin. . . . If it is successful I will repair the viola, which is in even worse shape.

August 14   It takes little to encourage us. I suppose it is true also that we are easily discouraged. Yet to see turnips and bush limas coming up, even amid so many failures in the garden, makes us happy about the whole thing. . . . A walk on the hill was encouraging, too. Elderberries are ripening now, fine heads of them and all we want. I found a few pawpaws not ripe yet, and have located persimmons. Some pecan trees have nuts on them, some do not. In spite of the absolute lack of apples and pears, we feel at present richly supplied.

August 19   I finally thought to ask Tom what the strange fruit was and learned it was muscadine. It is like a grape and a plum, between the two in size, plum color, grows on a vine. I must identify it closer. The taste is unique, plumlike.

August 21   Violin is performing well as ever now, and seems perfectly sound.

August 24   With the muscadines I feel like the explorer of a new continent must have felt, finding new fruits with new flavors. They had the pleasure of naming them.

August 26   A light shower before sunset. The sun at last came out, shining under the low cloud, a white faint light. A few minutes later the light flamed into glorious colors. . . . I must mention yesterday's dinner, shrimp gumbo and rice, with muscadine pudding. Crowder peas in abundance now, and we eat them every day.

September 3   I think of our visit to Smith Harbor. All the expanse of river and shore, and those three boats in a little pocket, hot and snaggy, with no view, dogs and children and gear everywhere, like an alley in the slums. Yet it was picturesque to ride into the narrow chute, the boats lined up like a watery town. . . . Mrs. Smith has a way with animals and fowls, making pets of a dove and two "Siberian ground squirrels." Young turkeys parade about the cabin and more on shore, with a big one or two. Also chickens, and ducks and geese swim about the boat. Three pigs roam the shores.

> *One Sunday we rowed up to visit the Smiths. . . . There was no resemblance here to the shiftless hand-to-mouth river rat so often pictured. The Smiths' standard of living was high—fresh meat and milk, ice, and store bread, a gasoline-powered washing machine. Their roomy boats were furnished much like town houses.*
> *. . .*
> *After glimpses such as these into other households, we looked at our own more critically. Even Tom and Rosie had an electric refrigerator and an oil stove. Yet we were in no way roughing it—our guests will vouch for that. Surely refinement of living does not consist in gadgets and machinery, but in such elements as leisure, contentment, lack of confusion, small niceties.*
> *Anna cooked on a wood stove. The two were in rapport, and turned out the best of food. . . . As for refrigeration, there was little to keep cool, with vegetables brought from the garden as needed, fish and shrimp fresh from the river. . . .*
> *I do not mean our way was better, and do not recommend it. To most, it would mean deprivation. To us it has an honorable simplicity and independence. We were living as we desired, and put out less than most, to get what we wanted.*

September 11 The river people here, who live on boats, that is, the ones we know, are not as much shantyboat as I expected. Nearly all their supplies come from town. They depend on their fishing for an income, instead of getting part of their food by gardening and foraging and barter. Yet they have chickens, they hunt, and in the case of the Truitts, have a deal with some farmers along the river. The country does not offer much in the way of forage, there are no roads, so their way is natural. They depend on their motorboats for fishing, trips to town and moving their houseboat. Their location depends on season and stage of river.

September 14 Yesterday old Jasper rowed by again. . . . To see him one would not know that he was old and crippled, he rows so easily. Yesterday also, the Smiths went in, taking grandma and Junior to town, where they will live this winter so the boy can go to school. They trailed the bateau, loaded with a bed, little stove and firewood, as well as other articles they will need for housekeeping. . . .

I see again, as often when the sun sets clear, or nearly so, with low clouds westward, the broad converging bands of light and shadow in the sky above the point the sun went down. Are they shadows of clouds below the horizon, cast into the sky by the low sun¿

I rowed down to Natchez and back yesterday for the first time. Crossed over to the other side first. . . . One appreciates the width of the river by rowing across. I tried to compare it with the Ohio at Brent, and guessed that this is 3 times wider. . . . Arrived downtown at 11 a.m., left 2 p.m., back at the boat well before sunset. . . . The last 2 miles hard pulling, but not so difficult as I had expected. . . . We now feel independent of our friends in the matter of transportation.

September 28 The summer season is over. Hear a brown thrasher singing this morning, I am quite sure, though I do not see him. Have seen several lately. Its song was soft and low, not the brilliant performance of spring. . . .

All summer we have had supper at dusk, finished our chores in the last light, then sat a while in the darkness before going to bed. Now, in the shortening days, we still have our supper at sunset or soon after, but take a little off of the night by lighting a light and reading a little while. This is a great pleasure for us, and the day seems better balanced, for we read little during the day, usually. The only regular time is after dinner when we try to have something to read together. Today we began *Romeo and Juliet*, the next play in our one volume edition. We have read all the historical plays, in our one volume edition, and now are reading the comedies and tragedies, first one then another, as they come in the book. We have recently read *El Cid* and *Cinna* of Corneille, and in between plays a fable or two of LaFontaine.

287

October 3   When this time of year comes around, I think of how we went to live on the river bank and built a boat.

October 4   A pleasant day, doing some inside chores, replacing one screen in the door with glass, playing, reading, writing.

October 5   I write this on the shore, in the afternoon, by a fire on which 4 pint jars of ladypeas are being processed. Hard to set up a lean-to, and build the fire in its lee, for a gale was blowing this morning. It began before daybreak, when, after a rough night, the SE wind shifted to south, with heavy squalls of rain. The wind became stronger, with ragged clouds in the sky. The sun broke through at times, but then dark rain clouds came up from the S. Boat pitched badly on the choppy water, but the waves were not large, no long rollers as there would be at Payne Hollow in such a wind. This afternoon is cloudy, cooler, wind not so strong. A red flush under the clouds at sunset, and a quiet evening. Clouds moving in from W, and we look forward to a fair day tomorrow.

October 7   Today I walked back from our spring, through the thick undergrowth and up the steep bluff. . . . A trail led back through the woods to the open fields—an agreeable prospect, reminding one of bluegrass country. Meadow larks and mocking birds singing.

October 13   The short days go by so quickly that one must take hold and forcibly insert that which he most desires to do. That which must be done consumes much of the time.

October 14   Truitt moved his houseboat up around the sand bar this morning. With his boat and the old snag gone, the upper shore is desolate as it was in the beginning. What a difference it makes to us! I feel that a guest has departed, leaving us alone again. Yet his boat was a small spot far away, and we heard nothing of him but the popping of his motor boat.

We laced the hoops on our net, working in the cabin. No trip to the garden, which is rare. After dinner, sweet potatoes and ladypeas, I explore further the hill behind our spring.

October 16   When we cease a joint activity, the implements connected with it are put in their places in a hurry, and in a few minutes both of us are busy at different tasks, showing that we are always thinking of what to do next. Diverse occupations follow closely, almost overlap. Today we played together long and happily. At the end, stands, music, instruments and benches are put away in a flurry of busyness and I take up a wood block, Anna a box to read a recipe, looking ahead to supper.

October 18 Another fair day, warmer almost summer heat. . . . Walked back through the woods, with the dogs, to a cornfield. Heard a plantation bell beyond. . . . Warm and sunny on the river. I swam as I drifted back. . . . Drifting back is a pleasure, always.

October 19 We get in our harvest.

October 24 We went to Natchez with Alfred and Helen Saturday, making a day of it. Landing on the bar they were met by Mrs. Smith and Bill's folks, Bill arrived shortly. What a family! Strong and lusty, outspoken, indelicate, frank. A flock of children, Sonnyboy, 26, a giant of a fellow, modest and shy, we like him very much. . . .

We notice a decided difference in our relations with the natives, black and white. We are not received unquestioningly, as we were in Kentucky. Everyone is put in a class here, and they have difficulty in placing us. Louise, of the tiny store at tile city front, is convinced we are well-to-do. First she thought we were poor folks, but soon changed her mind. Expressed this in picturesque language which I cannot remember or transcribe. Others, the Smiths and Truitts, cannot make us out. We were told of a piece about us in the Natchez paper. Mrs. Truitt said she often sees my picture in the paper, the New York paper. We are mystified too.

October 25 Geese ride the north winds now. Last night the noise of them seemed continuous. . . . I crossed the river today. . . . Walked back to the levee, about two miles. The levee is impressive, a smooth green hill. On the other side a gravel road, small houses along it, cotton fields, still green, and pastures, then more woods. A flat place, depressive. Looking the other way, at the irregular woods, the colored grass and weeds about the barrow pits is a lively scene. Returning to the river one feels its magnificence.

October 26 River fell a little, but another rise follows, they say.

Now there is a rising tendency to the river. It does not fall to its former low point, and rises to a new high one. All summer it was the reverse, falling more than it rose.

October 28   The shores of the Mississippi, I felt this across the river recently and on this shore, too, are scarred by the fierce conflict of river and land. The current cuts the shore to the bone. Huge logs are heaped in the drift. The bank is slipping, trees leaning at angles, wide fissures and steps back from the river. Ancient stumps and snags are uncovered, remnants of a forest which once stood there. The wind, too, scours the bank. At other places, however, on a quiet front there is no current, the shores are extending into the river, willows spring up thick as grass.

October 31   A gale blowing from the NW this morning. Cold, with dashes of fine rain. . . . In the night we heard the wind and waves. Made all tight, let in the dogs, and lay awake listening and thinking. In such times I go down to the underpinnings of existence. The life of man on this earth is not firmly established. One wonders how he can exist, how he can go on living in the face of the immense, hostile forces. The momentum which daily affairs and custom give to living is lost in the darkness. All the trappings of imagination and conceit are stripped away. However, when daylight comes, and action and accomplishment, the ego revives and with it the impudence to outface the empty caverns of the sky. Attention to immediate and pressing details occupies the mind, hope and cheerfulness return.

This was a shantyboat morning. I arose to find the johnboat full of water, the slack stern line fouled in a floating tree, plunder on the bank almost in reach of the rising water. Then Anna discovered some water in the bilge. I mopped it out, decided it was from waves slopping over the top of the gunwale, where it is not tight with the deck. The river is rising at a fast rate for the Mississippi, perhaps a foot overnight. . . .

I looked over Tom's tomato patch, the chance of frost and the unlikelihood of his coming down today making it ethical. Picked a bucketful of ripe or too ripe tomatoes. We are distressed by his corn and soybeans, too, which I fear will be lost. Yet we cannot help ourselves to them.

November 1 When the wind abated yesterday after sunset, we felt the relief from strain and looked forward to a quiet night of sleep.

We dug 3 buckets of peanuts today. There remains less than that now. How we labor at this crop, raking through the ground trying to get every one. Yet after a rain the ones we missed are exposed. We wash and dry them, sort them over, put them on the overhead rack inside to dry. Then they must be roasted. The final eating of them is a small part, and something of an anticlimax. Yet we get more out of it than the final product. If it were not so, it would be better to buy the peanuts with money earned by our labor.

Anna is put to it these days for salad material yet she continues to turn out excellent ones of considerable variety. We have discovered that parsnips can be used like carrots. Our various greens, cut up and mixed with peanuts, are delicious.

November 2 When Alfred raised the net just above our boat, which he was unable to lift in the wind Monday, he found a dead gar in it. This he gave us. It was one of those big ones we have seen diving like porpoises along here.

November 5 Alfred brought us two coots this morning, all cleaned and dressed. The common name for them here is "pull-do." Anna traced this to *poule d'eau*, which expression we found in the French dictionary.

Reading in *Cape Cod*, Thoreau's claim of the importance of French discovery along the New England coast over that of the English brought up the idea that he might be something of a Frenchman himself. His ancestry was partly French. Certainly he is no Englishman.

November 12 This has been one of the great days. So much has taken form, and opened before us. For one thing, our leaving here, which is now just a matter of doing a number of things. Our minds are ready, suddenly, for the first time. That seems to be all that is important, but there is a new air of confidence and achievement.

November 16   We turned the boat around yesterday, so the main deck would be in the sun, and out of the N wind. Thinking of the hot days of summer and the power of the sun then, this move makes it a new season beyond a doubt. There is still much green in the woods, especially in the low river banks, but all is mellowing. The higher woods show wonderful color, not as bright as the northern maples, but new hues are seen, of dark dull tones, very exciting, the dark magnolias mingled with the brighter trees.

November 18   We enjoy our midday meal on deck, in the warm sun. Wind has been steadily from N or NW and cold. Nights are cold, too, but the sun quite warm. It seems so sensible to have a dwelling that can meet the seasons most favorably.

November 20   Another trip to Natchez yesterday with the Alfred Smiths. We always start out so hopefully, but return worn out and upset. It is so good to be back here again. . . . Our living on the river, in this boat has reached a high degree of refinement. Yet we are always experimenting and improving, in minute details, and once in a while in a radical way.

November 23   The first fish smoking today since leaving the Cumberland. We have missed the smoked fish, too. This batch consisted of 3 goo and a spoonbill, split and skinned, which Alfred gave us. The smokehouse is the usual oil drum. I had noticed it at the top of the bank below the bayou early in the spring, but we hesitated to smoke fish in the hot weather, and seldom had enough fish, anyway. It took some searching to relocate the drum.

November 26   For Thanksgiving we had smoked spoonbill, baked potato, greens, tomato salad and sweet potato pie.

November 28   The SW wind has continued and increased in strength. We pitched about considerably. We carried over the old Model T Ford chassis and dropped it to windward as another anchor.

November 30   The excitement today was a deer swimming in the river. I heard the dogs barking from shore, above the boat, as they do at an odd piece of driftwood going by. When I looked the deer was swimming away from shore, but still within a stone's throw. The dogs were furious. I felt I must do something, so, after some hesitation, put out in the bateau with the intention of driving the deer back to this side, where it would have more chance. By now it was well out in the river, and the current had carried it below the boat. After a hard row I cut it off and it swam back toward this side, though with some reluctance, possibly remembering the dogs. I was surprised at its speed in the water. I could gain on it only by hard rowing. It was a large animal, with no horns. Very delicate and sensitive, with long pointed ears. It reminded me of a very delicately formed mule. Unluckily I had not considered the dogs. If I had taken them along, all would have been well. But they followed the chase down along the shore, and, when within 75 feet of land, the deer heard or saw them, and in a panic headed for the open river. I was not able to drive it toward shore, and as we had drifted down almost to the shoals above the wire crossing, I gave up the attempt, with a stiff row back against the current and wind. The deer swam out holding against the current. I saw it climb out on the sand bar, and run to the upstream end and continue running on the reef as far as the red buoy. Then I could see its head in the water. Not long after, perhaps 15 minutes, two hunters came up in an outboard, running along the outside of the bar. At first I thought they were chasing the deer, but evidently, and fortunately, they had not seen it, for they continued up the river. . . .

After dinner, on the deck in the hot sun, we printed woodblocks. I walked up on the hill, picking some cowpeas ahead of the pigs. A little playing at sunset.

I do not know whether the deer was swimming from the far shore, and was turned back as he neared the shore, by the barking of the dogs, or whether he began his swim from this side. In that case it seems strange he would enter the water so near a dwelling. If he was trying to make this shore, the current might carry him towards us. I say "he" but it must have been a doe, for it was full grown, without antlers. It grunted much like a mule when I grabbed its tail.

December 3   I have a present feeling of achievement. Today I completed the first draft of our writing about our time at Brent, and have gotten underway on our voyage.

December 5 Now we are ready to leave, and will do so in the morning if conditions are favorable. We are eager to go, now.

Tom was down this morning. He and Rosie really would like us to stay. We could never have better neighbors.

December 6 The great day of departure. We awoke with the full moon shining. . . . After breakfast, and considerable work with firewood, lines, fishboxes, planks and the like, it was well along in the morning before we cast off. . . . Wind had increased, but the current carried us swiftly into it.

Again we felt the glory of drifting with the river. The familiar shores were newly seen. . . .

11

River's End
---

*T*his *would be our last stretch of drifting on the Missis-sippi. . . . During our long layover we had forgotten how glorious it is to be adrift. The familiar shores were newly seen, and, released from land, we again became part of the river.*

December 6, 1949, Natchez.   We like this place much more than we expected. Behind a fringe of willows the sand cliffs rise, crowned by thick-growing pines, suggesting a Chinese landscape painting. A view out on the river looking up the old channel. The town and down river view is shut off by the sand bank, so we might be not at all near. Yet its sounds reach us, the varied hum of the saw mill, now in operation, voices, dogs, cars, train whistles, none of this frequent or close by. Once or twice I thought I heard firecrackers.

December 7   A thick fog, high and low, after a showery night. We heard a steamboat whistle, 3 times repeated at intervals. . . . Also heard a rooster crowing this morning, back in the hills.

December 8   I climbed up the hollow away from this eddy, a sort of a box canyon, very wild. Came out in the back yard of a negro cabin. There was a road, many houses, church, school and National cemetery. . . .

Anna reports that a white canoe passed downstream, with a load, and handled as if by experienced canoemen. A deep hulled two-masted schooner passed, too. It had a clipper bow. All sails were in place, furled. Auxiliary motor running.

December 10 This morning I walked up along the shore to the corral and open pastures, a mile, I guess. Rough and wild along the river, I was unprepared, as I returned next to the hill, to find cultivated fields and negro cabins. It was the real South, or the conventional or expected South. Many pecan and fig trees, some walnuts. The low spreading fig trees, with heavy twigs, trunk and all of a gray color, was a note of contrast among the dark bare trees. Yet colored leaves remain, the rich glossy reds of the gums. The pines, cedars, and magnolias come into their own now. Among all this the fig trees stand out unique. . . .

Mr. C.B. Ramsey called when I was away this morning. Last winter in high water, early in the spring, rather, we saw two ramshackle boats in this harbor. We thought what undesirable neighbors they would be. One was Mr. Ramsey, the other Mr. Warner, both honorable gentlemen, and our good friends.

December 11 A high wind from S. So warm I go about barefooted. . . .

This evening I pull the bateau out on the sand bar. Since we do not need it here, I will try to paint it, making some small repairs. This was not planned for, but since there is an opportunity, we will take advantage of it.

December 13 Tom appeared yesterday morning with a goose under his arm, a parting gift from him and Rosie. We set to work on it at once, had another meal of it today, enough for meat pie tomorrow, the cook says.

December 15 Sky cleared and sun came out at midday. Still a chill wind from NW. Yesterday was a dark, wet day, low clouds sweeping down from the N. Some sleet this morning. In the dark days the sun is not to be conceived. When it bursts forth it is a near miracle. Yet after an hour or two we accept it as a matter of course.

Some pleasant indoor work and play yesterday, with a little work on the boat in between showers. This morning I completed the reorganization of all our storage space, including the roof. Order and efficient use of space are essential on this or any boat, especially in our winter drifting. River rose faster last night.

December 18 River still rising sharply. Launched the johnboat this evening, after being out on the bank for just a week. . . . We feel more sure of ourselves with it afloat.

December 19 I was up by starlight to move the boat off the point which was no longer tenable. Now we are inside the cove, just able to see the river over the sandbar. River still rising, and we will no doubt be forced to move again.

Tom came down this morning, bringing the peanuts and ladypea seed, all that he had promised. He took the net away with him. His talk was interesting. About Dr. Shields' son, a year older than Tom. The black and white boy were raised together, and enjoy an intimacy still. . . .

We remember our recent conversation with Mr. and Mrs. Smith. It was a surprise to learn that neither came from river families. Mr. Smith's father apparently sold out his farm in Illinois, bought a houseboat. They started down the Illinois river, greenhorns, managing the boat with poles. Reaching Hardin, I believe, they were told the river below was too deep for their poles, so they rigged up some sweeps. Reaching St. Louis, they sold the boat, but all the family missed it, so that the father gave back the amount already paid. They continued farther down the river, sold out, and returned back up the river. They built, I think, a succession of boats, drifting down and selling out, returning. Mr. Smith first saw his wife (Costain) in Louisiana. Her family had just acquired a boat, and were timid and green.

December 20 River rose perhaps 2 feet the past 24 hours. The point is going under. Moved the boat ahead against a higher bank.

December 25 Made two trips to Natchez, both of us on Friday, to buy our winter reserves of food and supplies. Rowed down to Learned's mill where we loaded everything from the C & G truck. It was remarkable, how quickly all of it was stowed away in its proper place, no crowding, some storage space still available. The deck load is smaller and neater than it ever has been. . . .

H. Pritchertt stopped by yesterday with a mallard duck for our Christmas dinner. Yet it must be for tomorrow, as today we eat roast beef.

While I was out yesterday Anna did some Christmas baking—spice cookies very much like I used to expect at Christmas, even the traditional Santa Claus. . . . Also stars, moon, bells, a trio of string instruments, notes of music, a pirogue. Besides this, some pecan rolls that could not be improved.

December 27 Yesterday I made a trip to Bisland Bayou. I hailed Sonnyboy for a tow as he was passing in Bill's new boat. The bayou was an attractive place now, a good safe harbor. Strange how it felt farther from town than this place, even though we see here no sign of Natchez. I was struck by the wintry aspect. When we left 3 weeks ago it seemed late summer. Brought back a bushel of collard plants, a sack of mustard, parsley plants, fennel plants, both flourishing. This morning our breakfast cereal was ground hen feed, consisting of cracked corn, wheat, milo, maize, and oats. It was very good.

December 28 A fair day, with some of the attributes of winter, but without its bite, like a mild fruit or vegetable which has not the tang of wild varieties.

We were up and about in the darkest morning, eager to make an early start in the fair day promised by the quiet, starry night. After breakfast by candlelight I could see to lash the gangplanks under the guards and take in the lines. We pulled out of the eddy which had been our harbor for 23 days, into the main current of the river. As the sun rose we were slipping past Natchez, an unfamiliar place now, seen through the eyes of a traveller instead of a resident. We drifted under the shining bridge, without an oar's pull, waving to a solitary pedestrian who stopped to watch. We wished we could have seen ourselves from up there as we passed swiftly underneath.

Below the railroad ferry was crossing. The *James Y. Lockwood* was an old, tall-stacked Mississippi sternwheeler. The freight cars were carried on a track barge which was towed alongside. The barge itself, I had been told, was the hull of the dismantled Baton Rouge ferry. . . . Next a busy sawmill, with its picturesque grouping of stacks, derricks, logs, and clouds of jetting steam. St. Catherine's Creek, two miles below Natchez, was a good harbor, with open shores, yet we had the satisfaction of seeing nothing below Natchez, which was as attractive as Bisland bayou and the river above. Around a bend to the left, and Natchez could no longer be seen. The distant blue line of Magnolia bluff above the low shores, but soon that was cut off, and the reach of river which had been our home for ten months became merely part of the river above, a place where we had made a longer stop. . . .

The drifting was perfect, a sunny morning with no wind. The swift current shunted us from one side to the other as it swept around the points, but the shores were easy and we let the boat have her course. . . . We relaxed and enjoyed the passing shores, did some chores about the boat. We are always busy when drifting, always alert.

A fisherman with his outboard bateau pulled up to the deck, drifted with us until we reached his houseboat, on which he apparently lived alone. It was out of sight behind a small clump of an island. He had built a shed there, strange to see so close to the water on such a small island. This man knew about us, though he said he had not passed our boat. We were attracted to him at once, by his appearance and manner, so jaunty and good humored. His usual remarks intimated an unusual depth of understanding.

Our dinner came next, creamed smoked fish, turnips and cornbread. A meal while drifting is usually interrupted and this one was by our running close to a ragged shore at Ellis Cliff. I pulled at the sweeps while we barely cleared a barge and derrick boat loading logs, the black crew watching us. A ragged shore below, swift water and snags along old St. Catherine's creek. Then we entered Glasscock cutoff, with the enticing bend of the old river off to the west. This is a long cut, 4 miles, and the old bendway must be 20. It is the last of the made cutoffs we will pass through. The left shore was an inviting one, with some good coves, although the upbound boat ran close in there. Toward the lower end of the cut we pulled out of the swift current, drifted slowly down to an inlet called the Washout, which the fisherman had spoken of as a good harbor.

The open stream extended straight back into the woods for a long ways, directly away from the western sun. Across the Mississippi were the low close willowed shores of the old river. We pulled in beside the point, tied up for the night, or a week, if it should happen. It was midafternoon, yet we had drifted 23 miles. This was perfect drifting, no hard pulling at the sweeps and oars, a good harbor reached early in the evening.

December 30   A fair morning. We were up at the first paling of night. Cast off with daylight, a light dawn breeze and slow current carried us out into the river. Drifted past the best cypress swamp so far, on the left bank. Breakfast. A fine view back of the cut and old river, with its low closely willowed shores. . . .

Birds on shore heard yesterday and today—bluebirds, phoebe, spring note of chickadee. The morning perfectly still, hazy in the south. I write this on the roof. The Carolina wren sounds from afar. If a boat whistle was as loud in comparison it could be heard in New York. . . .

Dinner while drifting around Palmetto bend. At Palmetto point the current shot over against the right bank, making a series of whirls. We drifted fast, close to the edge of still water. A long reach down to Fort Adams now, to the SE, bluffs at the end showing like blue mountains. We pulled across to left bank, looking for Buffalo bayou. Could not make it out on the shaggy shore flatly lit by the afternoon sun. Came upon it suddenly, were lucky to be in close enough to make it. Landed around the upper point, which was open and grassy.

Tar vat, nets and fisherman's gear about. Bayou about as wide as the Washout, say 100 yards. Still much of the afternoon left, so we played and explored after chores were done. Talked with a passing fisherman. He advised the "Chafalay" for us. We will consider that. Cloudy this evening, warm and perfectly still.

December 31   Buffalo bayou. The weather cleared during the night and a stiff wind from SE sprang up. It blew all day shifting to S. We are satisfied to remain in port, after two fine days of drifting. It is remarkable—two perfect days just when we desired them. An easy morning, after two days of early getaways. I rearranged the deck load again making all ratproof, especially the pecans, which the rodent from Jones Hole bounces on the roof at night and often during the day. Anna cut my hair, with *Arabia Deserta* as accompanying reading. . . .

This Saturday afternoon we visited the town of Fort Adams. . . . The town was attractive as we approached, a cluster of gray buildings, mostly unpainted with gray metal roofs. Immense trees dwarfed the houses, and above all rose the line of bluffs. They offered a striking contrast with the lowlands with their lively color and sharp contours. We went in the store of Curry Brothers, also the post office. It was a fine example of country store and we liked the proprietor very much. As we walked back to the river we met him again, horseback, looking over some cattle. He pointed out the site of the old Fort Adams on the highest point of the ridge.

Tonight a chorus of peepers in the flooded swamp. Many doves in the fields, buzzards and unknown birds.

January 2, 1950 · Beginning as soon as I was out of bed, I worked under the deck, in the hold, so to speak, cleaning, inspecting, reinforcing and caulking. This last to keep out a small seepage of water which kept the corner of the bilge damp. The boat is sound and tight but must be watched now. The upper edge of the gunwale on that corner is rotted badly, when water leaked through from the deck. The deck is tight now, and I left alone the weakened timber, since it was above the water line. That, too, must be watched.

During the rest of the morning, while Anna wrote letters, I walked down the shore to the bluff. A ragged dirt road ran along the foot of it downriver. A delightful place, open, with big trees, even some mossy rock. . . . I liked the place and the harbor so well that we plan to move down there.

I am trying to recover from a cold, the first I have had in years. Anna suffered from one also, and we blame it on our trips to the crowded stores of Natchez.

The drifters' boats which put out from this harbor are very interesting. I think we have seen three operated by negroes. One, a match for Snookum's boat in Natchez, has the slowest turning engine I have even seen. Yet the boat moves right along.

A yellow butterfly today.

January 3 We made another trip to Fort Adams, rowing up

301

another slough. . . . Storekeeper said the town is flooded often now, rarely in former days. Said 1912 was the first bad flood they had. Does that mean the bed of river is higher, or as storekeeper said, that the levees concentrate the water?

Saw a redheaded woodpecker, the first one this winter.

January 4   The morning was threatening. The wind which had blown from SSW for an unbroken 24 hours, had ceased, but the sky was full of low, ragged clouds, with showers and fog on the river. We decided to try to make Clark's creek, 1.2 miles below, before the weather broke loose, and cast off before breakfast. It was an exciting run, with fog, gusts of wind and rain, the worst weather of the day. Made the creek mouth easily and tied up on lower bank. We can look out on the river and up a long reach to NW. . . .

To celebrate *[Harlan's 50th birthday]* we had a jar of pork tenderloin, parsnips, mashed potatoes, green salad, grape juice and chocolate cake, made yesterday. We are pleased with our traveling garden. The collards from Bisland bayou are still fresh, the parsnips and turnips sound, and the box of parsley, fennel and collards growing well. Sweet potatoes are in perfect condition. Our lack is corn, which so far we must buy. And wheat. . . .

This is a fine place. . . .

Night insects as in summer. . . . At night the navigation light hangs in the darkness like a star.

We did some good playing today. How satisfactory it is to send forth the music of Brahms into the woods.

January 5   In the rainy darkness yesterday, we were startled by a nearby voice. Dogs barked and I went out with the flashlight. A solitary figure had pulled alongside in a bateau. He came in, and after taking off his raincoat sat by the fire and talked, with difficulty. His name was Williams, and he lived a third of a mile above the creek in a sort of dug-out camp. I saw it when I walked along there 2 days before. He was a rather old man, not as crude and insensitive as he first appeared. He had gone down the river about 2 miles in the afternoon, apparently to run his traps. He had a live coon in a sack in his boat. Coming back, the rain, or something, stopped his outboard motor, and he spent a long time paddling around some swift points. Said if he had known or remembered we were here, he would have walked up, had us put him across this creek.

January 6 A wild night, the past one. The rain of the previous 24 hours continued and increased, with heavy thunder and lightning. I looked out, after we had been asleep, and saw current and drift moving down the creek past the boat. By the time I was dressed in complete rainclothes, the creek was flowing too swiftly for me to cross and loosen the line tied there. I cast off the line at the boat, let the boat swing around close to the bank. We were in a fortunate position, on the inside of a curve, and in almost slack water. The run-out reached the river, and at the mouth of the creek was a whirling mass of driftwood. This at times extended almost up to our boat. After I had been up an hour the run-out slackening, the rain coming in broken showers, I went back to bed and had a good sleep. . . .

The wind blew the drift up the creek today, most of it is above us, filling the stream completely. I made my way through it to retrieve the line tied to the other side. At the height of the run-out, there was a series of waves in the swift current, "haystacks," and some heavy trees were carried out. This was not as bad as it might be, say if the water in the creek was shallow. Yet I hope we are never in a worse run-out.

Another fortunate circumstance last night—it was but a night or two past the full moon. By its diffused light through the clouds I could see very well. Many birds were hopping around on the drift. Some crows at a distance from the boat. Outside our windows were many bluebirds. For the first time I heard them make a sound other than their alto warble—a dry unmusical chirp.

January 8 We think we do very well to manage a successful washday in a period of winter drifting. Yesterday's was near perfect— a sunny windy day, abundance of clear water, rainwater this time, a good place to hang the clothes. The only mishap was the breaking of the clothes line in a flapping wind, but little damage was done, the clothes being dry. By nightfall every piece was dry and stowed away, as was all the gear. . . .

We see many birds about. A flock of grackles in a long line

passed overhead, at least half a mile of them. We saw a mockingbird chasing a bluebird around and round in a thorn tree. Redheaded woodpeckers, as well as downy and red-bellied, Brown thrashers, and an occasional robin.

January 9 We walked to Fort Adams, rowing first up to the landing of Williams' camp, then followed the trail which runs along the base of the bluffs. On our left, the level river land thick with willows. On our right the varied scenery of the bluff, caving banks, evergreens, cedar except for half a dozen pines, holly and green vines, some hardwood trees, much spanish moss. I met a cowboy on a white horse, the man evidently part Indian, part negro. As we returned he was coming back toward town, calling the cattle by blowing on a horn leading them on by dropping something, perhaps salt, in the road. His horn was a cowhorn, its tone clear and ringing, but sweet.

January 10 No fire for warmth is necessary this morning. Yesterday we ate our dinner on deck, Anna in a thin, shortsleeved blouse. . . .

After an early dinner, eaten on deck again, we decided to pull out of Clark's creek in the face of uncertain weather. . . . Down Fort Adams reach we pulled over to the right bank, and stayed within reach of it the rest of the way, fearing an offshore wind. Drifted slowly along a caving bank. Rain began to fall, very dark sky. I saw ourselves as from a distance, drifting on that swift drift-carrying river, past the caving bank, amid rain and thunder, to an unknown harbor.

The Mud Hole, as our neighbor at Clark's creek called it, was a mean place. The swift current swept us by the point, we pulled out of it into the center of the eddy. Above us, the current of the eddy was running swiftly out into the river. I took our long cordelling line ashore, and pulled the boat in against some small willows out of the current and close enough to shore. Fog closed in, then darkness, so we know little of our position. The ominous sound of a whirlpool below us.

January 11 A most heavy day. Fog lay on the river from daylight to dark. At evening the clouds parted in the west, there was a red gleam of the setting sun, but the thick fog was unaffected. . . .

River rose about 14 inches in the past 24 hours. It is now sweeping directly into the old river. We wonder how we will get out of here without being carried down the Atchafalaya. It is a strange situation. In a run-out the Red river pours through the old river into the Mississippi. Its driftwood is piled on the west side of the bridge piers in the ditch. One thing is certain, the Atchafalaya never flows into the Mississippi. It drains both the other rivers. Thus the Mississippi at this point has water running out of it and into it.

January 12   A fog this morning heavier than yesterday's. It left at midday, and we had clear air after 2 nights and 11/2 days of fog. Now at nightfall the clouds are nearly all gone.

January 13   No fog today but a high wind from S. Very rough water in the swift current off the point, some low swells rolling in here, giving a nice motion to the boat, tied to a bending willow.

The same motorboat which went up the river day before yesterday, came by this morning. I hailed him in—a friendly fisherman. . . . Said the current always flows out of the Mississippi here. Gave us no hope of making it from our present position down the Mississippi. When asked he readily agreed to tow us out in the river when he would pass here again, day after tomorrow. . . .

We played again this morning, took a walk on shore in the afternoon, among many other pursuits during the day. On the ground by a trail in the woods I found a quantity of white chunks, about a bucketful, which appeared to be paraffin. It was paraffin by all the tests I knew. Made a small candle of it, which burned perfectly.

January 14   Last night in our restless sleep we attempted to cross time after time the rough water and contrary currents that lay ahead of us. Early in the morning we set on the real voyage. It was dark and still. The sudden beginning of a windless rain delayed us, while we donned rainclothes. We pulled out into the current of the eddy and rowed hard to hit the swift current of the river with as much momentum as possible, for not until we were through the whirls at the edge would we begin to cross the current which flowed westward. We pulled hard but sighting on the point above could see ourselves slowly slipping into the old river. At the parting of the current is the apex of a triangle of dead water extending perhaps 300 yards out from shore, its base along the reveted shore, current running along one side, down the Mississippi, along the other into the Atchafalaya. We were still in the Atchafalaya stream when we passed this point, but we were able to pull out of it, to our great satisfaction, and into still water close to shore. A hundred feet to the west we would have been irretrievably lost. Now we made our way along the newly reveted shore, and after considerable trouble with driftwood, and as the current increased, with eddies and swirling water, we were taken up by the true current of the Mississippi. . . .

We skimmed along the shores, and rowed almost constantly out into the river. Rain had ceased. We were past the chute which we thought might be the beginning of the old Raccourci bendway before settling down to breakfast and easy drifting. I filed a saw, Anna did the morning chores. A fine view of the Tunica bluff downstream.

A fisherman's motorboat pulled up along side, the man said he thought we might be Luther Gillison, which we took as no compliment. His name was Bass, fisherman and light tender. We passed his deep-hulled houseboat, beached out among some trees near an inlet at the lower end of Raccourci cutoff. A washing was hanging out, the womenfolk came out to wave. He was quietly friendly, inviting us to lay over with them a while.

A head wind sprang up and we approached Tunica bend with whitecaps. The place was attractive, houses and grassy slopes, another wrecked railroad bridge, a barge of logs being unloaded, the same one which was towed out of the Red River, judging the tug standing by. We were carried by current and wind over to the Tunica bluff in swift water past the Tunica bluff light, 290.6. Although we had just decided to run as long as we could, the inlet at the lower end of the bluff seemed so attractive that we pulled out of the swift current, and after some easy maneuvering entered a narrow ditch with grassy banks. We had our dinner and the afternoon was quiet and clearing. Yet we did not regret the short run, of 10 miles on a fine day, considering that our successful navigation redeemed it.

It was a drifter's dream of a perfect harbor. We looked for similar places, and nearly always found them, on the rest of the way down the river.

The final section of our voyage was of a carefree, holiday nature all through, full of novelty and pleasant surprise.

January 15 In this snug harbor the constant strain we were under at our last station is apparent. Through the fog and wind, and in the night, the roar of the waters across our path, the huge pieces of driftwood shooting past the point, made our further progress a matter of doubt and concern. The shore was inhospitable, the view bleak. The swiftly running river on its way over the bank. We were cheered by a trim phoebe who remained almost constantly about our boat.

This place in contrast is idyllic, a grassy bank, where not even a footboard is needed to step ashore. Above an open meadow, the bricks of an old chimney in the grass under a chinaberry tree, two figtrees nearby. The bluffs are low and rounded, with open woods like the classic groves and vales of antiquity. Clear water at the bend of the little creek.

Yesterday afternoon we walked to Brandon, half a mile, which turned out to be a lane against the low bluff lined with negro cabins, with an old plantation house where "white folks" lived. This is the first settlement entirely of negroes we have seen, all so friendly and good natured and picturesque. We feel far to the south now. Saw palmettoes and in the winter gardens, peas climbing sticks, "pomps" in the cabin yards, little mounds of earth ventilated at the top where sweet potatoes are stored. We were intrigued by the plantation house, a large two-story frame of classic form.

January 17 Late in the morning the rain stopped. We pulled out in the river under a cloudy sky but almost no wind. . . . The sound of a distant train whistle to the east—comforting and reassuring to one on the wilderness water. . . . Drifted down at edge of current, wondering where Bayou Sara was, when we saw the ferry boat come out of a hole in the willows, much closer than we expected. Pulled in close to shore, drifted and rowed down to entrance. . . . The motor boat *Red Cross*, run by two young fellows as friendly and obliging as could be, towed us perhaps 1/4 mile up, above their highwater landing. Tied up in a snug harbor before darkness and rain set in.

About 26 miles today. Many frogs in Tunica Swamp.

January 18 Fog this morning. We write letters, take them up to post office, a mile away. The town [St. Francisville] lies entirely on the hill, a railroad at the bottom. We felt we were in a far, strange part of the country, the character of the houses and gardens so new to us. . . .

Yesterday when drifting we noticed especially the varying speed of driftwood, and of the current. . . . There is a difference in surface currents and the deeper ones which gives a different speed to deep and light floating drift.

January 19 Here with people about, the noise of motors and the always-felt proximity of the town, we look back on the remote places behind us, where we were so close to river and sky, as we might think of some high place above the world where we had lived a free and hardy life, where our aspirations were somewhat realized.

Yet here we feel a comfort and safety from the proximity of people. The sound of cars and trains is natural to us, I root in the dumps and all is familiar. Found some pieces of belting which will make sandals and various items needed or potentially useful. There was a large cornfield down that way, in which, judging by the new sprouts, much corn was left last fall. Our failure to get corn was due to our situation, I think in a place where none was grown. If we had been adrift in the fall we would doubtless have found all we could use.

January 22 A second trip to St. Francisville this morning. . . . The fishermen at the levee end are friendly and helpful. This low levee once enclosed a square of land in which was a town, Bayou

Sara, a prosperous city in steamboat days. Ruins of the buildings are about us. Part of the levee has disappeared into the bayou with caving banks. We hear again that the river rises to greater heights often compared with half a century ago. Thus a town could be in this low land, now an impossibility. The increased height of floods and their frequency is no doubt due to levees as they say. Also, I think, to the silting of the riverbed.

A mocking bird looking in our windows yesterday. We did not at first recognize it close at hand. Watched closely today—a goldencrowned kinglet. We saw an eagle in the bayou, first since Missouri, I believe. Hear some spring bird notes and a great chorus of frogs in the swamps.

An interesting railroad with old engines, I believe with simple cylinders, hauling a few freight cars. I walked back that way, watched the convicts in striped clothing load cars.

January 23 River continues to rise at a good rate. We had already moved from under the live oaks to higher ground at the ferry landing. . . . We decided to leave, since that ground was going under, and we must move somewhere. Since last evening the bayou had filled solid with driftwood, carried in by an eddy, for more than 100 yards from the river. Exit that way was impossible. After considerable difficulty, struggling with submerged grapevines, dewberry bushes and trees, we pulled and pushed our way down to the low water ferry road, which was open to the river. Now, however, a wind came up, blowing in off the river. We tied up, wind increased.

A feature now is the prodigious multitude of ants on the vines and bushes, sometimes in clusters like a swarm of bees. Think of all the ants driven out of the ground by the water covering square miles of surface.

January 24 All yesterday afternoon we lay in the ferry road, a third of the way from the levee to the riverbank. Wind continued, even after sunset, though abating. I did not drop back to the levee, thinking to hold our position for an early start, but it would have been better if I had tied up and stayed there today. As it was, after a quiet and starry night, I pulled the boat out to the last trees at daybreak. There we lay, ate breakfast, waited for the fog to lift.

Fearing a wind would blow when the fog did break up, I towed out in the river to try and drift down the dim shores. Heavy, motionless drift. Fog became worse, and current was farther out than I realized. We lost sight of shore, let the light breeze blow us back in. I found we were 2 or 3 hundred yards below the opening we had come out of.

The fog breaking a little, we pulled out into the current again, drifted past a light and daymark without seeing it, made land at the next light. Swift current close in shore now. We pulled out of it, entered a cove which was all of the harbor we were to have.

January 25 We were invaded by ants last night, they swarmed all over the boat, infesting the food cupboard on deck heavily. We are thankful to have poison for them. They take advantage of any twig which will serve as a bridge to the boat. . . .

One day is never like another, except that something is doing every minute. Today, for instance, the battle with the ants, then a tussle with the drift about the boat. Anna wrote letters during that, and while she got dinner, of fish hash, fresh mustard greens and elderberry cobbler, I did some writing. After dinner, while Anna washed dishes, I and the dogs took a walk into the swamps. I could just wade the backwater in hip boots. It was a novel walk, high and dry through the flooded swamp. Ties and rails were all gone, only a grass grown embankment. While I was making a watercolor Sambo started up something, and went off down the right of way, his barking fading away like a receding locomotive. Soon he returned dripping wet, carrying a big rabbit, also wet. It was too big for a cottontail, probably a swamp rabbit. Anna had her work all done when I returned to the boat, and after cleaning the rabbit, we went off in the boat to the old house below to get some clear water out of its rainbarrel. A tug went by, running light downstream, and swamped our boat.

We did have time to play a little Purcell before dark.

January 26 Today I discovered on the farm across the creek, a few rows of cabbage just being submerged. . . . I gathered 15 or 18 heads, sloshing around in the water wearing rubber boots. Also pulled a peck of fresh turnips. So our stock of green vegetables is replenished. . . . Today for dinner we had steamed cabbage in quantity, along with fried rabbit. A delicious bit of cooking, that was.

We played some this afternoon, essaying the Brahms viola quintet (III).

One of the most cheering notes these days is the meadowlark's whistle. Yesterday we saw our first pelicans. First two or three, then a flock riding the drift. Their flight is marvelous. Flapping their great wings slowly, they skim the water, all in a long line, alternately flapping and sailing. The remarkable feature is that they do this in unison, like a well trained crew.

January 26 Fog all day. A fine session in the afternoon with the Brahms. In the evening the sky cleared and the fading sunset was a cheerful sight. These days of fog and flood, especially here in our exposed position, so open to storms, might be called trying. We seldom feel that they are, just a trace now and then. With the Brahms on our side, and so much else, we could easily put through a winter of fog.

January 29 We are fascinated by the changing formation of drift in our cove. There is an amazing difference in the current as the wind changes. In a stiff on shore wind, as today, the drift is packed in. The current of the eddy often shoves out the entire island, against the wind. This evening as the wind lessened, the whole mass to our surprise moved up the river around the point. Then it came sailing back down, crashing into the small willows below, then surging out into the river and away.

January 30 We pulled out of the cove, our harbor for 6 days, surely a ringside seat from which to watch the Mississippi river. The current, which a few minutes before was rushing past the shore line, was farther out when we entered the river, and we were carried upstream as we rowed out. Soon we were sailing by the shores of unbroken forest. . . .

I did notice one deserted farmhouse. No doubt when the river went over the banks less often, river bank farms were frequently seen. We see now only abandoned ones.

A stiff wind now, almost directly upstream. We followed the shore closely, and into Fancy Point chute. Now the wind was more

311

on shore, and both of us must row steadily. The waiting dinner was disregarded. Past Thompson Creek, an open aisle through the willows, no land to be seen. A log raft tied up. A rip of current over what was probably a bar in low water, slack water and heavy drift in our lee. It was a thrilling place.

Fancy Point Towhead standing off shore up the river. Point Menoir breaking off suddenly on the right. Ahead of us the clay banks of the bluffs, appearing as high land after the low shores of flood. A thick pine woods coming down to the water. To the north the shore was willows thick as grass, red in the sun, an unbroken hedge from Thompson Creek to the bluff at Port Hickey.

Wind increased, and we could not hold out of the eddy. After a long hard pull we gave it up, let the wind and backlash carry us into the willows, almost back to Thompson Creek. Dinner at last.

Then I rowed with the dogs out through the eddy into the current and down to the bluff, running into a narrow cove in the pine grove. It was a strange sensation, to land from the Mississippi river among the tall pines. The earth and air were different, the wind across the needles a sound from far off. Looking out on the river, its vast flatness was more impressive than ever. I walked up the hill through the grove, past some old headstones, to the road. The tall trees of its border, decorated with moss and mistletoe, made of the narrow road a magnificent avenue. . . .

The trip back to our boat was easy. The current divided at the pine grove, eddy and main river. The eddy, nearly a mile across, was swift along the clay bank. . . . The willows along the eddy were lined with driftwood, until our boat was reached. It was in a small cove, clear of driftwood. Thompson Creek is nearly 1/4 mile to the west, the nearest land, 3/4 mile to the east. We have never passed a night so far off shore.

A beautiful evening, clear and still, a bright moon.

January 31 We lay in our willow harbor.

February 1 Early, in the usual morning fog and calm, we towed the boat into Thompson Creek. . . . We had been tied up for 36 hours to the willows by the eddy, 3/4 mile from dry land. . . . As the fog thinned, still no wind, we headed out into the river. Hard pulling brought us into the current. . . . Soon we were at the Profit Island chute. Our plan was to go down the chute, but all the current seemed to be going the other way, so we were carried with the drift to the right of the island. . . . The current was swift, and we travelled fast into a stiff breeze, rounding the bend close to the left bank. On the east reach I rowed and Anna, too, toward the end, so the cross wind would not carry us ashore. . . . We suddenly saw the Baton Rouge bridge, a tower and smoke, across Devil's Swamp. Around Springfield Bend we ate our dinner and in peace. . . . On the final reach now, the bluff at Scotlandville in the distance and evidence of the city and industry, an exciting prospect. Approaching Baton Rouge bayou which comes out of Devil's Swamp on the left, we saw another eddy ahead, marked by the heavy drift collected there. We pulled out around it, and then into the trees at the lower end of the eddy, below Light 234.4, 20 miles from Thompson creek.

We did not feel restricted in any way, tied up far off shore. The dogs adapted themselves very well too, and our boat seemed truly a boat. We could make such a voyage seldom touching land. . . .

It is exciting to see the lights of the city, traffic on the bridge, some real trains. City noises, and smells. . . .

A full moon, I think, a warm, partly cloudy evening. This has been one of our best days of drifting.

February 4   After some investigation this morning, we dropped down the shore about a quarter of a mile to the landing below the abandoned Mengel plant. It was a rather tricky move, swift current and eddies along the shore, and a landing in an eddy. Hailed in a passing bateau before we started, the lamplighter who tends a few lights on this bend. He had experience with log rafts, and spoke of "making your check." We made our check all right, and eased into the grassy shore, a fine place for us. With a house on top of the bank where we can get water, a black top road running out to the highway, open fields for the dogs to run in. . . .

It is strange how we are affected by different landings—the others above were depressing and unfriendly. The lamplighter visited us again, for he leaves his boat here. He is a true riverman. He saw us come around the bend, said be was glad he was not in our place.

February 8 Paul Love, coming in from his lights, stayed to supper. We wonder what he thought of tortillas and tomato salad. He is the most assiduous light tender we have met. Out again yesterday. He has 4 lights, the Scotts bluff blinker, Ben Burman light above Baton Rouge bayou, the light on Free Nigger Point and the one below it. He says a blinker light is paid $3.60 per month, oil lights $12.40. I believe he is the first light tender we have seen using a rowboat. The eddy helps him after he reaches it, carries him up to the bayou. Then he crosses over to the point from the eddy. A hard pull back to this side in the present current, which he says is unusually swift.

Chores about the boat this morning for both of us. I planted some lettuce in our roof garden. The parsley and fennel do well—plenty of fennel for salads. Gathered a mess of poke, the plants 2 or 3 feet high.

Last night we heard the sound of machinery below the bridge, and when the fog cleared this morning, there was a freighter being unloaded. It is a definite harbinger of the ocean and salt water. From now on the river will not be the same to us.

February 9 This morning Mr. L. L. Ricks took me and the dogs in his car to the veterinarian, to have the dogs shot for rabies. Now they have jingling tags and look like responsible citizens.

February 10 Found a large cedar tree on the dump. It is a pleasure to burn after the smoky scraps that have made our fuel lately. I continue to marvel at the good material thrown away. I could build a good house of the bricks and boards available along this mile of river.

February 13 On Saturday we all walked out to the Scenic Highway, via roads and railroads. Found a feed store kept by a former shantyboat lady. Rainbow Feed Store. Her father a former river pilot, Brooks.

The *Jason* passed up with a heavy tow, running the bend wide. A fine sight, the water pouring from her great wheel. . . .

Saturday out on the highway, in a store buying some spareribs for a special treat, though we find that meat is not usually a good buy, I asked the butcher for dog bones. He said he had none, then

picked up a tray, asked if we had a big dog or a little one. I said,
one of each. So he cut the bone in two. It was a large one. When
we got it home it was so fresh that we cooked it for soup for ourselves. Delicious vegetable soup.

February 15 A cold wind yesterday, and today, with a warm
sun. We went to Baton Rouge today. From the tower of the State
Capitol we could look back up the river at our last day's run, the
bends and Profit Island chute, and the bluff and even the dark pines.
. . . It was like a glimpse into the past.

February 16 This day we left our anchorage above the Baton
Rouge bridge, after a stay of 15 days in that vicinity. A clear, chill
morning, underway at sunrise. We pulled hard at once, to clear the
bridge pier and the dock below, but at that had little room to spare.
Three tankers at the Standard Oil dock, one leaving, another loading,
the third just landing. They seemed huge ships as they loomed up
in the smoky air. . . . The current was very swift and we were
carried over to the right bank by it and a light breeze from NE. The
steam ferry *Louisiana* held up as it approached the Port Allen dock
to let us pass. . . . Soon we were drifting easily down midstream.

Nearing the sharp bend, I rowed steadily but we rounded Sardine
point with no trouble. This was the first bend of a huge S curve
the river makes around Manchac bend, to the west, a crossing current carried us over to the left bank, passing Manchac landing close
in. We recalled its significance in the early history of this country.
The English made a settlement here, and planned to use Manchac
bayou to reach the gulf though Lake Pontchartrain, thus avoiding
the Spanish bottleneck at New Orleans.

The day was bright and cool. A light wind from NW sprang
up, the last remnant of the blow of yesterday and day before. We
must pull to keep off the shore above Placquemine Point. Current
slow for aways and we passed two boats which were coming up
through the easy water. At the point the current increased, and
shot off to the right bank at the sharp bend at Placquemine. However
the wind carried us into and through an eddy on the left. A shantyboat, nice looking, in the slack water and a flat with a tent on it.
Motor boat with a canopy, crossing back from Placquemine stopped,

asked if we needed any help, advised caution at the bend below. Another boat up around the bend, the fourth passed close by. It is an uneasy time, when you see the head barge with a bone in her teeth coming out from behind the willow point, the towboat still out of sight.

Placquemine made a fine appearance in the bright sun, the entrance to the canal, lock close to river and an odd white building, a Dutch house Anna called it, as a lock building. . . . A square belfry in the town, possibly at a monastery, another high square building, a curious lift bridge. Strange to see only the peaks of the house gables sticking up over the levee. The last segment of the S now, a long run to the east, gradually carried over to the right bank by wind and current. Soon we were clawing off and about 7 miles below Placquemine, in slower current, seeing open water to the levee, I caught on to a tree and then warped the boat into the channel between trees and levee. We were at Golden Ridge landing, 201.4, about 32 miles below Mengel Landing. Only midafternoon when we had our dinner.

Going ashore and climbing the levee, surprised as usual to see road, houses and fields on the other side, seeming even more strange now, at a lower level than the river. . . .

We swing between the willows 200 feet off shore. A calm clear night.

February 17 This clear morning was of spring. We are confused about the season, with the warm winter, the green willow shoots coming almost before the yellow leaves of fall have disappeared, the summer birds about, the green grass. Yet there is now a difference in the sky, in the feel of the air. We notice many sprouting willows. It is a different land, too, a different river, narrow and deep and swift, already the feel of a delta in the flat shores with no entering stream. Anna figured that the last one was Baton Rouge Bayou out of Devil's Swamp.

The shores are more thickly settled than any we have passed. The sound of trains and highway from both sides, even when the levee is out of sight behind the thick growing willows. Then for a mile or more, on the outside of a bend, often, in other places, the levee is the river shore. Tops of houses, chimneys, gambits, church steeples rise above. Often tall chimneys back from the river, surrounded by buildings and tanks. They were sugar houses. At White Castle the curious spire of a church, suggesting Normandy. Old plantation houses, in thick groves of cedar and live oak. This is the river of the south that we have looked for all the way down. . . .

Yesterday in the warm afternoon sun as we lay off shore between the flooded trees, a marsh hawk, female, we decided, sailed and hovered about a tiny grassy island with such ease and grace that we were enchanted. . . .

We hauled ourselves out of our harbor this morning as the sun rose clear on the horizon. In the night, waking often from sound sleep, as I do on strange shores, I heard a sound which I knew at once was a ship. I wake Annie and we watched it pass not far out, slowly, looming high above us. It made hardly a wave!

Easy drifting even around the sharp bend at White Castle. . . . We had just remarked about the easy time we were having and that this last bend, around Philadelphia Point, should not be a bad one, when I heard rough water ahead, and we began pulling off shore. Then all hands were called but we went into the eddy after all. This was at Gem Light, not a big eddy, but as bad as any we have been through, with some swift deep whirls. We had to go up through it and make another try, which was successful. . . .

Below we followed the left bank and when almost to 81 Mile Point, saw the head of a tow coming around. When the boat saw us (it was a DPC, the *Kokoda*, with a big tow of barges) the pilot whistled once, so we hugged the shore, which was here nothing but trees standing in water, the current pouring through them. The boat passed us close in, many of the men out to watch us. A young fellow with glasses on the bridge shouted that another tow was following them. We thought it best to tie up, instead of rounding the point into the boat's path. I caught on to a sycamore, we got out two lines, the current being swift. The next boat was the *Harry Truman*, with its curious boxlike tow. It ran the bend wide, going up on the other side. While we waited for a little tug with two empties to pass down, we saw a tanker rounding the bend above.

So we ate the dinner which Annie had ready, a feast of baked ham, sweet potatoes, string beans. A splendid view of the tanker, *Esso Shreveport*, the one which had docked at Baton Rouge as we passed. It rolled a few large swells into the trees, not bad. We had to wait for another boat to come up, the *Lehigh*. Then we cast off, and drifted around the bend easily, though there were areas of rough water. . . .

It was midafternoon when we tied up to a small island, part of the old levee. The new one was perhaps 100 yards distant, a gay sight, the grass so green, people promenading, dipping for shrimp, for the current was quite swift, children playing. The peaks of the town rose above.

After all was made shipshape, we went ashore, all of us, late in the afternoon. A colorful shabby end of town, Port Barrow. Talked to an old man, Mr. Kane, and walked with him along the levee to his house. . . . We were delighted with the town, a clean, quiet place, with some old buildings and an air of quaintness. Galleries over the sidewalks, of wrought iron, as one would expect in New Orleans, some bizarre architecture. The chinaberry trees quite thick with leaves, figs well out. Bayou Lafourche once was connected with the river here, now the levee cuts it off, but the old bed is there, close to the river. . . .

February 18 A perfect day for drifting, one of the finest, but we remained in port with no inclination to travel farther on. Partly, I suppose, because there remain only two more days of drifting before reaching New Orleans and all its complications. Two days like this one might mean the end of our drifting. We feel also that our destination has been reached here. This is the country and life that we expected to find at the river's end. . . .

This place has many merits of its own, too. A small town, away from the main line. A perfect harbor for the boat, so we are not concerned about letting this fine weather go by, and will lay over another day at least. As for weather, surely the endless fogs of winter will not return, and fair days will be more frequent.

February 21 Mardi Gras. They observe this day, all through the country, a holiday for workers and schoolchildren, some stores closed.

318

We heard about this from a visitor at College Point, where we now are. He was Donald Saunier, 16, who came aboard from his little rowboat and then accompanied us on a walk to Jefferson College of the Jesuits.

We pulled in here, against the open levee, when the wind increased, with clouds and made the sharp bend below a hazardous place. Wind blew a little when we left Donaldsonville at sunrise, but the sky was clear and we hoped for another day like the 4 quiet ones spent at Donaldsonville. However, there was a good breeze as we rounded the bend below, and off Point Houmas. Along here the Coast Guard cutter *Salvia*, a handsome, deep sea craft, slowed down as it passed close to us, a voice shouted, through a loudspeaker, "Ahoy Houseboat! Are you all right?" We answered that we were, though with some reservations in our own minds. The bend below was very rough, but we rounded Brilliant Point and had a quiet passage down the reach toward College Point.

February 22 Another ship, tanker, passed up during the hard storm which preceded the dawn. A visit from Donald Saunier at breakfast, and now 5 boys and girls stand on the levee, watching us as they wait for their school bus. After a showery morning, and dinner, we cast off in early afternoon. Sky mostly cloudy, but no wind, an easy passage around College Point, some rowing to keep out of the eddy, then down the wooded left bank. . . .

Wind freshened around Belmont Bend, blew us in to willows, below Light 151.7. While tied up there, inside with shutters closed, reading, we were boarded by an outboard bateau, a man and a boy. Man introduced himself as Deslattes, fisherman. He lives over the levee just below here. We are waiting now for wind to slacken. If it does not, we will pull into this cove.

After some reading by the fire, we observed the wind to lessen, and cast off. Easily made it down the shore, for the wind stopped altogether. Ran by the hole in the willows, which was Deslattes' landing, and rounded the point. Another long eddy, which we skirted. Some openings in the trees before the levee appeared, and we pulled toward the left bank at the end of the eddy. However, a wind sprang up from N, directly off shore, so we had to give it up. Turned and ran with the wind for the right bank, far off. A quick crossing. The boat took the bit between her teeth and we could not turn her. Made a fine landing, just below the trees on an open levee. Wind strong on shore, but no current. We cordelled and shoved to move up and around an angle in the levee to sheltered water inside the trees. Darkness fell as we were tieing up. . . .

The *Delta Queen* up, lights ablaze. . . .

The contrary winds springing up as we were about to land, reminded us of the wilful, god-directed winds which hindered Odysseus. Where would we be now, if no wind had interfered?

> *Another day's run would have taken us to New Orleans. The shantyboater has an instinctive feeling for keeping out of the way, however. We decided to find a good harbor still in the country, but as close to the city as possible. . . . The nearness of the City was felt. . . . The river was unchanged, however. We did not like to think of leaving it.*

February 23 We will not mind if the weather holds us here, in fact, may stay a few days even in good weather. We have a fine harbor, the country is fascinating. . . . The houses are as closely built as in a city suburb, and a sidewalk extends as far as I walked. There are many old houses. Some might be called plantation houses, some are mere cabins. Most are unpainted. Nearly every roof is unpainted metal. This goes well with the weatherbeaten sides, giving the country a lichenous appearance. . . .

Talked some to the negroes who are on watch here for the body of a negro boy drowned 19 days ago. They have kept vigil every day.

February 24 A fair warm day, perfectly still. A better day for drifting could not be expected, yet we did not shove off. In the morning we rowed down to the ferry landing, left the boat there and crossed over to Lutcher. There we were taken by the name of the church—Our Lady of Prompt Succour. It was printed in large letters on a rectangular sign nailed to the steeple. Perhaps she is the patron saint of drifters.

February 25 Midmorning, the air clear and still, sunny for the most part, we cast off. An easy matter, with only two lines out, tied to trees, no gangplanks to handle, anchor and sweeps all in place. Old Mae Young, still on watch, waved farewell, called all the neighborhood, probably, for as we drifted down along the levee a group stood at the levee point watching us. Good drifting. Past Wallace, waving at Gerald Kliebert, who seemed to have posted two boys as sentinels to watch for our coming. . . .

A splendid view back up the river, from Bonnet Carré Point, the far-off strip of low shore appearing as land mist when seen from out at sea. . . .

Round the bend above the spillway well over to the right bank. An exciting view down this reach, with various craft on the river, a tanker at the refinery at Norco. . . .

At first the spillway could not be seen, as it was behind a screen of willows. The roar of water could be heard but not as loudly as we expected. We noticed no draw in the current on the far side. The spillway is about 11/4 miles long, and we could see it plainly along its lower end. All of it seemed open. It was an exciting passage. . . .

February 26 Soon we were around the bend, our thoughts on a harbor. . . . We crossed over with the current to the right bank, hung on to a tree, above the Luling-Destrehan ferry to investigate the batture. Found it too shallow, dropped down below the ferry, pulled in behind some thick, green willows at the lower end of Luling. One line to a tree, another to a spike driven in the levee. No great attraction to the place, but it was a harbor, and we were glad to be in.

February 27 A trip today by bicycle down the right bank, across the bridge and back to the Destrehan ferry, about 35 miles riding. . . . Anna had a busy day alone on the boat, accomplishing various chores for which a day alone seems necessary. The name of the ferry is *Joy.*

February 28 I picked up along the road yesterday—a loaf of bread, wrapping intact, a mess of spinach, a mutilated copy of Andersen's fairy tales. What I should have brought home is dog food. We scorn the baker's bread, will not buy it. Yet a loaf contraband is just to use—toast, french toast, bread in cooking.

March 1 A year ago today we entered Bisland Bayou. Today was another windy day. In the night it shifted to N, and blew hard until after sunset. Heavy showers in the morning, but the afternoon was of winter clearness and brilliance.

March 3 The N wind was blowing at earliest daylight yesterday, holding us to the bank. A near gale all morning, but by midafternoon it had dropped to a gentle breeze. We pulled out of our harbor behind the willows and drifted around the bend into a NE reach, from which no sign of city or industry could be seen. Skirted an eddy at the bend, then ran close to an old levee, past Ama Light 117.3. Half mile below we pulled through an opening into the quiet water within. This suggests in a mild small way the entering of a reef into the lagoon of an atoll. Almost dark when tied up. . . .

This levee is grassy and open, with scattered trees, and the whole situation appears very satisfactory. During the night the wind shifted to E with a cold rain and now the warmth of the fire is good.

A feature of our drifting yesterday was the passing of a large seagoing steam tug with some barges. Tall-stacked and fine lined, it had a grace which the new boats never achieve.

March 5 The strange relation between river and land is always felt. The river shores are usually the back side. Here the levee is the front, and one disembarking from a boat at once mounts to the highest and most conspicuous point in the countryside. He is faced with a road and close-built houses, barring his way to the fields and swamps. I found a way I could get through, and looking back toward the distant levee was surprised to see a tanker steaming along among the treetops and roofs.

March 7 At daybreak we found a ship tied up on account of the fog, just above us on the outside of the levee—just above the break in the old levee. I rowed out there, and around it, and later we both rowed up alongside. It was the Norwegian freighter *Folke Bernadotte* of Risor. A new, trim boat, steam, oil burning, well painted. Anna and I talked to the bow lookout, our conversation interrupted by his frequent ringing of the bell. He said he was Swedish, though the rest of the crew were Norwegian. Their cargo was bauxite from Venezuela, for the aluminum plant at Baton Rouge. They were about 2 weeks out of port. The sailor we talked to said he had left Sweden 12 years ago when he was 16. His English was very good, as were his manners, very polite, his smile almost a grimace. The ship drew 28 feet of water. It was held by one anchor....

When Anna and I rowed up to the ship, the dogs were left on our island. Sambo swam across to that part of the levee near us, and began digging at the water's edge. A few yelps brought Skipper. It was not an easy swim for the current was running out. By the time she arrived, Sambo had pulled a possum out of its hole.

March 10   Yesterday, March 9, we made our delayed entry into New Orleans. Had a fine day of it. Bus at Ama, 8 a.m., left New Orleans at 4:30. Fare, two round trips $2.51 (something like that).

The river is definitely falling now, after some days of hesitation. The first decided drop since the rise began, 3 months ago.

Today we ate the last of our Bisland bayou parsnips.

March 16   I play so many parts that they become confused and unconvincing. Yesterday we went to the city, visited libraries and the art museum, talked glibly of music and art, entered 4 pictures in the exhibition. Also, at the Engineers procured charts of the Intracoastal Waterway. Today I took fish over to the levee, offered them to the negroes for sale. However, it all seems logical to me, and one activity is as important as the other.

We slowly become acquainted on shore. Yet if this were Kentucky we would already have many friends. We live here with little interference from the rest of the world. It might be some remote isolated sand bar, instead of the fringe of a city. Our only visitors have been two boys, one of whom delivers papers along the road. If this were Kentucky, the inhabitants would be more friendly, and we might have made some intimate connections. We enjoy an unexpected freedom, as the levee, even this abandoned levee, seems to be public property. Yet the shoreland, roads and farms, are inhospitable and fenced.

March 21 This morning we left our mooring and dropped down through the lagoon and into the next opening through the old levee. We are now about 1/8 mile below our former landing at the lower end of the same island, a point to which we have often walked. It is good to look out on the open river, but we have lost some of our protection from waves and the N wind. . . .

Yesterday I rode the bicycle down as far as the Harvey lock, examining the shore for a possible next harbor, and making a first acquaintance with the Canal. Our future is difficult to lay out, since there is to be no more drifting downstream. We consider all possibilities.

This morning some more fish buyers, colored women and the old man who watches the stock on the levee. All we had was a small perch and a smaller sturgeon. The man talked me out of the sturgeon, saying, "Don't be stingy, now." The women bought the perch, at their own price.

March 25 Mockingbirds and brown thrashers in full voice along our old levee. . . . I rigged up a shrimp net and am catching some off the boat. They are like an old friend seen again.

April 2 Today I picked a bucket of dewberries along that T & P [Texas and Pacific] railroad. I walked back there, about a mile from the road, by an old lane between big trees, some brick ruins at one place. The ground becomes lower and wetter the farther one goes from the river, a curious experience. Heard many birds back there, red- and white-eyed vireo, orchard oriole, parula warbler, Maryland yellow throat, Carolina wren, titmouse and others—common birds, but not seen or heard along the river. This is another strange feature. Brought in a handful of carrots from a field by the lane.

There passed us today a new flat towed on a line by a small motor tug. Tied to the flat was a boat of familiar appearance. We soon placed it and its name, *Red Cross*. It was the launch which towed the St. Francisville ferry. They spoke of getting a new flat, and this was it, we suppose. The tall young pilot of the *Red Cross* came out on deck and waved, having recognized us. These slight connections are so important to us, who have so few contacts with people. Also they make the places we have been real.

April 5   Rough weather. Storms yesterday from all quarters, heavy clouds, thunder, lightning, rains, a dash of hail, and always wind. In the evening it shifted to N, blew a gale all night. We had to batten the door. Today is bright as can be, the wind still as strong, from N. Yet our little harbor is smooth. What weather this would be on the open river!

Saw a myrtle warbler, transformed, in full plumage, essaying his summer song.

> *Yet we were unwilling to consider New Orleans as the final destination of our voyage; nor were we ready to give up our shantyboat life. We could drift on past New Orleans—ninety-odd miles of river remained. Yet we figured it was no place for a drifting shantyboat—no land, no harbors in low water, and many ships passing. We gave up the idea of going to the river's end with reluctance, for we would like to see its entrance into the ocean.*
>
> *There was another way out—westward into the bayou country of Louisiana, by way of the Intracoastal Waterway. . . . Our enthusiasm was fired by this strange new region where the land is almost water and water is everywhere. We determined to leave the river and follow a new adventure in the land of the Cajun, where the towns face the waterways and every house has a slip for boats.*

April 7   An important date in our log. About 8 a.m. we cast off from Ama harbor, 116.5, which we had entered about 5 weeks ago. It was high time to leave, the falling river draining out the lagoon fast. Drifting again, so familiar, always a new adventure. . . .

The steam tug, *Independent*, crossing over from a ship it had just berthed to the Bisso landing on the left bank, ran full speed across the bow of a tow bound up, the *Mattie B. Simpson*. It cut across our path too, and made 2 or 3 high waves. The afterdeck went under, about a tubful of water going in through the open door. More rockings below, mostly from tugs. . . .

The Harvey lock. . . . Tug *Atlas* entered the lock ahead of us. Lockmen held gates open while we rowed at our best speed into the lock. The gates closed on our last view of the Mississippi from our boat, the line of New Orleans docks, ships scattered along. . . .

Lockman said there would be about 14 feet drop. When the gates opened we rowed out while the railroad and street bridge, two-thirds opened for the *Atlas*, were held up for us. Rowed about half a mile, past many boats and docks to a slip on right, west bank, between shipyard and sulphur dock. After some indecision we tied up there among some small fishing boats.

April 8 In the Harvey lock yesterday, the lock tender filled out a form in which our boat was called a quarterboat. Home port given as Brent, Kentucky, destination Morgan City. This I must sign. Our drifting was 1483 miles, 519 down the Ohio, and 964 down the Mississippi. We left the Mississippi at a point 98.2 above its mouth.

IV

Shantyboat in the Bayous

April 15, 1950 – July 1, 1951

12

New Country

Our shantyboating began on the Ohio River with no more thought of cruising into the bayou country of southern Louisiana than of navigating the upper Amazon. In fact, we undertook this venture with no definite intentions of any kind, except a vague notion of drifting downstream as natural as a piece of driftwood and as heedless of an ultimate destination. . . .

When at length New Orleans was reached, our shantyboat life was in full swing. The river had worked its change, and to live with flowing water beneath us seemed the natural and most desirable way. . . . To give up shantyboating at this high point was unthinkable. . . .

Yet to leave the river and go westward into the bayou country had at first seemed a wild and desperate move. It would mean a long voyage on the Intracoastal Waterway, which was a canal dug through an uninhabitable swamp, from all that we had ever heard of it, and not inviting or friendly to shantyboaters. The idea appealed to us only because it would allow the even rhythm of our shantyboating to continue. Our outlook changed completely, however, after one glimpse of the bayou country. . . . Then we became enthusiastic about the voyage, and eager to reach those waters which promised so much.

April 15, 1950 Boatyard, Harvey Canal. Our shantyboat life goes on even in these unfavorable surroundings. We seem to live leisurely, compared to the hustling men about us. Yet we are busy at something all of each day. It is pointless, you say, but so seems much of the activity about us, respectable and sanctioned as it is.

329

Crossing the Mississippi on the ferry yesterday, we felt no longing to be drifting there again. When we saw the muddy current swirling past the ferry dock. . . we felt relieved that our struggle with the current was over. Yet it was not a struggle, rather a going with it on its boisterous way. Perhaps when we tow through the canal, it will be so tame and mechanical that we will long for the continuous endless flow of the river.

Although in no hurry to get on with our voyage, we kept mulling over the possible ways of towing our shantyboat. . . . We have no fondness for a motor of any kind, unless it could be a steam engine, but a small motorboat having an inboard engine would be least objectionable. Though not caring how slowly it towed us along, we must have a boat that we could live with on pleasant terms, one with a sturdy engine that could be run all day without strain on either itself or us. . . . Remembering the number of small boats I had seen on Bayou Barataria, I determined to extend the search there. When I mentioned this to Landry, the fisherman, he offered me a ride to Barataria in his skiff. . . .

It seemed that the only boats available were too large, too powerful, or too expensive. At length, a young fellow from Bayou des Oies, or Goose Bayou, took me to see a boat belonging to a friend of his. . . . He lived in a neat white cottage, and a few steps from his back door, at a flimsy pier, was a small, gray-painted skiff which took my eye at once. It had an honest look about it, a character which promised willing and faithful service. Though heavily built and broad of beam, it was a good-looking boat, I thought, with graceful lines. The engine, small and unobtrusive, made a pleasant chucking noise on a trial run. The boat was slow, of deep draft, and awkward to handle, but these defects would not keep it from being an efficient towboat.

. . . A few days after the first trip, I bicycled down to Barataria with the money in my pocket. . . . I put the bicycle in the skiff and managed to get the engine started. It did not miss a beat, nor did I touch it, all the way back to Harvey.

330

April 18   This day I brought up the motorboat from Barataria.

April 23   Much tinkering with the motor in the skiff these days. I marvel at it. An intricate contrivance yet its parts are simple in design and action. But there are so many parts, even in such an elemental machine as this. The complicated economic structure behind it, which makes it run, the fact that this system keeps running is most remarkable. It does miss and backfire.

April 25   How simple it was to drift—the steady flow of the river—endless power, quiet and on a grand scale. How finicky are mechanical contrivances, how expensive in many ways.

May 2   Up at daybreak this morning. Dead calm, and we prepared to leave our harbor. Besides taking in lines and lashing gangplanks, the motorboat, the skiff had to be hooked up. Our tow was made up and we pulled over to the sulphur dock. Departure delayed by absence of both dogs. South wind, by the time we entered the canal. Some difficulty holding our course, but we were pleased with the speed and handling of our fleet in a head wind. . . .

Dinner on deck and a wild shore. How good it is!

May 3   A chorus of bird song this early morning. Cardinals and prothonotary warblers. A chat sang through the night.

The mosquitoes are formidable. They enter our inner defense, a screen of netting over our heads while we sleep. They are abroad only at night, so far, swarming about the boat at nightfall. It is hazardous business, opening a door.

May 4   We shoved out early this cloudy morning, ran down the canal a ways. . . . Found that by turning the skiff at a slight angle to houseboat that it would hold a straight course and we could both sit on the main deck, steering with the rudder there. Much traffic on the canal.

Well before sundown we pulled up at the entrance to Hero canal, tied up against the hyacinths. A beautiful place. To the south a great, open marsh. In this wild place we come to ourselves again. Carefree and joyous, our voyage becomes an adventure again. The limits of the city's blight have been passed.

May 5   We came down to Hole-in-the-Wall cut-off against a stiff wind. . . . We tied up to the island, in the back channel, where there was solid ground. To the east and north an expanse of grassy marsh. It is good to be in this wild place, off of the canal. At last no one can see us.

I swam in the bayou today and bathed. We bathe on deck this evening. At sundown I forced a way through the thick growth and unexpectedly found it more open within, and many blackberries. The blackberries are delicious—sweet and mild, having small seeds and still with a tang.

May 6 A late morning start, ran at cruising speed in light breeze from S. Our course SW. Entered shallow, pond-like cove on S.E. bank at mile 10. Ran down to Crown Point, Bayou des Familles and canal opposite on left. Decided to leave the boat where it was, though open to waves of boats coming down the canal. It is a fine place, a solid shore, level and grassy, barely above the water level. Some scattered willows, and a rounded knoll or two only as high as a tall man, but they count for something in this country. An open view on all sides. Prairie and marsh to the east and south level and open as the sea. The distant woods might be islands and a solitary tree looks like a square-rigger with dark green sails. Dark blue and white herons feed in the marshy grass with the cows. The sound of young lambs is imitated by certain frogs. Young frogs? Mockingbirds, a kingbird, jay, parula warbler. Redwings, Maryland yellowthroat and others.

May 8 It is full summer, to our notions. We went to bed with no light last night. To light a lamp with all the windows open, even though screened, is exposing yourself to an enemy in the darkness. At twilight we shut ourselves in, the dogs out. No door is opened. With this measure, and Anna's alertness, the mosquitoes are worsted. . . .

Luckily we are in such a good place—attractive, retired and convenient. The great openness is good, after the shut-in places. The expanse of marsh is like the sea. . . .

Perfect conditions for our washday, sun and wind, abundance of clear water to be dipped up, pleasant working on deck, a convenient shore. The shore is parklike, grassy and open with trees close enough for tying the line. All this helped us with the big washing.

332

May 11   Yesterday the first canning of 1950—71/2 quarts of blackberries. We are elated about it. I picked the berries in the jungle on the island at Hole-in-the-Wall cut-off, our night stop previous to this. The berries are of fine quality, very sweet. Also, these days, our cleaning and reorganizing goes on. Yesterday our first mess of crabs. It is a tedious job to prepare the meat, but very delicious. A fine concert of birds this morning.

May 12   Day before yesterday a boy came through the willow grove with his gun, came aboard and stayed a long time. His talk was unceasing but full of wit and good sense. His name is Roy Pressenbach.

I went berry picking this morning on the island at Hole-in-Wall cut-off. Brought back 10 quarts. What more restful occupation than picking blackberries, in a hidden place, the chat improvising overhead. An antidote to yesterday's crowd and noise. This was the annual pirogue race at Barataria, from Lafitte to the canal. 4 1/2 miles they tell us and it has been made in less than a half hour. 40 odd entrants. We were amused at the costumes of some—a work shirt, shop cap and jeans, for instance. Many of the entrants had no hope of winning, but since everyone who finished received a prize, everyone was a winner.

May 18   Hot summer days, thunderstorms ever imminent. The nights are delightful. The lightning bugs were never so thick, so bright, so slow moving. Some flash intermittently. Toward daybreak, when they have thinned out, a spectacle is a clump of tall grass standing in water near the shore. The lightning bugs congregate in it, not moving but flashing their lights on and off.

Last evening a visit from the Pressenbachs—Mrs. and five of the seven children and another boy. They came up in their skiff, swarmed over the place.

May 19   We arise before the sun these days. . . . These mornings are delightful, fresh and spacious. . . . We feasted on turtle today. It contained 21 hard shell eggs.

May 26   Every evening at dusk a mockingbird sings on our island, low and sweet.

May 29   On Saturday night Skipper had another batch of puppies, the 8th, I believe. She had skipped the time previous to this, making the last litter the one at Natchez, over a year ago. There were 7 pups this time 2 black, 2 brown, 2 white with brown spots, 1 white with black spots. They seem small, but perhaps we have forgotten. Skipper was inside Saturday night and made a nuisance of herself, climbing into the clothes closet and into our bed, everywhere but in the bed we had fixed for her. At last we put her out and in the night heard the squealing of puppies on the bank.

May 30 Bayou Vilars. Decoration Day somewhere. We left Crown Point yesterday after an early dinner. . . . Earlier a big white Coast Guard boat stopped, called to know if we had been visited by the census taker. We answered "no", and they were preparing to put the census taker ashore. I rowed out, to save them the trouble, and answered the difficult questions, difficult for us who are beyond their classifications.

We left the canal, followed Barataria bayou to the private slip beyond the shell cemetery, where we tied up. It was so private that we did not even ask for permission to lay there. Everyone is friendly.

May 31 Bayou Willow. We were welcomed here by an orchard oriole and a Carolina wren and redwing blackbirds. Have also heard a chat and seen at least one strange bird.

A rude thatched roof on four poles, sign of previous living here and a pleasing note in the green landscape as well, change the character of this place, making it an established landing, with a history, instead of an undistinguished part of virgin shore.

Caught a gar in the little net, the first catfish for a long time, if it was only a small fiddler.

June 3 I went to Barataria with Sambo in the skiff in the morning. It is almost a foreign land. The people mostly, are not like any Americans I have known yet I feel at home there, among the boats close to the water. Watched the building of a trawler, 46 feet long. The two carpenters spoke French to each other. The keel was of pine. Another keel, fir, for a 60 foot boat lay on the floor. The boats were built under an open shed. Nearby was a shed, much smaller, where a man was building pirogues. I must go in there.

June 5 Today a short expedition up the canal—poke and a few blackberries. We keep up our foraging, and still supply most of our food.

June 7 Yesterday a rainy day, first to last. The open fire in the afternoon was grateful. A little reading by candle light, as on a fall evening. . . . We are enjoying our new mosquito bar, a tent-like shroud over the whole bed, extended by strips which are tied to the carlings by long strings.

June 8 Catch a few softshell crabs, "busters," "cracked crabs" in our bushes. An innocent way to get your food. Yet very clever.

June 11 We heard the name of this canal from Mr. Adam Dufrene yesterday but not accurately enough to write. Sounded like BT. Adam Dufrene built our skiff, in 1937 for Irwin Belsom. He could speak of his work today with confidence. He is still building skiffs, of a different design now, with flat bottoms—faster he says, but not so good in rough water. Though not a very old man, apparently he showed a liking for the slower and more sturdy and simple ways of the past. He works alone, in an open-sided shed, with no machinery. Cypress is hard to get, he says, and not as good or as wide or long as formerly. We liked the man very much.

We spent most of Saturday in the stores, buying all we need for the next section of our voyage, where there are no towns or roads.

June 12 Today we moved down the canal to Bayou Perot, 5 miles. . . .

June 13 . . . . The canal offered more interest and variety of scenery than expected. The spoil from dredging had been all deposited on the left or SE bank. This was higher than the other which was marsh. The difference in vegetation on the two banks was remarkable. The higher bank was like the shore of rivers, grass, blackberry, elderberry and poke bushes, willows, even cottonwoods. There were several abandoned docks, and toward Perot some clearings and fences, one house seemed lived in and had, a wonderful sight, some rows of green corn. Masses of elderberry bloom, almost a palisade of ancient cypress stumps.

Arriving at Bayou Perot, we turned left around the point, and tied to a pole which we set up in shallow water. We were dismayed by the watery extent, for the bayou was as wide as the Ohio in its narrower parts. I rowed out to a fisherman who was tracing a trotline in a pirogue. He suggested two harbors, an oil well canal across the bayou and a small bayou off the canal. The man was kind and friendly, and gave us two small catfish. We towed across the bayou to the small canal, which was a short, new one leading to a dry well. Tied up at the entrance where we had a wide view. Miles of open country to the SE, some distant buildings, a blaze from an oil well, a boat anchored to the shore a mile below, where there was a building on shore. More buildings off toward Lake Salvador, which the fisherman whom we visited twice more and from whom we got a dozen fish, said were built on a shell pile. The only high ground is manmade. The shell pile attributed to the Indians, the levees of canals. Saw some black terns, adult and immature, and at our treeless landing, Carolina wren, kingbird and cardinal. The dogs chased rabbits all day. Fair, hot weather. A dim moon above the clear rising sun.

June 14 We took the skiff down the bayou to Lake Salvador. The scene was impressive—it might have been the ocean, since the far, low shore could not be seen. The wooded parts were like distant islands. An oil well standing far out in the water might have been some mystic structure with its blazing fire. The rainstorm had moved across the lake ahead of us, and now the lowering sun was breaking through with great spokes of light. There was a flashing light on a pole to mark the entrance to Bayou Perot. Looking back we saw how necessary it was, for no break showed in the low strip of green. Willow poles of fishermen were stuck up everywhere, evidence of the lake's shallowness.

Returning, we stopped at a group of houses on a shell pile. A narrow dock extended out from shore, and continued inland for a hundred yards or more, past a row of small board cottages built close together. They were tight and well constructed, with windows, often curtained, porches, cisterns and all the trappings. All neat and in good order with charming irregularities. The boardwalk of heavy planks ran across a low place to several more. Here the shells rose higher and there was a grove of live oaks, draped with moss. One could look out through the grotesque trunks and branches over miles of prairie. . . . Even here there is a concert of birds, reduced almost to a trio—Carolina wren, cardinal and red-wing. Heard a night hawk, the black terns skim the water.

June 16   Two unusual phenomena at first glance this morning before sunrise. A heavy cloud in the east cast its shadow clear across the sky, an arching band of dark blue. Then I saw what I thought was a new bird, yellow below, one with a black throat patch. Yet they turned out to be orchard orioles, female, and the one with black, immature. The interest excited by half-a-dozen kinds of birds equals that of many. . . .

This afternoon we went out to the lake in the skiff, picked up half a bucket of clams. The lake is exciting as ever.

June 17   Down the canal from Bayou Perot. Long straight reaches, marsh on the right, a higher bank on the left, where the spoil from the dredging of the canal was placed. The different character of the two sides is ever remarkable. The marsh is bordered by a row of elephant ear plants, dark green, as they stretch away into the distance. They seem of even height and unbroken. The yellow-green marsh grass rises above an occasional small willow. On the left the willows are continuous, and of good height. Elderberries, in full bloom, are thick in some places. In the far distance, a line of blue marks a turn in the canal. Boats approach and recede. I hear towhees on the willow side, a Maryland yellowthroat, chat, Carolina wren. In the marsh redwing blackbirds. . . .

We left Bayou Perot with some regret. It was a place of repose, the expanse of water, the impossibility of a road ever reaching it.

June 18   We heard some fishing skiffs go by before daybreak. They returned later in the day loaded with crabs. The skiffs, engines, and fishermen are not as fine or fast as the Barataria ones, but they had more crabs.

June 19   Current still flows into the lake. The drifting hyacinths recall floes of ice. They gather at the head of the boat and must be shoved out at times. They have been as steady as the current, about as thick as running ice.

June 20 A trip down the canal to Lake Salvador this morning. . . . Talked to a crab fisherman who was running his line. The line comes up over a large spool as the boat moves slowly along, the fisherman, if he may be called one, scoops the crabs into the boat with a wire paddle. They seem to do better here than at Lafitte, receiving $1.00 or more a basket. The man was friendly, gave us some valuable information. He says the current always flows down the old canal into the lake, that it is caused by the rivers in Texas flowing into the canal. This must be the Atchafalaya. If so, we have already met the descending current of the Mississippi. What a devious way!

June 24 In the late afternoon we went down to call on our fisherman friend, who had invited us. He lives halfway to La Rose in a new, modern white house, clean as a Dutch house. His name is Estay, has 10 children, all pretty well grown up. He was a farmer, his heart is still in that. A babble of French, of which we could get but a word now and then.

Returning at sunset, I found a big gar in the small net. 5 feet long and 50 pounds, I should say. Hard to understand how it got in or how the net held it. The net beyond the throats is chickenwire. The gar's beak was caught in that, the fish was dead, though not in the net many hours. An unpleasant unwelcome task to clean and cook it, on the bank, but it could not be lost.

June 24 Some big trees, hackberry, linden. The familiar sycamores and maples are missing on these shores.

June 25 We saw two downy woodpeckers this morning, close to the boat. Yesterday a bittern, a beautiful gold and brown bird. We had seen hardly one buzzard in this country, yet when I dragged the fresh gar's skin back along the canal, they appeared in numbers, 50 at least.

June 26 This morning we pulled out of the little side canal, and took down the straight reach of the Intracoastal. . . . We proceeded to Bayou Lafourche where we turned right. At once we felt the difference from the narrower, winding bayou, with higher banks, trees on both sides, willows next to the water, other trees above, wild grapevines. There was a relief from strain. The canal is like a highway or railroad. Charming views of cottages, some of them old buildings, gardens, the sound of cars and children swimming. . . . Good to be in a farm section again where there are no fishermen, where the water way is neglected, where we can pass unobserved along this hidden way.

June 27 Saw a painted bunting this morning and heard a bob-white. Gathered some green corn for breakfast. . . . To Larose in the skiff late afternoon, too late for the post office, our chief errand. Met Mr. Estay. Went to his house, visited, listened to the amazing French, got several buckets of water from their cistern. Talk of war. Their French is almost incomprehensible to us, even to Anna, who sits amid the lively conversation in deep concentration trying to understand the mouthing and mumbling.

These mornings the rooster's crow and the moo of the cow are mingled with the choir of birds.

June 29 Pulled in at Bollinger's Shipyard and Machine Shop after an hour's run. The location, on right bank, small tugs and quarterboat before the shop building and above all a small slip attracted us. Talked to Bollinger, proprietor, a young man, sympathetic and understanding. It looks like we might have found our harbor.

July 10 I have been painting these days, yet we plan to leave *[on a trip to Kentucky and Michigan]*. It is satisfying to go on such an extensive trip which requires so much arranging, no hurry or hard work. It has all been very gradual, due to the length of time at this station from which we will depart, and to the fortunate way our affairs have worked out. The people here make it easy for us—the Bollingers, Galianos and Melançons, even the boys on the boats and in the shipyard. The Melançon boy took us to Larose today for mail. How unpleasant, uncomfortable and disturbing is an automobile. And the radio on the *Gertrude* which was hauled out this morning! This is the sort of thing ahead of us.

339

July 11 Today the packing and final shifting of our fleet into its out of service position. We leave early tomorrow morning for the north.

September 27 Today we returned to Bayou Lafourche, having left I think on July 12.

September 28 A warm welcome from the Galianos, and men of the shipyard, most of all from the singing mockingbirds and the soft air. From the sharpness of fall, the cold rains, such a change.

I feel strongly the unique character of this gulf country. The train ran through the prairies and marshland. It seems like I have hardly seen the sky lately, or even walked on the earth, so subtly does the world come between. This is a barefoot, out-of-doors country, to me.

September 30 Each day we become more used to the old accustomed ways. Crab gumbo for dinner, crab chowder for supper.

October 1 Roast beef for our Sunday dinner, the meat given us by the captain (?) of the *Belfort*. The crew seems to be living aboard, but the refrigerator could not be kept running. They also gave us 4 steaks, which are keeping in Galiano's icebox and a quantity of liver which the dogs have eaten. The various fishermen have passed on to us 6 or 8 catfish. It is an easy place to live.

October 7 Went to town in the skiff yesterday, alone. Saw the wreck of a steamboat along the bayou, mostly under water, but the shape of hull, towing knees, upper deck with two holes for stacks, hog chain braces, rudder posts, and in the water astern the ruin of a sternwheel. . . .

Before noon today the boys of the shipyard pulled our boat out on the ways, end to the river, and blocked it up level. . . . The bottom should be at least inspected, even if the boat does not leak. I scraped it this afternoon, and aside from a little putty it is in fine condition. . . . We intend to paint the hull, below the waterline with copper paint. It will be a satisfaction to know that our boat is sound when we get underway again. . . . It is strange to be perched up here, level with the rest of the world, dry land all around us.

October 9 A hard day in the shipyard today—scraping, caulking, repairing and painting the hull. Now it is ready to launch. . . .

The moment we were pulled out of the water, we felt a security that we were unaware of when afloat. Even in this calm and sheltered water one is uneasy and wary, unconsciously.

October 10 They slid us into the water this morning, and about 11 a.m. we got underway up the bayou. Tied up in drainage ditch, surrounded by pastures on the north side of canal, across from the end of Lockport.

October 12 Our situation is a strange one. Three quarters of the compass is open wilderness, water. The other segment is Lockport, compactly built, ending abruptly at the canal and the pond. We are close to the houses and watch them in detail, yet we are detached as if looking at a picture, or through a telescope. The town is quiet all day, in the evening life stirs, children come out to play, men and boys talk and get out their boats, dogs bark. These are answered by Sambo and Skipper. After dark Sambo swims over to town, like Leander, coming home dripping sometime in the night.

October 15 An opening of some season or other today, for all the hunters and their dogs were out. Many went by in their skiffs—guns and dogs. Two cowboys rode down late in the afternoon, asked us to move our campboat so they could get a cattle barge in the canal. We are intrigued by all the activity on the canal—pirogues and skiffs coming and going. The Lockport shore is lined with boats and boathouses. These built out over the water for skiffs with doors like a garage. The pirogues are sheltered in long low sheds on the bank, like oversize doghouses. Several motorboats bring in women-folk and carry out supplies, as if the people lived down the canal somewhere, and the waterway was their route to town which is Lockport.

Some good playing today. Also more decorating inside the cabin, going over all the surfaces painted red, for the first time since the boat was built. Anna has made new covers for the cushions, of dark blue corduroy. It will be a general refurbishing, inside and out when completed.

Called on the Donald Bollingers Friday evening, a stimulating experience.

October 15 Yesterday afternoon I rowed up the canal, sketching.

October 21   A visit from two boys this morning. They, like their parents, waste no words, use no circumlocution. If they want to know something they ask directly. Their speech has a sharpness. They answer questions about themselves just as freely, and do whatever they can for you. They lack grace. Their voices are often harsh. They have a quickness of mind and of body too. . . . They were delightful guests, interested in the books which Anna showed them, after they had washed their hands. They asked intelligent questions and made sensible comments.

October 22   Yesterday when Anna and I were working at the table she was reading the directions for assembling the binoculars. One of the boys asked, "Can't your husband read?" and was not surprised. His own father could not, I believe. This last generation will speak less Cajun French. These boys, town boys, speak English entirely.

October 23   Today we tried navigating, after a final trip to Lockport in the morning. Half a mile down the canal we came to an almost solid block of lilies [water hyacinths]. Tied up there. . . . I scouted ahead, found we could make it to the next side canal, in open water along shore. Moved down there. The cattle flat came up the canal, said conditions were not so bad there, so we put out again, going south now. Within a mile we came to solid lilies, tied up to marshy shore on left. The lilies seemed to be moving so we went on, hoping to find a dry shore. Pushed through one block of lilies, crossed to right bank where there was open water, came to an open grassy shore, the grass very short, many horses about. Scattered willows, and willow groves. Tied up there. . . . Anna steered the boat while I rode on the roof to pick out a path. Splendid view across the golden meadow eastward. The blue water of the pond, some white houses of Lockport. . . .

How good to be away from town with no street lamps shining in the windows, only the moon in the clear sky. A perfectly still night, after a northerly or northwest wind today. Lilies seem to have stopped passing.

October 24   The favorable combination of circumstances was too good to pass up, so we washed clothes this morning.

October 25 We got our fleet in motion this morning, after a leisurely time of breakfast and getting ready. A light breeze down the canal, still. It was one of our best short voyages. Soon passed Eagle Island, houses on both sides. Cape Peters on the right. It might have been the western plains, extensive pastures and hay fields, cows, an old truck which looked like it might not run, a tractor, some pecan trees. The only cultivation a small garden between the house and the canal. A well and watertank, haybarn. I was on the roof, and could look over miles of prairie to distant lines of forest, which were no doubt willows. They grow only in the low wet places, inverted islands. The land with a little imagination appeared as cropland, the tall grass which Anna calls cattails as extensive and even as canefields, acres of lilies, and miles of a russet grass. One thing grows in one place. The land tapered off below, another house and a houseboat beached out on the last, low dry ground. Then swampy shores, lined with elephant ears. Soon we could see Long Lake, close to the canal, an oil well, tanks and buildings, and steam at the far end. An opening into the canal, a side canal, below the Lake, another house. Suddenly to our surprise, a huge tugboat and string of barges looking like a freight train shot out from the bank of the canal and across. It was the Intracoastal Canal. We tied up in a small canal in the NE shore of the Lockport canal. . . .

The inhabitants of Eagle Island use boats to go to town, which means Lockport. If there are any children what do they do about school? It is amazing, the heavy traffic on the Intracoastal. Like a busy railroad. The peace of the prairie is disturbed.

October 26 Bayou Terrebonne. . . . We were charmed by this narrow winding bayou, trees overhanging, Spanish moss and a few live oaks, neat farmhouses along the road, with great pecan trees towering above all. Sugar cane fields. Tied up for a midday stop, went ashore with the dogs, returned with a spindly bunch of bananas and some satsumas, the small tangerine-like fruit. The bananas were on a tree next the water and I stopped purposely to get them. Fishermen came along in a pirogue, stopped to talk. . . .

We followed the narrow bayou all afternoon, past the junction with Petit Caillow. Stopped short of Houma in an unpleasant place.

Yet the narrow bayou lined with cabins and fishing boats was fine, especially in the full moon.

October 27   Houma. We pulled up to town this morning, landed at 9:30 along the left bank, tied to a row of the piling in the dirtiest water ever encountered. Very picturesque, however, the narrow bayou lined with fishing boats, packing houses, houses, sheds, bridges everywhere. The bridge below town was a small swing bridge opened and closed by manpower. A footwalk with cleats extended over one quadrant of the bridge's circuit, a few feet under the end of the bridge. The tender was a husky young man who put his shoulder to the bridge. It was a little slow opening, for this reason I guess, and we had to shut off the motor. About to cross the Intracoastal, the siren for opening the bridges sounded and we lay by until a tug passed. We feel we handle our craft very well.

October 29   Last night at Bonvillain Canal, lightning bugs, definitely, and more than one. The peeping of frogs now and then these days. Mosquitoes very bad last night and in the woods. Set out at sunrise, breakfast while moving through the mist. Very quiet, but a noticeable current. Turned due west for a straight run of 6 miles. Entered small canal on right for a brief stop and run for dogs. Two large fishing boats passed, eastbound. Pogey boats, perhaps. High ground, pasture and willows on right. Some fine open canals. On the right, a road leading back to Bayou Black, motorboats, cars, a group of trappers' cabins, empty now, cane fields. A sign on one canal—"No Hunning Allow." This is written Cajun. A sign in a Lockport garage, "Bienvenue à tous," the only written French seen so far. . . .

We have lost track of the days of the week. Log says this is Sunday, but we would never know in any other way.

October 30   Discovered that the bottom of the boat had collected and held a mass of lilies, and while in the back channel tried to remove them by prying them out with an oar, by dragging a line along the bottom from one end to the other. Neither method was successful. The capacity of the lilies for floating held them tight against the bottom. At last took a stage plank and dragged it by a line at each end along the bottom. Scraped off a boatload of lilies,

matted together. A noticeable increase in the boat's speed afterward.
. . .

The canal now follows Bayou Cocodrie for more than 5 miles. At first it was wide, as wide as Bayou Perot, the canal following a channel marked by a long line of red buoys. It was fun steering our boat along the buoys in the expanse of water. The shores were mostly low and open, a great expanse of land and sky. The bayou narrows and winds among cypress swamps, with many canals and side bayous. The finest cypress we have ever seen, golden and red, long pendants of gray moss. The light gray trunks gleaming in the sun. Many other trees, gum with deep red leaves, maple, and trees we did not know. It was exciting to us, we felt we were in a new land, the bayous and cypress swamps of Louisiana at last.

13

The Creation of
an Environment

*L*ike our voyage, the passage of time and the change of
season seemed to have come to a stand. Who was it that, like us, had
stayed his course to watch the ripening forest, where the cypress became
an arrowhead of ruddy gold, where the maple, gum and oak blazed
among the restrained colors of ash and hackberry; where the dark,
glossy green of the live oak was a symbol of life everlasting?

October 31, 1950 Bayou Black. There is another campboat on
this shore. Soon after landing its inhabitant came to see us, an old
man, very friendly, gave us a little eel for bait, offered us a catfish
still struggling on a springline. He told us much about this place.
His name is Verret. . . .

Mosquitoes are bad but we ate on deck with not much discomfort and are bothered little in our sleep. We think we may stay here
a while.

November 1 A visit yesterday evening from Frank Verret, the
old man who lives on the campboat a hundred yards S of us. We
had asked him to come in when he came to see us in the morning
but he declined. He appeared in the twilight, when we were ready
to bathe and get supper. When we saw him coming over the water
in his long oared flatboat, like a man on crutches, we shoved things
out of sight and put on some clothes. He had dressed up for the
call, and sat and talked for an hour. We learned much.

These people have a different accent from those on Bayou Lafourche when they speak English. This morning we went down to the store kept by Curtis Verret. He was gone to town in his boat, but first his daughter and then his wife came out of the house, unlocked the store when they saw us coming. The store is a tiny, backwoods sort of place, well stocked in a sketchy way, the people friendly. Some flatboats at the dock, but not a pirogue.

The old man spoke of our way of rowing, sitting down and pulling on the oars, as if it were as strange to him as his way of standing up and shoving is to us.

November 3 Mr. Verret came up this afternoon, barely making it against the wind with his feeble strokes. He brought some eels for bait, a Beaumont, Texas, paper of today's date. He had been to Houma again today. His kindness is embarrassing. We will have to be careful about mentioning anything we want or he will bring it to us. Yet he ruined our afternoon.

November 4 Old Verret gave me a handful of small eels for bait but I caught nothing last night. He is extraordinarily generous, and does his best to make it possible for me to catch fish.

November 6 To Verret's store this morning, with more mail. There is little to buy there, yet we could live indefinitely on what the store offers. . . .

Yesterday down the bayou, as often before, it was hard to realize that behind the low shores was not higher ground. The truth is that the shores are the high ground and swamps lie not far away from the bayou's edge.

I woke up with this fever. I had had an active day but late in the afternoon I felt tired which was unusual.

November 7 Night—fever.

November 8 Fever continued. We decided to go in to Morgan City to see doctor. Went in the skiff to Bayou Boeuf, up to the highway bridge. Left the skiff with Mr. Lee who has a campboat just above the bridge. After an hour and a half wait we went in on the bus. Walked to Dr. Russo's office. . . . I had a fever of 102°. He was about to send us home with some medicine saying it was malaria but on second thought suggested I go to the hospital for 24 hours for observation. Took a taxi to the Morgan City General Hospital which is on the waterfront to the north. Had a bad attack in the afternoon—fever, then "chill," they called it—more like a spasm. Doctor came, took a specimen of blood to send away for a test. A bad night. But did better next day, Thursday, the 9th.

November 10 Did still better. Doctor said I could get up for a while. Mr. Curtis Verret came in the evening.

November 11 Dr. Russo said the report on the blood test came back and I have para typhoid and that we had to go home because it was contagious. However they decided to isolate us and let us stay.

November 14 Returned from the Morgan City General Hospital. . . .

Out on the highway, at the first sight of the autumn forest, the marsh, I was nearly overcome by the realization of its harmony, forgotten in the city. Not forgotten. In fact, I was sure I remembered it. Yet not the intensity of it, the pervasity, saturation. It is indivisible from the aspirations of the race of men, their contract with the unknown power they call God.

November 15 Verret says they have caught $15 worth of fish, one of them a 25 lb. blue cat. I thought of the old man when in the hospital. He seemed so humble among these proud men in sweeping action. I thought perhaps I gave him too much attention. Yet he is gentle and kind and thoughtful of us and deserves consideration and respect.

November 19 Services in the little church at Bayou Chêne this morning. It was over so quickly that I did not see it, out around the point cutting wood, but Anna watched through the glass. I saw Verret taking the young priest back to his car.

A high foreboding wind all day from SW. Yet this evening the sun sets clear, there is quiet. I have been quite lively today, grinding and sawing, carving, writing, reading, playing music, a sorry performance, knotting the rope mats.

Mrs. Verret called on us late yesterday afternoon, rowing up in their stand-up skiff, bringing a skinned coon for the dogs. An admirable woman, quiet and capable, of great integrity and understanding. Mr. V. says she taught him how to fish. She makes castnets, said she lived in a campboat a long time, until the children were grown. Frank Verret was here at the same time. He came up in his flatboat calling out, "How is the old man?" We went to the store in the morning, I rowing slowly. Procured two buckets of drinking water from the store cistern, of a doubtful appearance. Mrs. V. rinsed her bucket in the bayou before dipping out the water for us.

November 22 This afternoon Floyd Verret pushed his way up here with his usual vigor to bring us a rabbit. He had taken it, drowned, from one of his traps, said it was fit for us to eat. So we plan to have rabbit for our Thanksgiving dinner, thanks to the kindness of the Verrets. There is something touching in the way these people give. If you mention something you would like to have, they seem to feel obliged to get it for you.

November 23 Thanksgiving Day. Fried rabbit for us and the dogs, and very good it was. Anna made a coconut pie which we shared with Frank and Pete Verret. To the store in the skiff this morning and I spent the rest of the morning working on the motor which is still hard to start, and entertaining old Verret, cracking nuts the meanwhile. Pete is painting and overhauling his joeboat. Mrs. C. Verret is very friendly, invites us into the house. She said she had but two months' schooling but she seems to have no trouble keeping accounts at the store. They stretch the mink hides on a frame made of two thin boards. Three were hanging above the kitchen stove, yesterday's catch.

November 27 Today we had coon and owl to eat. The coon is tender and delicate. The owl good, but tougher and of less flavor. The breast, however, was very good.

November 28 This morning we prepared to leave Bayou Chêne. A farewell visit to the C. Verrets. . . .

A joy to get underway again. At Bayou Boeuf found wind and current in our favor so did not stop there. The old buildings on the southeast corner, under live oaks which look like big short-handled umbrellas. Fast time down Boeuf. On the right saw the stacks and pilothouse of a steamboat, apparently rising from the trees. It was a narrow slip and the boat was our old friend, *Greenbriar*. Evidently out of commission but not dismantled. . . . Turned into Bayou Shaffer, south. . . . Tied up on east bank, 1/4 mile south of Boeuf. . . . Got water from Tom's fish dock down to the Atchafalaya, making an acquaintance with Tom's son, name L.T. Ozio, Spanish. He guessed I was an artist, to my surprise.

November 29 To Morgan City. . . . The Atchafalaya really is a river. The point at Bayou Boeuf is pure sand and we have a drift-wood fire. How differently it burns from the set or sappy forest wood. . . . The waterfront is interesting, fishing boats and tugs lined up, one old two-masted schooner. . . . The net fisherman raised his nets this morning, skipping the two near the boat, however. It was a young man, alone, in a long, well-equipped joeboat. Using a long pole as long as the boat, at least 20 feet, he set the net stakes. All done very neatly—reminded me of a man on horseback, he controlled the boat so well.

November 30 Another trip to Morgan City. . . . The waterfront is a fine place, even the buildings. A river town.

December 2 No time to write yesterday, or rather no opportunity. We left Bayou Shaffer. . . . The boat had hardly power enough to make way against the current and wind and it looked like we would be blown on to the sandy point, which, by the way, may not be sand but dust from a plant above which seems to grind shells. I asked a passing joeboat to give us a tow. He said he would return to us when he had delivered the fish to the dock. Before he came back, taking advantage of a slackening of the wind, we worried around the point and headed north in the Atchafalaya, running before the wind. The boat made good time against the current. . . . A fine run past the Morgan City waterfront. It is a river town, the buildings might be in Pomeroy. Much to see—fishing boats and tugs and oil company motorboats, the LST being fitted for work in the Gulf, the whitened shell-grinding plant, Coast Guard, docks for selling gasoline and oil to boats, marine ways, (Intracoastal, in front of the hospital which we could not see); all manner of boat works—machine shops, net shop, fish docks, ice dock, propeller works, boat store, boat builders. A triangular red flag fluttering in the stiff wind, small craft storm warning, I think. Under the tall, three-span, highway bridge meanwhile where the river bends to right, we began to cross over, the Têche, or rather lower Atchafalaya river, floodgate in view on the far side. Very rough, especially toward the shore where it might have been shallow. I rode in the stern of the skiff to hold the propeller under water. The two boats rolled so that it was a question whether the lines would hold. Johnboat painter broke a strand. Then we were in smoother water, coasting the shore to the floodgate, which is approached by a short canal dredged through the mud flat. Some neat steering for Anna with the strong wind astern into the narrow passage which did not appear to be 50 feet. High walls, closed gates at each end, no one around. Current running out. Then we entered the wide river, it had the look of a river, no wider than the Cumberland, though. We were struck by the contrast of the heavy domes of live oak with golden feathers of cypress and yellow willows and pecans intermingled, the russet fields behind.

All went well until the course turned toward the south. Tried for a landing on the windward shore but it was too shallow. So was the lee side. Farther on the wind blew our fleet broadside on to a mud bank strewn with snags. Decided to remain, got out anchor and pulled stern of boat into wind, ran some lines to snags. Hard to reach shore because of shallow mud, found shaggy pasture land, a gravel road running SW from this the last house, some weatherbeaten houses in the sun, live oaks scattered about.

The countryside with so many deserted buildings, beautiful to see, has apparently gone to seed, the river without small boats or fishermen. Yet there are suburban houses on the left, where the highway (90) is, and across from our landing, a seaplane. Noticed a difference at once in the bird population. They had been scarce in the woods, but in the open country, many meadowlarks, singing, mockingbirds. I identified the vermilion flycatcher which I had glimpsed at Lockport. Also the loggerhead shrike. . . . Night warm and cloudy, gentle wind from southerly direction, a long low window in the eastern sky at daybreak. Then a flush of red.

December 3 Lower Atchafalaya River and Bayou Têche. . . . Evening. Clear and cool, fresh wind from west. The boat faces south now, as it has not recently. The firewood changes, too. At our last stop I picked up bleached driftwood, left on top of the bank by high water. Here we burn dry live oak, choice fuel.

December 4   This morning we saw a woman from the campboat near the levee taking several children across to the S. shore, no doubt to meet the school bus. She pushed on the oars like an expert. . . . Heard bluebirds this morning. Hawks over the open fields, kingfishers on shore, gulls over the water. . . . I sit out in the open sun, writing and watching the birds.

December 6   A touch of winter today and how good it is! I rise to a higher plane, in the sharp, clear air, the cold wind. Two fires this evening.

December 10   Yesterday morning we went to Patterson. . . . Liked Patterson, a town which seemed old. Spoiled somewhat because the narrow main street is a through highway. The fishing boats lining the bank the main attraction. . . . Caught an 8-pound bluecat on a bushline overnight, and a mullet in the castnet for bait.

December 12   Learned considerable about this place today, through visits from Mrs. Wilson, who had just taken the children to school and from Mr. Saux, on his way after them, both in the pushing skiff as he called it. He could not spell his name, nor did he pronounce it clearly. It sounded like "Soass." Mrs. Wilson is herself French, Simoneaux. Has three children in school, two younger ones at home. Both families formerly lived across Six Mile Lake, in Bayou Boutte. Moved here so the children could attend school, and to avoid floods which cover the swamp. They are "fishermans". . . . Saw the American egret atop a tall cypress tree this morning. He spent the day fishing, on first one shore then another.

December 13   Another trip to Patterson to mail the Christmas cards, all in a bunch, about 175 of them.

December 14   A mild barefoot day. I painted the screens. Mosquitoes returning, after the cold weather. We all crossed over at sunset to see the big oaks on the mound, a remarkable sight. The low sun shining through in great contrast of light and shade. . . . Got some fine vegetables from the field across. They were planted with the new cane—long rows of mustard, turnips, lettuce, carrots, radishes, spinach. The carrots are the best flavored we have had in many a month, very tender. Saw, I think, a short-billed marsh wren and blue gray gnatcatcher. Anna made hot bread of henscratch flour today. Very good. Light and fine flavored. A little white flour added. The henscratch is mostly corn with cracked corn and wheat. It is very good for breakfast cereal, toasted.

December 15 A thick high fog this morning, very dark and some rain but the day was mild, quiet and mostly fair. Some inconsiderable acts have such virtue connected with them, as today, washing out paintbrushes, sharpening all three planes, and at last, repairing my toolbox.

December 17 We had an idea of leaving this place today but the morning was taken up with much doing—a trip to the garden, bringing back a sackful of turnips, mustard, lettuce, carrots, a few beets; taking up the bushlines; preparing to leave; most of all, worming Sambo. He is a patient and reasonable dog. . . . We have been here a day over two weeks, have burned live oak in both fires—small dead trees which were pushed over by the bulldozers when the levee was built.

December 18 Left the oak trees this morning at sunrise. . . . Stopped after a mile for breakfast, dogs and myself ashore. Waste fields, they seemed, grown into weeds and grass and bushes. Three brick chimneys, in ruin, the old brick washed clean. This country is like that, the appearance of decay increased by the unpainted buildings, though they might be sound, and the raising of sugar cane is flourishing. . . .

At the top of the bend, 1/4 mile east of the Verdunville canal, where the Têche is quite close to Grand Lake, we moored the boat to some old sheet piling along shore. The water was so low all along that the shores were mud flats, unapproachable. At this place we ate dinner. Then I went out casting, caught five small mullet for the dogs. Also a big one which got away. Decided to remain overnight in this likeable place—open fields, from which rose great oaks, singly and in groups, no houses near or traffic.

December 19 A long and varied day, after a sunrise start. . . . The view of the lake was splendid, an expanse of water to right and left. Cypress Island, far across, divides Grand and Six Mile Lake. The near shore is all cypress, much fishing gear, tarring vats, net floats and piles of strange traps made of wire on a frame of welded rods. . . . A long run down the canal to Garden City. . . . Before, and beyond, a swinging bridge of unique design, operated by a negro who was hard to rouse. At the second, the wind and current carried us into a fender while the bridge was being opened and we drifted on through. The bridgetender is assisted by volunteers—a car stops, or someone walks out from shore. . . . I am sure I heard a bobwhite two or three times, whistling backwards. Favorably impressed by Franklin, a long established solid place, with old homes along the streets.

December 20 Franklin. A dark, unopened day, all through. Light rain at times, light breeze from east but mostly quiet and motionless. We thoroughly enjoyed it.

December 22 We went to Franklin in the skiff, arriving there 10:20, leaving about 2 p.m. after a trip to the lower end of town for feed. . . . A friendly reception from Franklin. On the way out is a grove of pine trees, some big ones with moss hanging. Also some cedars. Saw the bluegray gnatcatcher I thought I heard.

December 23 A perfect day, one might say. Summer warmth in the afternoon. We have never seen such smooth water, no wind, no boats. . . .

The A & P was a busy place, boxes and crates on the sidewalk, women picking stuff out. Heaps and boxes of trimmings from vegetables. We picked up a lot of it for the dogs. It was so fresh we cooked some for ourselves, outer leaves from cauliflower. A delicious vegetable dish. How much goes to waste, town and country.

Bayou at high tide. Does the full moon make it higher than usual?

December 24 Another fine morning. Chores done, I sit on the dock in the warm sunshine. . . . Hard to believe this is Christmas Eve, such a warm, fair day, perfectly still. This evening it is a full moon, which rises the color of copper.

December 25 We took a walk through the fields this afternoon, looked at the muskrat's house in the canebrake, the squirrel's nest in the live oak. . . . Played morning and afternoon. Anna prepared a fine dinner—ham, stringbeans, mashed potatoes, mince pie.

December 26   I met three boys, 14-15 years and down, very friendly chaps. . . . The boys came over to our boat with me, and I took them home in the skiff. The older boy showed me over the place, gave me some pecans and a mess of mustard greens. . . . Later in the afternoon the boys returned, paddling the little flatboat, inspired to fish by my catch this morning. Wherever we are, some contact with a native is soon made.

December 27   A storm of thunder, lightning and rain in the night. Up to close shutters, stuff rags in leaky places. A cold wind from N followed, and this day has been dark and chill. We made a good day of it, writing, playing, painting, writing letters, besides meals and chores, wood chopping, fishing. The Facheaux boy told me that the present plantation house replaces one which was destroyed or torn down because it was in the line of fire of gun boats on the Têche during the Civil War, firing on boats out on Grand Lake.

December 28   Yesterday, or day before I towed in a drifting log. Cut off the end of it today, and it is cypress, perfectly sound, though it appears to have been in the water or mud a long time. About 16 feet long, straight almost without knots. I wish it was up on the Ohio, sawed up.

December 31   Today ends a year, begun at or below Natchez on the Mississippi river. A year ago who might have guessed that we would be here now? I have no idea where we will be a year from now. Perhaps here, still.

January 1, 1951   This afternoon we packed 5 packages to send to our family and some friends—cypress knees, made into candle sticks or little hanging vases, candles to put in the holders, twigs with red berries for the vases, spanish moss.

January 2   A tornadic wind from SE last night and all day, with a little rain. A low wet, ragged sky. Bayou higher than ever, over the float and part of our walk ashore. I walked through the muddy cane fields on this side in the morning as far up as the old road which led to the site of the bridge, which once crossed to Oak Bluff.

Gleaned a few ears of corn from a field, to carry on the tradition.

January 3   Now at midday a dead calm. Last night was a wild one. The SE wind gave way suddenly to a blast from N, toward morning, and it rained hard, continuing until midmorning. Bayou went down with the change of wind.

The cypress sawlog drifted or blew out during the night. Now I do not have to decide what to do with it, or saw up good timber or wrestle with it in the mud.

January 4   The warmest, sunniest birthday I can remember. We ate dinner on deck, arms bare and almost too warm in the sun. What did I do today? Nothing that I would not have done yesterday or tomorrow, although Anna's love and attention set this day apart. Yet even that is my daily lot.

I did some writing this morning after the chores were done, sitting on the bank in the sun. . . . Immediately after dinner (roast beef, browned potatoes and carrots, the Galianos' jar of corn, peaches and a piece of the birthday cake), I set up my easel. Later we played together, and then it was time for the evening roundup. We all went out in the johnboat to cast, caught very little. Now I sit by the fire writing this, while Anna prepares supper. . . .

I am 51 years old today. As I painted I was sure that what I could do, what I could see and how I could express it was worth even longer years of living. My playing, the intimacy with certain music which Anna and I have achieved together, is a worthy accomplishment. The writing is an unknown factor, but it may amount to something. It is another expression of what I have felt and lived for. The creation of an environment in which it is possible to do this work, which allows the time and freedom, peace of mind, happiness, security—this in itself is a success which is not always achieved.

To mark the day, the bayou flowed westward for the first time, the water rose to a highter level. A new evening star low in the sky shone brightly just after sunset.

14

A New Beginning

It was a serene, contented time for us, the unmarred days flowed smoothly into one another. On many of them the warm sun rose and set clear, and the tawny-shored bayou, unruffled by a breath of wind, was of a more intense blue than the sky. There were dark days, too, when rain came in a misty drizzle, and we went about our indoor work before a cheerful fire. In all weather we found much work to do, but work and pastime were inseparable.

January 9, 1951 This afternoon I walked along the road across the bayou in the direction of Franklin. An unfenced road among the bare canefields, woods off in the swamps, live oaks and other trees along the bayou. A desolate country between and how muddy it would be! It is desolate because one feels nothing when he looks at it. It is not like an expanse of prairie or sand. One senses the hurried, profitable crop-raising, mechanized and done without love or humility. Coming back, I walked along the bayou side, and this was better, trees, pasture part of the way, and old houses. The old road must have run closer to the water. One fine place—one story on piles, long galley and dormers with big live oaks and pecan trees toward the bayou.

How strange our life here is—we are happy and content, enjoy the water, to look at constantly, as the sky, yet there is nothing on shore to interest us. Anna does not step ashore for days at a time.

January 12 It is only by this log that we keep track of the days of the week.

January 28 Today we left our landing on the east reach of Bayou Têche, 1/2 mile west of Oak Bluff, 21/2 east of Franklin. Our stay there lasted 40 days. Figuring up the results, the time seems to us well spent. A late start was made, but around the first bend the wind was astern and the boat sailed along. . . .

February 1 Last night was a rough one. Rain and wind, thunder and lightning. I got up in the night to bail out the skiff. It was cold then but continued to rain. Sometime before morning it became much colder. We awoke to frozen ground, a skift of snow and a cold NW wind. Blew hard all day and although the afternoon was sunny, ice and snow remained in sheltered spots all day. Two fires kept burning all day. Luckily there is plenty of wood at hand. How good the cold air, wind and winter sky. In a cluster of trees lie some old bricks scattered about and a fragment, with carved lines of poetry, of a gravestone, a large flat one. Perhaps the bricks are from the tomb or there may have been a house there. Swift current down the canal from the Baldwin side.

February 6 The shores of the bayou are becoming different from any we have seen since leaving the river. They often slope gradually up from the water to rolling knolls which might be called hills. The high ground seen before has been level at the top of a straight bank. The effect of this with the pastures and live oaks and clean water line is very fine. The high water covering all the mud and former water lines adds to the clean parklike appearance of the shores. Many small farms.

February 10 At last I got the motor to run smoothly. The new coil and plug did not help but there was a bad circuit somewhere which was obviated by moving the battery and coil box near the motor and using new wires. Now we are popping along. . . . Annie getting dinner, the dogs waiting patiently for the next landing. They seem to enjoy watching the shores near at hand and sleep little when we are running. Weather very thick, a dead calm.

Just tried to make a sketch of an old house, and let the boat run into some branches and aground before I could straighten it out. The house was a small frame weather-boarded and gray with age. Porch on long side, main roof overhanging it, as nearly always here, giving equal and unbroken roof lines. Only two columns re-main, wide and square with trim at top. These columns and the wide facer boards above give a dignity to the smallest house. This one had a door with side and overhead lights. The small paned win-dows had solid wooden shutters. Most strange was the stairway on the porch to the loft. It was at one end, beginning at the outside corner sloping about parallel to the roof. Thus one ascending it would have to go through a very low door. The stairway had no railing. . . .

Stopped above the Loreauville bridge for dinner. Candied sweet potatoes, our own canning at Payne Hollow, it must be, boiled red beans, cabbage raw and cornbread.

February 11 A foggy calm this morning, breaking up into a warm sunny day with a southerly wind. We made a Sunday of it—tinkering about with chores, a walk in the afternoon, some playing.

February 12 We got underway early in the afternoon and had hard shoving against current and wind, which was across and ahead. Picnic dinner on deck while running. The shores delightful. Woods and pastures on the left, only one house, an old one, for a long way. . . .On the New Iberia side some very nice houses, some large and expensive, some good small ones—one with much screened in space which took Anna's eye. . . .

This part of the Têche unlike any we have seen—very narrow, though not yet as narrow as Terrebonne, shores sloping down, often grassy, fine trees, willows overhanging the water, very little of the tall grass along the shore line. The country is almost rolling, no cane fields visible from the water.

We made slow progress on this 5 mile run to the east, but around a bend, heading N and then NNW, we did better. Tied up along east bank, just past Loreauville canal after sunset. The shore across is like Lafourche, a row of houses. A grassy slope from the road to water, children out playing in the twilight.

February 14 Started up this cloudy morning before it was full daylight. . . . The bayou is so winding here. Current swifter than ever. Passed through a bridge, promptly opened, a simple girder bridge, no truss. Stopped above, paddled back to bridge with empty gas cans. A neat country store, operated by the bridgetender. All

Frenchmen, amazed that a boat from Kentucky had penetrated thus far. Pronounced it like a French word. . . .

Bayou narrow and winding, with a faint suggestion of a gorge, up to the Keystone Dam. Just below a canal to left, into Spanish Lake. The lock and dam, much like those on the Kentucky River, smaller, made this a real river. We blew a long and short blast, a head looked over the wall, the valves in the gates were opened, soon the gates themselves. The familiar procedure of locking followed. We had to sign and fill out a paper, the lockman said, and when I asked about the Ruth canal, he took me to the lockmaster. He said it was definitely impossible, because of a watergate built across the canal, so that voyage is out of the question. Brent to St. Martinville, our papers said. . . .

St. Martinville bridge. . . . Landed below the bridge on left at the Evangeline oak. An old brick schoolhouse on the lawn, fine old church nearby. We started up after a short visit, blew for the bridge. Nothing happened, a boy said the bridgetender lived in town. I aimed the horn that way and blew again. The boy said I could phone the bridgetender from the powerhouse just below, then shouted that he was coming. We could hardly believe it, such a dressed up, important looking man, could have been the mayor. He asked when we would be coming back. I said, in several days. Siren sounded 3 times, bridge swung open, electric power, of course, with such an operator.

We soon left the town on a long straight reach. Landed in little cove on left bank at the lower end of Longfellow-Evangeline State Park, a perfect harbor for us.

February 16 We went to St. Martinville in the skiff after dinner. A charming place, very clean and neat, quiet and friendly.

February 17 In the afternoon we were visited by Mr. Bernard, photographer and free lance journalist of New Iberia. While he was here, other visitors, Mrs. Leana Martin Guirard and a little grand niece, and her brother, Wade E. Martin, Secretary of State of Louisiana.

February 18 In the twilight, I walked through the park, picking out of the trash cans scraps of picnic food for the dogs.

February 23 The mornings have the feel of spring.

February 24 I have been painting and writing every day, and we get in some playing.

February 26 A very dark morning, either rain or S wind to be expected. We pulled out, however, and the sun came out. . . . Wind came up as expected but we went on, making good time. . . . We notice much green along the bayou which we did not see on our up trip. I picked some wild plum blossoms. Grass is green, fields being plowed, with mules. . . . We are struck by the different character of the bayou below the dam—winding and narrow with steep banks, overhung with a thick growth of willows, shaggy borders. Above it is like a swamp bayou, here like a stream in hill country.

February 27 Anna spotted some poke. We moored the boat and got a fine mess at just the right stage. Good for Annie.

March 1 The watchman at the sugarhouse came around to welcome us back. When I told him how much we were enjoying the blackstrap he gave us on our other stop, he said he would bring us some more. This he did, after dark, in the same can, I believe. He asked if the dogs were mean. I said, no, just speak to them. He said "How de-do."

March 3 Most of the day given to trying to start the motor.

March 5 Mr. Reynaud works at the Red Fox Machine shop, at monotonous drudgery, what I have seen of it. How different was the work in his own shop, repairing and rebuilding engines and machines, helping people out of their trouble, using his imagination and skill to the utmost.

March 6 Caught six catfish, 8 or 10 pounds, on the bush lines last night. I was out in the dark at bedtime, and met three boys in a pirogue hunting frogs. Two of the boys came to the boat today— Laurence Melançon and Boutte (booty). They are interested in our boat, our trip, and look upon us as real fishermen.

March 8 We have eaten poke and catfish every day of our stay here, and poke even before that. We do not tire of it—we seem to require the juicy green stuff after our winter diet. . . .

How different is our downward passage of the Têche. It is like full summer, song of birds, leafing trees, green grass, wisteria often draped over the water, the yards of houses blazing with azaleas and camellias—an artificial looking flower to us. Blew for the first bridge and it was opened by the old man who has become our friend from frequent landings there. . . .

Lawrence Melançon was up yesterday at sunset and I supplied him with more sardines for bait. He tried to row the johnboat, was as awkward as a girl from the city. Yet he and his pals are perfectly at home in the pirogue, with its inch of freeboard. They spoke of our johnboat as a big boat, big enough for a cabin.

March 9 We got underway at sunrise, though the sun could not be seen for some time on account of the heavy fog, which lasted a long time. This is summer weather, even before sunrise when no clothes are necessary for warmth.

March 10 Down the long corridor of the canal lined thickly with green trees—willows, maples, bitter pecan, bush trees and the like, no big trees. The red and yellow trumpet vine in bloom. White-eyed vireo, parula warbler, titmouse, Carolina wren. American egrets flew back and forth, a gull, and possibly ibis. Crows, kingfishers. . . . The shores became lower after leaving the Têche, now nearly awash, palmettos showing. . . . We passed a wide opening southward through which we could look out into West Côte Blanche Bay. To the west a low blue smear, almost like a cloud, we decided was the Côte Blanche salt dome. It was thrilling to see, a decided elevation, like a Mississippi River bluff. It was five miles away. . . .

How good the wilderness is, after the weeks on the settled Têche. Now I realize that something was missing there. It was only a part, like a screen behind the actors. Here the scene extends infinitely far and deep. We admire the tall grasses with brown tufts on their tips—they shine "as burned gold with stremes bright."

March 12 The weather is the news, after weeks of insignificant fair weather. A wind came down from the N last night, slow at first, but this morning it was a gale, with heavy rains. Water is two feet lower.

Evening—this has been a rough day. No rain in the afternoon but a very strong wind from NW. Water level continued to drop, now about 31/2 feet lower, and we rest on the bottom, except when the water is pushed in by heavy boats. . . .

This afternoon the dogs, Sambo first, discovered a 'coon in a hollow tree. After a battle they succeeded in dragging it out and killing it. The 'coon got in some good bites. Now we will all feast tomorrow, all but the 'coon. . . .

Some good playing this afternoon. A Bach Prelude and Fugue, no. 19 I believe. Then two parts of the Brahms clarinet trio. Even the two parts played as we play them, reveal to us the beauty of this music. As we finished the adagio the sun shone beneath the dark clouds, low to the earth, lighting up the prairies and trees in a sudden brief flash of golden light.

March 15 Left Côte Blanche Island soon after sunrise. . . . We entered Weeks Bayou. . . . A wide bayou in the marsh, the island not far away. Very winding. Tied up at shell pile which had a ruined house on top, oak trees. Road back to the island and we would like to stay there. While eating dinner a tug came up from the Intra-coastal, dragging three empties. We were in a bad spot, on the outside of a sharp bend, or rather, on a short straight away between two right turns. Tug made first turn, came to us pretty well straightened out, but the second turn, and the South wind, swung the tail of the last barge into the bank. There wasn't much I could do. We should never have tied up there in the first place not knowing what sort of traffic there was, or I should have tried to get away when the tug was first sighted. When we saw it would hit we jumped ashore. A hard shell bank, deep water. The barge raked the outside of our boat, heeling it over, carried away a plank lashed there, and a short section of the guard. A dish broken inside. Apparently no other damage. I signalled the tug to come back, which it did, after tying up its barges. Tug *Ace,* Bonner Towing Co., of Houston, Texas, Capt. Farrington. A nice crew. They should not have come at us that way, however, without blowing a danger signal and making some attempt to stop. We got away at once. . . .

March 16 We lay in the little slip on Warehouse Bayou, quite at home now with the grotesque, noisy giants who are our neigh-bors. This morning I walked into the town of Weeks, all alone, rowing up to the bridge. A long walk, through rolling farm country, then the scattered town, an ill-at-ease, unnatural place, very striking to see, draped on the hill, A splendid view out into the bay, and the Gulf beyond. To look out over the mystic sea, where you cannot trust your eyes too much.

> *One year in the bayou country of Louisiana had slipped by; a short year, it seemed now, full of novelty and good living. Yet we felt that we did not want to make Louisiana our settled home. The attraction of a more northern air, of hills, gardens and a known and loved countryside was strong within us. If we were going back to Kentucky, and this we were certain to do in the end, it might be best to leave Louisiana now, before the long, hot summer.*

March 21 I tacked a "For Sale" sign on each side of the boat today.

March 23 Good Friday. On Good Friday in 1950 we drifted down the Mississippi from Ama into the Harvey Canal. Today we bid farewell to Weeks Bayou. An early start, for the S wind was already blowing. Wound over a devious course to Bayou Carlin, where we had breakfast. Tied up the boat in a little side bayou to the N. The marshes and prairies in the sun, the sky blue water, and sea breeze are delightful. Again we feel, coming from the midst of men and their works, that we have come out-of-doors, that without knowing it we had been confined.

March 25 Easter Sunday. Our only celebration was a raisin cream pie, after our dinner of creamed catfish, fried poke and baked potatoes; and an effort to play the cello and first viola part of the Brahms Quintet No. 111. . . .

A flock of little blue herons this afternoon. The song of the Maryland yellowthroat and the cardinal, and at evening an unknown twittering. The song of the cardinal, so unexpected in this marshy land, is lovely.

March 27 Went to the Intracoastal in the skiff, it would have been a hard row against the wind and current. A dry shore between

Carlin and Weeks Bayou. Eastward it spread out into a wide area of bare earth, cracked by the sun like river bottom land. The variety of grass and bushes is fascinating. Such a wealth of form and color, in a landscape which might be called monotonous, if ever any could. Nothing can grow here which is hurt by salt water. The whole land is covered. Were it not for the grass and bushes, the waves would run quite high, and we would be frightened by the extent of the sea on which we float.

March 28 Busy, profitable days. Writing, painting, chores, meals, reading, sleep. . . .

A new venture today. I trimmed Anna's hair—tentatively. The result is encouraging.

In this treeless marsh, in these day of rain and high tide, our reserve of firewood comes into its own.

March 29 I managed to get the bush lines baited this morning, caught one catfish. We decided to eat it right away—fish soup for our supper out of the backbone, the rest for the dogs. Our menus depend on what comes to hand, and are often changed suddenly, as this evening. It is a hand to mouth existence.

April 4 These nights are cool, the days not always warm. The brilliant mornings are inspiring.

April 7 I paint every day, today worked on a wood block also. Our playing is daily, too. Little work to do. A fishing trip morning and evening.

April 8 The dogs dug out of its underground canal an otter, and killed it. We will try eating some tomorrow. . . .

The bay was so rough that we went up Weeks Bayou to the shell pile, landed and walked through the woods. The change, so sudden, is unbelievably complete; different air, warmer, no wind, new sounds of birds, insects, wind in the tree tops, pines; smell of trees, of warm sun on leaves, of tender green plants crushed by a car which had passed. The gentle slope of the road is as startling as it would be if the earth suddenly tilted. A handsome pond, surrounded by forest. . . . Returned by the Powerline Canal in time to play. Good to be on the windy open marsh again.

April 10 The first draft of our account of the voyage down the Mississippi River, from the building of the boat at Brent, is now complete.

April 15   A dark night, that is, no oil field flares close by. They have tarnished the splendor of darkness for the past month.

April 20   Our situation is strange. For six weeks we have lived in the marsh alone, no one living for miles around, except on the islands. Except for our short and infrequent visits to Weeks Island, we have seen no one. Yet we are not isolated, nor do we feel so. Boats pass by often, and close by, fishing boats, tugs, motorboats. We can see the lights of oil wells at night, hear them by day, hear the siren of the saltmine at Avery Island, the whistle at Weeks. Through the glasses we can see houses in the island, structures to the north. Yet we are as much alone as if on a light ship anchored out to sea.

April 22   This afternoon we all made a johnboat trip on the dancing blue water.

April 24   We left our anchorage, on the tenth day after our arrival. Went up Petite Anse toward Avery Island. Very stirring to see the trees appear. . . . Suddenly the right bank, at the beginning of the slope on Avery, became cultivated—lawns, gardens, flowers in bloom, palms, the fragrance of honeysuckle and blossoming bushes. This was Jungle Gardens, extended for a mile.

April 25   Strange to awake and hear roosters crowing. And last night the droning frogs, and lightning bugs. Dust. The nearness of people and their works has made a different world. Yet the higher ground, the trees, have changed the country. To look at the Island, and see sloping pastures amid masses of dark green trees, to breathe a new air, hear different birds. One misses the sweep of marsh and sky already. A ragged horizon only, takes one's attention from the sky.

April 28   A short run to Five Points, where Bayou Carlin branches off. We anchored behind a small island east of Petite Anse. Now at sunset the South wind, which has been busy all day, goes to rest. The nighthawks buzz through the air, the few birds sing their evening song.

April 29   The storekeeper's wife asked Anna what sort of fancywork she was making. She had seen Anna working at the castnet from the road, having stopped at the dock to buy shrimp. We are observed much more than we realize, always. . . .

How good it is to be in the marsh again. One feels released from a pressure he did not comprehend.

April 30 A grand sky today, great white clouds, so soft and melting, a clear, blue sky, but soft in between. The wind makes us feel more than ever that we are afloat. The land here is insignificant, this small island now under water. Water in every direction. To the SSW in the low sunlight the little trapper's cabin gleamed above the grass, with its two trees a prominent landmark. Nearby is a tall straight pole. What prominence anything mechanical has in this landscape. The eye returns to a sign or a stranded box like a cadence in music.

May 1 The SE gale continued all last night and today, varying in intensity, but undeviating and relentless. Our island is all under the water now.

May 8 We left Petite Anse this morning after an early breakfast and proceeded up Bayou Carlin to Delcambre, 6 miles. . . . The harbor at Delcambre is a crowded busy place. I suppose the number of boats now in port is normal. I can see about two dozen out of the window. The town is small and shabby but answers our needs.

May 10 Visitors yesterday, Mr. Delcambre and Mr. Boudreaux. The latter, 89, would buy our boat, if priced low enough. Mr. Delcambre is 70, but looks much younger. He made an excellent impression on us. Talked much of the early days here, made us welcome to land he owns or looks after.

May 12 I put up signs—"Camp Boat For Sale"—at the bridge. I hate this publicity.

May 29 Yesterday I went to New Iberia, tramped the hot pavements looking for a car we could use with some honor and satisfaction.

May 31 Yesterday and today, part of the time, I have been working on deck, putting in new pieces on one side and under the post. For this I used the fir plank we have carried from Brent as a gangplank. Donald and I found it in the Coney Island drift pile.

June 1   Another trip to New Iberia today. I was picked up on the road by Broussard, state policeman. Another plodding march over sunny streets and roads, reading, memorizing, and reciting "Lines Written a Few Miles Above Tintern Abbey." So apt, I could have written it myself. . . . Heard a yellow billed cuckoo today.

At this point we let the sale of the boat rest for a while and gave our attention to another matter which was urgent. What if we did sell out? We would be left on the bank of the canal with all our personal property, three musical instruments, two dogs, pictures, books, tools and other possessions, some of little value, perhaps, but not to be abandoned for one reason or another. We considered ways and means of getting this stuff back to Kentucky overland, and came to the conclusion that it would be best to buy an old automobile; a decision made with reluctance, for we remembered what a relief it had been to get rid of a car we had once owned. But it seemed the best way out. A car would give us some measure of the independence with which we had traveled by water.

Our first thought was to get a station wagon; then a pickup truck was considered; but these ideas were abandoned in favor of a roomy four-door car with a trailer of some sort for the overflow. Now we had something to buy as well as something to sell, and no heads for business of any kind. . . .

In our perplexity we were visited at the boat one day by a good-natured Cajun with the unlikely name of Ike Romero. . . . Ike's specialty was selling cars to country people, and his easy-going, homely ways inspired confidence. For better or for worse we bought the car he had to offer, a bulging ten-year-old Dodge; in good shape as far as we could see, with a rebuilt motor.

The trailer was easier. In our rambling about New Iberia we had seen a two-wheeled trailer chassis built of steel pipe at a welder's shop. Designed to carry a small boat, it was ten feet long and four wide. I thought I could make something of this and we bought it.

June 10 I brought out the car and trailer on Friday, June 9. It is at the end of the street across the canal, as yet not made a part of our system. Yet we are changing, our interests are beyond the boat and water.

June 13 These are hot days, sultry, breaking storms cruising about. I grapple with the task of changing over and leaving here. Yesterday a trip to New Iberia for both of us—the first in the car. . . . Today I began work on the trailer. Bought $18.85 worth of lumber, low grade cypress at 18¢ a foot, some at 12¢. From A.P. Dooley, another one of the boys. I hope the trailer, all homemade, will take the curse off the automobile. Yesterday we sent by express to Fort Thomas, 273 pounds in 4 crates—bicycle, 68 pounds, 3 boxes of pictures, prints, watercolors, drawings.

> *We were proud of our trailer, built of cypress, varnished, neatly fit to the aluminum-painted frame and wheels. It gave our equipage a unique and individual character, and took the curse off the automobile. We would be able to live along the road as free as gypsies.*

June 28 Our shantyboat world has come to an end. The boat in turmoil, the familiar arrangements and routine breaking up, packing boxes standing about, nothing where it should be. The boats have been sold to Dr. Landry of Abbeville, the cash is in our pockets. $679.00, after giving the bank of Abbeville $21 on Landry's note. We do not feel bad about it, and look forward to new fields.

July 1 Left Delcambre at 2:30 p.m. Had already done enough for a full day—up at daybreak, moved our bed from boat into trailer, more loading, making ready for last voyage. Anna washed hair. Landry arrived about 8 a.m. By then wind and tide were against us. We got underway, inched under the bridge, through the narrow passage between three deep trawlers. Bumped the *Sailor Bob*. Landry shouting greetings in French to friends on shore. Slow going against wind and tide. Reached Bayou Tigre at last and glad to turn in. A narrow winding way through the grassy marsh. A natural bayou, yet Landry says that at one time Bayou Tigre had no outlet. Reached higher land and trees overhanging the water, green cypress, moss. A sharp turn into Bayou Duvall, or Dugall, tied up the boat at the little bridge.

Mrs. Landry had dinner about ready. How we ate! Fried corn, chicken, rice, lima beans, a mixture of eggplant, meat, etc., fig preserves and country milk in quantity. Coffee.

Then they brought us to Delcambre with a stop at Landry's *maman*. She lives in the old house on Main Street, which we admired from the first. She is the old lady whom we saw working in her flowers.

We were left alone at 2 o'clock. No boat.

Soon moving down the road. . . .

With the miles our spirits began to rise. After all, we were still together, still shantyboating, on wheels, with all the world before us.

Appendix

Diagrams of the Shantyboat

Exterior Diagram

The shantyboat is 20 feet long, 10 feet wide.

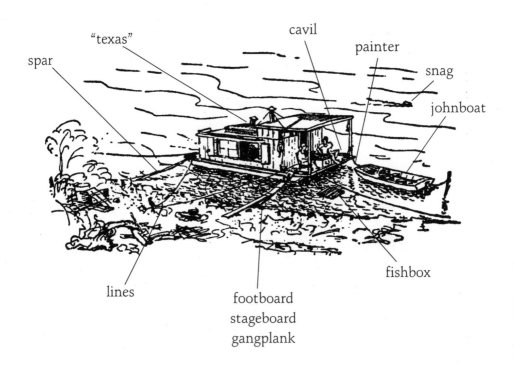

spar · "texas" · cavil · painter · snag · johnboat · lines · footboard stageboard gangplank · fishbox

cavil

cavil: a cleat on a boat deck to which lines are tied.

fishbox: a wooden box holding live fish recently caught until time to cook them or sell them (or give them away).

footboard, stageboard, gangplank: interchangeable terms for the wood plank or planks making a walkway from the boat deck to the shore.

johnboat: a rowboat, flat-bottomed, square-ended, 14' or 16' long. "Every shantyboater has one johnboat at least. It answers all his needs. It can carry a heavy load; its square ends make it easy to step into from the deck of a shantyboat; its scow bow is good for running up on a bank; and it is better for fishing than a skiff, being more steady and roomier. With the shantyboater, the johnboat corresponds to the farmer's wagon or the yachtsman's dinghy"— *Shantyboat.*

lines: ropes for tying up the boat.

painter: a line tying the johnboat to the shantyboat.

snag: a tree or tree branch caught ("snagged") in the muddy bottom of the river; a hazard to navigation.

spar: a wood plank or tree branch set between the boat and the shore to keep waves or wind from beaching the boat.

texas: a small, collapsible compartment on the roof of the boat where Harlan and Anna slept when guests occupied the boat's cabin. "Nights in the texas were delightful, so close to the stars and river," Harlan wrote in *Shantyboat*. The Hubbards called it the texas after the texas deck on a steamboat, a small deck on the top.

Interior Diagram

The cabin is 16 feet long, 10 feet wide.

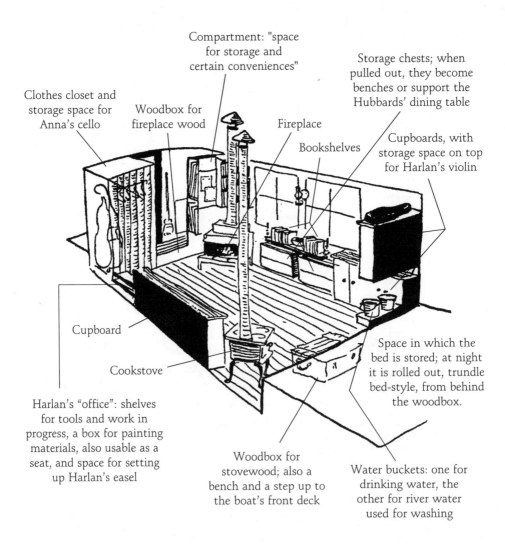

Compartment: "space for storage and certain conveniences"

Storage chests; when pulled out, they become benches or support the Hubbards' dining table

Clothes closet and storage space for Anna's cello

Woodbox for fireplace wood

Fireplace

Bookshelves

Cupboards, with storage space on top for Harlan's violin

Cupboard

Cookstove

Space in which the bed is stored; at night it is rolled out, trundle bed-style, from behind the woodbox.

Harlan's "office": shelves for tools and work in progress, a box for painting materials, also usable as a seat, and space for setting up Harlan's easel

Woodbox for stovewood; also a bench and a step up to the boat's front deck

Water buckets: one for drinking water, the other for river water used for washing

While I was busy outside, Anna was organizing the interior, developing a system of housekeeping which would fit our small quarters. The arrangement of the cabin was not planned but grew around us as we lived there, a more natural and efficient way, we thought, than to make figures and drawings beforehand and then fit ourselves to them. We had so much fun at all this that we sometimes felt like children playing at keeping house, almost as if we were playing at living. There was not a trace of the dead seriousness and worry that go with planning and building a house. Yet our cheerful cabin became a comfortable and convenient place to live and work in. . . .

Every possible bit of space has been put to use, but our cabin does not seem crowded. The center of the floor is entirely open, nothing is standing around. In fact, one sees so few objects on entering that the effect is one of bareness, almost emptiness. One visiting riverman, coming while we were away, looked in the window and decided that we had moved out. The bare windows without a trace of draperies or shades carry out this impression and make the room seem larger than it is.

The many problems of space arrangement which came up were like puzzles to work out, and often the solution was an ingenious one. Nothing is arbitrary or merely decorative. . . . Many innocent objects have unexpected uses, and our guests require some training and instruction in living with us. We sometimes think of our boat in the hands of a stranger. He would come upon puzzling contraptions and unexpected compartments one after another. The boat would fall apart with some of its secrets undiscovered.

—Shantyboat

Glossary

See also the annotated diagrams in the appendix, pages 372-75.

bateau: the Louisiana version of a johnboat; flat-bottomed like a johnboat but with tapering ends, making it easier to row but less stable: better for transportation, not so suitable for work.

carling: the shantyboat's roof joists.

Chippy: a small train, one or two cars and a caboose, that carried railroad workers to work and back to town; it went by the Hubbards' boatsite at Brent every two hours or so.

cordelling: pulling a boat along the shore against the current by lines tied to the boat and carried by persons on shore—hard work.

cribbing: timber pieces and blocks of wood used to support the boat on the shore as Harlan worked on it.

DPC: a rivermen's term, probably meaning "displacement craft," for huge steam towboats whose propellers churned up powerful waves that rocked boats moored at shore.

drift: anything carried off the shore by the rising or falling river and floating downstream; usually wood (**driftwood**), trees and branches and pieces of lumber, but also any floating debris.

driftpile: a pile of drift caught on a snag or on the shore.

"Driftwood": the Hubbards' name for their shantyboat.

driftwrack: another name for a driftpile, connoting large size; often dense enough to walk on.

gunwale: a wood plank running the length of the top of the hull side, where the topsides meet the deck.

keelson: a timber piece running the length of the hull to stiffen and strengthen it.

LST: Landing Ship Transport, a type of Navy craft built in the Ohio Valley during World War II, the biggest of all boats on the river; passing by, they created a suction force in the river that devastated shoreline boat moorings.

mule or **mud sail:** an underwater sail, a square of canvas about 8' x 10', lowered overboard off the bow; as a sailboat's sail propels the boat by wind power, the mule utilizes the power of the current, increasing the speed of drifting. (It pulls the boat, hence **mule**, and it is always muddy, hence **mud sail**.)

oakum: hemp fibers used to fill (caulk) the seams in the boat's hull to make it watertight.

plates: the shantyboat's hull joists.

rake: the slope of the boat's hull at the bow, stern, and sides.

running board: a plank running the length of the bottom of the hull on each side, easing the boat's movement (its "run") through the water.

shoe gunwales: timber pieces running the length of the bottom of the boat's hullsides, strenghtening the frame.

skiff: a small boat with a raised bow and often a V-shaped hull, easy to row or propel with a motor.

streamer: the longitudinal members of the hull framing; Harlan used twenty-foot-long timbers ripped in two to strengthen the boat's structure.

sweeps: long oars with large square blades that Harlan and Anna used to propel their boat away from danger or to navigate in tight places such as creek moorings—very hard work.

U.S.E.D.: United States Engineer District, the designation used then for what is now the Army Corps of Engineers; U.S.E.D. boats patrolled the river, setting buoys, dredging navigation channels, and so forth.

Whirly: the remains of a crane installation at Brent once used to unload logs from railroad cars into the river, where they were made into rafts and towed by boats to sawmills on the Cincinnati waterfront.

Breaux Bridge

Lafayette

Longfellow-Evangeline State Park

St. Martinville

ATCHAFALAYA RIVER

L. Peigneur

New Iberia

Bayou Teche

bbeville

Erath

Jefferson Island

Delcambre

Avery Island

Jeanerette

Charenton

The end of our shantyboat journeys

Petite Anse

Weeks

Baldwin

Bayou Cypremort

Franklin

Berwick

Morgan City

Patterson

INTRACOASTAL WATERWAY

Vermilion Bay

West Cote Blanche Bay

Wax L.

Bayou Shaffer

East Cote Blanche Bay

Sweetbay L.

Bayou

GULF OF MEXI